WRITING TO COMMUNICATE

WRITING TO COMMUNICATE

A RHETORIC, READER, AND HANDBOOK FOR COLLEGE WRITERS

MAUREEN P. TAYLOR
KALAMAZOO VALLEY COMMUNITY COLLEGE

Wadsworth Publishing Company
Belmont, California
A Division of Wadsworth, Inc.

English Editor: Kevin Howat
Production Editor: Gary Mcdonald
Designer: Cynthia Bassett
Copy Editor: Mollie Hughes
Technical Illustrator: Lisa Palacio
Cover Photo: Dow, Clement & Simison
Back Cover Photo: Gregory L. Taylor
Signing Representative: Jon Muir

© 1983 by Wadsworth, Inc. All rights reserved. No part of this book may be reproduced, stored in a retrieval system, or transcribed, in any form or by any means, electronic, mechanical, photocopying, recording, or otherwise, without the prior written permission of the publisher, Wadsworth Publishing Company, Belmont, California 94002, a division of Wadsworth, Inc.

Printed in the United States of America
1 2 3 4 5 6 7 8 9 10—87 86 85 84 83

Library of Congress Cataloging in Publication Data

Taylor, Maureen P.
   Writing to communicate.

   Includes index.
   1. English language—Rhetoric. 2. College readers.
3. English language—Grammar—1950– . I. Title.
PE1417.T35   1982   808'.042   82-11082
ISBN 0-534-01196-9

To my grandmother,
Lillyn F. Barclay,
whose dramatic readings from
<u>The Official Detective</u>
and
<u>The Five Little Peppers</u>
provided my first
lessons in style

CONTENTS

A NOTE TO TEACHERS xiii

ACKNOWLEDGMENTS xv

**PART ONE
RHETORIC
1**

CHAPTER 1 SOME PRELIMINARIES (WHY WRITE?) 3

How Writing Differs from Other Communicating 4
How Writing Is the Same as Other Communicating 6

CHAPTER 2 PREWRITING: THE SENDER (WHO'S WRITING THIS, ANYWAY?) 9

Roles and Our Self-Concepts 10
Practicing Defining Yourself 10
Labeling 12
Roles and Voices 14
Some Techniques for Prewriting about Yourself 15
Related Readings 18
One Valuable Value   Elizabeth DeKam 18
The Many Me's of the Self-Monitor   Mark Snyder 20
Writing Assignments 26

CHAPTER 3 PREWRITING: THE RECEIVER (AND WHO'S READING THIS?) 29

Analyzing Your Audience 30
The Writing Class as Audience 31
Practicing Audience Analysis 31
The Writing Instructor as Audience 32
What the Audience Knows about Your Topic 33
What the Audience Feels about Your Topic 33
What the Audience Knows about You 34
Another Technique for Prewriting 36

Related Readings 36
A Good Cigar Is a Smoke   Stan Green 36
The Audience as Creative Force   Richard M. Eastman 38
Writing Assignments 42

CHAPTER 4   PREWRITING: THE MESSAGE (WHAT DO YOU HAVE TO SAY?) 47

Getting from General to Specific 48
Stating the Thesis Sentence 51
Practicing Evaluating Thesis Sentences 53
Practicing Writing Thesis Sentences 53
Placing the Thesis Sentence 54
Related Readings 55
In Retrospect   Sherrie Dunham 55
Phooey on the Little Boxes Other People Put around Us   Nickie McWhirter 57
Writing Assignments 59

CHAPTER 5   WRITING: THE MEDIUM (WORDS) 62

Varieties of English 62
Words as Symbols 63
Two Kinds of Meaning 66
Practicing Achieving Variety with Connotations 68
Literal Language and Figurative Language 69
Practicing Recognizing Figurative Language 71
Practicing Writing Figurative Language 72
Related Readings 73
The Ticket   Roberta Thompson 73
A Growing Wealth of Words   Norman Cousins 74
Writing Assignments 76

CHAPTER 6   WRITING: THE MEDIUM (SENTENCES) 81

Content: Factual and Nonfactual Statements 81
Practicing Identifying Factual Statements and Inferences 83
Structure: Readability 84
Structure: Long Sentences and Short Sentences 85
Structure: Emphasis and Coherence 87
Practicing Writing Periodic Sentences 89
Structure: Repetition and Parallelism 89

Practicing Achieving Parallel Structure 91
Structure: Active and Passive Verbs 92
Practicing Achieving Sentence Variety 92
Related Readings 93
The Swamp David Kelsey 93
Men, Women and War Ellen Goodman 95
Writing Assignments 98

CHAPTER 7 WRITING: THE MEDIUM (PARAGRAPHS) 101

Grouping Sentences Together 101
Topic Sentences 103
Methods of Developing Topic Sentences 104
Practicing Methods of Paragraph Development 106
Holding Your Paragraphs Together 108
Special Paragraphs: Introductions 109
Special Paragraphs: Conclusions 110
Practicing Writing Introductions and Conclusions 111
Special Paragraphs: Summaries 111
Special Paragraphs: Dialogue 112
Related Readings 113
It Is No Secret Patricia Macklin 113
Competency Tests for Everyone Charles R. Larson 115
Writing Assignments 117

CHAPTER 8 WRITING: THE MEDIUM (SOME WAYS TO PUT IT ALL TOGETHER) 121

The Simplest Pattern: Chronology 121
Outlining for Other Patterns 123
Practicing Developing Outlines 127
Related Readings 128
Fighters Mark Giles 128
Labors of Love Brian Friel 129
Writing Assignments 132

CHAPTER 9 WRITING: THE MEDIUM (MORE WAYS TO PUT IT ALL TOGETHER) 137

Classifying and Analyzing 137
Practicing Analysis and Classification 139
Writing Cause-and-Effect Essays 140

Practicing Cause-and-Effect Analysis 142
Writing Argumentative Papers 142
Using Inductive Reasoning 143
Practicing Arguing Inductively 144
Using Deductive Reasoning 145
Practicing Arguing Deductively 147
Using Analogies 149
Dealing with the Opposition 149
Arguments to Avoid 151
Related Readings 152
Stars and Dollars: The Space Research Controversy   Rick Chambers 152
The Age of Indifference   Philip G. Zimbardo 155
Writing Assignments 161

CHAPTER 10   POSTWRITING: REDUCING NOISE 165

Testing Your Skills 165
A Checklist for Editing 169
A Checklist for Proofreading 170
Writing Assignment 171

CHAPTER 11   REWRITING: RESPONDING TO FEEDBACK 173

Interpreting Feedback 173
How to Rewrite 175
Writing Assignment 176

CHAPTER 12   SPECIAL ASSIGNMENTS: EXAMINATION WRITING 178

Preparing for the Exam 178
Writing the Exam 181
Practicing Evaluating Essay Answers 184
Writing Assignments 185

CHAPTER 13   SPECIAL ASSIGNMENTS: EMPLOYMENT WRITING 187

Presenting Yourself on Paper 187
Writing the Cover Letter 191
What Next? 194
Related Reading 194
Q: Why Do You Want to Work Here?   Theodore Pettus 194
Writing Assignment 198

CONTENTS

CHAPTER 14 SPECIAL ASSIGNMENTS: RESEARCH WRITING 200

A Sample Paper 200
Blind Obedience to Authority Linda Asmus 202
Prewriting the Documented Paper 210
Prewriting at the Library 212
Developing Your Outline 215
Writing the Paper 215
Postwriting Concern: The Format 217
Writing Assignment 220

PART TWO READER 223

FOCUS: SELF 225
Mommy Goes to Jail Judith Viorst 225
Memories of a Small Bomb Morton Sontheimer 231
Preparing for the Job Mary Jo Volosky 233
FOCUS: AUDIENCE 235
Decoding TV Commercials Hal Kome 235
The Arab Stereotype on Television Jack G. Shaheen 241
Brass Rubbings Tonia Mekemson 249
FOCUS: THESIS 253
The Sporting Spirit George Orwell 253
New Deal for the Academic Shuffle Stephen Crites 256
Safer at Any Speed John Kison 259
FOCUS: WORDS 262
Defining a Few Terms Sydney J. Harris 262
Memories of the Championship Ed Vital 266
Spare Me the Details Kathy Marsh 269
FOCUS: SENTENCES 271
The Band Plays On Melvin Maddocks 271
Snapshot of a Dog James Thurber 273
Keys and Me Julie Allen-Avery 276
FOCUS: PARAGRAPHS 279
Some Cheerful Words about Men Gloria Steinem 279
Body Language Spoken Here Art Buchwald 282
Male Attitudes in the Army Laurie Wardell 284
FOCUS: ORGANIZATION I (CHRONOLOGY, PROCESS, COMPARISON/CONTRAST) 287
How to Outsmart the Bureaucrats Jack Anderson 287
The Place of Sex among Human Values Bertrand Russell 290
The Best Teachings Michelle M. Marlett 292

FOCUS: ORGANIZATION II (ANALYSIS, CAUSE AND EFFECT, ARGUMENT) 295
Music to Get Pregnant By   Mike Royko 295
On the Meaning of Life   H. L. Mencken 297
The Case against the Drafting of Women   John Holler 300

PART THREE HANDBOOK 305

SECTION 1   PROBLEMS WITH CLAUSES 307

Fragments 307
Comma Splices and Run-On Sentences 310

SECTION 2   PROBLEMS WITH VERBS 313

Agreement 313
Wrong Principal Parts 315
Shift in Voice or Tense 318

SECTION 3   PROBLEMS WITH PUNCTUATION 323

Apostrophes 323
Quotation Marks 325
Commas, Semicolons, and Colons 327

SECTION 4   SOME OTHER GRAMMATICAL PROBLEMS 331

Pronouns 331
Dangling and Misplaced Modifiers 334
Faulty Parallelism 336

SECTION 5   SPELLING PROBLEMS 339

Surveying Your Spelling Habits 339
Steps toward Spelling Accuracy 341
A Note on Capitalization 347

SECTION 6   USAGE PROBLEMS 349

A NOTE TO TEACHERS

You've just picked up *Writing to Communicate,* and you're asking yourself, "What can this book do for my class?" I'll tell you what points I'd be interested in, if this were the first time I had ever seen this book.

First, the content covers both composition and communication. Writing is always discussed as a part of the process of communication, so it isn't as divorced from the "real world" as it is in some textbooks. Also, the dual emphasis makes the book appropriate for practical writing courses, communication courses that will include a number of writing assignments, and combined composition-communication courses.

Second, the organization follows the steps in the writing process: prewriting, writing, postwriting, and rewriting. Assignments grow progressively more difficult in each section. The chapter on rewriting (not found in most textbooks) should help your students to respond to your comments as well as to feedback from other students as they try to improve their essays.

Third, the writing assignments—generally four per chapter—have specific objectives that tell the students what they need to do to earn a good grade. Objectives are related to the chapter, and the grammatical objectives build from one chapter to the next, so that students begin by eliminating fragments and progress to eliminating a whole list of major structural errors. Of course, you can add objectives of your own or subtract from the objectives I have listed to meet the needs of your students. If your college has been promoting Competency Based Education, this feature of the assignments should make the program fit right in with *Writing to Communicate.*

Fourth, there are many models of good writing. Chapters 2–9 contain two essays each—one by a professional writer and one by a student writer. In chapters 13, 14, and the Reader, there are twenty-six more essays, including nine more by students. These cover a wide range of reading levels, listed in the Instructor's Manual.

Fifth, both the assignments themselves and the Handbook sections provide practical help with grammatical problems many students may be having. Each assignment contains a brief discussion of the new grammatical requirement and also refers students to the appropriate section of the Handbook for more assistance. In the Handbook, in addition to brief but clear explanations of the rules, exercises that "make sense"—not isolated sentences—give the students a chance to check their grammatical skills.

Sixth, three chapters on special assignments cover writing essay exams, employment writing (cover letter and résumé), and writing research papers. These come after the rewriting section, so you can omit any or all that do not fit into your course, but students may want to read them anyway for help in their other courses.

Seventh, most chapters contain exercises to help the students practice what they are learning. Instead of coming at the ends of the chapters, these are located right with the related material.

Eighth, the book follows its own advice to personalize writing. The examples come from my nineteen years as a student, my nearly twenty years as a teacher, and my forty years as a person.

ACKNOWLEDGMENTS

Four groups of people helped me immensely as I worked on this text, and I want to thank them all.

First, I must thank my family. All authors thank their families, deserving or not; but in this book, so much of the content comes from my family—illustrations that are family anecdotes, grammatical exercises about ancestral history—that the text would be entirely different if I had a different family. I'm glad I don't, and I appreciate the part played in this book by them all: my husband, Clyde, my sons, Greg and Nick, my mother, brothers, ancestors, and, of course, the dogs.

Second, I acknowledge the great contributions made to this text by the thousands of students I have taught since I began my career in 1963. The seventeen students whose essays are included here are obvious contributors, but many, many others also taught me something about teaching and about writing. I thank you all.

Third, all of my colleagues at Kalamazoo Valley Community College have contributed enormously to this book, and I really appreciate all of their help. John Corbin and Bill Lay both made perceptive, encouraging comments on the manuscript in early and late stages; Elizabeth Miller performed a readability analysis on all parts of the book; Patricia Baker, Russ Briggs, John Holmes, Raelyn Joyce, Rich Konieczka, Sadie Miles, Beryl Schicker, Jonnie Wilhite, and Joanne Wright all used the text in manuscript form with their classes (as did Corbin and Lay), and the excellent suggestions from all of them and from their students have helped to make it a much better book than it might have been. I can't omit my office mate, John Mulay; although he teaches speech and therefore couldn't use the book, he read it and provided tons of moral support with his wildly enthusiastic comments. Thanks, everybody!

Fourth, a great group of people provided assistance in turning this from a manuscript into a published book. In the book's reviewing stages, I benefited from the invaluable judgments of Laura Bernell-Zisser, Ohlone College; Robert Dees, Orange Coast College; Nancy Hoagland, Northern Virginia Community College; Susan Petit, College of San Mateo; Ramona Rhodes, George Corley Wallace State Community College; Lucille Thomas, Grand Rapids Junior College; and Susan Wolstenholme, Cayuga Community College. The whole staff of Wadsworth Publishing provided expertise and enthusiasm for the project, but I can mention only a few: Cynthia Bassett, Pete Cokinos, Diana Griffin, Jon Muir, and Steve Robins. My two incomparable editors deserve special acclaim: Kevin Howat and Gary Mcdonald made this book, and it has been a joy to work with them.

PART ONE
RHETORIC

CHAPTER 1
SOME PRELIMINARIES (WHY WRITE?)

CHAPTER 2
PREWRITING: THE SENDER
(WHO'S WRITING THIS, ANYWAY?)

CHAPTER 3
PREWRITING: THE RECEIVER
(AND WHO'S READING THIS?)

CHAPTER 4
PREWRITING: THE MESSAGE
(WHAT DO YOU HAVE TO SAY?)

CHAPTER 5
WRITING: THE MEDIUM (WORDS)

CHAPTER 6
WRITING: THE MEDIUM (SENTENCES)

CHAPTER 7
WRITING: THE MEDIUM (PARAGRAPHS)

CHAPTER 8
WRITING: THE MEDIUM
(SOME WAYS TO PUT IT ALL TOGETHER)

CHAPTER 9
WRITING: THE MEDIUM
(MORE WAYS TO PUT IT ALL TOGETHER)

CHAPTER 10
POSTWRITING: REDUCING NOISE

CHAPTER 11
REWRITING: RESPONDING TO FEEDBACK

CHAPTER 12
SPECIAL ASSIGNMENTS: EXAMINATION WRITING

CHAPTER 13
SPECIAL ASSIGNMENTS: EMPLOYMENT WRITING

CHAPTER 14
SPECIAL ASSIGNMENTS: RESEARCH WRITING

CHAPTER 1
SOME PRELIMINARIES (WHY WRITE?)

What have you written lately? Your immediate response may be, "Nothing. I'm not a writer," but think again. You have almost surely held a pen, pencil, or crayon in your hand in the last forty-eight hours and written something. Or perhaps, like me, you do most of your writing at the typewriter. If you really think about your activities for the last few days, they probably included writing at least two or three of these:

- A check to pay a bill
- A grocery list
- An excused absence note for a son or daughter
- Lecture notes in a college class
- A memo to a coworker about a job to be done
- A thank you note
- A limerick about someone you dislike
- A note to your wife, husband, or roommate to explain why you would be late coming home

Although you probably don't consider yourself a writer, you almost surely do spend some time writing practically every day. According to one communications researcher, Dr. Ralph Nichols, most of us spend 70 percent of our waking moments in some form of verbal communication. Although only 9 percent of this time is spent writing, this still works out to an average of an hour a day, allowing for eight hours of sleep. Of course, to make this average, we must balance journalists and creative writers who put in eight hours or more a day with others who never write because they can't. As a reader of this book, you're likely to be somewhere between these extremes.

Why did you write the check, list, note, or memo? Probably much of what you have written lately has been written for someone else to read. Of course the notes you took in the biology lecture may be comprehensible only to yourself, and the grocery list—unless you're not the one who does the shopping—may be designed only as a memory jogger. Even in these cases, however, the you who does the reading and who finally acts upon what you have written will be slightly different from the you who did the writing. If you could count on the you-reader to be as familiar with the term *phyllotaxy* as you were when you listened to the biology professor explain it, you would not need to take notes on the definition. Similarly, if you could count on the you-shopper to be as hungry for chocolate covered raisins as you were when you made the grocery list, you could depend on your hunger to jog your memory, and you wouldn't need the list. Because you change slightly between the Monday when you take notes and the Wednesday two weeks later when your knowledge of biology is tested, you need the lecture notes. Because your appetite grows or diminishes and your memory is fallible, you need the grocery list.

For most of your writing, however, the intended reader is not just a slightly different you but an altogether different person—a bank teller, Mehitabel's teacher, the second shift foreman, Great Aunt Sue. You write to convey information. You want $10.95 taken out of your account and paid to K-Mart, and it had better not be $109.50 or $1,095.00! You want Mrs. Peabody to know that Mehitabel was not goofing off; she missed school because she had the mumps. Jake needs to know which invoices are to be processed first, and Great Aunt Sue should be told that the antique mirror she sent for a wedding present arrived in seventy-two pieces.

HOW WRITING DIFFERS FROM OTHER COMMUNICATING

Of course, writing is not the only way to convey information. Some futurists even claim that writing is on its way out, to be replaced by the telephone, the tape recorder, and electronic data storage capacities beyond our wildest dreams. It is true that we all spend approximately three times as much time talking as writing. Still, in the 1980s writing is nearly unavoidable, and it has several distinct advantages over other forms of communication. One of the most obvious is the semipermanent record it creates. If there is some question over the amount to be paid to K-Mart, the bank teller can consult the actual check you wrote, or at least a photostatic copy of it. If Mrs. Peabody suspects that Mehitabel wrote her own excuse, she has the actual note she can compare to earlier examples of your penmanship.

At one time, writing had a distinct cost advantage over telephoning, but increases in postage rates have reduced this advantage in some cases. Still, we write notes rather than phone when the phone is inconvenient or inaccessible. If you know that your wife is headed home in rush-hour traffic, there is no way to call to explain that you are taking the neighbor's dog to the vet, so you leave her a note.

Another advantage of writing is its selectivity. When you take notes on a lecture, you probably write down only what you consider to be important points. You can review the notes on an hour lecture in twenty or thirty minutes—or even less, if the lecture is dull and repetitious. College students tended to forget this advantage when cassette recorders were first popularized, but they soon realized that it took just as long to review a boring lecture as it had taken to listen to it the first time. Note taking returned to the classroom.

One final advantage of writing is that you can change it. Now, I am not going to be so naive as to argue, in this post-Watergate era, that tape recordings cannot be altered, but I am going to argue that we can never eat our words. Once I have called somebody a damn fool, the damage is done. I can't unsay what I've said, unless my words are written. If my anger cools, I can always replace my written message ("You're a damn fool!") with a calmer one ("I think you're mistaken."), if the message is still in my hands.

Although I enjoy writing and have spent nearly twenty years teaching it, I am not going to pretend that the only differences between writing and other ways of conveying information are positive ones. Writing has two big disadvantages that keep many of us from spending more than an hour a day at it: It takes more time than speaking, and it requires a knowledge of different rules than the rules for speech. These two disadvantages are related. One reason we take longer to write a brief message than we do to speak it is that we have to decide what to do about punctuation and spelling when we write. If we speak the message, we need only concern ourselves with word order and pronunciation; and if we garble these, we generally have the advantage of an immediate reaction from our listener—a raised eyebrow, a "Huh?" or a direct question—that tells us to try again.

But even without concern for the mechanics of writing, we would still take longer to write down our thoughts than to voice them, because we almost always speak faster than we write. Actually, writing is a three-step process, whereas speaking is more like a one-and-one-half-step process.

Before we write anything, we must take the first of these three steps: We must get an idea. Something has to occur to us. This *prewriting process*, as it is generally called, can take anywhere from a second or two to years, depending on how complex the idea is. When I write a grocery list, the prewriting consists of checking the cupboard and refrigerator, looking at any new recipes to see what ingredients I need, asking the rest of the family what they'd like to eat, and doing an internal check to see what cravings I have. It takes only a few seconds to realize that I'm hungry for marshmallow fudge and perhaps a whole minute to argue with myself about the calories before I cross it off my list. Before I started to write this book, however, the prewriting process took several months—several months of thinking about all the things wrong with other books I had used, discussing with other teachers what they wanted to have in their textbooks, and stuffing ideas in a manila folder.

Doesn't speaking have a step comparable to the prewriting step of the writing process? Well, yes and no. In spite of generations of admonitions to "think before you speak," most of us don't do it very long. Most people speak about 150 words per minute, and they are thinking only a sentence or so ahead of themselves. When the speech catches up with the thinking, they fill in with "uh"s to let their listeners know they still want the floor. Of course, when we have something really important to say, we rehearse our speeches as carefully as we plan our writing, and then the prespeaking step may take a long time. Still, I know that when I do this, my words often come out entirely different from the ones I had so carefully planned, making much of this step wasted. In comparison to the prewriting step, prespeaking is only a half step, as far as I am concerned.

The second step in the writing process is the most obvious—*writing*. For many people—especially for poor writers—it is almost the only step. They begin writing before they have any definite idea of what they want to say, and as soon as they have a few words down on paper, they heave a sigh of relief and stop. If they had done a really thorough job of prewriting, the writing step might be nearly the end of the process; but there is always a third step that should be taken—*postwriting*.

There is really no comparable revision step in the speaking process, no postspeaking step. The main reason for this lack is the time differential. We speak so rapidly that we are generally not expected to go back over what we have said and correct it. Also, if our words are not clear to our listeners, we have the opportunity, most of the time, to say something else—a second message that will convey what the first didn't get across. When we write, we do not always know what ideas will be clear to our readers and what will be garbled, and we don't see the raised eyebrow or hear the muttered "Huh?" that tells us we haven't been understood. However, we do have the benefit of time to revise and clarify what we have written, so we can try to assure that the message is clear.

The distinction between speech and writing is a little like that between live television and taped television. Live television was exciting and spontaneous, but we viewers excused a number of fluffs and revelations of hidden microphones because we knew the producers had no chance to correct their mistakes. Today, almost all television is taped because of the obvious advantage of having time to redo a scene that goes badly on the first take. Even programs that are nearly live usually allow a delay of a few seconds before broadcasting, just in case someone comes out with one of the seven words you can't say on television and the censor needs to insert a bleep. Because we know the producer has time to make corrections in a taped show, we are more critical of uncorrected mistakes, and the same is true for mistakes made by writers. Because the writer has more time than the speaker to revise a message, we expect the time to be used.

Using this time to edit your writing, reorganizing sections, adding details, smoothing out difficult sentences, and improving word choices, is the first part of the postwriting step. The last part is proofreading, checking your spelling and reading exactly what you wrote to make sure you haven't omitted words, repeated words, or had problems with verb tenses or punctuation. This step is where the knowledge of rules that are a little different from the rules for speech comes in, and acquiring this knowledge is one of the main reasons you have studied English for twelve or thirteen years. It is one of the reasons you are in this class today.

HOW WRITING IS THE SAME AS OTHER COMMUNICATING

So far, I have been pointing out how writing differs from other ways of getting your ideas across to other people, ways of communicating. But I shouldn't overemphasize these differences, because writing is really much more like speaking than it is different from it. Writing and speaking are both parts of the communication process, and they can both be illustrated by the same *Communications Model*.

When we try to put our ideas into other people's heads, we go through an abstract process, one that we cannot see happening. If we want to visualize this process to understand it better, we have to create a model, using a specific instance of communication to illustrate the essentials of the process.

Since I am writing this book to try to convey certain ideas to you, the readers, I'll use my experience as writer and yours as readers to illustrate the communications model. As I write this book, my goal is to transfer certain ideas from my brain into your brains. To accomplish this, I sit at a typewriter and make marks on paper. These marks stand for the ideas I have, and I hope that they will mean approximately the same ideas to you when you see them—slightly altered by the process of publication—on the pages of your textbook. Whether or not I succeed in getting my ideas across is determined only in part by how carefully I have chosen my words and how accurately I have typed the symbols to represent them. Part of my success is determined by my readers. Your physical and mental state will influence how carefully you read; your past associations with certain words will determine whether they say the same things to you that they say to me. Your surroundings and the distractions they may contain will also influence your receptivity to my ideas. I will never be sure that you really understood my original ideas unless I get some response from you or from the instructors using this book.

In the brief description just given of one example of the communication process we have all ten essentials of the Communications Model:

1. Sender (me)
2. Message (my ideas)
3. Receiver (you, the reader)
4. Communication situation (the occasion for writing and reading, our surroundings while we do both, and our relationship to each other)

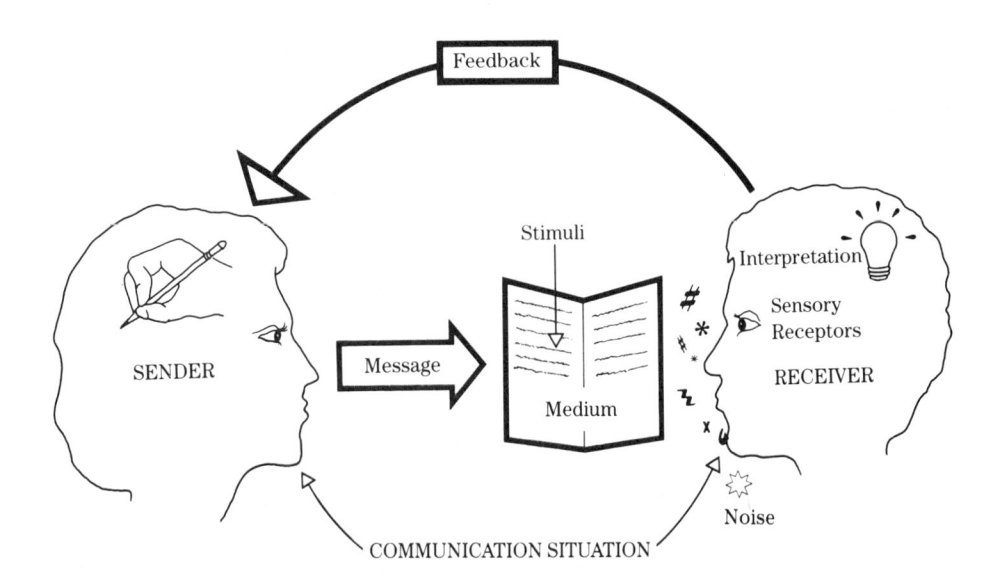

5. Stimuli (the letters typed out on a page and later reproduced in printed form)
6. Medium (the book itself)
7. Sensory receptors (your eyes that perceive the stimuli)
8. Interpretation (the meaning that you attach to the words you read)
9. Noise (distraction from your surroundings or even internal distractions, like a throbbing mosquito bite on your leg)
10. Feedback (the receiver's message back to the sender, indicating whether or not the message got through)

As you write papers for this class, you will become senders, and your goal will be to achieve a close match between your message and the receiver's interpretation. This model should help you to anticipate some of the difficulties. As the sender, you will have control over the message, the stimuli, the medium, and your part of the communication situation. If you are going to influence the interpretation put on your message, you will need to make some informed guesses about your receivers and their part in the communication situation. You will need to estimate how different they may be from you and how these differences may affect their interpretation. You must try to reduce noise as much as possible. Although you won't be able to eliminate distractions from within your reader or from the reader's surroundings, you can greatly reduce noise that is part of the stimuli or message itself: the coffee stains in the margin, the pale writing that can't be read, the misspelled words. To improve your communication, you will learn to rely on feedback more and more—feedback from other members of your class as well as from your instructor. From their comments you will be able to tell how successfully you have achieved your goal of putting your ideas into other people's heads.

Please keep this Communications Model in mind as you begin your study of prewriting, the first step in writing to communicate. Remember, there is nothing mysterious about the topic. Writing is something you already know how to do with some degree of success. You have been writing those grocery lists, lecture notes, and business memos for years. You have probably even written a few formal essays for high school assignments or other college classes. This book should help you to write more effectively in your daily life as well as in your college career.

CHAPTER 2

PREWRITING: THE SENDER (WHO'S WRITING THIS, ANYWAY?)

There are two parts to the prewriting of any written communication more complicated than a grocery list: the part in your head and the part on paper. If your instructor asks you to turn in your prewriting—as I generally do with my students—it is the second part you will turn in. The invisible prewriting is a kind of self-talk that may take the form of a dialogue. "What on earth do I have to say about such a dumb subject? I can't write about the time I went to Niagara Falls; that was too embarrassing! I guess I could write about the time . . ." This mental part is not what your instructor expects you to turn in; there is no way to demonstrate it. Even the enterprising student who turned in a copy of his brain waves recorded on an electroencephalogram would have no way of establishing the *content* of these brain waves. It is just taken for granted that some self-talk occurs before you begin to write. Studying this prewriting step should help you to make this self-talk more productive.

The second part of the prewriting is the visible part, and it is what you should turn in if you are asked for prewriting. Your prewriting should include the random jottings that help you get from nothing to write about to a well-formulated idea of something to say, from a blank page (panic time!) to a jumble of notes and a clear concept of the introductory paragraph. For many student writers, this step is the most difficult (as well as the most neglected), but studying prewriting techniques should provide you with several gimmicks to help you over the hurdle of getting the first words down on paper.

Just a word of caution here: The prewriting is *not* the same as the rough draft. Once you begin actually writing the paper, even if you are working on an early version that is changed quite a bit before you submit the final paper, you have proceeded to the writing step. You should not begin a rough draft until you have a fairly clear notion of what that draft will say. Any activity that helps you develop that clear notion is prewriting. The rough draft comes *after* the prewriting and is not a part of it.

As you go through the prewriting step, there are three elements of the communication process you need to consider: the sender, the receiver, and the message. This chapter will help you to think about the first of these—yourself—and to develop some techniques that will be useful whenever you are getting ready to write.

ROLES AND OUR SELF-CONCEPTS

You may be saying to yourself, "Why bother to spend a whole chapter on me? I know who I am; I just don't know what I want to say when I write!" This kind of self-talk is only partly accurate. You can test it by jotting down a one-sentence answer to the question, "Who are you?"

Now look at your answer. Does it sum up *all* of you? Is this always the person you are when you write or speak? Can anyone be capsulized in one sentence? Part of the problem of defining yourself is the real complexity of any individual. We all have many different social positions that we fill at various times throughout the day. These social positions are called *roles*. (Even though the term implies a kind of artificiality, as if we stepped into parts created for us by some playwright, there is nothing essentially insincere about taking several roles. In fact, we cannot avoid multiple roles. We are all children of our parents, but once we reach maturity we take on other roles with our responsibilities. As workers, home owners, lovers, voters, athletes, and parents ourselves, we cannot behave exactly as we did as children. Adapting our behavior to our social responsibilities is a part of growing up.) Generally, when we become the sender in any particular communication situation, we are involved in only one or two of our social roles. These roles affect the choices we make as we write or speak.

PRACTICING DEFINING YOURSELF

Before you can decide which one of your many roles is taking part in a specific communication situation, you need to analyze what some of these roles are. The following questions may help. It should be interesting to write down your answers and share any that are not too private with other members of the class. (Answer quickly, "off the top of your head." This rapid-fire thinking is a good prewriting technique; sometimes your answers will surprise you!)

1. What six nouns name roles you take in your life right now? (For instance, *father, electrician, neighbor, softball coach, Democrat,* and *student*.)
2. What six adjectives best describe you? (*Short, serious, studious, religious, talkative,* and *generous*, for example.)
3. What activities have taken up most of your time in the last two weeks?
4. What do you do that you would like to quit doing?

> **5.** What do you do that you would keep on doing, even if nobody knew anything about it?
>
> **6.** What was the most expensive thing you ever bought?
>
> **7.** What accomplishment do you have to look back on with pride? What plans do you have to look forward to with hope? (I owe these two questions to a couplet in Robert Frost's "The Death of the Hired Man": "And nothing to look backward to with pride,/And nothing to look forward to with hope."*)
>
> **8.** What kind of person do you dislike most?
>
> **9.** What do you do to avoid being that kind of person yourself?
>
> **10.** How have you changed in the last three years?
>
> **11.** How would you like to change in the next three?
>
> You can probably think of some similar questions that will help you visualize the roles you take in life and the attitudes you have toward these roles. Share these questions with the class.

* From "The Death of the Hired Man" from *The Poetry of Robert Frost* edited by Edward Connery Lathem. Copyright 1930, 1939, © 1969 by Holt, Rinehart and Winston. Copyright © 1958 by Robert Frost. Copyright © 1967 by Lesley Frost Ballantine. Reprinted by permission of Holt, Rinehart and Winston, Publishers.

All of the attitudes you have about yourself and your roles, taken together, go to make up your self-concept. "Self-concept influences the people we choose to talk to, what we talk about, what we decide to listen to, and what we remember," according to Taylor, Rosegrant, Meyer, and Samples (*Communicating*, 1977). It also influences our writing and reading choices.

The relationship between self-concept and communicating behavior—both spoken and written—is complicated and interesting. Much of our self-concept develops because of the experiences we have in communicating, and at the same time, the self-concept we have already developed helps to determine which communicating experiences we will have.

This circular process begins in infancy; the early childhood years are the most crucial in the development of your self-concept, but you will never reach a point when you can say, "Now, my self-concept is *finished!*" Your view of yourself will continue to change as you and your circumstances change. (It had better. The eighty-five-year-old who still views himself as he did thirty years before may learn a new self-concept only when shoveling snow brings on a heart attack.)

It is easiest to see how your self-concept develops if you analyze just one idea you have about yourself, rather than taking the whole complex of ideas and attitudes. For example, I'll take a negative (but accurate!) idea I have about myself: I am unathletic. How did I come to think of myself as unathletic? Before I started school, the word was not even part of my vocabulary, nor did I think of myself in simpler language as "rotten at sports." I guess I never really had experienced any sports; I played Pinochle and Canasta before I started school, but nobody in my family did anything more physical than that unless it was work, not play. At school the games more complicated than jacks or jumprope were beyond me. I didn't know the rules, I was slow, and I was uncoordinated. The kids laughed when I came up to bat, and I was usually the last girl chosen, amid groans, for any team. The laughs and groans were definite communications to me; my interpretation was to tell myself I was "rotten at sports." Of course, the more I told myself this, the more nervous and embarrassed I was whenever I had to attempt anything athletic, and the worse my performance became. This "unathletic" self-concept became a self-fulfilling prophecy. I was bad at any game not just because I lacked experience but because I expected myself to be bad. Because I expected to be bad, I avoided games as much as possible.

Many students have similar negative ideas about their abilities to communicate. "I just can't speak in front of groups," or "I never can write what I want to say" can become self-fulfilling prophecies, too. Realizing how these attitudes became parts of their self-concepts can help them to change them.

How do our self-concepts, both positive and negative, affect our writing? They help to determine what stand we take on issues we are discussing, and they give our writing that personal flavor that is lacking in writing done by a committee or by a computer. They account for the difference in perspective which makes each writer's approach to a topic different by a few degrees from any other writer's approach. Imagine an entire class of freshman writers expounding on the topic of sports. At least one of the students may have an "unathletic" self-concept similar to mine; his paper may be filled with torn ligaments, sweat, strain, and disappointment. The jock sitting next to him has visions of playing in the Superbowl, so he writes about the straight path to glory, and his paper includes the bands, the cheering fans, and the adrenalin rush of victory. All the students' insights about sports will be determined by their own past experiences and their feelings about themselves, so their papers will all be personal. Only one paper is likely to be objective, totally without individual perspective. That is the essay written by the computer whiz who has programmed her latest birthday present to produce a reasonable facsimile of the English language. Since the computer has no self-concept, its prose would have no point of view. It might be technically correct, but it would be wooden.

LABELING

When I say that a part of my self-concept is that I am unathletic, I am using a *label*, a term used to describe one aspect of my behavior. Although I cannot describe myself or anyone else without using labels, this process of labeling, or *stereotyping*, is dangerous. One of the dangers is that it is self-fulfilling, but that is not its only danger.

Labeling, in its negative sense, occurs when we attach a term to someone's behavior and then apply that term to the whole person. If we label a person as "unathletic," we see her as terrible at all physical activities, even dancing, although she might be very good at that. We stereotype someone else as "conservative" because of her politics, and we assume she will also be conservative in her religion, her child-rearing practices, and her financial dealings. It is always possible for one person to be so consistent, but it is unlikely. We tend to forget people's inconsistencies when we label them, and this forgetting is almost always a mistake.

I often try to illustrate the problems of labeling to my classes by describing Mrs. X and Mrs. Y. I tell my students that the two women have much in common: both are married, in their mid-thirties, with school-age children. Then I begin labeling them by listing several details about them in parallel columns. When my list is completed, it looks like this:

Mrs. X—
has a professional job, earning over $25,000 per year.

won many scholastic honors and earned three degrees.

is a very bad housekeeper.

is a vegetarian.

is an agnostic.

is active in the Democratic Party.

Mrs. Y—
comes from a twice-broken home.

married in high school.

makes most of her own clothes.

loves to bake.

teaches Sunday school.

is active in the PTA.

Given this minimum of information about Mrs. X and Mrs. Y—but still more information than we often have about people when we begin forming opinions about them—the students start drawing conclusions. Some have told me they would feel more comfortable with Mrs. Y than with Mrs. X, and others have noted that Y is probably a better mother. One even started to psychoanalyze her, explaining that her unhappy childhood probably made her emphasize home and family more than Mrs. X did. They have begun to label Mrs. X as an intellectual oddball and Mrs. Y as a happy homebody. I have not yet had a class see, on their own, the whole point of this exercise, and so I have to tell them: I am both Mrs. X and Mrs. Y.

After the students get over feeling slightly cheated, we go on to discuss the limitations of the labeling process. When we use it, we put people in pigeonholes based on a few observations we have made about them in certain circumstances or a few bits of information we have picked up from some of their acquaintances. Had we seen them in other circumstances or talked to different acquaintances, we might label the same person differently. It is not that I have a split personality that enables me to be seen as both Mrs. X and Mrs. Y. We all have multifaceted selves; when the observer chooses only a half-dozen facets to focus on, he must see an incomplete picture.

The labeling process occurs when we read and write, too; in fact, it is almost inescapable. I used labels just now when I described the essays written for the hypothetical assignment on sports: Their writers were the unathletic student, the jock, and the computer whiz. As you get ready to write, try to visualize how your readers might label you, and think about how you would like to be labeled. Do you want to come across in your writing as a cool logician, a sentimentalist, an intellectual, a charismatic leader? Do you want to present yourself as a dutiful son, an avid hunter, an executive-in-training, or an enraged consumer? You may be all of these, but you aren't likely to draw upon all of these facets of your life in any one communication situation. Your reader is most likely to label you as you want to be labeled if you give some thought to the role you are taking *before* you write.

Of course, it is impossible to see the complete picture of anyone, even yourself. Your self-concept is necessarily incomplete and changing; some people spend years in analysis "finding themselves." The more experiences you have and the more people you meet, the more you will see yourself reflected in the eyes of someone else, and these "mirrors" provide you with new ideas about yourself. These reflections of you are only partial, as each person notices and reacts to some quality about you that is important to her or to him. None of these acquaintances can know and respond to the "real you" any more than you can know and respond to their real selves.

W. B. Yeats, the Irish poet, summed up this impossibility clearly in the last verse of "For Anne Gregory":

I heard an old religious man
But yesternight declare
That he had found a text to prove
That only God, my dear,
Could love you for yourself alone
And not your yellow hair.*

ROLES AND VOICES

So, we all learn many roles in life, beginning in early childhood and continuing as long as we are alive, and these roles, together with our attitudes toward them, go to make up our self-concepts. But the self-concept is somehow more than just a listing of our many roles; the whole is greater than the sum of its parts. So what? What does all this have to do with writing?

Well, one of the prewriting decisions you generally have to make is which self is doing the writing in any particular communication situation. When I write an assignment for my students, or when I write this book, I use the voice of my teacher-self; this is a little different from the parent-self voice I use when I write a note to my son's teacher. And that parent-self voice is even a little different from the parent-self voice I use when I write a note to one of my sons. (And there may even be a difference—at least in vocabulary—between the voice I use when I write to the ten-year-old and the voice I use when I write to the fourteen-year-old.) The differences in the parental voices depend upon the audience (the receivers), so they really belong in the next chapter. In this chapter I just want to caution you to make good decisions about which self is speaking before you write.

Writing in the wrong voice can produce ludicrous results. If you have ever written a love letter, you probably knew instinctively not to use the same phrases and tones you would use in a letter to the editor. However, people don't

---

* From *Collected Poems* by William Butler Yeats. Copyright 1933 by Macmillan Publishing Co., Inc., renewed 1961 by Bertha Georgie Yeats. Reprinted with permission of Macmillan Publishing Co., Inc., M. B. Yeats, Anne Yeats, and Macmillan London Ltd.

always realize what voice they are using. Some of the humor in literature is created by mismatching the voice of the writer and the communication situation. Jane Austen used this device over 150 years ago in the novel *Pride and Prejudice.* Mr. Collins, a pompous and not-too-bright minister, mistakenly used his pulpit voice in this proposal to Elizabeth, the novel's main character:

> Almost as soon as I entered the house I singled you out as the companion of my future life. But before I am run away with by my feelings on this subject, perhaps it will be advisable for me to state my reasons for marrying—and moreover for coming to Hertfordshire with the design of selecting a wife, as I certainly did. . . . My reasons for marrying are, first, that I think it a right thing for every clergyman in easy circumstances (like myself) to set the example of matrimony in his parish. Secondly, that I am convinced it will add very greatly to my happiness; and thirdly, which perhaps I ought to have mentioned earlier, that it is the particular advice and recommendation of the very noble lady whom I have the honour of calling patroness.

Need I say that the proposal was turned down? Of course, that would probably have been the result even if Mr. Collins had chosen a more romantic voice for the proposal, but at least he would not have made such a fool of himself!

SOME TECHNIQUES FOR PREWRITING ABOUT YOURSELF

So far, we have been discussing the first part of prewriting, the thinking or self-talk that goes on in our heads before we write anything down. What about the second part? Do we still need to be concerned about the sender of the communication once we start scribbling down ideas in preparation for the actual writing?

You need to keep in mind the voice you will be using in the actual writing in order to keep from switching your tone in mid-page. A student of mine recently had problems with this when he wrote a letter to the parents of the boys he would be coaching in Little League. He started out writing to them as peers, using a friendly but businesslike tone and speaking in a one-adult-to-another voice. But at one point he switched to the dictatorial coach's voice and began telling them what he "would not permit." I cautioned him that the voice appropriate for addressing the boys might not be the best one to use with the parents who paid his salary.

If you are writing something lengthy enough that you might make the mistake of switching voices in the middle, it probably would help you to jot down which voice you will be using. Do this as part of the prewriting. You can put down something like this: "Sender's voice: I am writing as supervisor in charge of the night shift." (Or as the president of student government, as a technical expert on floppy disks, as a member of the PTA, or whatever.)

Generally, when you have gone this far, you can forget about the sender, temporarily, and concern yourself with the receiver and the message. Still, there will be times when these overlap because you will be writing about yourself, so it will be difficult to separate the sender from the message. When this is the case, the "jotting down" part of the prewriting will be all about you, and you may need some special techniques to help you get your thinking organized.

The first technique which might be helpful is a narrowed form of *freewriting*. The idea behind freewriting is borrowed from the group technique of brainstorming. When a group gets together for problem solving, it often uses this procedure, which emphasizes quantity of ideas rather than quality. The group sets a time limit and tries to come up with as many possible solutions as it can; all solutions, no matter how far-fetched, are recorded; no criticism of any solution is allowed until after the time limit expires. The reason for lack of criticism is that criticism frequently cuts off creativity; sometimes the most ridiculous idea will lead someone in the group to the best solution, and if the ridiculous idea had been squelched, the solution would not have appeared.

Freewriting makes use of the time limit and the lack of criticism, although it is not generally done in a group. (It can be, however.) In totally freewriting, you set an alarm clock or stove timer to warn you when the time is up—choosing ten or fifteen minutes, generally—and you begin to see how much paper you can cover with words. You let your mind wander to any subject that comes to your consciousness, not trying to make complete sentences, punctuate in the proper places, or spell the words correctly. You strive to write as much as possible, hoping that in the quantity of ideas your mind will produce there will be some one idea worth developing when you begin the actual writing. When your timer goes off, you begin to review what you have written down, underlining parts that seem worthy of further development.

Freewriting in the narrower or more limited form differs only because you try to stick to one subject—in this case, yourself. There is still no criticism of your wording, ideas, or organization. You are free to write any gibberish that pleases you, so long as it has something to do with the topic—you. You may even begin by writing your name over and over again until something else occurs to you.

To illustrate how this narrowed freewriting might work, I'll try it with you. Let's assume that we have been assigned to write a paper entitled "What I Value." For this, we will need to prewrite for ten minutes on the topic of our own values. You do your prewriting on scrap paper, and I'll do mine right here. (I haven't written this out in advance; I'm really doing it, and I won't know whether it succeeds or fails until the ten minutes are up. Here goes.)

Right now I value the cookie I'm eating—light, flaky, and with just a hint of peanut butter. Yum! Think I'll have another—but if I eat too many cookies in ten minutes, my prewriting won't be done. Well, what do I value? I guess that boils down to what I like to spend time doing. Soaking in a very hot tub with an interesting book to read and nobody hollering at me. Paradise! I must be really lucky, because I get to do this almost every night—the perfect way to end the day. How many people get to do what they most enjoy every day? Of course, if I did it all day long, it wouldn't be the same. It is the contrast with routine that makes it valuable (certainly not the cleanliness; I'm not one of those who believe that cleanliness is next to godliness, as my house will attest!) If I didn't have work to do, deadlines to meet, and people around to holler at me most of the time, I wouldn't enjoy the solitude, the relaxing warmth, and the book as much as I do. Contrast is important to me. Great spells of busy-ness (business?) followed by total lethargy—only the mind working, and that working only on deciphering the work of someone else, some other author. I think I have hit on what I value and a possible topic without using up my ten minutes. At least a paper on leisure made meaningful by its contrast with work, solitude made meaningful by its contrast with family and work life, will probably be different (and therefore, more interesting) than all the papers on my parents, my church, and my home. And when I started doing this, I had the idea I'd probably wind up writing about reading! Maybe this focused freewriting really does work!

How did yours turn out? Can you go back over yours and separate the usable material from the unusable ideas? That is pretty easy to do with mine. The peanut butter cookie can go, and the hot tub and book can stay, but only as an illustration of the main idea, the "leisure made meaningful by its contrast with family and work life."

Although my prewriting has produced a narrower topic for me to write about than just my values, it still isn't quite finished. I really haven't decided which voice I will use in this paper or what labels I want my readers to attach to me as they read about my values. Will I be presenting myself as Mrs. X or Mrs. Y? To show the multitude of activities in my life, the frenetic pace that makes the leisure and lethargy so valuable, I probably need to combine X and Y. Perhaps I can describe a typical day of teaching classes, grading papers, attending a committee meeting, rushing home to make date bars for the parent conferences at the high school my older son attends, waiting in lines for two hours at the conferences, and coming home in time to type up one more test for tomorrow's classes. Is it any wonder that the tub and the book look so good at midnight? I guess I want my readers to label me as the modern woman: wife-mother-professional-community activist—superwoman without the steel brassiere. For this paper I will speak in a professional-but-human voice, using vocabulary appropriate to my role as a college instructor, but avoiding jargon and overly academic statements.

This narrowed freewriting approach is not the only technique for prewriting, of course. A second approach to the same topic—you and your values—could also begin with your name. It is a bit more gimmicky than freewriting, but it should be helpful for writers who need a more structured approach. This is a word game I call Acronym. A word is not truly an acronym unless its letters are made up of the first letters of other words for which it stands. (For instance, *UNESCO*, which stands for United Nations Educational, Scientific, and Cultural Organization.)

For this prewriting approach, you write down the letters of your topic in a vertical line, leaving one line for each letter. Since your topic is you, write down your name, using just your first name to start with, but progressing to your whole name if you get carried away. Now the task is to think of one word for each letter, and the words must describe you. As in freewriting, put down the first descriptive word that comes to mind, unless you quickly think of a better one. Here is my first name as an example.

M essy (My first idea was "motherly," but this is more accurate.)

A rgumentative

U nathletic (You guessed it!)

R elaxed
E nthusiastic
E ducated
N earsighted

If you also have a seven-letter name, you should have seven ideas you could develop about yourself, using an example or two for each one. (You'll have more ideas about how to develop these when you read Chapter Seven on paragraphs.) If I had to use this prewriting for a paper about my values, I would reject "nearsighted" right away; that is a physical fact and has little to do with values. I could write about the value of education, but I always try to steer away from topics I expect other people to write about, so I probably wouldn't use that one. "Messy" and "relaxed" go together pretty well, and so do "argumentative" and "enthusiastic." I could choose between writing about the lack of value I put on good housekeeping (justified when the most immaculate housekeeper I ever knew died of a stroke at age thirty-seven) or the great enthusiasm I have for an intellectual argument. These two papers would call for slightly different voices: the first, that of a woman married for twenty-two years and no longer caring about "ring around the collar" or "housitosis" (a kindred spirit to Erma Bombeck, perhaps); the second, the voice of someone rational, well educated, and—to explain the love of argument—definitely Irish!

Narrowed freewriting and the Acronym Game should get you started writing. You'll learn some other approaches in Chapters Three and Four.

RELATED READINGS

Student Essay

ONE VALUABLE VALUE
Elizabeth DeKam

Points to Consider

As you read the essay that follows, try to answer these questions:

1. What were some of the points that probably appeared in the author's prewriting?
2. How many of the author's roles are revealed in this paper? Which ones seem to have influenced her writing on this occasion?
3. What values, other than horse ownership, are revealed in this essay? Do these seem consistent with the roles of the author?
4. Does this essay seem carefully organized? What ties the first and last paragraphs together?

Used with permission of Elizabeth DeKam.

I learned in my Earth Science class that the scientific name for horse was "equine." I learned that it meant a large, solid-hoofed, herbivorous mammal. There is no way those words could begin to describe that big, fuzzy horse that comes trotting and nickering up to me when I whistle.

To me, owning a horse means more than just shoveling the barn and going riding. Merely spending time with her is an attribute to the ownership. Running out to the barn in the morning to do chores reminds me that there is more to this rut-filled world than just sitting behind a desk pushing a pencil. On the mornings when chores do not need to be done, it is a pleasure to walk up to the fence—all dressed up for the day at the office—and call to my horse and have her come to me for a pat on the nose.

At times when dates are slow, school is over, and friends are busy, boredom never sets in. On rainy days there is always equipment to clean or clippers to take apart and re-oil. On snowy nights there is always a how-to article that has not been read yet, or an experience that has not been recorded in my journal.

There are more reasons than never being bored and having a rejuvenating experience before going to work for horse ownership's value to me. Take one 14-year-old niece; toss in two upset parents; also, add one problem like wanting to date at the ripe old age of 14. The result will be a breakdown in not only the communication between parents and child, but also the communication between aunt and niece, because I disagreed with her on the topic of pre-16 dating. Now take one common bond—our horses—and she will be waiting Saturday morning ready to go for the weekly excursion. At first, talk is non-existent. But given a three-hour ride and a lunch beside a remote lake, the barriers will come down and conversation will start. Answers are not necessarily given and problems not solved, but caring is shared. It is times like those that make me realize how valuable my horse is to me.

I value my horse, and through this value other values have grown. Being an avid horse lover, I wanted to give my horse the things she needs. Also, being a person who watches the pocketbook, I wanted to adjust her needs to my means. So I went out and bought a small farm of ten acres: five acres of pasture to give her plenty of room to roam, and five acres of hay field to feed her all winter so no hay bill comes out of my pocket. It did not take too long before I realized that while I valued my land for what it could do for my horse, it also had other possibilities. Now, every spring I am anxious for the snow to melt to see how the pine seedlings fared over the winter. It has been said, simple pleasures for simple people. Well, perhaps I am a simple person, because I get great joy out of seeing those trees grow.

I consider myself to be a straight person—no bars, never take drugs. There is no virtue in that to me. Where the virtue lies for me is, in part, in the fact that my dollars go into my home, which stemmed from the value I placed on my horse. My joy is in coming home from work and seeing my horse out in the pasture grazing, looking as pretty as a picture. My pride is built up when at horse shows I realize my horse is a first-place winner—perhaps not in the eyes of the judges, but in my eyes. My contentment is found in using my horse as a stepping stone in meeting new people. For me it does not take a can of beer in my hand to loosen my tongue around strangers. For me it helps to have my horse at the end of the lead rope in order to break the ice with strangers.

Often others have wondered about the high cost of a hobby such as the ownership of a horse. They have often asked me about how wise it is to hold such a thing so valuable, especially when to them my value just eats away at the most valuable value: money. But what they do not realize is that what I receive back from my value is worth more than their most valuable value to me.

My value enlarges my appreciation for the countryside. While riding down a road I have often traveled in my auto, I have been surprised to see a house that I really like a lot but have never noticed before. While riding in the fields, I have been thrilled by finding oil wells that are still being pumped. While riding around lakes, I have been in awe at nature when I see three pairs of herons flying in. While riding in the woods, I have been excited at the sighting of a deer. Sometimes if we are close enough we give chase, never getting very close, but just enjoying the sport.

Enjoying my horse is what I do, and as a result I am rewarded in many ways even when I am not looking for reward. Lend an ear and keep an eye on the lookout, for come early Saturday morning, you'll be able to hear a whistle and a few minutes later see a bib-overalled person aboard what she considers to be a very valuable value. We will be cantering down the dirt path to the pines en route to experience serendipity.

Professional Essay

THE MANY ME'S OF THE SELF-MONITOR
Mark Snyder

Points to Consider

As you read the essay that follows, try to answer these questions:

1. How do you rate on the Self-Monitoring Scale? Does this score appear to be an accurate evaluation of your "impression management" ability?
2. Does the author use an appropriate voice for a psychologist writing in *Psychology Today*? Why or why not?
3. Although he cautions against assuming people to be consistent, the author goes on to label people as high or low self-monitoring. Is this form of labeling likely to be as inaccurate as other forms? Is your own level of self-monitoring fairly consistent?
4. The conclusion of this essay presents two definitions of *self*, Jourard's and Goffman's. Contrast these two ideas. With which do you agree?
5. The author discusses the self as an "*integral* feature of personal identity" (paragraph 3) and later comments on a "*canon* of modern psychology." What do *integral* and *canon* mean in these contexts? (Watch the spelling of the second one if you look it up!) Are these words appropriate for the voice

the writer is using here? Could he expect readers of *Psychology Today* to understand them?

Adapted from "Impression Management" by Mark Snyder in the book *Social Psychology in the Eighties*, Third Edition, by L. S. Wrightsman and K. Deaux. © 1981 by Wadsworth, Inc. Reprinted by permission of Brooks/Cole Publishing Co., Monterey, California.

The image of myself which I try to create in my own mind in order that I may love myself is very different from the image which I try to create in the minds of others in order that they may love me.—W. H. Auden

The concept of the self is one of the oldest and most enduring in psychological considerations of human nature. We generally assume that people are fairly consistent and stable beings: that a person who is generous in one situation is also likely to be generous in other situations, that one who is honest is honest most of the time, that a person who takes a liberal stance today will favor the liberal viewpoint tomorrow.

It's not always so: each of us, it appears, may have not one but many selves. Moreover, much as we might like to believe that the self is an integral feature of personal identity, it appears that, to a greater extent, the self is a product of the individual's relationships with other people. Conventional wisdom to the contrary, there may be striking gaps and contradictions—as Auden suggests—between the public appearances and private realities of the self.

Psychologists refer to the strategies and techniques that people use to control the impressions they convey to others as "impression management." One of my own research interests has been to understand why some individuals are better at impression management than others. For it is clear that some people are particularly sensitive to the ways they express and present themselves in social situations—at parties, job interviews, professional meetings, in confrontations of all kinds where one might choose to create and maintain an appearance, with or without a specific purpose in mind. Indeed, I have found that such people have developed the ability to carefully monitor their own performances and to skillfully adjust their performances when signals from others tell them that they are not having the desired effect. I call such persons "high self-monitoring individuals," and I have developed a 25-item measure—the Self-Monitoring Scale—that has proved its ability to distinguish high self-monitoring individuals from low self-monitoring individuals. . . . Unlike the high self-monitoring individuals, low self-monitoring individuals are not so concerned about taking in such information; instead, they tend to express what they feel, rather than mold and tailor their behavior to fit the situation.

My work on self-monitoring and impression management grew out of a long-standing fascination with explorations of reality and illusion in literature and in the theater. . . . But I was also interested in exploring the older, more philosophical question of whether, beneath the various images of self that people try to project to others, there is a "real me." If we are all actors in many social situations, do we then retain in any sense an essential self, or are we really a variety of selves?

Here is a 10-item abbreviated version of the Self-Monitoring Scale that will give readers some idea of whether they are low or high self-monitoring individuals. If you would like to test your self-monitoring tendencies, follow the instructions and then consult the scoring key.

These statements concern personal reactions to a number of different situations. No two statements are exactly alike, so consider each statement carefully before answering. If a statement is true, or mostly true, as applied to you, circle the T. If a statement is false, or not usually true, as applied to you, circle the F.

T F 1. I find it hard to imitate the behavior of other people.
T F 2. I guess I put on a show to impress or entertain people.
T F 3. I would probably make a good actor.
T F 4. I sometimes appear to others to be experiencing deeper emotions than I actually am.
T F 5. In a group of people I am rarely the center of attention.
T F 6. In different situations and with different people, I often act like very different persons.
T F 7. I can only argue for ideas I already believe.
T F 8. In order to get along and be liked, I tend to be what people expect me to be rather than anything else.
T F 9. I may deceive people by being friendly when I really dislike them.
T F 10. I'm not always the person I appear to be.

Scoring: Give yourself one point for each of questions 1, 5, and 7 that you answered F. Give yourself one point for each of the remaining questions that you answered T. Add up your points. If you are a good judge of yourself and scored 7 or above, you are probably a high self-monitoring individual; 3 or below, you are probably a low self-monitoring individual.

Skilled Impression Managers

There are striking and important differences in the extent to which people can and do control their self-presentation in social situations: some people engage in impression management more often—and with greater skill—than others. Professional actors, as well as many trial lawyers, are among the best at it. So are successful salespeople, confidence artists, and politicians. The onetime mayor of New York, Fiorello LaGuardia, was particularly skilled at adopting the expressive mannerisms of a variety of ethnic groups. In fact, he was so good at it that in watching silent films of his campaign speeches, it is easy to guess whose vote he was soliciting.

Of course, such highly skilled performances are the exception rather than the rule. And people differ in the extent to which they can and do exercise control over their self-presentations. It is the high self-monitoring individuals among us who are particularly talented in this regard. When asked to describe high self-monitoring individuals, their friends say that they are good at learning which behavior is appropriate in social situations, have good self-control of their emotional expression, and can effectively use this ability to create the impression they want. They are particularly skilled at intentionally expressing and accurately communicating a wide variety of emotions both vocally and facially. . . .

High self-monitoring individuals are also quite likely to seek out information about appropriate patterns of self-presentation. They invest considerable effort in attempting to "read" and understand others. . . .

Although high self-monitoring individuals are well skilled in the arts of impression management, we should not automatically assume that they necessarily use these skills for deceptive or manipulative purposes. Indeed, in their relationships with friends and acquaintances, high self-monitoring individuals are eager to use their self-monitoring abilities to promote smooth social interactions. . . .

Detecting Impression Management in Others

High self-monitoring individuals are also adept at detecting impression management in others. To demonstrate this finely tuned ability, three communications researchers at the University of Minnesota made use of videotaped excerpts from the television program "To Tell the Truth." On this program, one of the three guest contestants (all male in the excerpts chosen for the study) is the "real Mr. X." The other two who claim to be the real Mr. X are, of course, lying. Participants in the study watched each excerpt and then tried to identify the real Mr. X. High self-monitoring individuals were much more accurate than their low self-monitoring counterparts in correctly identifying the real Mr. X and in seeing through the deception of the other two contestants.

Not only are high self-monitoring individuals able to see beyond the masks of deception successfully, but they are also keenly attentive to the actions of other people as clues to their underlying intentions. . . .

How can we know when strangers and casual acquaintances are engaged in self-monitoring? Are there some channels of expression and communication that are more revealing than others about a person's true, inner "self," even when he or she is practicing impression management?

Both scientific and everyday observers of human behavior have suggested that nonverbal behavior—facial expressions, tone of voice, and body movements—reveals meaningful information about a person's attitudes, feelings, and motives. Often, people who engage in self-monitoring for deceptive purposes are less skilled at controlling their body's expressive movements. Accordingly, the body may be a more revealing source of information than the face for detecting those who engage in self-monitoring and impression management. . . .

One way that prejudice can be revealed is the physical distance that people maintain between themselves and the target of their prejudice. To demonstrate this phenomenon, psychologist Stephen Morin arranged for college students to be interviewed about their attitudes toward homosexuality. Half the interviewers wore "Gay and Proud" buttons and mentioned their association with the Association of Gay Psychologists. The rest wore no buttons and simply mentioned that they were graduate students working on theses. Without the students' knowledge, the distance they placed their chairs from the interviewer was measured while the interviews were going on. The measure of social distance proved to be highly revealing. When the student and the interviewer were of the same sex, students tended to establish almost a foot more distance between themselves and the apparently gay interviewers. They placed their chairs an average of 32 inches away from apparently gay interviewers, but only 22 inches away from apparently nongay interviewers. Interestingly, most of the students expressed tolerant, and at times favorable, attitudes toward gay people in general. However, the distances they chose to put between themselves and the interviewers they thought gay betrayed underlying negative attitudes.

Impression Managers' Dilemmas

The well-developed skills of high self-monitoring individuals ought to give them the flexibility to cope quickly and effectively with a diversity of social roles. They can choose with skill and grace the self-presentation appropriate to each of a wide variety of social situations. But what happens when the impression manager must effectively present a true and honest image to other people?

Consider the case of a woman on trial for a crime that she did not commit. Her task on the witness stand is to carefully present herself so that everything she does and says communicates to the jurors clearly and unambiguously her true innocence, so that they will vote for her acquittal. Chances are good, however, that members of the jury are somewhat skeptical of the defendant's claims of innocence. After all, they might reason to themselves, the district attorney would not have brought this case to trial were the state's case against her not a convincing one. . . .

It often can take as much work to present a truthful image as to present a deceptive one. In fact, in this case, just being honest may not be enough when facing skeptical jurors who may bend over backwards to interpret any and all of the defendant's behavior—nervousness, for example—as a sign of guilt.

The message from research on impression management is a clear one. Some people are quite flexible in their self-presentation. What effects do these shifts in public appearance have on the more private realities of self-concept? In some circumstances, we are persuaded by our own appearances: we become the persons we appear to be. This phenomenon is particularly likely to occur when the image we present wins the approval and favor of those around us. . . .

The reactions of other people can make it all the more likely that we become what we claim to be. Other people may accept our self-presentations at face value; they may then treat us as if we really were the way we pretend to be. For example, if I act as if I like Chris, chances are Chris will like me. Chris will probably treat me in a variety of friendly ways. As a result of Chris's friendliness, I may come to like Chris, even though I did not in the first place. The result, in this case, may be beneficial to both parties. In other circumstances, however, the skilled impression manager may pay an emotional price.

High self-monitoring orientation may be purchased at the cost of having one's actions reflect and communicate very little about one's private attitudes, feelings, and dispositions. In fact . . . correspondence between private attitudes and public behavior is often minimal for high self-monitoring individuals. Evidently, the words and deeds of high self-monitoring individuals may reveal precious little information about their true inner feelings and attitudes.

Yet, it is almost a canon of modern psychology that a person's ability to reveal a "true self" to intimates is essential to emotional health. Sidney Jourard, one of the first psychologists to hold that view, believed that only through self-disclosure could we achieve self-discovery and self-knowledge: "Through my self-disclosure, I let others know my soul. They can know it, really know it, only as I make it known. In fact, I am beginning to suspect that I can't even know *my own soul* except as I disclose it. I suspect that I will know myself 'for real' at the exact moment that I have succeeded in making it known through my disclosure to another person."

Only low self-monitoring individuals may be willing or able to live their lives according to Jourard's prescriptions. By contrast, high self-monitoring individuals seem to embody Erving Goffman's view of human nature. For him, the world of appearances appears to be all, and the "soul" is illusory. Goffman defines social interactions as a theatrical performance in which each individual acts out a "line." A line is a set of carefully chosen verbal and nonverbal acts that express one's self. Each of us, in Goffman's view, seems to be merely the sum of our various performances.

What does this imply for the sense of self and identity associated with low and high self-monitoring individuals?

I believe that high self-monitoring individuals and low self-monitoring individuals have very different ideas about what constitutes a self and that their notions are quite well-suited to how they live. High self-monitoring individuals regard themselves as rather flexible and adaptive people who tailor their social behavior shrewdly and pragmatically to fit appropriate conditions. They believe that a person is whoever he appears to be in any particular situation: "I am me, the me I am right now." This self-image fits well with the way high self-monitoring individuals present themselves to the world. It allows them to act in ways that are consistent with how they believe they should act.

By contrast, low self-monitoring individuals have a firmer, more single-minded idea of what a self should be. They value and strive for congruence between "who they are" and "what they do" and regard their actions as faithful reflections of how they feel and think. For them, a self is a single identity that must not be compromised for other people or in certain situations. Indeed, this view of the self parallels the low self-monitoring individual's consistent and stable self-presentation.

What is important in understanding oneself and others, then, is not the elusive question of whether there is a quintessential self, but rather, understanding how different people define those attributes of their behavior and experience that they regard as "me." Theory and research on self-monitoring have attempted to chart the processes by which beliefs about the self are actively translated into patterns of social behavior that reflect self-conceptions. From this perspective, the processes of self-monitoring are the processes of self—a system of operating rules that translate self-knowledge into social behavior.

WRITING ASSIGNMENTS

In doing any of the assignments for this chapter, you should strive to meet the following objectives. If you meet all four, you will get a satisfactory grade.

Objectives

1. Turn in your prewriting, showing that you used one of the techniques discussed in this chapter, narrowed freewriting or the Acronym Game.
2. In the essay itself, use examples to illustrate what you are saying.
3. Use standard American spelling.
4. Proofread to eliminate any sentence fragments (unless they are intentional and are marked with asterisks).

Nothing in this text so far has prepared you for this last objective, so I'll give you a little help with it now. If you need a fuller description of fragments, see the Handbook, Section 1.

To avoid being a fragment, a sentence needs a subject, either stated or implied, and a verb. "Stop!" is a sentence, because the subject—the person who is supposed to stop—is clearly the person you are speaking to (implied). A sentence must also *not* have an introductory word that leaves the reader hanging in mid-air. "Prices increase." That is a sentence, but this is not: "Although prices increase." To make it into a sentence, you must complete the thought by adding another subject-verb combination that does not begin with such an introductory word. Here are two suggestions: "Although prices increase, wages do not." "Although prices increase, people continue to buy cars." A sentence will be okay as long as *one* of its subject-verb combinations can stand alone. It can do this if it does not have one of the introductory words that make the idea sound incomplete. There are a number of these introductory words, called "*sub*ordinating conjunctions" because they introduce a clause (a subject-verb combination) of a *lower* order than a sentence. Watch out for these, the most common ones in student writing: *after, although, because, before, if, since, when,* and *whereas.* When you begin a sentence with one of these words, make sure you add another subject-verb combination to complete your thought. If you have some reason for wanting your sentence to sound unfinished, go ahead and write a fragment, but put an asterisk in front of it to show that you do know what you are doing.

2 PREWRITING: THE SENDER (WHO'S WRITING THIS, ANYWAY?)

Writing Assignment 2-1 An important part of your self-concept consists of your values. In this chapter's student essay, "One Valuable Value," you saw how one student described her values. For your prewriting step, use narrowed freewriting to focus on some of your personal values.

When your prewriting is complete, choose one value that you have identified to develop in a more detailed essay. Try to find something tangible you can describe, as concepts like "family" or "religion" are difficult to describe concretely. Instead of discussing family, you could describe a family reunion; instead of discussing your religion, you could describe the stained glass window in your church that means so much to you. This descriptive essay will be the writing step.

For your postwriting step, proofread the essay—not the prewriting—carefully. Be sure to correct any spelling errors and to check for complete sentences.

Writing Assignment 2-2 When you were a very small child, you probably said, "When I grow up, I want to . . ." No matter how fantastic this goal was, it was part of your self-concept at that time. You were the kid who would eventually become chief justice of the Supreme Court, Wonder Woman, or a superspy—or perhaps all three at once! Use the technique of narrowed freewriting to try to recall some of these early ambitions, both career goals and personal goals.

When you have done enough prewriting to have some ideas, choose three or four of these early ambitions to develop into a more detailed essay on your goals in life and how they have changed since you were small. Try to be quite specific about both your early and current goals. This essay will be your writing step.

Proofread the essay, but not the prewriting, for your postwriting step. Check for sentence fragments and spelling errors, and eliminate these.

Writing Assignment 2-3 For the prewriting step of this paper, play the Acronym Game, using at least five letters of your name (either first, last, or a combination).

Then develop these ideas, or some of them, into an essay about yourself, giving examples to show why you think these descriptive terms apply to you. You may use the acronym as an organizational device if you wish, making one paragraph for each letter of your name. This is the writing step of your assignment.

Proofread the essay carefully for the postwriting step. You do not need to proofread the prewriting. Check for sentence fragments and spelling errors, and eliminate these.

Writing Assignment 2-4 Choose one role that is very important in your life right now. For the prewriting step of this paper, play the Acronym Game, using this role as the word you spell out. Try to think of descriptive words that apply to you when you are in this role.

When you have done enough prewriting to have some ideas, develop these into a detailed essay about yourself and your important role. Be as descriptive as possible when you explain this role. This essay will be the writing step of your assignment.

For your postwriting step, proofread the essay—not the prewriting—carefully. Correct any sentence fragments or spelling errors.

CHAPTER 3

PREWRITING: THE RECEIVER (AND WHO'S READING THIS?)

If you wrote only for yourself, you could skip this part of prewriting. You can write in your journal, make a grocery list, or jot down your list of things to do today without being concerned about the person who will read these being able to understand what you mean. For most writing, however, you do need to be concerned about your audience—the person or persons who will read what you have written and who may receive your intended message or may get some other idea altogether.

You are your ideal reader. To you, your observations are perceptive, your phrasing is brilliant (most of the time), and your arguments are convincing. You know exactly what you meant to say, and you will usually read anything you have written as if you had said just that—even if you have omitted or repeated words in such a way as to trip up another reader. If you could be sure that all the readers of your writing were clones of you, you could almost guarantee accurate communication.

The reason communication is nearly perfect when you read your own writing lies in the interpretation section of the Communications Model: When you are both the sender and the receiver of a message, the interpretation you attach to the stimuli when you receive them is the same meaning you attached to the stimuli when you created them. Communication is 100 percent.

Misunderstandings occur when the receiver's interpretation is not what the sender intended. The greater the difference between the two people, the greater the chance of such a failure in communication. Two different people perceive stimuli differently because the process of perception is learned. Because we have different experiences, we perceive differently. Our backgrounds influence our reactions. Two examples should illustrate this principle.

When my younger son had almost finished first grade, he came home one day with more enthusiasm for the school lunch program than he normally displayed. He explained to me that there was going to be a special lunch the following week, and all of the kids would be able to help themselves to unlimited amounts of ketchup. I understood that he would be pleased with this emphasis on one of his favorite foods; but it seemed unlikely to me that the schools could throw concern for good nutrition to the winds, so I questioned him further. "How do you know about this, Nick?" His response clued me in: "Well, Miss King told us we were going to have a special ketchup day on Tuesday!" His enthusiasm disappeared when I had to tell him that such a day was a time when students could *catch up* on school work they hadn't completed. Never having been behind, Nick had no experience with catching up; when he heard the term, he pictured French fries. The teacher's message needed an interpreter.

When the sender and the receiver are from different cultures, failures in communication are frequent and can be humorous. A British friend of mine used to tell many stories about communication mixups when she first married her American husband. One of the most humorous of these involves the British equivalent of the request, "Wake me up." Now, when British villagers used to depend on the town constable to wake them up by tapping on their windows with his nightstick as he passed their houses, they developed the expression, "Knock me up." This was what my friend's sister meant when she visited in America and said to her brother-in-law, "Sammy, will you knock me up about seven tomorrow?" Sammy, not having a British background, misinterpreted the message. Luckily, his wife knew both the British and the American meanings, so she explained the confusion. (In case some of you readers are new to American slang, *knock up* means, in America, to get somebody pregnant.)

ANALYZING YOUR AUDIENCE

Perception is *selective* as well as learned. You have probably realized this if you have ever asked a friend to read a paper before you turned it in and have had the friend find none of the spelling and grammatical errors later found by your instructor. Although it is possible that your friend deliberately let you down, more likely your friend's past experience and your instructor's past experience were so different that the two of them selected different features of your writing to notice.

To write effectively in most situations, you should include a careful analysis of your audience as part of your prewriting. How is your intended reader different from you? What knowledge of your subject do you have that this reader may lack? What attitudes toward your subject can you expect your reader to have? What details of your writing is your reader likely to focus on?

Of course, if you are to answer questions like these, you must first have a fairly definite audience in mind. You cannot write for *everybody*. Even the newspapers seldom are written for everybody. The general news sections are often written to be read by someone with at least an eighth-grade education. The special sections—sports, concert reviews, stock market analysis—are written for more limited groups with particular interests in those topics, and their level of reading ability may be higher or lower. It is nearly impossible to write on any topic so that your ideas can be understood by everybody and will appeal to everybody. Don't try. Select a smaller audience that seems appropriate for your topic, and write with that audience in mind.

3 PREWRITING: THE RECEIVER (AND WHO'S READING THIS?)

THE WRITING CLASS AS AUDIENCE

Many writing texts recommend that students think of the other students in their writing class as their audience. This often has an advantage, but some classes are so diverse that writing for them may not really be so different from writing for everybody. Before you decide to write for the other students in your class, give some thought to how they are like you and how they are different. If you attend a community college, you may find an especially large number of differences in your audience. It might help you to compare your class with the following description of a typical college writing class:

> They're all in their late teens, for instance, and attending the same college. Consequently, they're likely to have other things in common. Probably they're all high school graduates. They all did well enough in high school, know enough about math and American history, read well enough, are bright enough to have been admitted to that college. They all know their way about the campus. They all know that Public Health 101 is required for graduation, that the food in the union cafeteria is ostentatiously unappetizing, that the dean of students is a windbag. Almost all of them were born in the United States—perhaps in the same part of the country, even in the same city—and therefore are likely to share certain interests and values. They are likely to have some interest in national, state, or local politics, for example; and they almost certainly think democracy a better form of government than dictatorship. What is perhaps most important, they all bear a certain relationship to you. They're your fellow students.*

Unless you attend a small private college, you are not likely to find so many similarities in your own writing class. However, if you are going to use the class as audience for any of your papers, it is important that you realize the amount of diversity that exists.

PRACTICING AUDIENCE ANALYSIS

Analyze your writing class as an audience for your papers by answering these questions. (I suggest you answer them in small groups first, responding only for the members of your group. Then the instructor or a group of volunteers can compile a "Class Profile" from the groups' answers.)

1. What is the age range of the group?
2. What is the range in number of credits carried this semester?
3. How many in the group have jobs?
4. What is the range in number of hours worked per week?
5. How can you categorize their jobs? (For instance, two garage mechanics, one horseback riding instructor, three accountants.)

---

* From *Words In Action* by Martin Steinmann, Jr., Harcourt Brace Jovanovich, 1978. Reprinted by permission.

> 6. How many in the group have children? How many children do they have?
> 7. How many were born in this state? How many in other states, and what other states? How many in other countries, and what other countries?
> 8. How many speak a language other than English, and what languages are these?
> 9. What curricula are group members majoring in?
> 10. What political parties do they represent?
>
> You can add to this list any questions that seem particularly appropriate for your class or your interests. Once you have at least a numerical profile of your group, you will be better prepared to write essays using your classmates as your intended readers. You will have some idea of how they are like you and how they are different.

THE WRITING INSTRUCTOR AS AUDIENCE

Since you will be writing papers in response to assignments made by your English instructor, and you are hoping to satisfy the instructor's requirements and to receive a good grade, why not just consider that you are writing for an audience of one—your instructor? Consciously or unconsciously, many students do this. Even if they do not say their audience is the instructor, you know this is the case when you hear this complaint: "I just can't figure out what that teacher wants!"

It is certainly wise to consider your instructor as you write your paper, especially when you do the proofreading that is part of the postwriting step. If you know that the teacher is a bear about spelling, you would be foolish not to make consistent use of a dictionary in this step. It may even help to be aware of any strong reactions your instructor may have to certain words. My professor for Advanced Composition 340 had conniptions when anyone used the word *field* to refer to anything that didn't have a fence around it and grass growing in it, so we all wrote about the subjects we were majoring in, rather than our fields. My own strongest bias is against the phrase "in terms of." It pays to know such details about your composition teacher.

However, I think it is a mistake to go further than this and tailor the entire content of your writing to your instructor's views—or to what you presume to be your instructor's views. Generally, when you write for an audience of one, it is one you know really well—your brother, sister, parent, lover, or close friend. You know many of this person's views, and you can come fairly close to predicting the reaction some of your ideas will receive. Most students never come to know their writing teachers this well, so many of their assumptions about their audience will turn out to be faulty guesses. Also, the instructor may resent what appears to be a phony attempt to please. Paul Roberts's advice (from "How to Say Nothing in 500 Words") is still valid:

Don't worry too much about figuring out what the instructor thinks about the subject so that you can cuddle up with him. Chances are his views are no stronger than yours. If he does have convictions and you oppose them, his problem is to keep from grading you higher than you deserve in order to show he is not biased. This doesn't mean that you should always cantankerously dissent from what the instructor says; that gets tiresome too. And if the subject assigned is "My Pet Peeve," do not begin, "My pet peeve is the English instructor who assigns papers on 'my pet peeve.'" This was still funny during the War of 1812, but it has sort of lost its edge since then.*

WHAT THE AUDIENCE KNOWS ABOUT YOUR TOPIC

Whatever audience you select—a particular individual, your classmates, your town's registered voters, the youth group at your church, alumni of your high school, for example—an important part of your prewriting step will be to answer one question: How much does this audience know about my topic?

Your answer to this question will determine the amount of background information you will present, the level of language (general or technical) you will use, and even the way in which you will narrow the topic. For instance, if you wanted to write a paper on your hobby of bowling, and you selected your classmates for your audience, you might decide, wisely, that a discussion of the effects of humidity and temperature on lane conditions and thus on the bowling score would be too narrow and technical to interest any but the most avid bowlers. Instead, you might limit your topic to the joys of bowling or to how to choose the best bowling ball.

Although you can't always know positively how much any audience will be familiar with a topic, you can estimate by asking yourself certain questions. How did *you* first learn about the topic? (Personal experience, hearing about others' experiences, reading?) How much time have you spent acquiring the knowledge you have now? Is it likely that many in your audience will have had similar experiences and have spent a comparable amount of time? If your answer is yes, your audience may be quite a bit like yourself, at least in respect to this topic, and you may be able to count on their needing only a brief explanation of the subject and no definition of terms. If your answer is no—and it often should be, as you will write about topics you have special interests in—you had better plan to spend more time explaining your topic, to use fairly simple words, and to define any specialized terminology you really need to use.

WHAT THE AUDIENCE FEELS ABOUT YOUR TOPIC

For some subjects, the audience's emotional response to your topic is more important than their knowledge of it. Almost any audience will be familiar with topics such as abortion, the military draft, mercy killing, the drinking age, or the fuel crisis, but any two audiences—or two audience members—may have very

---

* From *Understanding English* by Paul Roberts. Copyright 1958. Reprinted by permission of Harper & Row Publishers, Inc.

different views on what should be done about them. Do not assume that your audience will necessarily agree with you. You cannot even assume that a controversial topic is understood by everyone in your audience. There is a story, possibly fiction, about a student assigned to write on euthanasia who gave up after a few minutes and confessed to the instructor that he "didn't know anything about the Chinese." Also, I once graded a final exam that was supposed to be on stereotyping but that really dealt with hi-fi components!

If you are writing on a controversial topic, you will need to analyze the variety of opinions your audience is likely to have about it. What appear to be the goals and values of any group are called the group's *perceived norms*. These are fairly easy to judge for a special interest group, so long as you stick to their area of interest. You do not have to be a fortune teller to predict the stand on abortion that a Right to Life group will take or the stand on the fuel crisis that a group of Volkswagen sales representatives will take. But when you go beyond that narrow area of agreed interests, watch out! It is too easy to make the mistake of stereotyping (discussed in Chapter 2) and assume that anyone in the Right to Life group will be conservative on issues other than abortion, or that the Volkswagen people will agree on other national issues. Groups may be held together by a very thin thread; although they agree on one issue, they may disagree widely on almost every other topic. If you mistakenly assume a cohesiveness that doesn't exist, you may alienate your audience.

If you are writing for an audience of your classmates, you may want to take a quick survey of their opinions on your topic. You can do this by selecting a few representative students—not all the same age, or all from the same high school—and asking what they think of your subject. If you are choosing some other audience, you may want to select one that will not be an entirely mixed bag of opinions. For instance, a paper on property taxes to support the schools could be written for an audience of members of the PTA, rather than for an audience of everyone in your school district. (This topic is discussed at greater length in the professional essay by Richard M. Eastman in the Related Readings section at the end of this chapter.)

WHAT THE AUDIENCE KNOWS ABOUT YOU

Almost as important as what the audience knows and feels about your topic is what the members know about you. If they are to accept your statements, they must first accept you as having *credibility*. In other words, they must see you as (1) knowledgeable about your subject and (2) trustworthy.

We all have credibility on certain subjects and with certain people. If your younger sister is going to enroll in the same college you attend, she may come to you for advice about what classes to take and which instructors to avoid; your personal experience gives you credibility on this topic. If she plans to buy a used car, however, she may consult your older sister, because the older sister's experience in buying and fixing up several used cars gives her greater credibility on the subject than you have. (I still remember the response one student gave me on a quiz, when I asked for an example of credibility: "My dealer has high credibility with me. When he says it's good dope, it's good dope." I'm not sure whether he was telling the truth or just trying to shock the instructor, but he obviously understood the concept!)

Both knowledge and trustworthiness are essential if you are to have high credibility. Knowledge without trustworthiness is suspect, and that is why I would be reluctant to accept any judgments on government that came from a former president who resigned to avoid impeachment. Trustworthiness without knowledge is no more valuable than a very sincere belief that the world is flat.

So how can you convey to your readers that you are both knowledgeable and trustworthy? There are several ways of conveying your knowledge without sounding like a conceited oaf. A brief description of your own background, including how you came to be interested in the subject and what you have done to learn about it, can be helpful. Mentioning experts whose works you have read or whom you actually have worked with may help, but do not go to the extreme of sounding like a name dropper. Generally, doing a thorough job of your homework, so that you have the facts on the topic, will show up in the finished writing. The only time you should have real difficulty convincing your audience that you are knowledgeable will be when you aren't. Then, you should do one of two things: (1) become knowledgeable or (2) change your topic.

Trustworthiness is sometimes more difficult to convey—especially today, when people tend to be skeptical of other people's motives, always wondering if a writer does not have some secret axe to grind. Anything that you can do to increase your audience's identification with you, to convince them that you and they have something in common, will generally increase your perceived trustworthiness. If you do have some special personal interest in the topic, it is usually best to admit it at the outset, rather than to leave the audience wondering what that interest might be. For instance, if you are writing about mainstreaming the handicapped in the regular classroom and you are handicapped yourself, you would do best to relate your personal experiences early in the paper. Both your knowledge of the subject and your candid approach would enhance your credibility.

Sometimes the language that you choose and the tone of voice that you use can affect your perceived trustworthiness. Simple, direct statements make your writing appear believable. Complex imagery and pompous wording may make it appear that you are deliberately confusing your readers. You may be sincere in your opposition to foreign-made cars, but your sincerity is likely to be questioned if you state your case like this: "I have come to the conclusion that, for dyed-in-the-wool Americans, true blue patriots, the purchase of a motor vehicle not produced and assembled within the confines of this great nation is a counterproductive action." Instead, say, "Patriotic Americans should buy American-made cars," and improve your credibility.

As a part of your prewriting step, you should consider what your audience already knows about you and what additional information you should give them to increase your credibility.

ANOTHER TECHNIQUE FOR PREWRITING

One systematic approach to audience analysis is to use the technique of the five Ws and the H taught to journalism students. The six questions—Who? What? Where? When? Why? and How?—can be applied to the topic as well as to the audience. Applied to audience analysis, they look like this:

Who are my intended readers? (Or, who is my intended reader?)
What are my readers' views on my topic?
Where did my readers get these views?
When were these views developed?
Why did they develop these views? (In other words, what are their reasons for accepting these views?)
How can I convince my readers to accept my views? (Or, how can I convince them to buy what I'm selling?)

Do not expect to be able to answer all of these questions about every audience and every topic. Still, if you have considered all of them, you will probably have done a thorough job of analyzing your audience before beginning to write.

When applied to the analysis of a topic, this technique of prewriting works best for essays that will be predominantly fact based. A paper that explains or analyzes a historical event (Why Napoleon Lost at Waterloo) or a scientific development (How a Test-Tube Baby Is Born) can benefit from this prewriting technique.

RELATED READINGS

Student Essay

"A GOOD CIGAR IS A SMOKE"
Stan Green

Points to Consider

As you read the essay that follows, try to answer these questions:

1. Do you think the author knows a great deal about cigars? Does his knowledge give him credibility on the topic of cigar smoking? Why or why not?
2. Are there any indications that the author took into account the differences between himself and his audience? What details seem to be addressed to his intended audience? What details seem to be addressed to a more general audience?
3. The title and the conclusion are playing on a well-known saying. See if you can identify it. Is the conclusion meaningful to a reader who is unfamiliar

with the saying? Compare the opening and closing paragraphs; are they tied together in any way?

Used with permission of Stan Green.

The advances in the women's liberation movement have led to women pursuing many activities that have traditionally been reserved for men. In today's world a woman may enjoy smoking a cigar if she will follow three simple steps: selecting the right cigar, preparing to smoke, and smoking the cigar. The joy and satisfaction of smoking cigars have been the domain of men for too long; it is a relaxing and rewarding experience that any person should feel free to enjoy.

The first step is finding a good cigar. Any tobacconist should have a wide variety of cigars, but a dark Central American cigar would be best for one's initial experience. Cigars of a larger diameter smoke more easily and will stay lit better. A relatively large, dark cigar will be suitable to start. A good cigar will cost at least as much as a pack of cigarettes, and a truly fine cigar will cost about $1.50. Choose a cigar that you feel you will be comfortable smoking.

Once a good cigar has been purchased, the next step is preparation for smoking. The cigar is prepared by removing the wrapper and clipping the end. To clip the end you may use a cigar clipper or a pocket knife. If neither of these is available, a pair of cuticle scissors or a seam ripper should serve quite well.

The final part of preparation for smoking is deciding on the time and place where you will try your first cigar. This is to be a relaxing and enjoyable occasion, so a peaceful environment should be found. If this is your first cigar, it would probably be best to enjoy it in the solitary comfort of your home. This will allow maximum attention to enjoying your first cigar.

Smoking the cigar is the final step and is the reason for the careful selection and preparation that you have made. When you light the cigar, take care to see that the flame never comes into direct contact with the cigar. The reason for this precaution is that the delicate flavor of the cigar will be ruined if it becomes too hot. You should hold the match slightly below and slightly in front of the end of the cigar. Puff gently while turning the cigar; lighting the cigar in this manner will make certain that the entire end is lit. Once the cigar is burning, you should smoke it slowly, making sure not to overheat it. The length of ash is a good indication of how cool you are keeping the cigar; the longer the ash grows, the cooler you are smoking.

If you have followed the above steps, you are now enjoying the pleasure of smoking a cigar. You now have about an hour to relax and let the troubles of your life drift away, while you gently puff and relish the aroma of your cigar. You should occasionally inhale to get the full impact of the nicotine, but be careful not to overdo it. Remember that cigars are much stronger than cigarettes.

The enjoyment of a fine cigar may be attained by any person willing to follow three simple steps: selecting a good cigar, preparing to smoke the cigar, and slowly smoking it. An activity that was once reserved for men may now be enjoyed by women and men both. And you may say something similar to what I heard a liberated friend say after following the above steps: "A man is only a man, but a good cigar is a smoke."

The audience that this paper was written for is the group of liberated women who have never experienced smoking a cigar. I did not expect many to be tempted by these instructions so chose to use a serious tone in an attempt at deadpan humor. The purpose of this paper is to explain the proper steps for enjoying a cigar.

Professional Essay

THE AUDIENCE AS CREATIVE FORCE
Richard M. Eastman

Points to Consider

As you read the essay that follows, try to answer these questions:

1. The author presents a "map" of moral pressures affecting the audience. If you were preparing to write a paper on the vaccination program discussed, would such a map be helpful to you? Why or why not? How could you use this technique as a part of your prewriting?
2. Which side would you find it easier to address about the vaccination program: its supporters or its opponents? Is this the group that is more like you or less like you?
3. The author suggests that there are audiences you can't write for effectively. Do you agree? If so, what are some of these?
4. This author uses some words in a slightly different way than you may use them. Two of these are *disposition* and *moral*. What do you mean when you use these words? What do you think the author means? Where does he make his meaning clear? Do you think he considered the vocabulary of his audience before he used these words?

From *Style: Writing and Reading as the Discovery of Outlook*, Second Edition, by Richard Eastman. Copyright © 1970, 1978 by Oxford University Press, Inc. Reprinted by permission.

Writing is discovery. Because this discovery takes place publicly in the sense of being shared with an audience, different audiences will shape different discoveries. For example, you may hold fairly consistent premises about campus radicals; but when you're writing home, you may come up with different reflections about them than when you're writing to the campus newspaper—not because you're hypocritical or flighty but because different audiences press you to explore your meanings in different terms. Hence you need to know how this relationship to an audience can work.

Two qualities of an audience to which a speaker or writer should respond are its knowledge of and its disposition toward the subject at hand.

The Knowledge of the Audience

The knowledge of an audience derives from its past experience of the subject and from its general command of information and language—all of which you ought to get clearly in mind since it will open up the levels of material and language you can use. Suppose that you're making a research report to your classmates on a new cure for some disease. You might open:

> Despite a common belief that Morse's Disease is a minor childhood ailment, medical research has uncovered the serious damage which often sneaks up on the victim after the mild primary symptoms have vanished. Weakened vision, slowed-up reflexes, and even brain damage may occur, but so slowly that heretofore they have been ascribed to other causes. [Drop a footnote to show source.] The cause lies in a secondary virus which slowly multiplies after the primary virus has temporarily depleted the white blood corpuscles. . . .

Your language here can be mature ("primary symptoms," "ascribed," "virus," "white blood corpuscles"). Your classmates are both intelligent and skeptical enough to expect documentation of your facts, so that you have actually accumulated sources which you can cite. If your audience already knows Morse's Disease by its common symptoms, you are spared from a detailed recital of them and can go directly to more advanced matters.

As a medical student a few years from now, you might be asked to report again on the same topic. You would naturally reach much deeper for conceptions and terms which would answer the professional interests of a medical school audience.

> Morse's Disease is one of a small number of known diviral diseases in which the primary and secondary stages are caused by two separate viruses or by two morphologically distinct stages of one virus. (See Strauss *et al.*, *JAMA*, 1965.) The primary virus, designated TK-112, retards diffusion of beta-keto acids from cells, particularly in the epidermis. The secondary virus, TK-113. . . .

Still later as a doctor yourself, you might face a grade-school audience waiting to be vaccinated. You might find yourself proceeding thus:

> For most kids Morse's Disease isn't bad. You get a pimply skin which itches. During the next couple of days you may feel almost too weak to cross the room. Then it's over. But some kids aren't that lucky. Morse's Disease sometimes leaves behind a slow poison in the body which. . . .

The basic topics for all three openings are the same—the hidden dangers in Morse's Disease. Each audience helps the writer to discover a different significance as he writes—the college student's intelligent but general concept, the medical student's technical comprehension, the child's simple concrete awareness. Each meaning is a different *human* projection of what began as objective information.

The Disposition of the Audience

The disposition of an audience means its initial readiness to feel and to act on the issues you will be treating. [People] do not feel and act from logic and knowledge alone. They feel and act from their virtues and vices as engaged by specific hopes and fears. If you know what these are for the audience you have in mind, you can open up your subject with maximum stimulus from it.

There is nothing complicated about virtues and vices considered as abstract lists. The standard virtues are generosity, courage, self-control, justness, reverence, and so forth; the standard vices are their opposites. These qualities do become alive and complicated through what [people] most hope or fear, praise or condemn. Most commonly praised and hoped for are usually health and youth, friendship and love, independence, wealth, prestige, knowledge, group welfare. Their opposites are most commonly feared and condemned.

What you would need to learn, then, is what are the morally sensitive areas in your topic which a given audience will press you to cover. Suppose that you want your community to adopt a public vaccination program against Morse's Disease. Taking the list of virtues, vices, hopes, and fears just proposed, try applying them to the vaccination issue:

Question What objects do people usually hope for that vaccination would favor?
Answer Health. Community welfare.
Question What virtues would be needed to obtain these objects?
Answer Courage to be vaccinated. Generosity with time and money. Loyalty to community.
Question What would people fear about a vaccination program?
Answer Government regulation. Impoverishment by taxes. Pain of being vaccinated.

For a really full understanding of the moral pressures exerted on you by the audience, you could map out this systematic coverage:

	Among Supporters of a Public Vaccination Program	**Among Opponents of a Public Vaccination Program**
What Would Be Hoped For	Health Community welfare	Freedom from gov't. regulation Wealth by avoidance of taxes

	Among Supporters of a Public Vaccination Program	**Among Opponents of a Public Vaccination Program**
What Would Be Feared	Sickness Loss to community through disease	Loss of freedom Impoverishment by taxes Pain of being vaccinated
What Virtues Would Be Needed	Courage to be vaccinated Generosity with time and money Loyalty to community	Independence Courage to resist
What Vices Might Enter In	Injustice (invasion of others' rights)	Selfishness (indifference to welfare of others) Avarice (unwillingness to give)

Having surveyed the "moral field" of the vaccination issue, you would be equipped to respond to your particular readers. Some common-sense questions to ask about them would be: To what important group do they belong? What are the special interests of that group? What is its power to affect the outcome of the issue being raised?

"Membership in an important group" can be defined by any connection you find relevant according to the issue before you. Age, nationality, political party, social level, occupation, place of residence, religion, sex, tastes—any of these could affect audience disposition at one time or another. For example, if you're addressing sixth-graders on the value of a vaccination program, you would do well to reflect that they belong to the group of those to be vaccinated. Accordingly, their special hopes are to avoid pain and to secure health. Their power is to accept the vaccine cheerfully. Their good will toward your subject can increase if you show how they can use this power to realize their interests.

But if you're writing to old retired people, you ought to remember that they belong to a voting group which is exempt from vaccination. Their special hope is to save money by avoiding new taxes. Their power is to vote in a vaccination referendum. Still, old people also need and hope to be recognized for their experience and their record of civic contribution. Their good will can increase if you show how they can realize their best interests by using this power.

What if the disposition of your audience is distinctly hostile? You're probably lucky. A perfectly disposed, "sweetheart" audience allows sloppy thinking, as many political rallies have demonstrated. It is the hostile reader, the skeptical reader, or at least the normally biased reader who helps you test out the subject. Eventually a drastic gap between you and your readers can disrupt that process. Maybe you oppose further taxation so strongly yourself that you can't sincerely write about your readers' possible generosity in submitting to new taxes. Or you may despise the conservatism of certain readers so much that you can't take seriously their apparent hysteria about government regulation. Then you've discovered the limits of your rapport and hence the limits of the "meaning" which you can find with this audience. But the discipline of checking out these questions of audience disposition as it bears on your topic will make an optimum relationship possible.

The Relative Importance of the Audience in Different Kinds of Writing

This close insight into the knowledge and disposition of your audience can help most directly in persuasive writing—both that which aims to influence the judgment of the audience and, even more, that which seeks action. In explanatory writing, the readers' knowledge deserves much more of your attention than does their disposition. When writing fiction, poetry, and drama, you may not be explicitly addressing your readers at all. Still, their knowledge and disposition must have much to do with your creation if you're to realize all the impact possible in imaginative writing. Remember that the readers of a great writer can say, "He talks from our heart, not his."

WRITING ASSIGNMENTS

In doing any of the assignments for this chapter, you should strive to meet the following objectives. If you meet all four, you will get a satisfactory grade.

Objectives

1. Turn in your prewriting, showing that you used one of the three techniques discussed so far—focused freewriting, the Acronym Game, or the journalistic technique.
2. In each description, show by your word choice, your sentence structure, and your point of view toward the subject, that you have considered your different audiences' knowledge and interests.
3. Use standard American spelling.
4. Proofread to eliminate any unmarked sentence fragments, comma splices, or run-on sentences.

The only new proofreading requirement here is that you eliminate comma splices and run-on sentences. If you need a full discussion of these problems, turn to Section 1 of the Handbook. Here is a quick review of the essentials. If it isn't enough, be sure to study the Handbook section carefully.

Writers mistakenly create fragments by trying to put too little into a sentence. When they do the opposite and try to put too much in without knowing how to connect the pieces, they create comma splices and run-on sentences. These errors are related because both result from cramming two would-be sentences into one sentence. The comma splice occurs when the two subject-verb combinations are spliced together with a comma the run-on sentence occurs when they are spliced together without punctuation.

The sentence you just read contains a run-on sentence error. Here are four ways to correct it:

1. The comma splice occurs when the two subject-verb combinations are spliced together with a comma. The run-on sentence occurs when they are spliced together without punctuation. (This correction makes two sentences.)
2. The comma splice occurs when the two subject-verb combinations are spliced together with a comma; the run-on sentence occurs when they are spliced together without punctuation. (This correction uses a semicolon to replace the period after the first sentence.)
3. The comma splice occurs when the two subject-verb combinations are spliced together with a comma, and the run-on sentence occurs when they are spliced together without punctuation. (This correction adds a coordinating conjunction, *and,* after the comma.)
4. While the comma splice occurs when the two subject-verb combinations are spliced together with a comma, the run-on sentence occurs when they are spliced together without punctuation. (This correction changes one of the sentences into a dependent clause—no longer a would-be sentence—by starting it with a subordinating conjunction, *while.*)

Whatever you do, *do not correct a comma splice by simply taking out the comma.* That would be turning a comma splice into a run-on sentence, an even more serious error than you started with!

Writing Assignment 3-1

For this assignment assume that two friends have asked you the same question: "Should I go to your college next year?" Select your friends from this list:

1. A brilliant student who graduated from your high school at fifteen and proceeded to flunk out of one of the prestigious New England colleges due to social immaturity.
2. The girl who was voted Miss Social Butterfly of your graduating class.
3. A displaced homemaker, suddenly divorced in her mid-thirties and in need of skills that will help her support her young children.
4. A top athlete whose badly broken leg meant the loss of an athletic scholarship to the state university.
5. An actual friend of yours whom you describe briefly as part of your prewriting.

For your prewriting step, use the journalistic technique discussed in this chapter, or one of the techniques from Chapter 2, to help you analyze your selected audiences, their interests, and the facts you would need to give them about your college.

When your prewriting has generated enough ideas, write a well-developed, detailed answer to each of your two selected friends. Be honest about your college, but consider how it would appeal—or would not appeal—to each of your friends. Make the two answers noticeably different for your writing step.

When the writing step is completed, proofread the paper carefully for the postwriting step. Correct any spelling errors and eliminate any unmarked fragments, comma splices, or run-on sentences.

Writing Assignment 3-2

For this assignment assume that you have joined a lonely hearts club or a computer dating service, and you have been sent the following descriptions of four members of the opposite sex:

1. Conservative, career-minded thirty-five-year-old with a good income. Likes to travel, but only in the United States. Interested in photography.
2. A self-styled "swinger," twenty-six years old. Likes partying, partying, and more partying. Interested in "unique experiences."
3. A twenty-three-year-old who lives on a farm and loves dogs, horses, and pigs. Raised the prize-winning pig at last year's State Fair. Enjoys playing Scrabble and all sorts of card games.
4. A good churchgoer who is "fortyish." Likes a variety of people, as long as they are not atheists. Does not believe in disco dancing but loves to square dance. Also enjoys reading biographies and other inspirational books.

Select any two of these four as your penpals, or write descriptions of two other potential dates. (If you choose to describe your own penpals, include these descriptions with your prewriting.) Use one or more of the prewriting techniques you have learned so far as a way of analyzing your different audiences and selecting details about yourself that will appeal to each.

For the writing step, write two letters, one to each potential date. Without telling any lies (except to alter your marital status, if necessary), try to make yourself sound as attractive as possible to each reader. Of course, you will choose different characteristics to emphasize for your different audiences. If the ages are all inappropriate, you may change them, but do not alter the other parts of the descriptions. Be sure to label each letter with the appropriate number, although you may invent names for your potential dates, if you wish.

Proofread the two letters carefully for the postwriting step. Eliminate any unmarked fragments, comma splices, or run-on sentences, and correct any spelling errors.

Writing Assignment 3-3

For this assignment you will be writing two descriptions of the city or town where you live. Assume that two relatives who live quite a distance away have written to you to discuss their interest in a possible move to your town. They have asked for your advice on the move. Select your two relatives from this list:

1. A thrice-divorced uncle who thinks a move from the wicked city where he lives might help him find the right wife at last.
2. An older brother who has been living in quite a primitive area of Alaska for the last ten years but who wants to return to civilization to raise his two young children.
3. A perpetually out-of-work cousin who is always moving in search of the right executive job.
4. Your mother's younger sister, a photographer who is married to a sculptor and who wants a place to live where they both can pursue their artistic careers.

5. Two actual relatives who do not live in your town. If you choose to write to real relatives, you will need to describe them briefly as part of your prewriting.

Use one of the techniques you have learned so far to analyze your two audiences for the prewriting step. Try to decide what details of your town would be important to each relative.

When you have generated enough ideas through your prewriting technique, write the two letters you would send in response, one to each relative. The letters are the writing step. Try to be honest about your town, but make your descriptions vary to suit your audience.

For the postwriting step, proofread both letters carefully. Correct any spelling errors, and eliminate any unmarked sentence fragments, comma splices, or run-on sentences.

Writing Assignment 3-4 For this assignment your first step is to make a design from a five-inch square cut into eight pieces like this:

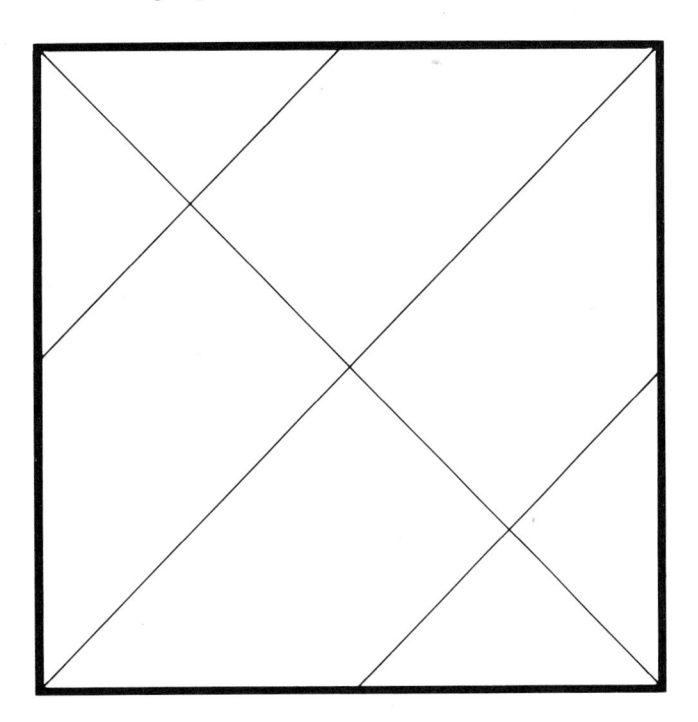

After you have cut up the square, move the pieces around until you are pleased with the design they make. Trace this design so you will not forget it. Now your job will be to write two sets of directions telling two different people how to make an identical design from the eight pieces they will be given. Choose your two audiences from this list: your mother, a seven-year-old child, a college instructor other than your English teacher, an architect.

For the prewriting step of this paper, in addition to making the design, use one of the prewriting techniques you have studied so far to analyze your two chosen audiences.

The writing step of this assignment will consist of the two sets of directions. Although the design will be the same for both sets, the directions should be noticeably different. It should be obvious which reader the directions are written for, but you should still label each set of directions to identify its audience.

Proofread both sets of directions carefully for the postwriting step. Check especially for correct spelling, and be sure to eliminate any fragments not marked with asterisks and any comma splices or run-on sentences.

If your instructor approves, you may check the effectiveness of your written directions by exchanging papers, either before or after grading, and trying to reconstruct another classmate's design. You may even go so far as to indulge in some role playing, trying to follow the instructions the way an architect or a seven-year-old would do.

CHAPTER 4

PREWRITING: THE MESSAGE (WHAT DO YOU HAVE TO SAY?)

Some communication situations exist only because you have a message to convey. Whether you are writing to protest an error in your credit card billing or to recommend a former employee for another job, your message is established by the situation itself. "I have never purchased a fur-lined barbecue mitt, and I want the $29.95 I was charged for one removed from my bill." "Bobby Ewing was an excellent employee for me, and I'm sure he would be for you, too." In these situations you may spend some time figuring out the exact wording of your message, but its content is clear from the start.

At other times you are asked to write, but you really don't know what message you want to convey. Many of the writing situations you encounter in college—in English and in other classes, too—will be of this type. Usually you will be given a general subject to write about, but you will have to come up with the ideas you want to express on this subject. On a history exam, for instance, you may be asked to contrast the War of 1812 with the American Revolution. You know that your message must contain some facts about the two wars if you are to earn credit, but what can you say about them? "The War of 1812 was different from the American Revolution." That won't do; it's too broad to give you any direction for your supporting statements. Any war, after all, is different from any other war. To write an acceptable answer, you must come up with a few specific differences—the way the war was financed, the civilian attitude toward the fighting, the battle plans. You are not really ready to write until you have decided upon these specifics.

The simplest approach to discovering your message is called "waiting for inspiration." It is simple because it requires nothing of you. You can wait for inspiration while you're driving to work, attending a basketball game, or playing gin rummy. You can wait for inspiration right up until the paper is due. In cartoon strips, the little light bulb above the character's head lights up, but it may never light above your head unless you take some definite steps to make it light. These steps are the prewriting technique you use to get from the general topic to the specific message.

GETTING FROM GENERAL TO SPECIFIC

Students often go blank when they are given a general topic for an essay. I remember the feeling well from my first composition assignment in a tenth grade English class—an essay about the outdoors. (I can still hear Crazy Gracie barking out the details: "Now, it has to be about the outdoors, and it has to be *controversial*—with an introductory paragraph, three paragraphs supporting your thesis, and a concluding paragraph." Those were not the days when students were encouraged to write freely; but almost all of us learned to write from Gracie's dictatorial methods, and a number of us even enjoyed the experience.) Although I have long ago forgotten what point about the outdoors I finally decided to argue, I can vividly remember my quandary. I had absolutely no opinion about the outdoors that could serve as the basis for a paper, and I had not much hope that inspiration would finally strike me. I must have muddled my way through to some sort of essay, as I'm sure I turned the paper in, but I could have saved myself much anxiety if I had known then a few systematic approaches to prewriting.

Suppose I had known then about narrowed freewriting (similar to brainstorming)? I might have approached the subject of the outdoors with a ten-minute timer and produced these results:

> The outdoors—I just don't have any opinions about it at all. How can you have any opinions about such a dumb subject? It's been around forever, I guess, except nobody called it the outdoors when everybody lived right in it. It didn't become the outdoors until there was an indoors, and the indoors was really carved out of the outdoors by early people who wanted to wall in part of it for their own. Should people be able to own the outdoors? Maybe everything will be indoors someday, if scientists put plastic bubbles over entire cities so they can control the environment and get rid of bad weather. Then where will the outdoors be? In outer space? I think it is silly for decorators to talk about "bringing the outdoors in." They only make the indoors phony putting rocks or trees inside; the indoors doesn't suddenly become the outdoors. That's an impossibility. I wouldn't want to live in the outdoors anyway, unless it had plumbing.

Well, that didn't take quite ten minutes, but it probably would have taken that long when I was a beginning composition student. Also, I didn't really get into the topic of ecology, because back in 1957 when I was given the assignment that was not the popular subject for discussion that it is today. When I look back at the paragraph to see if any ideas emerge for a possible paper, I see one with some promise: The outdoors is disappearing. With a little more thought, I probably could support that with an appropriate five-paragraph paper.

Another systematic approach to the topic (also covered in Chapter 2, as freewriting was) is the Acronym Game. If I had used that back in 1957, I might have come up with these words:

4 PREWRITING: THE MESSAGE (WHAT DO YOU HAVE TO SAY?)

O verpowering
U nknowable
T imeless
D angerous
O rganized (by scouting groups and travel agencies)
O versold
R avaged
S ecluded

Several of these ideas aren't particularly controversial, and I always like to write something different from what I expect other people to write, so I'd probably reject all but "dangerous" and "oversold." I could support a thesis like "The outdoors is too dangerous for me" with the required three paragraphs: dangers from the elements (drowning, being blown away by a tornado), dangers from wildlife (getting stung by bees or bitten by snakes), and dangers from humans (being attacked by muggers who lurk behind every third tree). "The joys of outdoor life are oversold" could be supported with a vivid description of any picnic, complete with hungry ants and poison ivy.

The journalistic approach to prewriting (covered in Chapter 3) also could have helped me seek inspiration on the topic of the outdoors. I might have used the approach this way:

Who uses it? Everybody, at some time.

Who needs it? Everybody.

Who enjoys it? Outdoorophiles (lovers of the outdoors).

What is the outdoors? Everything that isn't indoors.

Where is it? Outside.

When do we use it? For play, but some use it for work.

Why call it *outdoors*? Because we spend most of our time in buildings, and we have to go through a door to get to it.

How did the concept develop? I don't know, but I could find out.

Two ideas from this list strike me as "possibles." If I had the time and wanted to do some research on the term, I could consult the *Oxford English Dictionary* in the library to see how old the word *outdoors* was and how the use of the term had changed, if it had. I'm not sure I could make this controversial, but perhaps I could argue that we are currently misusing the term; at least the paper would surely be different from any other paper written for the assignment. Another approach I could take would be a kind of definition paper, working with the term *outdoorophile*. My thesis might be this: By the time we reach school age, we are all either outdoorophiles or outdoorophobes. The contrasts between those who love the outdoors and those who hate it would be good for at least the three paragraphs and a conclusion, and I suspect that Gracie, who positively salivated when she came across coined words, would have loved the paper.

These are all of the techniques of prewriting we have covered so far, but they do not exhaust the possibilities. One other technique that might help you (and might have helped me with my difficult assignment on the outdoors) is the drawing of a *classification tree*. (I am indebted for this suggestion to Martin Steinmann, Jr., author of *Words in Action*.)

To build a classification tree, you begin with a group of things that have something in common, in this case outdoor environments. Then you decide on a basis for subdividing them into smaller subclasses with more elements in common. You must divide them so that everything in the larger group of things belongs in one and only one of the subclasses. Here is one classification tree you might make:

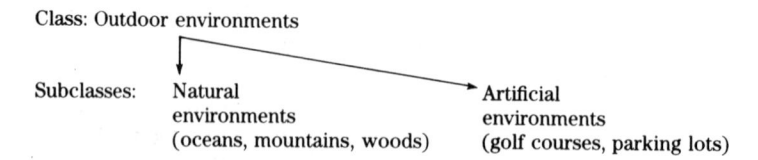

Class: Outdoor environments

Subclasses: Natural   Artificial
              environments   environments
              (oceans, mountains, woods)   (golf courses, parking lots)

Basis of Division: Origin

This tree suggests another thesis: Artificial environments are rapidly taking over the outdoors.

A second example goes back to the idea of writing about the dangers of the outdoors:

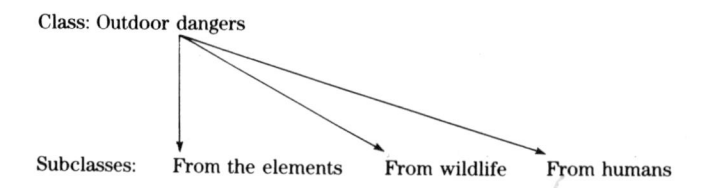

Class: Outdoor dangers

Subclasses: From the elements   From wildlife   From humans

Basis of Division: Origin or Cause

Something more like a tree emerges when you go a step further and analyze the subclasses, breaking them down into their separate parts:

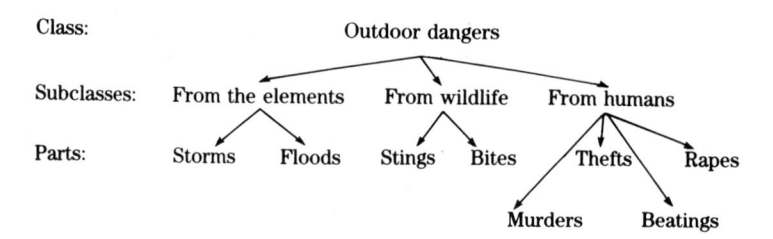

Class: Outdoor dangers

Subclasses: From the elements   From wildlife   From humans

Parts: Storms   Floods   Stings   Bites   Thefts   Rapes
                                                   Murders   Beatings

From such a tree comes another idea for a thesis: The most dangerous creature we are likely to encounter outdoors is another human being.

4 PREWRITING: THE MESSAGE (WHAT DO YOU HAVE TO SAY?) 51

Taking this same class, Outdoor Dangers, we could have produced an entirely different tree by choosing a different basis of division. For instance, Degree of Danger could have been used. However, it would have been difficult to keep the subclasses from overlapping. Suppose I had decided on the categories Trivial, Serious, and Catastrophic for my subclasses. Now, everyone would agree that being stung by a bee—assuming no fatal allergies to bee stings—belongs in the Trivial subclass, but how about being bitten by a snake? Do you need two categories for this, depending on the kind of snake? The point is not to produce the perfect classification tree; the point is to come up with some ideas for the next step—writing. Classification trees provide some writers with inspiration. They are probably particularly helpful to people who have a visual orientation—people who like maps, diagrams, and flowcharts. If they work for you, use them.

STATING THE THESIS SENTENCE

Using these four approaches to prewriting—narrowed freewriting, the Acronym Game, the journalistic method, and classification trees—I have come up with six ideas for essays. I've formed these into six statements about the outdoors, and I've called them *thesis sentences*, without explaining what a thesis sentence is. In case the term is unfamiliar to you, let's look at the six statements to see if we can discover a meaning.

1. The outdoors is disappearing.
2. The outdoors is too dangerous for me.
3. The joys of outdoor life are oversold.
4. By the time we reach school age, we are all either outdoorophiles or outdoorophobes.
5. Artificial environments are rapidly taking over the outdoors.
6. The most dangerous creature we are likely to encounter outdoors is another human being.

Each of these sentences is a *statement*, not a question (Should I spend more time outdoors?), an order (Go outdoors!), or a title ("The Pleasures of the Great Outdoors"). To be a thesis sentence, a sentence must first be a statement: That is, it must claim something about a subject.

Each of these sentences is, more specifically, a particular kind of statement—a statement of opinion. A statement that is merely an observation about a fact can't be a thesis sentence. For instance, you could make this observation about the outdoors: There are thirty-mile-an-hour winds today. This could *never* be a thesis sentence, because you would have no way to support it in a paper. If you doubted the truth of the observation, you would verify it or disprove it by checking a weather report—or, if you were a meteorologist with the proper equipment, you would go outdoors and measure the wind velocity for yourself. Neither of these actions would give you much to write about in a paper. Facts and observations about them do not make thesis sentences. Once you have stated them, you have nowhere to go in your paper. Facts make excellent support for theses, but the theses themselves should be statements of opinion. Opinions need support; they need to have the reasoning behind them brought into the open and discussed. This discussion becomes your paper.

To be a good thesis sentence for a particular paper, an opinion statement also needs to be the right size. If you are supposed to write a two-to-five-page paper (the average length in a freshman composition class), your opinion should be one that you can support in five to ten paragraphs. It should not be so broad as to require a short book to prove itself, nor should it be so narrow as to be proven in only one paragraph. "Each of the fifty states has a slightly different approach to conservation" suffers from the first problem. The writer would need to devote a minimum of one paragraph—and a pretty detailed one, at that—to each of the states, and a fifty-paragraph paper is too long for most freshman writing assignments. "Many people don't cut their grass often enough," on the other hand, is both too limited and too obvious to provide the basis for even a two-page paper.

Most importantly, the thesis should cover everything you put in your paper. The thesis should control the paper, giving direction to your thoughts as you write. Almost every writer has been confronted with this dilemma: Midway through the paper, a brand new idea appears. It doesn't really fit the thesis, but it has class, originality; it just calls out to be put in the paper. If you are the writer, what do you do? The easy way out is to stick it in anyway, hoping the reader won't notice that you changed direction a bit. This almost never works; you are likely to get a poor grade and a comment like this: "Your thinking seems disorganized here. Starting with paragraph four, you lose track of your thesis." If you want to avoid this comment, you have two choices: (1) You can practice self-control and cast out the tempting idea, perhaps jotting it down somewhere for future papers, or (2) you can scrap what you have already written and revise your thesis sentence so that the new idea can be used to support it. Neither choice is easy, but the resulting paper—and the resulting grade—should be worth the effort. A really thorough job of prewriting might have helped you to avoid this dilemma, for the brilliant idea might have come to you before you started to write, saving a great deal of time. Still, some ideas do present themselves in the middle of the writing step, so be prepared to deal with them.

As part of your prewriting, you should formulate a thesis sentence. Here are some questions about your thesis that you can use as a checklist to determine whether or not the sentence is likely to result in a good paper:

1. Is it a statement of my opinion? (Could I put it after the words "I think that . . ."?)
2. Is it clearly defined, or will I need to explain some important terms in the paper?
3. Is it narrow enough to be covered in the length of paper I will be writing?
4. Is it broad enough to include the important points I want to make?
5. Do I have enough information to support it?

PRACTICING EVALUATING THESIS SENTENCES

Before you construct your own thesis sentences, test your understanding of the concept of *thesis sentence* by applying the first four questions on the checklist to the following ten items, all submitted as theses for an assignment in one of my classes. If you think the sentence could be developed into an effective paper, mark it "OK." Try to think of some modification which would change the unacceptable items into usable thesis sentences.

1. In many ways First Chance Community College is a much better school than Sociability U.
2. Your own ideals can sometimes ruin you.
3. Mrs. X is a great teacher.
4. There is something wrong with the Japanese way of teaching English.
5. A suspension from school is a violation of the student's constitutional rights.
6. Students are required to attend school until they are sixteen.
7. My high-school experience leads me to believe that handicapped teachers put forth a great effort to know their students on an individual basis.
8. Should a coach be a teacher or a friend?
9. A job as a governess helped me to understand children as an important part of life.
10. History classes would be much easier to take if the teachers made them more interesting.

PRACTICING WRITING THESIS SENTENCES

Now you should be ready to compose your own thesis sentences. Select four general topics from the list below and try out each of the four prewriting techniques (one technique per topic), generating ideas until you have at least *two* for each topic that you can state as thesis sentences. When you have your eight theses, check them against the checklist to see if they are worthy of being developed into essays.

General Topics

Education
Entertainment
American Eating Habits
Newspapers
Guns
Relatives
Art
Vices

The Opposite Sex
Consumer Rights
Car Safety
Money Management
Professional Sports
The Four Seasons
Clothing
Virtues

PLACING THE THESIS SENTENCE

Although technically you are already into the writing step once you begin to worry about where you should put your thesis in your essay, you may be concerned about this problem right now. That makes now a good time to talk about it.

Relax! There is no one place where the thesis must go. In fact, there are six possible places, and all are appropriate at least some of the time.

1. The thesis can be the very first sentence, but this is often not the best place for it, although beginning writers tend to put it here almost automatically. Unless your thesis is so interesting that it would involve your reader right away, you will be wise to choose one of the other five places.

2. The thesis may end your first paragraph. This is a good place for it in about two-thirds of the papers you will write. It allows you to make a few more general, possibly more intriguing, statements before you have to commit yourself to the opinion the rest of the paper will be developing.

3. It may begin your second paragraph or whatever paragraph begins the body of your paper. This is also an excellent position, as it allows for an opening dialogue or brief anecdote which gets the reader's attention before the commitment is made.

4. It may conclude your paper. This is a difficult position for the unsophisticated writer to use because it is easy to get lost—and to lose your reader—on the way to the thesis. Still, for certain papers, such as one with a logical argument in favor of an unpopular position, this can be a good choice. It allows you to postpone a statement that might turn off your reader until it is too late—the paper has already been read.

5. You can put the thesis anywhere else that makes sense for your particular topic and your particular organization. Just be sure that you have a reason for the place you choose.

6. You can omit it from the paper entirely. This kind of paper is a difficult one to write, too. For certain approaches, it is the only sensible choice, however. If you are writing a tongue-in-cheek argument, a sentence that says what you really think would clash with the rest of the paper totally. For instance, you might be developing this thesis: The fifty-five-mile-an-hour speed limit should be retained because it has saved many lives. Now, suppose you decided to approach this satirically by showing that the speed limit was creating a population problem because we were no longer killing off sufficient numbers on the highways. Would your thesis have any place in this paper? Of course not. You might think that in this situation you would not really need a thesis. You'd be wrong. To write a difficult essay like this, you need to be in control at all times, knowing exactly where you are going. Although the thesis doesn't appear, its existence in your prewriting helps to keep you on track and helps you to write a paper in which you will not lose your reader.

4 PREWRITING: THE MESSAGE (WHAT DO YOU HAVE TO SAY?)

RELATED READINGS

Student Essay

IN RETROSPECT
Sherrie Dunham

Points to Consider

As you read the essay that follows, try to answer these questions:

1. What sentence in this essay makes the most effective thesis? Can you give reasons for its position? Should it have come first? Why or why not?
2. What ideas probably occurred to this writer in the prewriting stage? How does she bring these in to support her message?
3. This was written in a journalism class, as an editorial to be sent to a magazine for music students and educators. Does it seem appropriate for this audience? Is there evidence that the writer considered her audience in writing the editorial?
4. If you have had any performing experiences, musical or otherwise, have they substantiated this author's main point? What thesis sentence about student performances would your own experiences support?

Used with permission of Sherrie Dunham.

It's December again. When I turned my calendar over, I couldn't help thinking about what this season used to mean to me when I was an adolescent. No, I'm not talking about Christmas. It's the time of year I used to begin preparations for what was my annual nightmare—the district Solo and Ensemble Festival.

For anyone who has never participated in one, Solo and Ensemble is a public competition and judging for student musicians before a live audience.

I believe musical training for children, at its best, can give a lifetime of enjoyment and increased appreciation for music. At its worst, it can create unbelievable anxieties and pressures and ruin a child's attitude toward music. The intensely competitive environment of Solo and Ensemble Festivals is an example of musical education at its worst.

From my own experience as first-chair flutist in our high school band, I was told by my music teachers that I had some talent. My reward for practicing conscientiously to develop this talent was a thrust from well-meaning parents and teachers into the arena of Solo and Ensemble. I was never one to seek the spotlight and protested loudly over this turn of events.

However, they argued that it was simultaneously an "opportunity" and an "obligation." They said it would be a good experience for me; and if I continued to perform and to compete publicly, it would become easier each year. I would gain in poise and self-confidence.

I soon discovered that whatever stuff performers are made of, I apparently lacked. I was terrified on stage, and far from finding it easier to do with each passing year, I found it more difficult. Each year there were more weeks of sleepless nights and days of working in a fearful frenzy in preparation for the dreaded day.

There were two results from this so-called "good experience." The immediate result was that I became greatly envious of the last-chair flute player in our band, who had not practiced her lessons and thus did not have the benefit of my "opportunities." I strove to be more like her.

A more far-reaching result was that as soon as I escaped the influence of parents and teachers, I gave up my music completely. For 12 years, I didn't touch my flute; there were just too many rotten memories associated with it.

I have finally begun to play again—cautiously, selectively, and preferably in a sound-proof room with no audience but myself.

In retrospect, I have often wondered if I suffered this trauma alone. I mean, maybe I was overly sensitive and others participating in this event thought better of it.

Then I read an excerpt from a book entitled *Uptaught*, by Ken Macrorie. Macrorie compiled opinions and writings of students on subjects of interest to them. One student wrote about her performance of a clarinet solo at Solo and Ensemble where she got so nervous she thought she was going to faint. She wrote:

> I began wondering what would happen if I did faint right there. It would wreck the reed for sure. No reed, no sound, and the hellmost torture for a clarinetist is wrecking a reed, because the good ones cost 45 cents apiece and only come in boxes of ten and only two or three of these will work with luck, and two or three won't work at all, and the rest will just kind of thud a lot. So when I thought of falling over on my only good reed, I decided I better stop. . . . The judge was a heavy man with dark rimmed glasses who looked at me over them like what was I doing stopping in the middle of a piece like that? I was supposed to play and not interrupt his judging routine with sudden stops. He took my elbow and my clarinet, which he put on his desk after checking the make of instrument and mouthpiece I had because he was a devoted clarinetist and probably hated fainting, whimpering females.

Well, I guess things could have been worse for me. At least flutes don't have reeds to worry about, but the feelings are the same.

I don't think that any student should be pressured into a musical competition such as Solo and Ensemble against his/her will. As psychologist-author Haim Ginott said in his book *Teacher and Child*, a good teacher does not force "a dancer to sing or a singer to dance." A good teacher allows "each of us to light his own lamp."

It's understandable that parents get gratification out of having their children perform and compete in public. It's like they've finally gotten something in return for all those hours of listening to sour notes and clinkers and for the small fortune they've spent over the years on instruments and music lessons.

But it might be wise for them to consider that there can be a higher cost to these events. Music is, first and foremost, to be enjoyed. If that objective isn't met successfully, it will indeed be an expensive lesson!

Professional Essay

PHOOEY ON THE LITTLE BOXES OTHER PEOPLE PUT AROUND US
Nickie McWhirter

Points to Consider

As you read the essay that follows, try to answer these questions:

1. What sentence in this essay makes the clearest thesis? Does it cover the entire article? Can you give reasons for its position?
2. What do you think is the purpose of the inserted dialogue between Irma and Frank?
3. Students sometimes have trouble deciding on the sex of this author. As you read, look for details that should provide clues for them. What sex is the author?
4. You can understand sections of this essay better if you can identify the references to Galatea and Pygmalion and to the house of many mansions. Can you find these in a dictionary or other reference book? Do you think the author assumed that readers of a syndicated column in the *Detroit Free Press* would recognize the references? Do you assume they would? Why or why not?

Copyright © 1979. Reprinted by permission of The Detroit Free Press.

I used to live in a lot of little boxes. Now I live in one, and it's commodious. I designed, built, and decorated it. Sometimes I kick out a side or two and rearrange the dimensions and decor. I do this when I get tired of the same environment or it becomes uncomfortable or I get excited about some change I have observed or envisioned and decide to experiment. The box may not suit you at all. It suits me, and I live in it. It's my life. It's labeled "Nickie."

As noted, I used to live in a lot of little boxes. They had labels too. One was "The Kids." One was "Husband." There were "Relatives," "The Boss," "Neighbors," "Friends & Associates," "Church & Society." There may have been some others, but these were the important ones, as I recall.

I remember spending a lot of energy climbing from one box to another and catching my breath after each scramble. I was often disoriented. I frequently felt cramped and uncomfortable.

"What's she talking about, Irma?"
"I have no idea, Frank. McWhirter is sometimes hard to follow."

I'll try to explain. You see, these little boxes were all constructed by other people. They were made out of ideas and concepts. The one labeled "Relatives" was constructed by my parents and other relatives, and when I was inside I had to contort and ooze myself into a configuration which fit the interior. I had to become a person who conformed to these relatives' ideas of what constituted the best possible me. When I was in the box labeled "Husband" or "Kids" or any of the others, I had to become a person to fit that box, even though there wasn't room for my elbows or knees and my head kept bumping the top.

Get it? Good.

You see how uncomfortable living in boxes can be, especially since I had to keep skipping from one to another, and a stance which worked well in one box might be totally unlivable in the next.

I mean, what do you do when the kids expect the Perfect You to play backyard baseball and at the same time husband wants you to entertain customers and boss expects you to be at work and the family thinks it's time you invited them up to have a backyard cookout with the neighbors before going to the church ice cream social where you are expected to play hostess—after you have put in your time as a volunteer at the library, naturally, and collected money for the Pigmy Relief Fund? Never mind your friends who say you never see them any more and have gotten "uppity."

Phooey on boxes. A person can get terminal shin splints climbing in and out and trying to conform. I quit some time ago.

It wasn't because I minded the energy required or was unsympathetic with the box makers. I quit living in the boxes because disappointment and discontent were inevitable all around.

It is possible for any human being to live in a single box, designed by its occupant or even by somebody else, but it is not possible to live in more than one box at a time. I decided that after years of research and observation of others engaged in this struggle.

It is difficult to become a Contented You in a box designed by someone else, but there is evidence that this is sometimes possible. It has been accomplished by some nuns, priests, and assorted other clerics and religious persons. Beyond this, I know of a few women who play Galatea to their Pygmalion husbands and appear to thrive. (I know of no male-female reversal of these roles which has succeeded but am willing to concede the possibility.)

For most of us, however, what happens is that we disappoint the many who construct boxes for us to occupy because, in fulfilling the demands of one, we leave empty places in the constructions of others. And when we try to fulfill the expectations of only one person or group outside ourselves we find we have to stretch uncomfortably to reach some of the corners and cramp ourselves up unnaturally to fit into some of the tight spots.

It's much better if each of us designs his or her own box, or life. It can be spacious or cozy. It can have many compartments or few; they can be locked and private or open to the public. The important consideration is that the life is comfortable and pleasing to the occupant. It is custom-made, one of a kind. It doesn't pinch and bind or require the person to go about stooped and bent, anxious, hurting, worrisome, and feeling inadequate to the demands and expectations of others. If we do not learn to construct our own lives and reject the pre-fab jobs so eagerly foisted off on us by others—even for good and noble reasons—we'll never feel comfortable in the house that has many mansions. We won't recognize which one is ours.

WRITING ASSIGNMENTS

In doing any of the assignments for this chapter, you should strive to meet the following objectives. If you meet all five, you will get a satisfactory grade.

Objectives

1. Turn in your prewriting, showing that you used one of the four recommended techniques.
2. Somewhere in your essay, include and underline a thesis sentence that satisfies the five-question checklist on page 52. (For this assignment do not attempt the type of paper that calls for an omitted thesis.)
3. Include personal experiences as at least part of the support for your thesis.
4. Use standard American spelling.
5. Proofread to eliminate any unmarked sentence fragments, comma splices, run-on sentences, or subject-verb agreement errors.

If you are really confused about how to eliminate subject-verb agreement errors, the addition to the grammatical objective this time, you should turn to Section 2 of the Handbook. If you just need a quick review, here is a brief explanation.

In every subject-verb combination in every English sentence, you have either a singular subject (one whatever-it-is) or a plural subject (two or more whatever-it-ises). Most agreement problems occur when you are using the *present tense*, talking about something happening now, because the form of the verb you use depends on the number of the subject in this tense. When the subject is a he, a she, or an it, you need a verb ending in s, called a *singular verb*. When the subject is a they, you need a verb not ending in s. This is called a *plural verb*, even though it is also the form used for all first- and second-person forms (*I*, *we*, and *you*), whether they are singular or plural. (Pay special attention to the effect of adding this s to a verb; it is just the opposite of what you would expect. Putting s on a *noun* makes it plural, but putting s on a *present-tense verb* makes it singular!)

If your ear is well trained, you can use it as a guide. Test yourself by saying these sentences:

- The boy don't live here any longer.
- The children isn't my concern.
- The coach of both teams are my father.
- There is three reasons you should vote for Kumquat.

If all four sentences sound wrong to you, you may be in pretty good shape on the subject-verb agreement problem. If any sentence sounds correct, you probably need to review the section in the Handbook.

Here are the problems in the four sentences just given. The subject of the first sentence is a he, *boy,* so you need a singular verb ending in *s, does not* or *doesn't. Children,* the subject of the second sentence, is a plural word, so the verb should be *are not* or *aren't.* The third sentence is confusing because the subject, *coach,* is not next to the verb, *are.* If you put them together, you would see that the verb should be *is.* In the last sentence the verb, *is,* comes before the subject, *reasons.* Since the subject is plural, the verb should be *are.*

Writing Assignment 4-1

For this assignment you are to narrow the general topic of Education down to one you could cover in a two-to-five-page paper based largely on personal experience.

For the prewriting step, try at least one of the four approaches discussed in Chapters 2, 3, and 4. Take notes on this step to turn in with your essay. When you have a narrower topic, state your main idea about it in a thesis sentence. Test this thesis by answering the checklist questions on page 52.

Use details from your personal educational experiences to support your thesis when you write the paper. Include the thesis and underline it so that your reader can identify it. (For this paper you may assume that your audience consists of your classmates, or you may select another appropriate audience if you identify it in your prewriting.) The essay itself will be the writing step of the assignment.

For the postwriting step, proofread the paper carefully, being sure to correct the spelling and to eliminate any unmarked fragments, comma splices, run-on sentences, or subject-verb agreement errors.

Writing Assignment 4-2

For this assignment you are to narrow the general topic of Money Management down to one you could cover in a two-to-five-page paper based largely on personal experience.

For the prewriting step, try at least one of the four approaches discussed in Chapters 2, 3, and 4. Take notes on this step to turn in with your essay. When you have a narrower topic, state your main idea about it in a thesis sentence. Test this thesis by answering the checklist questions about it.

Use details from your personal money management experiences to support your thesis when you write the paper. Include the thesis and underline it so that the reader can identify it. (For this paper you may assume that your audience consists of your classmates, or you may select another appropriate audience if you identify it in your prewriting.) The essay itself will be the writing step of the assignment.

For the postwriting step, proofread the paper carefully, being sure to correct the spelling and to eliminate any unmarked fragments, comma splices, run-on sentences, or subject-verb agreement errors.

4 PREWRITING: THE MESSAGE (WHAT DO YOU HAVE TO SAY?)

Writing Assignment 4-3

For this assignment you are to narrow the general topic of The Opposite Sex down to one you could cover in a two-to-five-page paper based largely on personal experience. (Remember that this is a very big topic; it even includes one of your parents!)

For the prewriting step, try at least one of the four approaches discussed in Chapters 2, 3, and 4. Take notes on this step to turn in with your essay. When you have a narrower topic, state your main idea about it in a thesis sentence. Test this thesis by answering the checklist questions on page 52.

Use details from your personal experiences with the opposite sex to support your thesis when you write the paper. Include the thesis and underline it so that the reader can identify it. (For this paper you may assume that your audience consists of your classmates, or you may select another appropriate audience if you identify it in your prewriting.) The essay itself will be the writing step of the assignment.

For the postwriting step, proofread the paper carefully, being sure to correct the spelling and to eliminate any unmarked fragments, comma splices, run-on sentences, or subject-verb agreement errors.

Writing Assignment 4-4

For this assignment you are to narrow the general topic of Consumer Rights down to one you could cover in a two-to-five-page paper based largely on personal experience.

For the prewriting step, try at least one of the four approaches discussed in Chapters 2, 3, and 4. Take notes on this step to turn in with your essay. When you have a narrower topic, state your main idea about it in a thesis sentence. Test this thesis by answering the checklist questions on page 52.

Use details from your personal experiences as a consumer to support your thesis when you write the paper. Include the thesis and underline it so that the reader can identify it. (For this paper you may assume that your audience consists of your classmates, or you may select another appropriate audience if you identify it in your prewriting.) The essay itself will be the writing step of the assignment.

For the postwriting step, proofread the paper carefully, being sure to correct the spelling and to eliminate any unmarked fragments, comma splices, run-on sentences, or subject-verb agreement errors.

CHAPTER 5
WRITING: THE MEDIUM (WORDS)

You've decided who you are, who your readers are, and what messages you want your readers to understand about your topic. You're ready to write.

Although much of the hard work of writing is finished by the time you have completed the prewriting step, there are still many decisions to be made in the writing step. As you write, print, or type the first draft of your essay, there are many choices to make, consciously or unconsciously. These choices will help to determine how closely the readers' idea of your message matches your intended message. Keep in mind that there is almost never a perfect match, because there are always differences in experience between writer and readers that affect the readers' interpretations. Still, if you make your choices carefully, remembering the prewriting analysis you made of your readers, you can make it more likely that good communication will occur. Some of the first and most important choices you need to make are about words.

VARIETIES OF ENGLISH

Although you must be familiar with the English language to be reading this book, you may not realize that there are several varieties of the language used in different communication situations in America. All of us can speak at least a couple of these, and some people are able to use nearly all of them effectively, depending on circumstances. Increasing your knowledge of the varieties can increase your versatility.

General English is the most common variety. People speak it and write it, and it is appropriate in the largest number of situations. It is the language of most educated people, speaking in private or public. When you listen to Dan Rather or Tom Brokaw report the day's happenings, you are hearing general English. When you read the newspaper or *Reader's Digest* or a letter sent to you by your bank, you are reading general English. Since general English is acceptable in so many contexts, it is important to know it and be able to use it. A good rule to follow is this: When in doubt, use general English.

Formal English is more academic and scientific than general English. It is more often written than spoken, and it is written for educated adults. If you were ever taught not to say "I" in your writing and never to use contractions, you were being taught to write formal English. It is the language of dissertations, literary criticism, and scientific reports. Do not use formal English when you talk to your friends—unless you want to be considered a pompous showoff.

Informal English, like formal English, has a more limited use than general English. It includes slang, and the structure of the sentences is much looser than in the first two varieties. It is the language of much casual conversation and conversational writing. You probably use it when you write to friends. If you include dialogue in an essay, you will probably write the conversation in informal English. However, most essays that don't include dialogue are written in general English. For some more scholarly papers, such as research papers, you may need to be able to write formal English.

These three varieties together make up what we call *standard English*. A fourth important variety is *nonstandard English*. Not often written, this is the spoken language of thousands of people. It is not much influenced by the schools, but it is influenced by local speech patterns and regional dialects. If you check the word *ain't* in a large dictionary, you will probably find it marked "nonstandard." Double negatives ("I don't get no respect") are also a part of nonstandard English, as they were of standard English 600 years ago. In fact some of the sentence structure of nonstandard English has changed less over the centuries than standard English has changed. Although these historical links might lead us to consider it a "purer" form of the language, it is not the variety to use when applying for a bank loan or interviewing for most jobs. It is generally not the variety taught in the schools.

For most of your writing, you should avoid nonstandard English. It would only be acceptable if you were recording the speech of people who actually speak in nonstandard English. I remember reading of a brilliant West Point cadet who had a mental block about spelling (or thought he had) and who feared that he would never be able to pass his final exam in English. He solved his problem by writing the entire essay as a dialogue between two farmers who spoke a southern dialect, so he got away with spelling everything just the way his farmers pronounced it!

WORDS AS SYMBOLS

Whatever variety of English you choose to use, you will have to express yourself in *symbols*. All words are symbols because they represent something other than themselves: They stand for people, places, things, actions, and ideas. If you tried to convey an idea to another person without using symbols, you could resort to only the most primitive kind of sign language. You could point to something you wanted—a glass of water, for instance—but if you started gesturing, pantomiming the action of drinking, that gesture would be a symbol.

In *Gulliver's Travels*, written more than 250 years ago, one of Jonathan Swift's characters proposed a novel way to eliminate the confusion caused by symbolic language. His suggestion was that we all carry large, Santa Claus-style packs on our backs, and in these packs we carry everything we might want to talk about. Then, instead of using a word to describe an object, and running the risk of misinterpretation, we could merely remove the object from our pack; and everyone who saw it would know immediately what we wanted to "talk" about. This proposal to eliminate language was obviously unsuccessful.

A simple example can show why word symbols sometimes cause us trouble. If you have an aquarium at home with little scaly creatures swimming around in it, you probably call those creatures *fish*. If German is the native tongue in your home, you call them a very similar name, *fisch*. But just because two languages call them almost the same thing, do not be deceived into thinking that there is some innate *fishness* in these creatures that determined that their name should have this particular sound. After all, the French call them *poisson*, and their choice is no more right or wrong, no more nor less arbitrary, than ours.

Now suppose you want to get rid of your aquarium. You might say to an acquaintance, "I have some fish at home I'm giving away. Would you like some?" That's a perfectly clear communication, isn't it? Well, no—not if your acquaintance is hungry for baked trout and answers with this kind of fish in mind. To her, the symbol has a different meaning.

Short of carrying your aquarium on your back, how can you talk about it more clearly? One step you can take is to use less abstract words. *Fish* is a fairly abstract word because it can be applied to a large category of things rather than to a specific few. *Trout* is a more specific term, and so is *guppy*. If you offer to give some guppies to your friend, she is not likely to visualize eating them. Generally you can convey an idea more accurately by using concrete, specific words to replace vague, abstract ones. That is why your writing instructions usually tell you to use specific illustrations, concrete examples, and details. However, there are some exceptions to this principle, and we can see these by looking at what is called the *ladder of abstraction*.

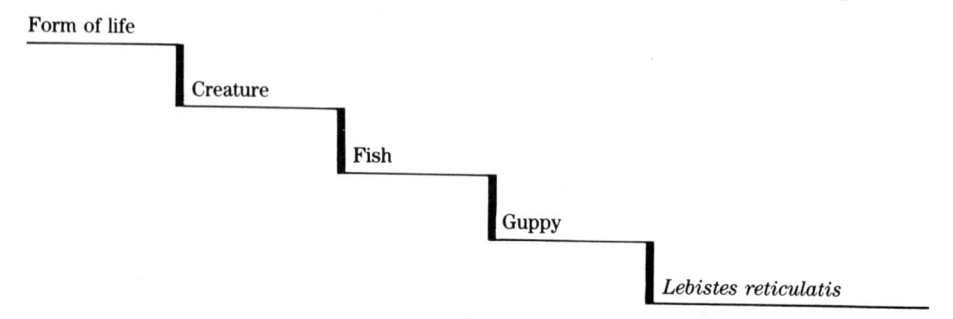

```
Form of life
    |___
        | Creature
        |___
            | Fish
            |___
                | Guppy
                |___
                    | Lebistes reticulatis
```

As you progress up the ladder of abstraction from the most concrete term (in this case, the Latin name for a particular kind of guppy) to the most abstract, each step marks a more inclusive word than the word on the step below. You can see that offering someone *creatures* or *forms of life* would be even more confusing than offering *fish*. I don't recommend it at all. But on the other hand, not many people would jump at the chance to get a free *Lebistes reticulatis*, unless they were true guppy fanciers. Consider your receiver's knowledge when you try to convey a message, as terms from either extreme of the ladder of abstraction can cause misunderstandings.

If, instead of speaking about your aquarium, you choose to write about it, you become even more deeply involved in the symbolic process. If the spoken word *fish* is only an arbitrary symbol we have learned to associate with the aquarium inhabitants, what are the printed letters *f-i-s-h*? Why, an arbitrary symbol of an arbitrary symbol! There is no reason, other than convention, why *f* should stand for the sound we make by putting our front teeth on our lower lips and forcing air out between them. In fact, George Bernard Shaw argued that the word *fish* could just as easily be spelled *ghoti*—the *gh* getting the sound it has in *cough*, the *o* the sound it has in *women*, and the *ti* the sound it has in *nation*.

The English alphabet is an invented tool that has changed over the centuries, losing some of the symbols it once had—the two letters for two different *th* sounds, for instance. Its very age prevents us from knowing who invented it, but alphabets have been invented in modern times. The great Indian leader Sequoya invented an eighty-five-letter alphabet to record the Cherokee language, and it was officially adopted by the tribe in 1825. If an alphabet can be invented, it must consist of arbitrary symbols assigned to sounds, not symbols mystically connected with them and waiting to be discovered.

If both letters and words are arbitrary symbols, only connected with the things they stand for because we agree to connect them, why do we so often confuse the word with its meaning? To see how much you tend to confuse the two, take a simple test. Before reading any further, jot down the three most beautiful sounding words that come into your head. Now jot down the three ugliest sounding words.

A poll once came up with the most beautiful sounding word in the English language—*mother*. Apparently the respondents were unable to separate the sound and the meaning, as the *oth* sound in that word is not one many people would call beautiful. When I have asked my students these same questions, I have gotten many answers, including these:

Beautiful Words	**Ugly Words**
ammonia	Xerox
banana	child
ripple	quiet
antediluvian	toes
leopard	cow
dawn	worm
sunshine	whining
melody	vomit

The words at the top of both these lists seem to be chosen on the basis of sound alone, but our reactions to the last three may be determined by the meaning as much as the sound. Confusing meaning and symbol is easy to do. Most of us are not really able to separate them all the time, or we would not react so positively to the word *kiss* and so negatively to some of its rhyming words.

When we confuse words and the things they stand for, we are indulging in *word magic.* We may use this magic to give a false picture of reality. When the generals in Vietnam referred to their use of napalm as *defoliation,* they were counting on people to react to the mildness of the term rather than to the harshness of the reality. One of my former students acknowledged a similar confusion on her part when she described her youthful escapades of shoplifting, which she had never before called by that name. To her group of friends, their activities were merely *cobbing some stuff.* She had changed her version of reality by substituting a pleasant-sounding word for an illegal act. Although we cannot entirely avoid falling under the spell of word magic, we should be aware when other writers use it on us, when we use it on our readers, or when we use it on ourselves. Not all beautiful sounding words represent beautiful concepts, and a concept does not become more acceptable simply because we have chosen a prettier name for it.

Use of such *euphemisms* (words chosen to cover up a harsh reality) was especially common in Victorian times (the last century), when arms and legs were abstractly called *limbs,* and underwear was absurdly mentioned as *unmentionables.* Today it is still very common in the language we use for death. A dead person is seldom called *dead;* he has *departed,* has *passed on,* or has been *lost.* His *number was up,* so he *cashed in his chips, kicked the bucket,* and *bought the farm.* If he died of cancer, *the big C got him.* In the *funeral home*—where nobody lives—there are *slumber parlors*—where nobody sleeps. Perhaps if we realized that *dead* is just a four-letter word, we would not fear it and avoid saying it so much.

Most of us deny we are superstitious, and we refuse to believe in the power of words to cast a magic spell. Still, we have to acknowledge the power of word magic when we choose our written words. If it were not for this confusion of the symbol with the reality, certain words would not have the power to shock certain readers. After all, there are no dirty words. Although we would like to consider ourselves too sophisticated to be swayed by word magic, we should remember that our readers—even the most intelligent and educated of them—will probably react illogically to certain words. Our job as writers is to figure out which words these will be for our chosen audience and then avoid these words—or use them only when we intend to shock.

TWO KINDS OF MEANING

When we read, we are able to interpret the symbols we see on the page because we have learned to connect a meaning with each. Through past experience, we have stored this meaning in our brains, and each time we see the same symbols, we retrieve that meaning from stored memory. But the meaning is not always the same each time we see the symbols for a term or a phrase; sometimes it depends on context. Take the phrase *a long time.* You probably have some abstract idea of what it means, but without a context for it, you would have difficulty defining it. What does it mean to you in each of these sentences?

- She waited a long time for the check to arrive in the mail.
- He waited a long time for his millionaire aunt to die.

- We waited a long time for our car to warm up.
- He waited a long time for his girl to warm up.

If you compare your answers with those of your classmates, you will probably find that your definitions are not the same. What seems like a long time to some would be a fairly short time to those endowed with more patience. You can expect differences of definition of abstract words, but even the most concrete terms also arouse different responses from people.

Let's look at a term fairly low on the ladder of abstraction—*horse*. Now, all speakers of English would surely agree on the basic definition, although they might not phrase it the same way. A horse is a four-legged mammal with hoofs; it is used for riding and for farm work. This meaning is the word's *denotation;* it is approximately what you would find in a dictionary. ("A large hoofed mammal, *Equus caballus,* having a short-haired coat, a long mane, and a long tail, and domesticated since ancient times for riding and to pull vehicles or carry loads," according to *The American Heritage Dictionary of the English Language,* 1973.)

Although many words have several different denotations and can thus be misinterpreted, this is not the kind of definition that causes the most communication problems. In addition to denotations, almost all words also have *connotations,* the personal, emotion-laden definitions given them by individuals. Three people may all agree on the denotation of the word *horse*, but they still might give it very different connotative definitions. Perhaps the first person owns several expensive race horses and is considered a good judge of an animal's value; for him, *horse* means financial asset. The second person may have fallen off a horse when he was a child; the terror he experienced then still remains, and *horse* to him means dangerous creature. If the third person has had very little experience, either good or bad, with horses, her reaction to *horse* may be completely neutral; her connotation is basically the same as her denotation of the word. Connotations can be positive, negative, or neutral. (This discussion purposely omits the slang meaning—heroin—because that is a different denotation.)

Sometimes you may wish to use a word in your writing and have all of your readers understand it to mean one and only one of its denotations. You may even want to change its denotation slightly. When this is your intention, you need to stipulate exactly what you mean by the word. In other words, define your terms in your paper. You can do this for even the commonest words. For instance, take the words *dog owner.* Everyone knows what a dog owner is, right? Well, apparently the dog license bureau wasn't sure, or at least it wanted to eliminate any legal problems caused by misunderstandings, because it put a forty-one-word definition on the back of the dog licenses printed for Kalamazoo County. Just in case you're curious to know what a dog owner *really* is, here is the definition: " 'Owner' defined as, 'Every person having right of property in a dog and every person who keeps such a dog, or has it in his care or who permits such a dog to remain on or about premises occupied by him.' " This stipulated definition is designed to prevent the owner of the unlicensed dog from claiming,

"Oh, he's not my dog. He just wanders in and out whenever he pleases." If the dog is permitted to remain, he is *owned* and must be licensed.

Writers who are unaware of the differing denotations and connotations of words sometimes get just the opposite of the reactions they intended from their readers. I am sure that the writer who wrote the copy on a package of pantyhose I once purchased wanted to make the stockings sound superior and hoped I would buy them again. I never did buy that brand again, however. What he (she?) had said was this: "These are the most effeminate pantyhose you will ever buy." Even though the denotation of *effeminate* in the dictionary is "having the qualities associated with women," most people have negative connotations of the term. Actually, a good dictionary could have helped this writer. My *American Heritage* (1973) says, "See Synonyms at *feminine*." The entry at *feminine* lists five other adjectives—*female, womanly, womanish, effeminate,* and *ladylike*—that might be used to replace *feminine*. (A synonym is a word that could be used in place of another word, even though the two are seldom, if ever, completely identical in meaning.) Then, a long paragraph spells out the different shades of meaning. The comment on *effeminate* is quite clear: "*Effeminate* is largely restricted in reference to men or things, and implies lack of manliness or strength: *an effeminate walk.*" This explanation might have saved the writer, and the pantyhose company, some embarrassment. If they had read it, they probably would have settled for *feminine* in their description. I would have bought feminine pantyhose a second time, but I won't waste my money on effeminate pantyhose.

If you want to choose the words that will stand the best chance of conveying your meaning to your intended reader, you need to get a good dictionary and use it often. It does not have to be an unabridged edition; that would probably be both too expensive and too heavy to be practical. Besides, you can always consult one in a library when you really need a complete discussion of a word. A desk dictionary weighs only four or five pounds and is considerably cheaper than other books of comparable size. There are many good ones available. In addition to the *American Heritage* already mentioned, there are *The American College Dictionary, Funk & Wagnalls Standard College Dictionary, Random House Dictionary of the English Language: College Edition, Webster's New Collegiate Dictionary,* and *Webster's New World Dictionary*. Any one of these is a good buy, and it will provide at least ten times the information found in the student dictionary with holes punched in the sides so it can be clipped into a three-ring notebook. Even though these are fairly cheap, don't waste your money on them.

PRACTICING ACHIEVING VARIETY WITH CONNOTATIONS

When you describe something or somebody, you probably choose words with connotations that reflect your general attitude toward the thing or the person—positive, neutral, or negative. For most ideas, you can find words that have the same denotation but have different emotional charges, so that they fit into one of the three categories. For instance, you have your choice of what to say about your English teacher.

(Positive) His assignments always have clearly stated expectations.
(Neutral) His assignments include a list of requirements.
(Negative) His assignments are encumbered with a list of picayune demands.

To test your skill with connotations, make two revisions of each of the following sentences; you should supply one version for each of the two emotional charges not given already.

1. (Neutral) Jake drove ninety-five miles an hour down Main Street.
2. (Positive) They dined on a nutritious variety of natural foods.
3. (Negative) When I rang the bell, two scruffy-looking mutts lunged at me, nearly tearing down the screen.
4. (Negative) By manipulating his vast financial holdings, C. Z. managed to exploit every loophole so that his tax bill was a mere pittance.
5. (Positive) Clara exercised her willpower and succeeded in trimming off ten pounds in just two weeks.
6. (Neutral) At the party last night, our new neighbor spent forty-five minutes telling my wife about his three speed boats.
7. (Negative) The neighborhood brat persists in careening through my immaculate hedges on his rattletrap bicycle.
8. (Positive) The new secretary's blonde, wholesome good looks will brighten up the office.
9. (Neutral) Whatever the topic of conversation, Sandra always has something to say.
10. (Negative) He was such a grind that he devoted his whole existence to maintaining his 4.0 average.

LITERAL LANGUAGE AND FIGURATIVE LANGUAGE

When you write a description, you can make use of the literal meanings of the words, saying as precisely as possible what you mean. For instance, you can describe an accident this way:

I heard the sound of metal and glass hitting the pavement. I saw the Land Rover turned upside-down with its headlights pointing straight up. The gas and oil leaked out into a puddle.

But you also have another choice to make your descriptions more vivid: *figurative language,* based on implied or stated comparisons. The same accident can be described as it was by John Irving:

Once I went to investigate an obvious accident—the darkness suddenly streaked with headlights pointing straight up and exploding; the silence pierced with a metal screaming and the shriek of ground glass. Only half a block away, in the dark and perfect middle of my street, a Land Rover lay upside-down and bleeding its oil and gas in a puddle so deep and still I could see the moon in it. The only sound: the *ping* of heat in the hot pipes and the dead engine. The Land Rover looked like a tank tumbled by a land mine.*

This description is easier for us to visualize, easier to feel. Its effectiveness should be evident without tearing the passage apart, but if you need to classify the figures of speech, you can see that Irving uses several kinds of figurative language. "Metal screaming and the shriek of ground glass" is *personification;* normally, screams and shrieks come from people or animals, but Irving gives these characteristics to inanimate objects, metal and glass. The Land Rover is also personified, "bleeding its oil and gas." The *metaphor* implies that it is like a wounded animal without actually saying this. If the author had said, "like a wounded animal," this would have been a *simile.* Irving uses a simile in the last sentence, where he compares the Land Rover to "a tank tumbled by a land mine." Because he uses *like* in this sentence, the comparison is a simile rather than a metaphor; metaphors only imply what similes come right out and state. Even the reference to the "dead engine," although common in our talk about automobiles, is a kind of personification. Engines stall; people and animals die.

Sometimes writers use a kind of personification-in-reverse, comparing the people to the machines. In a recent review of a novel, Dolly Katz, writing in the *Detroit Free Press,* criticized the characterization in this way: "Aside from swearing, people . . . express emotions by shuddering and shivering, which they do more than a '55 Chevy with a misaligned front end."

Many metaphors and other figures of speech started out as fresh comparisons but have been repeated so many times that most readers are bored with them; the expressions have become clichés and should be avoided. See how you would complete the following comparisons. If the answer comes to your mind immediately, it probably comes to your readers' minds just as quickly. Don't use the expression unless you want to bore your readers and give the impression that your ideas are just as lacking in originality as your language is.

Happy as a _____   Cute as a _____
Quick as a _____   Ugly as a _____
Slow as _____   Dull as _____
Busy as a _____   Lazy as _____
Sly as a _____   Sharp as a _____

Student writers do not need to fall back on clichés in their descriptive writing. If they are observant and playful with language, they can produce images that are just as fresh as those of the professional writer.

---

* From *The World According to Garp* by John Irving. Copyright © 1976, 1977, 1978 by John Irving. Reprinted by permission of the publisher, E. P. Dutton.

PRACTICING RECOGNIZING FIGURATIVE LANGUAGE

All of these passages come from students' essays. Identify their use of simile, metaphor, and personification, and decide whether these figures of speech are effective or ineffective for you, the reader. Which works best? Which is least meaningful?

1. Ahh, what a relief! I feel as though I have just been bathed in the first warm spring rain, and the clouds have drifted off to uncover the sun. I can smell the heavy, pervading scent of warm, fertile soil promising color and new life. Cold, drab winter has subsided, and now I have hope. I can think of tomorrow as an opportunity instead of a never-ending list.

    Marriage made me feel like a vegetable: a radish, a few droopy leaves above ground, with the spicy, delightful fruit hidden under the soil.

2. [To her daughter, who has announced that she is dropping out of college] One semester will turn into the end of school for you! You have so much talent! You love children! You would make a terrific teacher! Don't be like the kernels in the bottom of the popcorn bowl, the ones that didn't make it. I want you to be like the white, fluffy popcorn, the cones that exploded and realized their full potential!

3. Our tap shoes flew across the floor like a fast tune on a xylophone. Of course, our confidence came to a screeching halt when Mom announced she wanted to show us off by giving a recital for the parents. We were so nervous opening night our tap shoes felt like blocks of cement.

4. Her hands move faster than the lips of an auctioneer.

5. I had tossed the night before on the bed we had shared; hot, salty tears drenched my pillow. My eyes appeared as if they needed to give a blood donation at the Red Cross.

6. The January wind whistles around the home, its cold fingers testing each door and window, each possible crack for ways to cool this building.

7. The trapeze artists are airplanes winging their way through the air with the greatest of ease.

8. It seemed to me that my girlhood had dissolved at that moment, and, like the Phoenix, I arose, a fully grown woman, out of the ashes of my former self.

9. I look to the east where I behold the woody slopes waiting patiently like a devoted audience.

10. The house becomes your security blanket, and stepping outside is like walking into a jungle. You feel like a caged animal in a zoo.

PRACTICING WRITING FIGURATIVE LANGUAGE

The last section listed ten clichés, expressions that come to mind immediately when you want to describe a certain characteristic. Take your list of ten and write a new comparison for each one. (For instance, you might decide to be "happy as a coach whose team has just broken its losing streak.") Here are the beginnings of the similes again:

1. Happy as a _____
2. Quick as a _____
3. Slow as _____
4. Busy as a _____
5. Sly as a _____
6. Cute as a _____
7. Ugly as a _____
8. Dull as _____
9. Lazy as _____
10. Sharp as a _____

Now try your hand at metaphors or personification by thinking of effective ways to describe the following situations. Write two or three sentences for each.

1. When Jose picked up his paycheck, he was surprised to find a blue note attached to the stub. With some anxiety, he read the note: His job had been evaluated and moved up to the next classification; he was to receive a 7 percent raise. How did he feel?

2. You are finally going to trade in your ten-year-old jalopy on a new car. Still, parting with old Freddie the Ford is not easy; he has served you well for so long. Describe your farewell to the car.

3. Your six-year-old daughter has been hospitalized with spinal meningitis. Tests have been taken to find out if she has the variety which is frequently fatal. You wait two agonizing days for the results, but finally you get the good news: Her disease is the less serious kind, and she should be well in a week. How do you feel?

4. Lou spent every spare minute for the last two weeks studying for a really tough final in Anatomy 101. When the test results were posted, Lou saw that his grade was the highest in the class, 97! How do you think he responded?

5. Assume the same circumstances as in situation no. 4, but a different result—a grade of 62. Now what was his response?

5 WRITING: THE MEDIUM (WORDS)

RELATED READINGS

Student Essay

THE TICKET
Roberta Thompson

Points to Consider

As you read the essay that follows, try to answer these questions:

1. To describe her feelings in this situation, this author naturally used a variety of figures of speech. Which two or three seemed most meaningful to you? Did any of the figures of speech strike you as ineffective? If so, which ones were they?
2. What assumptions do you think the writer made about her audience before she wrote this essay? Do you think she was writing for an audience of drivers who had received parking tickets? What opinions about parking tickets might she expect her audience would have before reading her essay?
3. As you read this narrative, try to imagine it told from a different point of view—the meter-maid's. If she were telling the tale, what words with particularly negative connotations would she eliminate? How could she describe her part in the scene more positively?

Used with permission of Roberta Thompson.

It was a lovely May morning with the sun spreading its blanket of warmth across the land, bringing new life wherever it lay. My son, Greg, and I decided to go to the park, where we could take full advantage of the pleasures mother nature was providing.

As we were about to drive off in our car, which was parked at the curb, a meter-maid approached the car. "You can't drive off with this car," she said.

"Why not? It's mine!" I retorted, frustrated with the delay of my plans. My mind was a spinning top. What is wrong? Why can't I leave? Is this lady nuts? I mentally questioned. My son was a caged animal, seeking the freedom to relieve his bottled energy, but, instead, sitting, waiting to go.

The voice, again, reached out and like a huge hand suddenly stopped my spinning top. "You have an unpaid parking ticket on this car," it said. "You must either pay me the money or have your car impounded!"

My tongue became a ball of cotton, my throat felt as if it were in a hangman's noose, and wells of water began springing out of my hands. Quickly I catalogued my finances and realized I was worth a big $10 until the next day, which was payday. "How much is the fine?" I managed to croak.

"It's $25," replied the woman.

"I only have $10 until tomorrow. Couldn't I come in and pay the fine then?" I pleaded.

The scavenger who had swooped in on my son and me went back to her vehicle, talked on her radio, then returned and said, "You either pay now, or have your car impounded. . . . There is no other way!"

"I haven't enough money to pay! I need my car to go to work!" My voice screeched with the hysteria that was gripping me like a vise.

Again the top began spinning with thoughts like, what can I do? I need my car for work! I read somewhere they can't take your car for tickets if it's on private property! Oh! My God! She's back in her cart calling a wrecker to take my car! Suddenly I became a mindless machine starting its car and putting it into motion. In the recesses of my mind I heard the vulture scream, "Hey! You can't move that car!"

The machine I was ignored her and drove the car up into the driveway. My son and I got out of the car. "There!" I said. "Now take my car!" As Greg and I retreated into the house, I could see the meter-maid was talking on her radio.

In about five minutes, my gaze went toward the front window. What I saw made my heart beat so fast it was like a hummingbird's wings. There were five police cars in front of my house! I heard a knock on the door—the hummingbird's wings became a statue of rock.

When I opened the door, there was a nice-looking gentleman standing on my steps. "Did someone commit a murder?" I queried.

"No, ma'am," he replied, "but when an officer states they're having trouble, we never know." The blush of pink roses had come to his cheeks. "Could you tell me what happened, ma'am?" he asked. I told him my story. He said, "I think we can arrange for this to be paid tomorrow." The arrangements for payment were made via telephone, and all of the officers left.

After everyone was gone, I became a bowl of jello. I had come to the realization that paying parking tickets promptly can save much embarrassment. I definitely never wanted to repeat the traumatic experience of being a criminal.

Professional Essay

A GROWING WEALTH OF WORDS
Norman Cousins

Points to Consider

As you read the essay that follows, try to answer these questions:

1. Look through the list of words given here as twentieth-century words. If there are any you don't know, check a dictionary. Then, consider the connotations; are most negative, positive, or neutral? What, if anything, does your answer reveal about twentieth-century America?

2. Can you find a thesis sentence in this essay? Are the examples in the essay sufficient to prove this thesis?

3. Where would you place most of the new words on the ladder of abstraction? (See p. 64.)

4. Can you think of any other new words not included in this essay?

Copyright © 1981. Reprinted by permission of *Saturday Review.*

Fair warning: I write here unashamedly about a book project with which I have been personally involved—*March's Thesaurus-Dictionary.* Originally published in 1902, it represented a significant advance over *Roget's.* It combined dictionary definitions with a wide array of synonyms and associative words. Perhaps its most unique feature was a special system of juxtapositions it employed to bring out the full flavor of a word. The work was the product of one of America's most gifted lexicographers, Francis A. March. It dropped out of print somewhere during the Thirties and quickly became a collector's item. I prized my copy, which became the single most useful reference work in my personal library, and called the book to the attention of Doubleday, which brought out a revised edition in 1958. After 20 years, that edition, too, dropped out of print. Then, in 1978, the late Harry Abrams brought out an updated edition under the imprint of his Abbeville Press.

What to me is most fascinating of all about the new edition is a supplement by Stuart Berg Flexner and R. A. Goodwin containing words that have come into the language since the original edition 80 years ago. The new supplement, therefore, is a guide to the language of the 20th century. Thousands of words have come into the language in a comparatively short time. Most of these words are by now so commonplace that it is difficult to imagine how people ever got along without them. It hardly seems possible that words like *activate, displacement, empathy, documentary, heartland, escalate, defeatist, disposable, euphoria, decibel, deflate, demote, imbalance, immobilize, intelligentsia, inoperable, deadline, foolproof, editorialize, highlight, threshold, thumbnail, addict, bypass,* and *backlash* are all of comparatively recent origin.

Many words, of course, are the products of 20th-century civilization. The automobile alone is responsible for a vast addition to the language. Consider *backup, convertible, jalopy, hot rod, trailer, van, hit-and-run, back-seat driver,* etc. Similarly, the world of aviation has enriched the vocabulary with *airport, blimp, glider, helicopter, runway, tailspin, jet lag, skywriting,* etc. Hardly less enriching to the language is the vocabulary of the space age: *blast-off, countdown, launching pad, splashdown,* and *moonshot.* Immediately adjacent is the entire new world of atomic energy: *antigravity, chain reaction, electron, fission, fusion, isotope, nuclear, radioactivity, reactor,* and *SALT.*

The advent of the Psychological Revolution has not been without its effects on the language. Witness *catharsis, escapism, extrovert, introvert, fixation, hang-up, id, identity crisis, inferiority complex, superiority complex, crack-up, flip out, freak out, go haywire, batty, bananas, masochism, sadism, hallucination, inhibition, libido, narcissism, Oedipus complex, neurosis, overcompensation, stream of consciousness, trauma,* and *wishful thinking.*

Words like *burnout, psych-out, psych-up, rationalize,* and *maladjusted* are the product of an age that is trying to understand itself. Closely related, of course, is the medical vocabulary that has spilled over to the general language, where we freely use words like *allergy, blackout, shut-in, whiplash, black lung, hormone,* and *holistic.*

As for uncomplimentary references, the 20th century is not lacking in derogation: *bonehead, boob, crackpot, dimwit, dumbbell, goof, kook, misfit, nitwit, punk, nut, rattlebrain, sad sack, screwball, zombie.*

Few developments in recent years have been more characteristic of American life than the arena of publicity and communications: *ballyhoo, blurb, buildup, centerfold, cheesecake, handout, hoopla, hype, plug, promo, public relations, sponsor, skywriting, throwaway, columnist, want ad.*

It is important to be reminded that the human species is in a constant condition of experimentation, adaptation, and adventure; and that language is a way of keeping astride change. It is also the currency of communication; we become richer in direct proportion to our linguistic capital. Progress for the individual or the group depends not just on purpose and action but the use of the right words. The greater the ability to express abstractions and nuances, the wider the thinking ability and the more effective the command of complex situations.

In recent years, we have seen the growth of the cult of incoherence; it is considered fashionable in some circles to grunt and stammer and to litter the language with stale expressions (*you know, I mean,* etc.). But the contraction of language is a temporary phenomenon. Far more significant and enduring is the infusion that comes from new ideas and new thrusts. The language has never been richer than it is today and it will become richer still.

WRITING ASSIGNMENTS

In doing any of the assignments for this chapter, you should strive to meet the following objectives. If you meet all five, you will get a satisfactory grade.

Objectives

1. Turn in your prewriting, showing that you used one of the four recommended techniques.
2. Include and underline a thesis sentence, as called for by the specific assignment.
3. Show that you understand the differences in the various kinds of language by using carefully chosen words that fit the kinds of language called for by the specific assignment and the audience you have selected.
4. Use standard American spelling.
5. Proofread to eliminate any unmarked sentence fragments, comma splices, run-on sentences, subject-verb agreement errors, or errors in verb form.

5 WRITING: THE MEDIUM (WORDS)

The addition to the proofreading requirement, eliminating errors in verb form, is covered in detail in Section 2 of the Handbook under Wrong Principal Parts. You can tell whether or not you need to study that section immediately by reading this brief explanation.

An error in verb form usually occurs only with irregular verbs, those that do not form their past tense and past participle (the form used with *have* or *has*) by adding *-ed*. There are only a few dozen irregular verbs, but they are used frequently, and they can give you trouble. Misusing them is one of the surest clues that a person is speaking nonstandard English. The most frequent error is the use of a simple past-tense form with a helping verb (though the use of a past participle without a helping verb is common, too).

Her father really should have came to the wedding. (*Come* is the past participle; he should have *come*.)

I could of gone to the party if I hadn't been in jail. (*Could of gone* is nonstandard because it uses *of*, a preposition, for the helping verb form *have*. *Could have gone* is correct.)

If I had wrote sooner, she would have answered. (*Wrote*, the simple past tense, can never have a helping verb; the form is *had written*.)

The whole family has went there before. (*Gone* is the form to use here: The whole family has gone there before.)

They done their work quickly. (Here the past participle, *done*, is used without the needed *have*; the form you need here is *did*.)

If you can read these errors without inwardly screaming in pain, you have become too accustomed to hearing faulty verb forms. Read the Handbook section right away!

Writing Assignment 5-1 For this assignment you will need to write some fairly simple explanation of something—perhaps some task you do at work, some household chore, a method of studying for an exam, or a technique that you use in getting to sleep. Choose something simple, for you will need to describe it in no more than two paragraphs. The hard part will be that you will write this description three times, using three of the four varieties of English—formal English, general English, informal English, and nonstandard English.

For the prewriting step, try at least one of the four prewriting techniques you have learned. When you have a good idea of what task you'll be describing, an audience to describe it to, some details to include, and the three varieties of English you'll use, you should be able to state your main idea about the task as a thesis sentence. You will need to restate this thesis idea in three sentences, actually—one for each of the varieties of English you will be using. Here are three samples:

(Formal) The most arduous task one must perform in laundering soiled clothing is separating items which should not be processed together.

(General) The hardest part of doing the washing is sorting it into piles.
(Nonstandard) It ain't the wash that's hard to do; it's makin' the piles I hafta make first.

For the writing step, write the three descriptions, including the thesis in each and underlining it. It will probably be easiest to write the middle variety—either general or informal English—first, and then write the more extreme descriptions. All three descriptions should give the same explanation, but the differences in word choices and grammatical structure should show that you understand the different varieties of English. (For instance, when you write formal English, you will not include the first person singular, *I*, and you will eliminate any contractions.)

For the postwriting step, proofread all three explanations carefully, being sure to correct the spelling and to eliminate any unmarked fragments, comma splices, run-on sentences, subject-verb agreement errors (except in the nonstandard version), and errors in verb form (again, except in the nonstandard version).

Writing Assignment 5-2 This assignment involves writing a brief description of an event—something simple like a parade, a music recital, a school open house, or a neighborhood dog fight. You are to describe it in no more than a page, using concrete terms from close to the bottom of the ladder of abstraction (see p. 64). Then, you are to write two more brief descriptions, moving one step up the ladder of abstraction in your word choices each time. It is perfectly okay if the event is no longer recognizable by the time you are describing it for the third time. (After all, "My neighbor's little black poodle bit my big Doberman on his right ear" may have become simply, "One creature wounded a part of the other creature's anatomy.")

For the prewriting step, try at least one of the four techniques you have learned. When you have a good idea of what to describe, an audience to write for, and some details to include, try to state your main idea about the event as a thesis sentence. (You will need to use this only in the first version, the concrete one.) Here is a possible thesis for the dogfight description: In my neighborhood, a dogfight involves more people than dogs.

Once you have a good thesis, you are ready to begin the writing step by writing the concrete description. Be sure to include and underline the thesis somewhere on the page. Also, use specific words, chosen from the lower end of the ladder of abstraction. To complete the writing step, you will rewrite the same description with more abstract terms, and then write it a third time, using very abstract terms. In the third version, the descriptions may be so general as to be ridiculous. The second and third descriptions need not include thesis sentences.

For the postwriting step, proofread all three descriptions carefully, being sure to correct the spelling and to eliminate any unmarked fragments, comma splices, run-on sentences, subject-verb agreement errors, and errors in verb form.

Writing Assignment 5-3

For this assignment you will be describing a person you know to a reader who does not know the person. You will write three descriptions, choosing your words so that the first description will make no emotional impression, the second description will be very favorable, and the third description will be very negative. The content of the three descriptions should be basically the same; what should change will be the connotations of the words. For instance, if the person you are describing is skinny and tight-fisted in the negative description, she should not become curvaceous and generous in the positive version. Instead, she can be slim and a careful spender.

For the prewriting step, try at least one of the four prewriting techniques you have learned. When you have a good idea of what person you'll be describing and what details you'll include, try to formulate *two* thesis sentences, one for the positive description, and one for the negative description. The neutral description will not reveal what your opinion of the person is, so it will not need a thesis.

The writing step will probably be easiest if you write the neutral version first, choosing words with little or no emotional content. Then, the description that comes the closest to what you really think of the person should be written. (In other words, if you're describing someone you like, write the positive version next.) Be sure to include and underline a thesis in this section of your essay, and include details that will support that thesis. The most difficult part should come last—the description that is the opposite of what you really think of the person. For this section of your paper, you will need to include basically the same details, but try to word them to achieve the opposite effect by choosing terms that have the opposite connotations. This section also needs an underlined thesis sentence.

For the postwriting step, proofread all three descriptions carefully, being sure to correct the spelling and to eliminate any unmarked fragments, comma splices, run-on sentences, subject-verb agreement errors, and errors in verb form.

Writing Assignment 5-4

For this assignment you are to write two descriptions of a place or an experience. The first description is to use only literal language, and the second is to incorporate at least three figures of speech, preferably well chosen and creative ones. Select a place or a happening that you know well or have experienced recently for this description. Describe it to a reader who does not know it or has not experienced it. You may use the same thesis sentence in both descriptions, but most of your other sentences should be different. The shorter description should be about a page long; probably the figurative description will be somewhat longer. Some good places to describe are the supermarket where you shop, your old elementary school, or the block where you live. Appropriate events include registration day at college, a rock concert you have attended, a family or school reunion.

For the prewriting step, try at least one of the four prewriting techniques you have learned. When you have a good idea of what you will be describing and some of the details you will include, try to state your main idea in a thesis sentence.

The writing step involves writing both descriptions. Be sure to include and underline the thesis in both versions. In the first version, use vivid details, but use only literal descriptions. Do not put similes, metaphors, or personification in this description. When you write the second description, do put in at least three of these. In the margin, identify the figures of speech you have used.

For the postwriting step, proofread both descriptions carefully, being sure to correct the spelling and to eliminate any unmarked fragments, comma splices, run-on sentences, subject-verb agreement errors, and errors in verb form.

CHAPTER 6

WRITING: THE MEDIUM (SENTENCES)

You write in word symbols, but you have to put these words into patterns before they make much sense to anyone, including yourself. You almost never write—or think—isolated words. Your ideas break down into pieces that are roughly equivalent to sentences; when you write, you group these into paragraphs. As you write sentences, you need to make decisions about both their content and their structure.

CONTENT: FACTUAL AND NONFACTUAL STATEMENTS

Although some sentences ask questions (Did you clean up the mess?), some give orders (Clean up the mess!), and some express strong feelings (What a mess this is!), by far the largest percentage of written and spoken sentences is declarative: The sentences make statements about something.

I have a dog. His name is Toby. He is a mix of black Labrador and some other breed. I have owned him since 1977.

All of these sentences are statements. They are observations about something that exists in the physical world—my dog, Toby. The physical object, the dog, is a fact. All of these statements about the fact could be checked for accuracy, so we can call them *factual statements*. (They are sometimes called *reports* or *observations*, too.) Now, checking the accuracy of these statements might not be easy—we had to take Toby to a veterinarian to find out the third one—but it is possible. The dog warden's office runs a door-to-door survey every year to verify just such factual statements.

We call any statement *factual* if it describes facts in such a way that its accuracy can be verified. Suppose in the statements just listed I had said that Toby was a goat. Would that be a factual statement, even though it was inaccurate? Interestingly enough, it would be. When we say that a statement is factual, we do *not* imply that it is accurate. We only imply that its accuracy can be determined; we can find out for sure whether the statement is true or false. Toby either is a goat, or he is not. His goatness is not a matter of opinion. He is not a goat on Tuesdays and Thursdays and a dog the rest of the week. Both statements—"Toby is a dog," and "Toby is a goat"—are factual statements, even though only one is an *accurate* factual statement. (Note that this definition of the word *factual*, used by those who study language and communications, is narrower than the word's everyday meaning.)

Many factual statements are second-hand reports, or third-hand reports, that we still accept as accurate. I can tell you that I have a dog named Toby, and I am reporting my personal experience. If I tell you that Richard Nixon had a dog named Checkers, I am reporting second-hand experience. I never saw Checkers, but I remember reading the famous Checkers speech of the 1952 vice-presidential campaign, and I even have vague memories of listening to it on the radio. Of course, if you wanted to verify this second-hand report, you would have to rely on other second-hand reports, such as comments on the speech in history texts—unless you had enough nerve to telephone Nixon himself to inquire about a dog he owned three decades ago.

But many of the statements we make are not second- or even third-hand reports. They are not factual statements at all, because they are not verifiable observations about physical reality. When a statement goes beyond what is observed to an interpretation of the cause or the meaning of that observation, we call it an *inference*. Although you cannot definitely check the truth of an inference, some inferences are better than others. If several observers draw the same inference from the same set of factual statements, the inference is more acceptable than a statement on which no two observers could agree.

Let's suppose I observe Toby's behavior during a storm and make the following factual statements:

Toby is shaking. Right after it thundered, he began to whine. He pushed open the closet door and curled up in a back corner behind the coats.

Based on these observations, I might infer that Toby is frightened by the storm. Other observers, noting the same behavior, might agree with me, helping to substantiate my inference. Still, their agreement would not prove the statement true in the same way that a factual statement is proven true. With inferences there is always an element of guessing involved in the interpretation. There is always some other explanation possible: Perhaps Toby is behaving in this way because he is sick. Still, my statement that Toby is frightened is a better explanation of his behavior than another inference might be. If I tried to explain his whining and shaking by saying, "Toby is happy," not many observers would agree with me. Whining and shaking are not generally signs of happiness. The important point is that whining and shaking can be observed, so we can make factual statements about them. Fright and happiness can't be observed; we can only infer them from the behaviors we do observe.

How do we use factual statements and inferences when we write? In writing we should not depend exclusively on inferences. We should back up our inferences with appropriate observations whenever possible. Then our readers can judge for themselves whether or not they would have drawn the same conclusions, given the same observations. We should also avoid writing that is entirely factual observation; after a certain point, facts without inferences can become very dull. Readers want to know what point we are making. They want to know what all these observations mean to us.

One type of inference needs special attention, as it is particularly important in writing. When I say, "My dog, Toby, is a better pet than your goat, Hercules," I am making a *judgment*. A judgment is an inference that reflects more about the speaker's value system than it does about the subject (Toby and Hercules). Like other inferences, it cannot be proven true or false, although it can be given support by listing factual statements about the subject. For instance, Toby is housebroken. If Hercules is not housebroken, these two factual statements would weigh heavily in Toby's favor. For most people, the definition of a *good pet* includes that the animal be housebroken. Still, Hercules is your pet, so perhaps that is not part of your definition. Perhaps to you a good pet is an animal that will eat anything in sight and run off undesirable guests by butting them with its horns. In that case, Hercules fills the bill admirably. "Hercules is a better pet than Toby"; that is *your* judgment.

You already learned that a thesis statement should not be a factual statement. A good thesis statement should be a judgment; it should reflect your values. What else is worth arguing about? You will use inferences to support your thesis statement. How will you back up the inferences? With factual statements, of course.

PRACTICING IDENTIFYING FACTUAL STATEMENTS AND INFERENCES

In order to see how you might use different kinds of statements in your writing, do two activities with each of the ten statements below. First, identify the sentence as either a factual statement or an inference. Second, for the factual statements, write an inference that could be partially supported by such a statement; for the inferences, write a factual statement that could be used to support such an inference. (The first one is done for you.)

1. Sonia is a very snooty girl. (Answer: Inference. Supporting factual statement: Sonia passed me three times in the supermarket today and didn't speak once. Note that another inference could be based on this statement; perhaps Sonia was not wearing her contact lenses.)
2. Hank must be an alcoholic.
3. There are four colleges in Kalamazoo.
4. Grandma is throwing a temper tantrum again.
5. All of the cupboard doors are open, and the pots and pans are in the middle of the kitchen floor.
6. I subscribe to eleven magazines.

> 7. There is a strong odor coming from that green package in the back of the refrigerator.
> 8. That teacher is mentally unbalanced.
> 9. Your new dress displays four and one-half inches of cleavage.
> 10. The basketball team is bound to have a better season this year than last year.

STRUCTURE: READABILITY

If you want to convince people to agree with your judgments, in addition to supporting them with factual statements, you must also make them readable. Readability depends somewhat on content—if the subject matter is totally unfamiliar to the reader, no way of stating the ideas will make much sense—but it also depends on word choice and sentence structure.

What makes one passage more readable than another? Scholars have tried to answer this scientifically only in the last forty years. The first scale to measure readability was developed by Rudolf Flesch at Columbia University in 1943 and revised five years later. It is still one of the most widely used measures, but it is very technical and depends upon a formula too complex to carry around in your head. The easiest rule-of-thumb measurement is the Fog Index, developed by Robert Gunning.*

The steps are simple. I'll apply them to the opening of this chapter on p. 81, just to show you how it works.

- First, count one hundred words. This is the length of the excerpt you will be evaluating. If you want to evaluate a whole book, choose three excerpts from different sections of the book, and average your results. The first hundred words in this chapter—not counting headings or subheadings—ends with the word *percentage* in the second paragraph.

- Second, count the number of sentences in the passage. If one sentence has two independent clauses joined by colon, semicolon, or comma and *and*, *but*, or *or*, count the sentence as two sentences. In my one hundred words, there are almost ten sentences—six in the first paragraph and four in the second. (The tenth sentence doesn't end until the word *declarative*, but I'm counting it as ten.)

- Third, figure what the average sentence length is. To do this, divide the number of sentences into one hundred, the number of words. Since I have ten sentences, the sentences average ten words.

- Fourth, count the number of "hard words," words of three or more syllables (unless they are proper names, two-syllable verbs with *-ed* endings added, or simple combinations, like *insofar*). There are eleven of these in my one hundred words: *anyone, including, isolated, ideas, equivalent, sentences* (three times), *paragraphs, decisions,* and *percentage*.

---

* From *How to Take the Fog Out of Writing* by Robert Gunning, The Dartnell Corporation, 1964. Reprinted by permission.

- Finally, add the number of hard words to the average sentence length and multiply this figure by 0.4. For my sample, the result is 8.4 (21 × 0.4). This is the approximate number of years of education required for a reader to understand the passage easily. Numbers to the right of the decimal are ignored, and any number over 17 is read as 17+, since not many readers have education beyond a graduate degree. A reader with an eighth-grade reading level should be able to comprehend this text, if my one-hundred-word sample is typical of the rest of the book.

For contrast, evaluate a sociology text or a chemistry text. Books with more technical language than this one will usually rate higher on the readability scale. If they also include many complex sentences, they probably really do make high-level demands of their readers. Of course, this whole text is not written at an eighth- or ninth-grade level of understanding; some of the readings are quite difficult. Look back at the one you considered most challenging so far. Apply the Fog Index to it to see if your gut-level reaction can be substantiated scientifically. Was it indeed quite high on the readability scale?

Now that you see how the Fog Index works, try it on your own writing. Count out a one-hundred-word excerpt from your last paper. Find the average sentence length, the number of hard words, and the total of these two figures. Multiply this number by 0.4. How does your writing come out? Whether your score is a good one or not will depend on who your intended audience was for that paper. If your score is over 14, I hope you were writing for a pretty specialized audience.

You should be able to come up with your own suggestions for raising or lowering the score now that you understand how the Index is applied. If the score is higher than you would like it to be, work on shortening the sentences and finding two-syllable equivalents for some of the longer words. In the unlikely event that the score seems too low, look for synonyms with more syllables rather than fewer, and try to combine some of the short, choppy sentences into more complex ones.

STRUCTURE: LONG SENTENCES AND SHORT SENTENCES

Of course, good writing does not always consist of short, easy-to-read sentences. Even the reader who is most comfortable reading passages that would score a 7 or an 8 on the Fog Index can, with a lot of concentration and the occasional use of a dictionary, decipher much higher-level writing. There are occasions when very long sentences are necessary to develop a point or create an atmosphere. Consider this 333-word gem from *Shikasta* by Doris Lessing:

> And this is what an eye tuned slightly, only slightly, differently would see looking out of the window at that tree which shed the leaf on to the pavement—since it is autumn and the tree's need to conserve energy against the winter is on it—no, not a tree, but a fighting seething mass of matter in the extremes of tension, growth, destruction, a myriad of species of smaller and smaller creatures feeding on each other, each feeding on the other, always—that is what this tree is in reality, and this man, this woman, crouched tense over the leaf, feels nature as a roaring creative fire in whose

crucible species are born and die and are reborn in every breath . . . every life . . . every culture . . . every world . . . the mind, wrenched away from its resting place in the close visible cycles of growth and renewal and decay, the simplicities of birth and death, is forced back, and back into itself, coming to rest—tentatively and without expectation—where there can be no rest, in the thought that always, at every time, there have been species, creatures, new shapes of being, making harmonious wholes of interacting parts, but these over and over again crash! are swept away!—crash go the empires and the civilisations, and the explosions that are to come will lay to waste seas and oceans and islands and cities, and make poisoned deserts where the teeming detailed inventive life was, and where the mind and heart used to rest, but may no longer, but must go forth like the dove sent by Noah, and at last after long circling and cycling see a distant mountaintop emerging from wastes of soiled water, and must settle there, looking around at nothing, nothing, but the wastes of death and destruction, but cannot rest there either, knowing that tomorrow or next week or in a thousand years, this mountaintop too will topple under the force of a comet's passing, or the arrival of a meteorite.*

Although this sentence strains the limits of most readers' comprehension, its length is probably necessary to fit its content. The cyclical patterns of creation and destruction and the restlessness felt by the human mind when confronted by these could not be shown appropriately in short, concise sentences. Because we are caught up in the fiction, we can read a sentence like this once in a while. If all the sentences looked like this, most readers would not get beyond the third page. Actually, the readability score on this passage is not as high as you might expect. For the first hundred words, it turns out to be 15. There are two reasons for this: Although the whole excerpt is punctuated as one sentence, by the rules of the Fog Index, there are three sentences here, so the average sentence length is thirty-three. Also, there are few multisyllable words in the first hundred—only five. The passage is difficult to read because of the unusual punctuation and the stringing together of many short words, not because the words themselves are difficult.

Very short sentences are easy to read, but they, too, have their drawbacks. With their choppy, monotonous rhythm, they will make your writing sound as if it belonged in a beginning reading text.

Look at the cat. See the cat run. The cat runs fast. The cat runs after the mouse. The mouse runs fast. The cat runs faster. The cat catches the mouse. Do not look!

Of course, there may be times when you want to convey monotonous routine, and short sentences will do the job perfectly.

They got up in the morning. They got dressed. They ate breakfast at the same table. They left the house. He drove the Ford to his job in the city. She drove the Chevette to her job in the city. They never spoke.

---

* From *Shikasta* by Doris Lessing, Alfred A. Knopf, 1979. Reprinted by permission.

Generally, a really short sentence is most effective for emphasis after a series of longer sentences.

He decided that he had done everything interesting there was for a man to do in the twentieth century. Starting his own companies, flying his own planes, marrying his own wives (three of them), earning his own millions—he had done it all, and he was bored because none of it required an effort any longer. So he died.

STRUCTURE: EMPHASIS AND COHERENCE

Varying the length of your sentences is one way to achieve the emphasis you want, but there are several other ways. They often involve playing around with the words. You should try out various ways of saying the same thing, just as you would try out several pairs of shoes before buying any. Do not settle for any wording unless the rhythm feels comfortable to you.

One way of changing the rhythm and the emphasis of a sentence involves coordinating or subordinating ideas. When you *coordinate* ideas, you join them together in such a way that you indicate their equal value. Let's start with the sentences from the phony beginning reading text example just given and see how many different ways we might coordinate them.

As the sentences are written, they are all *simple sentences*. They are called this because they each contain only one clause, one combination of subject (or subjects) and verb (or verbs). Since these clauses can stand by themselves, as they are doing in the simple sentences, they are called *independent clauses*. When we join two of these independent clauses into one sentence, we create a *compound sentence*. We can coordinate the ideas of two of these simple sentences into one compound sentence in at least three ways:

1. With just a semicolon: The cat runs after the mouse; the mouse runs fast.
2. With a comma and a coordinating conjunction (*and, but, or, nor*—sometimes *for,* and *yet*): The mouse runs fast, but the cat runs faster.
3. With a semicolon and a conjunctive adverb (a word such as *consequently, however, moreover, nevertheless,* and *therefore*): The mouse runs fast; nevertheless, the cat runs faster.

Although we have coordinated ideas in these three examples, we haven't really made our writing much more complicated. Remember that in the readability formula, the independent clauses in a compound sentence are treated as if they were separate sentences. Apparently, reading "The mouse runs fast, but the cat runs faster" is not any more difficult than reading "The mouse runs fast. The cat runs faster." What does make writing more complicated—and therefore more sophisticated and often more effective—is *subordinating* ideas.

Subordinating ideas involves joining them in such a way that you indicate that one is more important than the other. The important idea is usually stated in an independent clause, while the other is stated in a *dependent clause*, usually—but not always—beginning with a *subordinating conjunction*. Subordinating conjunctions include such words as *after, because, if, since, that, when,* and *while*. This combination of independent clause and dependent clause creates a *complex sentence*, a type of sentence very popular in current writing. Let's look at some complex sentences made by subordinating some of the simple sentences from the same passage we used above.

- Although the mouse runs fast, the cat runs faster.
- Because the cat runs faster, the cat catches the mouse.
- The cat, who runs faster, catches the mouse.

Notice what happens to *the cat runs faster* in each of these examples. It is the emphasized clause in the first sentence, as it is the independent one. In the other two examples it is the dependent clause, so the other clause gets the emphasis in each case.

There is still another way you could express the ideas in the last two complex sentences. You could turn the idea in the dependent clause into a *modifier*.

Running faster, the cat catches the mouse.

Running is a participle (an *ing* form of the verb used as a modifier). Because *running faster* is not a clause, you still have a simple sentence, but it is a simple sentence with more variety than the original sentences had. When you begin a sentence in this way, make sure that the modifier and the thing modified are close together. (For help with this problem, see Section 4 of the Handbook.)

One other kind of sentence involves de-emphasizing certain clauses; it, as you might guess, is a combination of the last two sentence types—a *compound-complex sentence*. This kind of sentence includes at least two ideas of equal value and one of lesser value, so it will have at least two independent clauses (to make it compound) and a dependent clause (to make it complex). Let's finish off our cat-and-mouse story with a couple of examples of compound-complex sentences.

- The cat runs after the mouse; while the mouse runs fast, the cat runs faster.
- The mouse runs fast, but the cat, who runs faster, catches it.

Just because an idea comes into your head in certain words and certain order, you should not think that these words and this order are the only way of saying it. You are not limited to one phrasing or word order just because that is the way the idea appeared in your head the first time.

What is the difference between the two sentences you just read? Both mean the same thing, and both are complex sentences. However, the first is *periodic;* you have to read all the way to the period before you get to a place to stop. The second sentence has several places where periods could have been put: after *phrasing*, after *order*, after *appeared*, after *head*, or where one was put, after *time*. The second sentence is a *loose sentence*.

Loose sentences sound more conversational, more informal than periodic sentences. They appear to be made up as they go along, rather than planned. Periodic sentences are uncommon in general English, so they draw attention to themselves while they add variety. Generally, they raise the readability level of a passage. For emphasis, you should occasionally try one. Contrast the emphatic value of these two sentences:

Cora lied because she couldn't think of any other way of getting out of the situation gracefully.

Because she couldn't think of any other way of getting out of the situation gracefully, Cora lied.

PRACTICING WRITING PERIODIC SENTENCES

Experiment with the rhythm of complex sentences by forming two different sentences for each pair of simple sentences given below. The first complex sentence of each pair should be loose; the second should be periodic. (Sample answers are given for number one.)

1. I can't buy a new coat.
   My checkbook balance is $2.15.
   (Loose sentence: I can't buy a new coat because my checkbook balance is $2.15. Periodic sentence: Since my checkbook balance is $2.15, I can't buy a new coat.)
2. The spectators throw fish to the seal.
   The seal snaps up the fish and applauds with her flippers.
3. Velma broke their engagement.
   Velma learned of Horace's social disease.
4. I can't afford the repair bill.
   The car needs a whole new transmission.
5. The kids are fighting constantly.
   The kids are bored with summer vacation.
6. The senator bought 5,000 votes.
   The public never learned of his dishonesty.

STRUCTURE: REPETITION AND PARALLELISM

Repetition is another device for emphasizing certain ideas. Look back at the long sentence from *Shikasta* earlier in this chapter. Repetition holds much of it together:

- slightly, only slightly, differently
- smaller and smaller creatures feeding on each other, each feeding on the other, always
- every breath . . . every life . . . every culture . . . every world
- forced back, and back into itself,
- but these over and over again crash!
- looking around at nothing, nothing.

Ideas are repeated, too. The word *rest* appears four times, *resting* appears once, and *settle* appears once.

Repetition makes your writing emphatic; parallelism makes it coherent. (Parallelism also helps emphasize certain points, but my parallel structure would have been thrown off if I had said, " . . . parallelism makes it more emphatic and coherent.") Whenever the same grammatical pattern is used two, three, or more times in a short passage, we call the resulting effect *parallelism*. Sometimes repetition is necessary to achieve parallelism, as in the case of repeated infinitives (*to* plus a verb).

He found it hard to study, to read the text, to take notes, to review for a test—in short, he found it hard to be a student.

Although we may note, in the backs of our minds, a certain *neatness* about a sentence with parallel structure, parallelism is much more noticeable when we expect it but it is missing. Doesn't this sloppily structured sentence have a grating effect?

My duties were helping the teacher prepare lessons, listening to reading groups, designs for the bulletin boards, to do playground duty at recess, and individual students would come to me with math problems.

To repair the parallelism in a sentence like this one, we can take each separate duty and state it after the sentence's beginning, like this:

My duty was helping the teacher prepare lessons. (OK)

My duty was listening to reading groups. (OK)

My duty was designs for the bulletin boards. (Not OK—*designs* could not be a duty, so this needs to be changed to a word like *helping* or *listening*. We can say, "My duty was designing the bulletin boards.")

My duty was to do playground duty at recess. (This one would be OK alone, but paired with *helping, listening,* and *designing,* the infinitive form sticks out awkwardly. It should be changed to *doing playground duty.*)

My duty was individual students would come to me with math problems. (Again, not OK—*students* could not be a *duty*, as duties are actions, not people. To make this one parallel, we need a word describing what you did with these individual students: "My duty was *assisting* individual students with math problems.")

Now that all five duties are stated in the same form, we have one more decision to make. What order should we use in stating them? There is no right answer to this question, but some order should be followed. Don't just plop the ideas down in the order they occur to you. My choice is to list the more important duties first, beginning with tasks that applied to the whole class. The parallel sentence that results from all this repair work is this one:

My duties were helping the teacher prepare lessons, listening to reading groups, assisting individual students with their math, watching the playground at recess, and designing bulletin boards.

Doesn't that seem easier to read and more pleasant than the first confusing sentence we had? It took some time to achieve that coherence, but future repair jobs should be less time-consuming. Once you develop the knack of parallel structure, you will be able to visualize different possibilities quite rapidly. For instance, you could have achieved a similar effect with this sentence:

To fulfill my duties I helped the teacher prepare lessons, I listened to reading groups, I assisted individual students with their math, I watched the playground at recess, and I designed bulletin boards.

The basic difference between these two sentences is that the first achieved parallelism with a list of gerunds (verbs turned into nouns by adding *ing* endings to them), while the second used a list of clauses to create its parallelism. (If you think I have four comma splice errors in the second version, you are nearly right. However, when you string together a whole series of clauses, you can join them with commas even though you are not using *and, but,* or *or* to start each new clause. You punctuate the series of clauses the same way you would punctuate three or more nouns or adjectives: Use commas after each, and put *and* before the last one.)

PRACTICING ACHIEVING PARALLEL STRUCTURE

Follow the same steps taken in the example just used to correct faulty parallelism in the ten sentences here.

1. At the New Year's Eve party, people were drinking, eating, they danced to records, while some were playing cards, and others necked.
2. The new neighbor is wealthy, ostentatious, and a bore.
3. The American public wants not only a car that gets good gas mileage but also safety.
4. There are two kinds of lecturers: Those who are well prepared, and dull ones.
5. Bringing up a child requires more energy than to own a pet.
6. George had three goals in life: running his own restaurant, marrying his childhood sweetheart, and to own a houseboat.
7. To estimate your housing expenses, you need to figure your house payments, your taxes, your insurance costs, and what you will have to pay for utilities.
8. The most popular movies today are either space adventures, movies about spies, or ones that take you to a world of fantasy.
9. Growing old is harder than to grow up.
10. To lose is hard, but so is winning.

STRUCTURE: ACTIVE AND PASSIVE VERBS

You may have been advised to use more active verbs in your writing. If such an instruction confused you, I'm not surprised. It can have two different meanings, but both are good advice. The first meaning calls for choosing vivid verbs rather than bland verbs: "He *punched* me, and I *collapsed* in a heap," rather than "He *hit* me, and I *fell* to the floor." By following this advice, you can make your writing more lively without overloading it with adjectives and adverbs. The second meaning calls for choosing verbs in the *active voice* rather than verbs in the *passive voice*. This concept may need some explanation.

"Cancer devoured his liver." "His liver was devoured by cancer." Which sentence would you write? Both are grammatically correct; the difference is between an active verb (*devoured*) and a passive verb (*was devoured*). The first verb is called active because the subject (*cancer*) does it. In the second sentence, the subject (*his liver*) is not doing anything. Instead, something is being done to it. When the subject just sits there passively having something done to it, the verb is said to be passive.

How can you choose between active verbs and passive verbs? For most purposes, active verbs are considered superior. They make the writing seem fast paced, whereas passive verbs slow it down and create a plodding effect. Still, passive verbs are preferred when the doer is unknown ("The gymnasium was demolished by vandals who left no clues as to their identity.") or when you do not want to take responsibility for an action—usually for political reasons. If you use the passive voice too often for the second reason, you can expect your reader to be suspicious. Laurence Gonzales, writing in *Playboy* ("Airline Safety: A Special Report," July 1980), stated the case against the passive voice well:

> The people responsible for air crashes . . . like to couch their descriptions in vague, official locutions . . . until it seems that the entire affair was a simple bookkeeping error in no one's favor. "Fatalities resulted" is a favorite, or, "Lives were lost," using the passive verb forms to suggest that, well, like earthquakes and cholera, these things just happen.
>
> . . . When an airline announces that lives were lost, it makes it sound as if, even at this very moment, every effort is being made to locate them and it is only a matter of time before the misplaced items are returned.

Check your own writing. Does it sound specific and lively or vague and dull? If you want to add pep to your writing, try using verbs that are active in *both* senses of the word. (For more help with the active and passive voices, see Section 2 of the Handbook.)

PRACTICING ACHIEVING SENTENCE VARIETY

To apply many of this chapter's concepts to your own writing, you must first find a sample of your writing to use as a starting point. Go through the papers you have written for this class, and select one of your weaker paragraphs. Make sure it contains at least four sentences, and copy them on a new sheet of paper, numbering the sentences so you

6 WRITING: THE MEDIUM (SENTENCES)

can comment upon them by number. Then, answer the following questions about your sentences:

1. How long are the sentences? Do you have a variety of sentence lengths? If you don't, could you combine some of the sentences to achieve a greater variety of lengths?
2. Do you have all four types of sentences (simple, compound, complex, and compound-complex)? Identify each sentence as to type. If any type is missing, could you create it by combining sentences or by streamlining sentences?
3. Do you have both periodic and loose sentences? Identify each sentence as either periodic or loose.
4. Do any of the sentences use repetition or parallelism? If they don't, do they contain any ideas that could be expressed through repetition or parallelism?
5. How many active verbs do the sentences contain? How many passive verbs? (Some verbs will not be either because they will be *linking* verbs, as in this sentence: "His plight *seemed* hopeless.")

Now that you have analyzed your own paragraph thoroughly, rewrite it. You should try to achieve as much variety as possible—variety in sentence length, in sentence type, in periodic and loose sentences, in parallel structures and repetitions, and in verb choices. Of course, try to make your paragraph *sound* good, too. Don't strive for variety for its own sake; make the structure of your sentences appropriate to their content. When you are finished, the weak paragraph should be a strong one.

RELATED READINGS

Student Essay

**THE SWAMP
David Kelsey**

Points to Consider

As you read the essay that follows, try to answer these questions:

1. Notice the simple style, almost like a story told to a child. What details of the sentence structure account for this effect?
2. What assumptions can you make about the audience for this essay? Does the style seem appropriate for such an audience? Does the style seem appropriate for this topic?

3. Find examples of repetition and parallelism. What points are they used to emphasize?
4. What figures of speech can you find in this essay? Which are effective for you, and which are not? Why?

Used with permission of David Kelsey.

It fascinates me to think that the fertile, tillable soil that is now Gun Plains was once a wet swamp. Gun Swamp was one of the last truly wild areas near my home town of Martin, Michigan. The swamp has been dead many years now, killed long before I was born. It was claimed by man in the name of progress.

I grew up in or on the edge of what had once been the swamp. From the time I was knee high to a grasshopper I heard stories told by the old men who could remember the original swamp. I could only imagine it, maybe the only one of my generation to give it a thought, and I mourned its passing. Gun Swamp lives on in the minds of these old men. Most of the old men are gone now, and with the passing of each one, a little more of what is known about the swamp's history is lost. If only the stories could be written down before it is too late, the swamp could live on forever in memory.

My grandfather could remember the swamp when no roads crossed it and few roads penetrated beyond its edge. It was wild then. The outlying areas were settled, but not the forbidding swamp itself. The river meandered through it. The river was the swamp's life, its aortic artery. The plentiful wildlife depended upon the swamp for its livelihood, the swamp depended upon the river, the river upon Gun Lake, the lake upon the springs that fed it. The springs, the lake, the river all remain. The river is crippled. The swamp is dead.

Another old man once told me that the swamp spread out all over the lowlands. Water of the swamp came all the way up to a knoll on the back edge of my father's farm. That knoll is three-quarters of a mile from the present river, although the original winding river certainly came a little closer. Yet another old man said that the knoll had been an Indian campground many years before the swamp died and probably had been a campground for many years before the coming of the white man. This would seem reasonable, as the knoll would have been a good place to camp. It was gravel, so well drained. Its location made it a perfect jumping-off place for travel into the swamp's waterways. We found arrowheads on the knoll occasionally, a testimony to the old man's word.

Grandpa told many stories about the snakes in the swamp. I was always all ears, and he stretched the stories to fit the occasion. Still, there must have been some impressive snakes in the swamp. He told of black snakes that stretched clear across wagon trails and then some. That's a fair-sized snake in anybody's book. He told of as many as three dozen rattlesnakes under one stump. These tales used to send chills up and down my spine. But I never missed a chance to hear them.

Grandmother and my great aunt Blanche used to reminisce about the area, too. About how Hooper had 500 people and many houses. Hooper now couldn't have more than a dozen buildings and three dozen people.

That was during the logging boom. It was the beginning of the end for the swamp. First came the loggers to clear the valuable timber from the swamp. Then the farmers cast their covetous eyes upon the rich, black earth, and more clearing took place. For a while the river kept the farmers from using much of the land. It flooded in the spring and made it impossible to farm.

Then they dredged the river—straightening it and deepening its channel. It would never flood its banks again. The swamp was now at man's mercy. It fell to the ax and the plow. It fell to man's ingenuity and determination. Probably some of those who knew the swamp were saddened by its passing, but they have joined it. Except me: I wish I could have seen it and recorded on paper what the swamp was like when it was alive and well.

Professional Essay

MEN, WOMEN AND WAR
Ellen Goodman

Points to Consider

As you read the essay that follows, try to answer these questions:

1. Can you see any reason for the repetition in the first three paragraphs? Is this device effective? Where else does the author use it?
2. At what point do you realize the thesis of the essay? Is the sentence structure at this point effective?
3. Look at the section where the author supports the contention that a male-only draft could not stand a court challenge (paragraphs 10–12). Does she use factual statements or inferences to back up her point? Do you agree?
4. What is the readability level of this essay? Does this seem appropriate for the audience (*Redbook* magazine readers)? Does the content seem appropriate for this particular audience? Why or why not?

© 1980, The Boston Globe Newspaper Company/Washington Post Writers Group. Reprinted by permission.

My daughter is 11 years old, and as we watch the evening news she turns to me seriously and says, "I don't like the way the world is doing things." Neither do I.

My daughter is 11 years and 9 months old, to be precise, and I do not want her to grow up and be drafted. Neither does she.

My daughter is almost 12 and worries about unkindness and evil, about slaughtered seals and whales. I don't want her to be brutalized by war—as soldier or civilian.

As I read those lines over they seem too mild. What I want to say is that I'm horrified by the very idea that she could be sent to fight for fossil fuels or fossilized ideas, that I can imagine no justification for war other than self-defense, and that I am scared stiff about who has the power to decide what calls for self-defense.

In recent months there has been talk of registering young people for a possible draft. There has been fervent debate about young women as well as young men. And so I have found myself wondering: Would I feel differently if my daughter were my son? Would I be less anguished at the notion of a son drafted, a son at war?

Would I beat the drums and pin the bars and stars on his uniform with pride? Would I look forward to his being toughened up, be proud of his heroism, accept the risks that he's subjected to as a simple fact of life?

I cannot believe it.

So when I've been asked about registering women for the draft along with men, I've had to nod reluctantly. I don't want anyone registered, anyone drafted, unless we are in a genuine crisis. I am far from convinced that we are in a genuine crisis.

But if there is a draft again, it can't touch just our sons, like some civilized plague that leaves daughters alone to produce another generation of warriors.

The courts might not allow a male-only draft anyway. Even without the ERA, the highest courts, one by one, have passed judgment against most laws that affect only one sex. Alimony is no longer awarded just to women; the Supreme Court ruled that men may receive it also. Social-security rights have been extended to widowers as well as to widows.

If a male-only draft were passed, some man no doubt could challenge it successfully. And would. There are simply no reasonable grounds for a male-only draft today. There are 150,000 women in the military services already. They have proved to be tough and essential members. More than half of the first 62 female West Point graduates requested assignment to combat branches of the Army.

Even if women were not used in combat, there were, I am told, seven soldiers for every combat soldier in Vietnam. Many of the jobs noncombatant soldiers did were precisely the kind we traditionally define as "women's work"—jobs demanding precision, eye-hand motor coordination and mental skills related to technological warfare.

Still, it was ironic to hear Phyllis Schlafly suddenly sounding horrified at the draft and blaming the ERA proponents.

"Carter's proposal proves what we have been saying for the past seven years," she remarks, "that the ERA proponents want to draft women and treat them just like men in the military."

Suddenly this pro-military hawk takes flight as a dove, spreading her verbal wings over women only. Her comments remind me of that harsh anti-male streak that lurks under the thin veneer of femininity in the anti-ERA movement. Many anti-feminists feel a deep reluctance to share the lives and problems of and with men; they express a bitter refusal to "let men off the hook."

I am sure the anti-ERA people know that drafting women would eliminate the very last argument against passing the ERA. The pro-ERA people know this too. But they note again, with irony, that women have "won" virtually all equal responsibilities with men. If women are drafted, we lack only one thing: equal rights.

But I think that if we ever do begin registering again for a draft, in this crisis or any other, women must be included along with men, not only because the courts might demand it, but also because our society demands it. For too long, warfare was seen as men's business only, and was one cause of the rage that so many men have harbored against women.

War is in the mind of the man who yells at an equal rights rally: "Where were you at Iwo Jima?" War is in the mind of the man who is absolutely enraged at a woman who challenges the laws that give job preference to veterans. War is in the mind of the man who chides his wife for having led a "soft" life.

War has often split couples and sexes apart, into lives built on separate realities. It has been part of the grudge resulting from self-sacrifice, the painful gap of understanding and experience between men's and women's lives. It is the stuff of which alienation is made and novels are written.

But even more awesome, as a male activity, a rite of passage, a test of manhood, war has been gruesomely acceptable. Old men who were warriors have sent younger men to war as if it were their birthright. Women were supposed to wave banners and sing slogans and be in need of protection from the enemy.

We all pretended that war was civilized, that war had rules and isolated battlegrounds. War did not touch the finer and nobler things of life—such as women.

This, of course, was never true. The civilians among the losers, the enemies, were casualties as surely as were the soldiers. The women in Vietnam were not "safe," nor were the women in Hiroshima. When under duress, or defending their homes, women have always fought. And in a push-button war, women could not be protected.

But perhaps, stripped of its maleness and mystery, its audience and cheerleaders, war can finally be deglorified. Without the last trappings of chivalry it can be seen for what it is—the last, deadly resort.

So if we must ever have a draft registration, I would include young women along with young men. I would include them because they can do the job. I would include them because all women must be in a position to stop as well as to start wars. I would include them because it has been far too easy to send men alone.

I would include them because I simply cannot believe that I would feel differently if my daughter were my son.

WRITING ASSIGNMENTS

In doing any of the assignments for this chapter, you should strive to meet the following objectives. If you meet all five, you will get a satisfactory grade.

Objectives

1. Turn in your prewriting, showing that you used one of the four recommended techniques.
2. Include and <u>underline</u> a thesis sentence of the type called for by the specific assignment.
3. Show that you understand the differences in the various kinds of sentences by including and identifying the kinds called for by the specific assignment.
4. Use standard American spelling.
5. Proofread to eliminate any unmarked sentence fragments, comma splices, run-on sentences, subject-verb agreement errors, errors in verb form, or faulty tense shifts.

For help with tense shift problems, the new proofreading requirement, see Section 2 of the Handbook. Here is a brief review.

The tense of a verb is only wrong if it doesn't make sense with what has gone before; no tense is wrong in isolation. If English is your native language, you can probably depend on your ear to help you catch errors in sequence of tenses. Classes in English as a second language generally spend time learning the appropriate sequences. A shift in tense usually sounds wrong, like these:

I slammed on the brakes and swerved to the left, but the big van still hits me right in the passenger door. (*Hits* is out of step with *slammed* and *swerved*. Say, ". . . the big van still *hit* me right in the passenger door.")

When I first got my charge card, I had run up big bills each month. (The *had run* seems to have occurred before the *got*, but you could not run up the bills before getting the card. Say this: "When I first got my charge card, I *ran* up big bills each month.")

You can often catch shifts in verb tense by reading your papers aloud; I recommend this practice!

Writing Assignment 6-1

For this assignment you will need to write a description of something you consider the best or worst of its kind. Consider anything you know a great deal about—the best or worst magazine, pet, houseplant, TV show, dessert, city to visit, place to buy groceries. Since your thesis will be your opinion of the thing you are describing, it must be a judgment. You should support this with other sentences that are inferences, and you should back these up with factual statements.

For the prewriting step, use any one of the techniques you have learned to generate ideas on your topic. Your prewriting should result in a thesis you can support.

The writing step involves writing the description of the best or worst whatever-it-is. Use plenty of details to support your judgment, and make sure you have included both inferences and factual statements. When you write your final draft, number your sentences. Include with the paper you turn in a sentence identification sheet which lists the numbers of your sentences and codes them *J* for judgment, *I* for inference, and *F* for factual statement. For instance, if your first paragraph consists of a judgment followed by an inference followed by three factual statements, your sentence identification sheet would begin this way:

1. *J*
2. *I*
3. *F*
4. *F*
5. *F*

For the postwriting step, proofread your description carefully, being sure to correct the spelling and to eliminate any unmarked fragments, comma splices, run-on sentences, subject-verb agreement errors, errors in verb form, and faulty tense shifts.

Writing Assignment 6-2 This assignment requires that you write two short explanations, in story form, of an experience that taught you something. Choose a fairly simple experience, preferably something that took place all in one day, so that your explanation will not need to encompass too long a period of time. You might consider writing about a shopping trip, an accident, a visit to see someone in the hospital, or an incident that occurred in one of your college classes. Your first explanation of it should stick to simple sentences as much as possible; you could write it for a fourth- or fifth-grade student to read, if this will help you to achieve a low readability level. The second description should include the same details but should be related in much more sophisticated language and sentence structure, including complex sentences, compound sentences, and compound-complex sentences. When you have finished both descriptions, you should measure the readability level of each by applying the Fog Index to the first hundred words of each. If you have done well, there will be at least a five- or six-point difference in the level of readability of the two pieces.

For the prewriting step, use your choice of techniques to help you get started. You should be able to state your thesis in two forms, one suitable for the low-readability-level version, and one for the high-level version.

The writing step involves developing the thesis into two short but detailed descriptions of your experience and what it taught you. Since your thesis will be explaining what you learned, you may want to consider leading up to it as part of your conclusion, but this is just a suggestion, not a requirement. When the writing is finished, check the readability level of each description, and include the score at the end of each one.

For the postwriting step, proofread both descriptions carefully, being sure to correct spelling and to eliminate any unmarked fragments, comma splices, run-on sentences, subject-verb agreement errors, errors in verb form, and faulty tense shifts.

Writing Assignment 6-3   This assignment calls for a description of a job you have done at some time in your life. The job need not have involved pay; you may write about the time you organized the PTA garage sale, the repair work you have done on your own car, or the summer you spent painting the house. Your thesis sentence should be an evaluation of the job, so it should be a judgment; it should also be either a complex sentence or a compound-complex sentence. Here are a couple of sample theses that could be developed nicely:

Running the PTA garage sale was a thankless task that took three weeks of planning to net $37.82.

I learned the hard way how to repair a water pump on a '78 Buick, but at least I got the satisfaction of knowing I did it myself.

For the prewriting step, use one of the four techniques you have learned to generate some ideas for your thesis sentence. When you have a thesis that is either a complex or a compound-complex sentence stating your judgment, you are ready for the next step.

The writing step requires you to develop the description of your job. Support the thesis you have chosen with details. At some point in the essay, use parallelism in your list of the steps you took or the duties you performed. When you write your final draft, mark this section with asterisks in the left margin, so that your instructor can identify it easily.

For the postwriting step, proofread your essay carefully, being sure to correct spelling and to eliminate any unmarked fragments, comma splices, run-on sentences, subject-verb agreement errors, errors in verb form, and faulty tense shifts.

Writing Assignment 6-4   For this assignment you will write an essay describing your *first* something—day in college, day on the job, traffic ticket, formal dance, caught fish, apartment of your own—anything that was a first for you. You should take special care to include a variety of sentences, some effective use of repetition, and at least two periodic sentences (marked with asterisks in the left margin).

For the prewriting step, use whatever technique works best for you to help in remembering details about your "first." When these details suggest a main idea to you, state this as your thesis.

The writing step involves composing the actual description to support your thesis. As you write or rewrite your sentences, be sure to include a variety of structures. Look for a place to include repetition effectively. Finally, check to be sure at least two of your sentences are periodic ones, and mark them with asterisks in the left margin of your final draft.

For the postwriting step, proofread your essay carefully, being sure to correct spelling and to eliminate any unmarked fragments, comma splices, run-on sentences, subject-verb agreement errors, errors in verb form, and faulty tense shifts.

CHAPTER 7
WRITING: THE MEDIUM (PARAGRAPHS)

You could write a two-page paper by writing every sentence on a separate line or by beginning at the left margin and writing all the way to the end, with no breaks. But only the most unsophisticated writer does either. Why don't you use either approach? Perhaps you tried one in the past, and you would like to avoid a repetition of the grade you received on that occasion. More likely, you are too considerate of your reader. You don't want the reader to think that every sentence is unconnected with any other sentence, or that all the sentences are connected equally with each other. So you try to group your sentences into clusters that belong to the same idea, keeping both content and appearance in mind.

GROUPING SENTENCES TOGETHER

Some paragraph divisions are based solely on appearance. Modern newspapers insert paragraph breaks frequently, adding white space to what would otherwise be a long, gray, dull-looking column. Even if one idea extends through twelve or fifteen lines of type, the newspaper editor will usually break it into paragraphs that average seven lines. Two of the writers whose work you have read so far in this book are newspaper columnists. If you look back at the essays by Nickie McWhirter (Chapter 4) and Ellen Goodman (Chapter 6), you may notice that writing fairly short paragraphs has become a part of their style. Paragraphs written by high-school students often average about the same length as newspaper paragraphs—fifty words.

If you are not writing for a newspaper, and you want your writing to appear more mature than your high school writing, you can take one apparently arbitrary step: Write longer paragraphs. This step only appears to be arbitrary, however, for you will soon discover that there is more to writing longer paragraphs than just putting in fewer indentations. If you are going to lengthen your paragraphs sensibly, you will need to follow the lead of professional writers and find more to say. Make your paragraphs full-bodied with details, as Judith Krantz did in this example from *Princess Daisy*:

It is not often that the creative people who make television commercials have a chance to break the rules. Normally they are limited, almost entirely, to working in a world in which moldy grout can ruin a woman's life, while at the same time, perfectly white teeth can guarantee her love and happiness; a world in which her husband's morning is destroyed by a weak cup of coffee yet his virility can be validated by the brand of beer he drinks; they inhabit a cosmos in which thick, bouncy hair is life's dearest treasure and moist underarms are a constantly lurking menace; a territory in which best friends exist only to make critical remarks, and the choice between one kind of tampon or another is the difference between a carefree, athletic existence or being haunted by relentless anxiety. It's a threatening world in which the only real hope is the right kind of life insurance or a new set of steel-belted radials; a world of unending physical effort in which perfectly nice women are given life sentences in which they must produce immaculate floors, pristine toilet bowls, and even impeccable laundry; a world in which the people who depend on iron supplements to give them vitality barely look old enough to vote, in which the best filled medicine cabinet is certain to lack that one particular preparation which will make pain and head colds not just bearable but almost enjoyable. When this world isn't scary, it is frustratingly filled with too-healthy people having impossibly delightful fun in far away places, all thanks to an aftershave lotion or the right eye make-up. In advertising land it's quite all right to use obscenity to sell cigarette lighters—they couldn't dare mean anything dirty by "Flick my Bic," could they? But bra ads can't show women wearing bras, navels don't exist, and a pregnant woman may never seem to have the desire for physical contact with a man, not even her husband. There is even a regulation preventing a woman from sucking her own forefinger on camera. Singing cats can sell cat food better than any other commercial in history and creative advertising men write their copy in a cold sweat of fear and angst, not knowing whether a new idea will make them a hero or get them fired. With ten-second commercials becoming more and more popular, with research showing that viewers don't remember commercials that contain more than one single message, and with prime *seconds* on television costing hundreds of thousands of dollars, the opportunity to make expensive mistakes continues to multiply and the pressure to play it safe grows.*

That paragraph, a mini-essay all by itself, is worth close inspection. It begins with a general statement of opinion, an inference: "It is not often that the creative people who make television commercials have a chance to break the rules." From this it goes on to a concrete description of the unrealistic, rule-bound world of TV commercials. We are able to visualize this world because the paragraph contains twenty-three examples. Although most refer only to categories of products—coffee, beer, steel-belted radials—and only Bic is mentioned by name, the reader has no trouble supplying brand names for the sales pitches Krantz depicts. The last two sentences summarize the panic that this situation

---

* From *Princess Daisy* by Judith Krantz. Copyright © 1980 by Steve Krantz Productions. Reprinted by permission of Crown Publishers, Inc.

creates in the commercial writer, and the paragraph ends with a more specific statement of the opening idea: ". . . the opportunity to make expensive mistakes continues to multiply and the pressure to play it safe grows."

That concluding sentence ties up the whole paragraph into one neat, unified package by its echo of the opening point. Still, the paragraph could have been treated differently. If Judith Krantz had been a writer with a penchant for shorter paragraphs, she might have made as many as four out of this one. The first two sentences would make a well-developed beginning, followed by two sentences explaining about the threatening, frustrating world of TV commercials. The third paragraph would probably include the next four sentences, from "In advertising land" to "get them fired." The final paragraph would contain just that long concluding sentence.

Which organization is best? Should that mini-essay be one paragraph or four paragraphs? The decision is, of course, up to the author. In making the decision, the author should keep the audience in mind. The really long paragraph requires a fairly sophisticated reader; if *Princess Daisy* had been written for elementary students, four paragraphs would have been the better choice. Since the novel was written for an adult audience, the lengthy paragraph was fine.

TOPIC SENTENCES

Imagine that description of the world of TV commercials without the first or last sentences. The examples would still fit together, but wouldn't you wonder what was the purpose of collecting so many examples? If that paragraph were an essay, you would call the first sentence the *thesis statement* and the last sentence the *restatement of the thesis*. The first sentence states the purpose of the paragraph, and everything else in the paragraph supports that idea. The sentence does the same thing as a thesis sentence, but because it does this on a smaller scale (paragraph instead of essay), it is called a *topic sentence.*

Now I'm not going to tell you that every paragraph must have a topic sentence any more than I will insist that every paragraph must have at least three sentences. (I had one composition teacher who did insist on that, but I think his purpose was to make grading easy: One paragraph of less than three sentences meant a B, two such paragraphs meant a C, and so forth.) There are times when your whole paragraph may be only one sentence, a transition or bridge from the idea in the previous paragraph to the idea in the next paragraph. There are other examples of paragraphs that do not need topic sentences because their development follows a clear, chronological order with little room for doubt about their main idea.

Although some paragraphs operate very well without topic sentences, there are definite advantages to topic sentences for most paragraphs. When the paragraph has several short examples, a topic sentence ties them all together for the reader. A topic sentence also helps you, the writer, as it keeps you on track as you write the paper, giving you some idea of what to include in the paragraph and reminding you to indent again when you begin to develop a slightly different subject.

METHODS OF DEVELOPING TOPIC SENTENCES

Suppose you have an idea for a topic sentence, and you can think of five or six details for supporting it. Does it make any difference what order you use in listing these details? Sometimes it doesn't, but usually some orders are clearer and more sensible than others. Try to avoid just stringing one example after another so that the organization appears as random as a laundry list. If your details are physical ones, you might consider *spatial order*. This can be left to right, top to bottom, north to south, front door to back door, or any similar order based on location. Here is an example, with the topic sentence underlined:

Herkimer's strange appearance resulted from a total lack of proportion. His tiny head perched on top of a six-foot-six frame. Since he was nearly bald and had miniscule eyes, the only noticeable part of his face was the bony protuberance of his nose. There seemed to be no chin below the nose and no shoulders below where the chin should have been. Still, he had extremely long arms—they hung below his knees—and his hands were enormous. His arms were matched by long legs, but his feet didn't match his hands: he wore only a size seven shoe!

For details that are steps in a process or happenings in a story, the best order is *chronological* or *time order*.
Here is a sample paragraph organized chronologically.

Sunday was one of those days when everything goes wrong. First, the dog woke me up at 5:30 to take him out. When I got out in the yard, I discovered that the raccoons had been at the garbage cans again, and half the patio was buried in tin cans, bread wrappers, and soggy coffee grounds. After spending fifteen minutes sweeping the patio, I was too wide awake to go back to sleep, so I decided to read the paper, if it had been delivered. It had been delivered, all right—delivered up and down the street by the wind. That was another fifteen-minute job assembling the paper, and I never did find Section *B*. I decided next to make coffee, and I filled the pot with water for ten cups. Guess what? There was only enough ground coffee for six cups, so I had very weak, tea-colored coffee. In a grumpy mood, I set out for church and a little spiritual uplifting. That must have been too good to hope for, as I never made it. The left front tire blew when I had driven two miles, but I had at least one piece of luck—I was right in front of a service station. An hour later I was back home with my tire repaired but with no improvement in my mood. I decided to go back to bed. Monday would have to be better.

Sometimes your details will be brief examples or anecdotes with no real spatial or chronological connection. What then? There are several possibilities. Here are a couple of examples that go from *least serious* to *most serious*. (Again, the topic sentence—or partial sentence—is underlined.)

In order to lighten the burden of calculation and to decrease the chance of error, scientists have turned to machines. The new machines are supposed to be infallible, but they only remove the responsibility one step, making humans guilty only indirectly for the errors made by machines. The catch is that humans must design the machines and must prepare the scientific data for the machines. Perfection has not yet been reached. When a simple milk-dispensing machine returns the price of its milk and ejects chocolate milk before any selection button has been pressed, the human tendency to err is displayed. It is not surprising that in 1962 the United States had to blow up an $18,500,000 *Mariner I* which was off its course because of a misplaced hyphen in the calculations.

<u>Associating with so many students, teachers, and administrators requires poise and a sense of humor, but the experience of substitute teaching also helps to develop these attributes.</u> The more classes I meet, the more easily I am able to introduce myself and to start the lesson. Even having two observers from Flint College does not disturb me. I can laugh when Central's dean of women, mistaking me for a Central student, tries to send me on errands. I am no longer easily shocked by the vulgar language first graders know and use. The tricks which students play on teachers no longer surprise me. One day when I was substituting at Central, I noticed that one of the boys had apparently vomited on my desk. When he sat down in the front seat, he was red in the face, but he was trying hard not to laugh. Not knowing what to do, I did nothing but stare at him. When he saw that I did not react, he picked up the plastic replica he had hoped would fool me and returned to his seat. While I joined the class in the laugh which followed, I congratulated myself for not attempting to wipe my books.

That last paragraph also illustrates another possible order—*shortest example* to *longest example*. The final example, which takes the last six of that paragraph's eleven sentences, is actually a brief anecdote. The whole story is right there. When you have a long example to be included in a paragraph with shorter examples, it is usually best to save the longest for last, after the shorter examples have already clarified your point.

When you build detail upon detail until you get to an especially impressive, surprising, or horrifying one, you are using *climactic order.* This is often used for descriptive writing, as Joyce Carol Oates uses it here in a paragraph from *Bellefleur:*

<u>In the end the storm was to be somewhat less severe than the Great Flood of twenty years previously; but it was still a hellish thing</u>, and took away the lives of some twenty-three people in the Lake Noir area alone, and caused damage of upward of several million dollars. The roads *were* washed out, many of the bridges damaged past repair; trains were derailed and train beds torn away; Lake Noir and the Nautauga River and Mink Creek and innumerable nameless creeks and runs and ditches flooded, propelling debris along: baby buggies, chairs, laundry that had been hung out to dry, lampshades, parts of automobiles, loose boards, doors, window frames, the corpses of chickens, cows, horses, snakes, muskrats, raccoons, and parts of these corpses; and parts of what were evidently human corpses (for the cemeteries once again flooded, and relief workers were to be astonished and sickened by the sight of badly decomposed corpses dangling from roofs, from trees, jammed against silos and corncribs and abandoned cars, washed up against the foundations of homes, in various stages of decay: some aged and leathery, some fresh, soggy, pale; and all of them pathetically naked); and spiders—some of them gigantic, with bristling black hairs—ran about everywhere, washed out of their hiding places and frantic with terror.*

---

* From *Bellefleur* by Joyce Carol Oates. Copyright © 1980 by Joyce Carol Oates, Inc. Reprinted by permission of the publisher, E. P. Dutton.

Sometimes the details you wish to include in a paragraph support two different ideas. In cases like this, you will need to structure your paragraph carefully, following *contrasting order*. In addition to the topic sentence, you will generally need a *bridging sentence* to tie the two different ideas together. In this example, both the topic sentence and the bridging sentence are underlined:

<u>Although Ethelberta appears to be brilliant, she is failing in her first semester of college.</u> She came here with a 3.82 average from high school and fine recommendations from several teachers. Her SAT scores were in the top four percent of scores for incoming freshmen. According to her high school transcripts, her IQ is 145. <u>Still, her intellectual promise is not being fulfilled in the classroom.</u> She has averaged only 61 percent on her first three tests in Biology 101. Her scores in American History 104 are only slightly better—65 percent. Her English professor reports that she has turned in only half of her assignments. Ethelberta will probably be placed on academic probation when the grades come out.

Note that the bridging sentence points in both directions in the contrasting paragraph. In this case, *intellectual promise* refers to the details in the first part of the paragraph, while *not being fulfilled in the classroom* summarizes the problem presented in the second part.

PRACTICING METHODS OF PARAGRAPH DEVELOPMENT

Examine the following paragraphs (all taken from *The Ann Landers Encyclopedia*) to see what methods of development their writers used. Do the paragraphs contain topic sentences? If they do, are these sentences placed in the most effective position? How are the supporting sentences organized?

1. If you are going to groom your dog yourself, be sure you want to do the learning and the equipment-buying that goes with it. Take, for example, a Poodle. It takes more than brushing. There is trimming and designing. It's a hobby in itself if done well and if the Poodle is to look smashing at all times. With other breeds brushing is the thing—Spaniels and Setters, for instance. They have feathers on their legs and their ears are subject to terrible tangles. They really must be brushed very often, vigorously, too. And not just for a minute or so. Is that what you want to do with your dog? The shorter-haired dogs, those with hard, close coats, need a quick going over from time to time but nothing compared to what we have been talking about. A sloppy dog is like a sloppy house, an unmade bed, a soiled rug or a spot on your tie. It reflects on you.

2. All learning is motivated and there are essentially two methods of participating in this process. In one, the learning takes place for someone else (such as parents or teachers), or for honors or rewards, and is called extrinsic learning. Intrinsic learning, on the other hand, is done for oneself, is inner motivated, gives pleasure, and may take place in any setting at any time. When life is going well in a loving and accepting atmosphere, both the actual process of learning and the accomplishment of having done a good job bring pleasure. However, when the child becomes unmotivated, his ability to learn becomes impaired.

3. I believe if twenty-five couples were selected at random and their marriages examined under the glaring light of truth, it would be discovered that one marriage out of twenty-five is "very good." Four are "okay"—which means they get along fairly well most of the time. Seven are bad—much bickering, many fights, poor communication—but the situation is tolerable. Eight of the twenty-five are unrewarding—a real drag, both parties fed up and wishing there were an easy way out. Five are disasters—they share nothing, not even a bed. Yet they plug along year after year, like a pair of matched mules, putting up a front, or not even bothering to pretend—needling each other at every opportunity, battling in the presence of family and friends. Or sadder still, they simply ignore each other: no sex; no conversation; no communication. They turn to hard liquor, white wine, work, hockey, golf, gambling or sleeping around. I've discovered, too, that millions of marrieds escape their boring—or punitive—partners by hooking their eyeballs into the TV set.

4. The symptoms of both forms of hepatitis are somewhat similar. There is an initial period of feeling just plain "lousy," with a headache, upset stomach, loss of appetite and vomiting. It may last one or two weeks and is followed by the onset of "yellow jaundice" which first becomes apparent to the patient in the form of a darkening color to the urine, an increased yellow pigmentation to the whites of the eyes and then full-blown yellow change in the skin color. By this time the patient is really sick. This lasts two to three weeks with continued loss of appetite, nausea, vomiting, headache, fever, etc. The symptoms gradually subside as does the jaundice and in uncomplicated cases the patient is well in four to six weeks but invariably requires several more weeks or even months to fully regain his strength and the feeling of well-being experienced during his pre-hepatitis days.

5. School phobia can be prevented by encouraging independence. When a child is six months old, the parents should be having evenings out alone. By age two, every child should be left at home with a babysitter while he is still awake. By age three, every child should experience being left somewhere other than his home—such as with neighbors while the mother shops, or in the home of a friend or relative.*

After you have analyzed the methods of development used in these paragraphs, choose one of the methods to imitate in writing your own paragraph. Use one of the topic sentences listed below to develop. (You may change the wording slightly, if you wish.)

* Excerpts from *The Ann Landers Encyclopedia* by Ann Landers. Copyright © 1978 by Esther P. Lederer. Reprinted by permission of Doubleday & Company, Inc.

> 1. Some cars are more trouble to repair than others.
> 2. There are two easy ways to avoid studying.
> 3. All college professors can be classified as lecturers, talkers, or wanderers.
> 4. All infatuations develop in much the same way.
> 5. Good study habits can be encouraged from an early age.

HOLDING YOUR PARAGRAPHS TOGETHER

Often your topic sentence is a judgment or other inference, supported in the rest of the paragraph by factual statements, statistics, quotations from experts, or detailed anecdotes. In addition to arranging this support sensibly, you need to include words from time to time that will indicate the relationship of one supporting detail to another supporting detail. These words are called *transitions*.

Sometimes the transitions function in much the same way that the bridging sentence did in the contrasting paragraph: They show that your thinking has changed direction. Such words as *however, nevertheless, still, on the other hand, on the contrary,* and *in spite of this* all indicate such a change in thought. If you look at the paragraphs from *The Ann Landers Encyclopedia*, you should be able to find some of these words.

Other transitions show that you are continuing along the same line of thought. You can indicate this continued progress with words like *for example, therefore, furthermore, thus, hence, in other words, in fact,* and *so.* If you have several points to make, you can even count them: *first, second, third.* (If you do this, be sure to keep your structure parallel; don't switch from *second* to *thirdly,* and don't count "first, second, fourth," listing the third point without its indicator.) Look for these transition words in the sample paragraphs you have already studied.

Although transition words help your reader to see how the sentences in your paragraph relate to each other, they can't rescue a paragraph whose sentences are really unrelated. If you are struggling with a paragraph, read it aloud—to a friend, if possible. Ask him or her if the sentences all sound as if they are about the same topic. Try reading the following problem paragraph out loud to discover where the problem lies:

I regret the day last June when I parted with all my savings in exchange for a little yellow Datsun. The car was only two years old, but it had to have a whole new transmission the second week I owned it. Then, in August the brakes started to whine, and I did without the car for ten days while I waited for repairs. It's a really sporty-looking car, and the girls all seem to like it. As soon as the weather began to turn cold, my Datsun refused to start. Again I shelled out money for another expensive repair job. I only work part-time, and I really can't afford to have major car repair expenses every other month. I'm going to sell it, if I can find a buyer.

If you read that out loud, the fourth sentence probably jumped out at you. It doesn't fit; it presents the car's one good point, and the rest of the paragraph is about the car's bad points. What can you do with that sentence? Here are three suggestions:

1. Throw it out.
2. Use it as your second sentence, with alterations—Although it's a sporty-looking car that attracts girls, it's a real lemon.
3. Change your ending, and use it there—I'm going to sell it, if I can find a buyer. Do you want to buy a little yellow Datsun? It's a really sporty-looking car, and the girls all seem to like it!

SPECIAL PARAGRAPHS: INTRODUCTIONS

Your challenge in writing your first paragraph is to be sufficiently interesting, stimulating, and provocative that your reader will want to continue reading. You must lead, but you must not mislead. You want to interest the reader in your subject, but you don't want to promise something that you can't deliver. If you have ever read an article and then complained, "Well, that wasn't what I thought it was going to be about," you know that you don't want your reader to be equally frustrated after reading your paper. Of course, if you are writing for an audience of one, your English instructor, your reader has to read the paper, like it or not. Still, your chances of getting a good grade are improved if the introductory paragraph makes your instructor *want* to read what follows.

There are many techniques for getting attention without making false promises. You can see several of these in the following examples, most taken from student papers. (Thesis sentences are underlined.)

1. Beginning with a quotation or dialogue:
   "Ah, yes, back in the good old days I walked miles through snow drifts as high as fences to get to school." All of us have probably smiled and politely listened to Grandpa retell this all-too-familiar story. Common sense alone tells you this one-room school education couldn't have been all bad: Grandpa was only able to complete the eighth grade, and yet he had the basic science knowledge to treat his cattle and hogs himself when they were sick, he could cipher any of us kids down until he died at age seventy-eight, and he could write letters to legislators that influenced the rural laws of the state. My personal elementary education, of course, does not date back to the one-room schoolhouse, but I honestly believe that <u>we as elementary students in the 1940s received a better basic education than is available today</u>.

2. Asking a question:
   Remember the days when cheating meant peeking at a friend's test paper or signaling answers on a true-or-false test? Let's see, it was crossed legs for true and uncrossed for false—or was it uncrossed for true and . . .? <u>These tactics appear primitive when compared to the incidents of cheating we hear about today</u>.

3. Making a comparison:
   Being married is like visiting an amusement park. Both provide experiences that are exciting, frightening, amusing, disappointing, and more. A marriage can flourish or fail, just as a day at the park can be either fantastic

or frustrating. <u>The expectations of each participant play a major role in the outcome of the adventure.</u>

4. Relating your topic to other happenings:

The year was 1926. . . . Roald Amundsen was on his way to the North Pole in a dirigible to look for land. . . . The president of the University of Michigan was denounced from pulpits for delivering a speech considered to be "neutral" on Prohibition. . . . The discriminating new car buyer could own a Hudson for $1,234. . . . And in Kalamazoo, Roosevelt Junior High School published the first edition of *The Rough Riders Annual.* <u>With Roosevelt School closing its doors to classes this year, the annual contains some of the few tangible memories of the city's oldest school.</u>

5. Starting with a dramatized scene:

I watched my doctor's face for his reaction. I had just told him that I had surgical polyaches. He stood quietly digesting what I had just said. "What are surgical polyaches?" he asked. (With an introduction like this, the thesis usually comes later. Here it was the definition of *polyaches:* <u>Polyaches is a word that could be used to describe numerous aches in various parts of the body.</u>)

SPECIAL PARAGRAPHS: CONCLUSIONS

Although conclusions are usually easier to write than introductions, some writers appear to forget all about them. Perhaps they are just exhausted from writing the introduction and the body; they have no steam left for a good ending. The most important characteristic of a good ending is that it should sound finished. Reading your paper aloud is always a good idea, but it is especially good to read the ending aloud so that you can tell whether or not it has this characteristic. Even if you are writing in class, do not be embarrassed to lip-read your conclusion.

What makes a paper sound finished? Well, sometimes it ends with a strong restatement—not a repetition—of its thesis, but this is not always appropriate, especially in a very short paper. Another choice is to end with your strongest or second-strongest point. Do not say anything in your conclusion that is not supported by your paper. Also, do not lecture your reader. Remember, your reader's lasting memory of your paper is partially determined by the last thing you say; make sure it isn't trivial or preachy. You don't want to write a clumsy, meaningless, or insulting final sentence any more than you want to stumble and fall out the door when you leave an important interview.

Often you can make your paper sound particularly well unified by echoing the idea of your introduction. For instance, here is the last paragraph from the paper that started with example no. 3 above:

People enter this marital "tunnel of love" fully expecting to emerge with the partnership intact, even though the future is hidden from view. If couples will remember to hold on fast to each other and refuse to let go, from entrance to exit, no matter how turbulent the waters inside may be, their expectations will undoubtedly be met.

For another example of this technique, see Ellen Goodman's "Men, Women and War," in Chapter 6.

> ## PRACTICING WRITING INTRODUCTIONS AND CONCLUSIONS
>
> Choose two of the thesis sentences listed and write just the introduction and conclusion for essays that would develop them. (You may be able to use these for the next assignment.) Try to use two of the five different techniques suggested for introductions, and make your conclusions echo some part of the idea you express in your introductions. Here are some possible thesis sentences:
>
> 1. Gardening is a hobby for the rich.
> 2. If a woman wants to succeed in the business world, her choice of clothing is very limited.
> 3. Physical fitness is being carried to extremes.
> 4. The competent secretary has almost disappeared.
> 5. Well-trained attack dogs are the best insurance a property owner can have.
> 6. A knowledge of history makes the difference between a person who is educated and a person who is merely trained.
> 7. Just as we plan for several careers in a lifetime, we should also plan for several marriages.
> 8. Condominiums are changing the rhythm of family life.
> 9. Mass transit will replace automobiles within our lifetimes.
> 10. Travel is no longer worth what it costs.
>
> Now apply one of these techniques for writing good introductions to your own writing by choosing one of the papers you have already written for this class and rewriting the introduction. When you are satisfied that you have a beginning that will make your chosen audience want to continue reading, look at your conclusion. Does it need revising to match your new opening paragraph? If it does, rewrite it also, trying to tie the end to the beginning and to produce a finished sound.

SPECIAL PARAGRAPHS: SUMMARIES

For some assignments, perhaps reviews of technical articles, you may be asked to write a one-paragraph *summary* of writing done by someone else. This kind of summary paragraph is quite different from other paragraphs. Here are some specific guidelines to follow:

1. In your first sentence, identify the book or article or chapter you are summarizing and state its main idea. *Identify* means name the author and give the title, underlined if the source is a book, or put in quotation marks if the source is a chapter or an article.
2. In your own words, state all of the author's important ideas. Follow the same order, but condense them. (A summary should not be more than one-third as long as the original, and often it is much shorter.)

3. If you use any of the author's phrasing for ideas that are especially well put, be sure to enclose words that aren't yours in quotation marks.

4. Do *not* include any of your own opinions. When you write what is supposed to be a summary, do not evaluate the writing. Some assignments may ask for a summary followed by an evaluation; if you have this kind of assignment, be sure to separate the two parts. Whatever you do, be sure to avoid the typical junior-high-book-report conclusion: "I really enjoyed reading this, and I'm sure you would enjoy it, too."

For an example of a good summary paragraph, here is one student's summary of the article included in Chapter 2, "The Many Me's of the Self-Monitor."

The article written by Mark Snyder, "The Many Me's of the Self-Monitor," states that each of us may have not one but many selves, and that the self is a product of the individual's relationships with other people. Through research, Snyder has found that some people have developed the ability to monitor their own performance by signals received from the audience. Snyder calls such persons "high self-monitoring individuals." The opposite kind of person is called a "low self-monitor" and tends to express what he feels rather than mold his behavior to fit the situation. Snyder has developed a scale by which he determines whether an individual is a high or low self-monitor. High self-monitors are able to detect impression management in others and can see through the masks of deception successfully. Snyder believes that high and low self-monitors have different ideas about what constitutes a self. High self-monitors are flexible people who believe that they are whatever they appear to be in any situation. Low self-monitors have a firmer idea of what a self should be and react according to their feelings and beliefs, and also regard a self as a single identity that must not be compromised for anyone, anytime. Snyder has noted that high self-monitors may pay a high price: They may be unable to communicate their private feelings.

SPECIAL PARAGRAPHS: DIALOGUE

There is one time when the normal conventions for paragraph breaks do not apply—when you are writing dialogue or quoting a speaker. The rule to go by here is that you change paragraphs every time you change speakers; never have two speakers in one paragraph. Following this rule may produce some very short paragraphs, but it still helps your reader to know who is speaking. Note the effect in "The Ticket," the student essay in Chapter 5.

"It's $25," replied the woman.
"I only have $10 until tomorrow. Couldn't I come in and pay the fine then?" I pleaded.

That entire essay is a good one to study for the paragraphing and punctuation of dialogue. Another example, slightly different, is "Music to Get Pregnant By," in the Reader section of this text. Most of that essay is written as an interview, but only the responses are in quotes. The questions spoken by the interviewer are not put in quotation marks. This method is also correct and also makes it easy for the reader to differentiate between the interviewer and the interviewee.

You should note one other peculiarity of paragraphing speech. When a speaker talks for more than one paragraph, the quotation marks go at the beginning of each paragraph, but the only paragraph that *ends* with quotation marks is the last paragraph the speaker said. A lengthy quote would look like this:

> According to Senator X, "Blah, blah, blah, blah, blah, blah. Blah, blah, blah, blah.
> "Blah, blah, blah, double-blah. Blah, blah, blah, blah. Blah, blah, blah.
> "Blah, blah, blah."

RELATED READINGS

Student Essay

IT IS NO SECRET
Patricia Macklin

Points to Consider

As you read the essay that follows, try to answer these questions:

1. What technique does the writer use to get your attention in the first paragraph? Does it work?
2. Which paragraphs have topic sentences and which do not? How do you account for the differences between the paragraphs with topic sentences and those without?
3. What transitional words are used in paragraphs 4 through 7? Do they make this section more coherent?
4. What assumptions can you make about the audience for this argumentative essay? Do you think the paper would be effective for that audience? Why or why not?

Used with permission of Patricia Macklin.

"More than half of the 21 million young people aged 15 to 19 are estimated to be sexually experienced—almost seven million young men and four million women. In addition, about one-fifth of the eight million 13-to-14-year-olds have had sex. Among sexually active teenage women who do not use contraceptives, seven in ten think that they cannot become pregnant."

"Along with increasing sexual experience, teenagers are also contracting venereal disease in growing numbers. . . . One of the major causes of unwanted teenage pregnancy is ignorance about human reproduction and the risk of pregnancy."

These statistics, from Planned Parenthood of Kalamazoo and Family Planning of Allegan, are proof enough that a well-developed sex education program should be incorporated into all schools, starting at the elementary level.

As alarming as the statistics on teenage sexual experience are, the statistics regarding teenage pregnancy are even more alarming. "Each year more than one million teenagers aged 15 to 19 become pregnant—one in ten of the females in this age group. In addition 30,000 girls younger than 15 get pregnant annually. More than two-thirds of all teenage pregnancies are believed to be unintended."

"Both the adolescent who gives birth and her infant face greater risk of death, illness, or injury than do women in their early twenties." Also, "pregnancy and motherhood are the major causes of young women leaving school."

Still, many people are opposed to public teaching of sex education because they feel knowledge of sex will lead to experimentation with sex. But already 11 million teenagers are sexually active, and this is without proper education. I believe that knowledge of sex may make teenagers at least more inclined to use birth control, if not more inclined to lessen their sexual activity, because with their new knowledge of sex they would have to make decisions, commitments, with all the facts and consequences in mind.

Parents also feel that they should be the only sex educators. In essence, I agree with this statement. The problem lies in the fact that most parents are embarrassed to talk about sex. Some parents have themselves been victims of sex misinformation and would be unable to give their children the correct facts.

It has been stated, by a counselor from Family Planning of Allegan, that teenagers feel cheated by their parents because sex was a taboo subject in their homes. This counselor also stated that when teenagers teach each other about sex they misinform one another regarding their ability to get pregnant. ("You can't get pregnant if you have intercourse standing up," or, "Your ovaries aren't mature until you're 16, so you can have intercourse without worry until then." These are just two ideas teenagers pass along.)

Parents also feel that they cannot depend on the schools to teach their children proper morals regarding sex education. They fear their children may learn the biological facts but not the moral (or their religious) beliefs concerning sex. With the teenage pregnancy rate as high as it is now, I believe the biological facts are most important now. Perhaps with a good sex education program where students are well informed, parents can then introduce their moral ideas and discuss the facts with their children, broadening the subject to responsibility, maturity, and morals.

We must incorporate into our schools classes especially geared toward teaching and answering students' questions about the basics of male and female biological differences and functions, reproduction, birth, birth control, and venereal disease, dispelling all fallacies regarding sex and pregnancy. We should also go one step further and have classes where students can learn and explore their own self-worth, relationships, marriage, and child raising.

We have a responsibility to our young people to give them the information they need to make responsible decisions regarding their sexuality and individuality.

Professional Essay

COMPETENCY TESTS FOR EVERYONE
Charles R. Larson

Points to Consider

As you read the essay that follows, try to answer these questions:

1. Where is the thesis sentence in this essay? Is it repeated or restated in the conclusion?
2. What order does the author seem to be following in paragraphs 2, 3, and 4? Is this order effective?
3. Does the fifth paragraph have a topic sentence? What is used as support in this paragraph?
4. In paragraph 7, look at the first sentence. What is it accomplishing? Is it needed there?
5. How do you respond to the author's recommendation? How would you expect the readers of *Newsweek* (his audience) to respond? Why?

Copyright 1981 by Newsweek, Inc. All rights reserved. Reprinted by permission.

Along with the recent publicity about the crisis in American public education, we hear an understandable refrain: the need for competency tests—not only for the students themselves but for their teachers. How else can we be certain of the excellence of our children's education unless there is quality control for their teachers? With this suggestion I heartily concur but proclaim the need for similar checks and balances for other trades and professions. The erosion of our basic skills has gone that far.

The initial blame rests on our universities. During the late 1960s and throughout most of the 1970s, I was often horrified at the indulgences of certain of my colleagues whittling away at our traditional educational system—built to its strength over several hundred years. Open admissions never bothered me as long as the students who entered the university under those conditions were expected to attain an equivalent level of performance with their more qualified peers. Much worse than open admissions was the mania for eliminating so many of the previously required courses—especially in English and math. Each year the skills of our incoming freshmen eroded a little further (from similar abuses that had filtered down to the public schools), yet far worse was the fact that we began graduating students from the university we wouldn't even have admitted a few years earlier.

In my own field of English, I watched the skills of our majors visibly disintegrate. Certainly, this was no surprise, since many professors proclaimed that content was far more important than form. Let students express themselves in any manner they wanted (or could). Skills didn't really matter. One of my colleagues jests that some universities stopped passing out degrees at commencement for fear that parents might ask their children to read aloud what was printed on them. Not only did many of these graduates then accept teaching positions in the public schools, but, as should have been expected, a certain number of them entered graduate programs.

By the mid-1970s, I noticed that a sizable percentage of my graduate students could not write a coherent paragraph, yet many of them were teaching assistants who regularly staffed our sections of freshman composition. Somewhat later, these graduate students completed their M.A.'s and Ph.D.'s and were turned loose upon university communities across the nation. They'd been passed along throughout their entire educational career—a little like those athletes one reads about who are functionally illiterate yet are awarded B.A.'s from distinguished universities.

Don't get me wrong. Some of these students were as competent and as gifted as graduate students have traditionally been. I take particular pride in one of them who—faced with the realities of an overcrowded job market—set up his own consulting business, teaching the skills that he had mastered to those who clearly had not. Two or three years after he had received his Ph.D., he was earning far more money than I was after nearly twenty years of teaching. His clientele? Middle-level executives in major corporations throughout the country whose writing skills were stunted at the ninth-grade level.

So we academicians indulged ourselves in a manner the educational system should never have tolerated. We eliminated any semblance of quality and standards, and now we're faced with a nation of marginal literates, taught by teachers who do not possess the talents to determine whether their own students are competent or deficient. This is an impossible bind. What should we do about it? Recall all the teachers we graduated in the 1970s? The system could never tolerate anything so dramatic. What it's going to take instead is mandatory competency tests for all teachers within their disciplines—with options for those who fail their exams (re-education, summer institutes, teachers working in harmony with one another, *teaching one another*)—in other words, concentrated effort from everyone.

But as I hinted earlier, there's more to the question of competency tests than examining our current students and their teachers and requiring that they reach an accepted standard of excellence. It's not only in the field of education that things have broken down but in too many other fields of endeavor. I'd like to see similar examinations (tests of the basic skills needed to do the job at hand) required of the people who provide our public services. To use only one example, I'll mention postal employees. Shouldn't it be demonstrated that all mail carriers can read the names and the numbers on the letters they are expected to deliver? (The evidence from my mailbox appears to suggest the contrary.)

I'd like to see comparable examinations required of all people trained for computer services. Though these professionals may have the superior mathematical skills necessary for the technical aspects of their jobs, of what use are these skills if they cannot express themselves comprehensibly to people in other fields? Why is it that they seem incapable of responding to a simple letter, explaining the computer error on a monthly bill or bank statement? Shouldn't these people be literate in English as well as in their own professional skills?

Although I do not want to belabor the issue, I would go so far as to require mandatory tests of special competency for people in the trades—repairmen and automobile mechanics, for instance. It's absurd that we've admitted the need for exit examinations for high-school seniors, yet as soon as these graduates begin their employment we tolerate shoddy work. If garage mechanics can charge $35 an hour for the labor involved in repairing your car, isn't it reasonable to expect the same level of expertise in that area as in that of other crafts?

Unfortunately, the examples are unlimited. The crisis in education has sadly affected every trade and profession. What this country needs to acknowledge—and what the current Administration must admit—is the need for a total commitment to basic educational skills. To do otherwise is to admit that incompetence is now the norm.

WRITING ASSIGNMENTS

In doing any of the assignments for this chapter, you should strive to meet the following objectives. If you meet all six, you will get a satisfactory grade.

Objectives

1. Turn in your prewriting, showing that you used an appropriate technique.
2. Include and underline a thesis sentence of the type called for by the specific assignment.
3. Include either several paragraphs of realistic-sounding dialogue or several paragraphs that provide well-organized support for underlined topic sentences, depending on the assignment you choose.
4. Make sure that your introduction is appropriate to the assignment and that your conclusion sounds complete.
5. Use standard American spelling.
6. Proofread to eliminate any unmarked sentence fragments, comma splices, run-on sentences, subject-verb agreement errors, errors in verb form, faulty tense shifts, or errors in use or omission of apostrophes.

To satisfy the addition to the proofreading requirement, you need to understand apostrophes. They are discussed in more detail in Section 3 of the Handbook, but this brief explanation will help you eliminate the most common problems with them.

By far the most frequent error in using apostrophes is writing *it's* when you do not mean *it is* or *it has*. If you form the habit of always reading *it is* or *it has* when you come to *it's*, you can catch this error every time you proofread. *It's* is a contraction, with the apostrophe replacing the *i* or the *ha*. If you write it when you mean *belonging to it*, you are forgetting that *it* is a pronoun, not a noun. *Its* is like *mine*, *his*, *hers*, *ours*, and *theirs*. Notice that these possessive pronouns do not have apostrophes in them. Nouns are made possessive through the use of apostrophes, but personal pronouns change their forms; they never have apostrophes in them!

The other problem with apostrophes is deciding whether they go before the *s* or after it. You are too old to get away with perching the apostrophe on top of the *s*, as you may have done in third grade, and hoping that the reader will assume you meant to put it in the proper place. It is time to learn one simple rule (which you may already know): The apostrophe goes after the basic word, and then an *s* is added only if one is needed to give the *zzz* sound. You can always find the basic word by converting your possessive noun to the object of an *of* phrase. It works like this:

The cat bit the mouses tail. (*Mouses tail* becomes *tail of the mouse*, so your basic word is *mouse*, the apostrophe comes after it, and *mouse' tail* still needs a *zzz* sound, so you say this: "The cat bit the mouse's tail.")

The cat bit the mices tails. (Now it's *tails of the mice*, and you say this: "The cat bit the mice's tails.")

The mice bit the cat's tail.

The mice bit the cats' tails.

You will note that plural nouns do not always make their possessive forms in the same way, as *mice* puts the apostrophe before the *s*, and *cats* puts it after the *s*. But if you follow the rule I just gave you, you do not need to worry about irregular plurals. You will always be right!

Writing Assignment 7-1

For this assignment you will need to refer to the work you did for the Practicing Writing Introductions and Conclusions section in this chapter. Select one of the two pairs of introductions and conclusions you wrote for that exercise and develop it into a full-fledged essay. To do this, you will need to think of at least three topic sentences that will support the thesis you have chosen. Each of these topic sentences should be developed into a paragraph of from four to eight sentences. These supporting sentences will probably be factual statements, while the topic sentences, like the thesis sentence, should be inferences. These well-developed paragraphs should fit smoothly between the introduction and conclusion you have already written, forming your essay.

For the prewriting step, use any of the techniques you already know to generate ideas for the thesis sentence that you have chosen. Your prewriting should produce at least three good topic sentences and some ideas about how you can support these.

The writing step involves developing the paragraphs for the middle of your essay. You may need to work on transition from your introduction to this middle or from this middle to the conclusion. Feel free to change the introduction and conclusion you wrote originally, if you have some better ideas while you're working on this assignment. As you write the essay, keep in mind the various approaches to organizing paragraphs, and try to use at least a couple of these. In your final draft, make sure you underline your thesis sentence as well as your topic sentences.

For the postwriting step, proofread your final draft carefully, being sure to correct the spelling and to eliminate any unmarked fragments, comma splices, run-on sentences, subject-verb agreement errors, errors in verb form, faulty tense shifts, or errors in use or omission of apostrophes.

Writing Assignment 7-2 You will begin this assignment by writing a summary of Nickie McWhirter's "Phooey on the Little Boxes Other People Put around Us," in Chapter 4. This paragraph will be the introduction to an essay that shows how McWhirter's ideas do or do not relate to your life.

For the prewriting step, brainstorm or use some other appropriate technique to come up with examples from your own life that can be used to prove or disprove McWhirter's point. You should also come up with a thesis sentence that explains whether the ideas in the essay do or do not apply to your life. (To be clear, this thesis will need to include either the name of the essay or the name of its author.)

For the writing step of this assignment, you need to compose a very structured five-paragraph essay. The first paragraph should be a summary of the main ideas in McWhirter's essay. It should follow the guidelines for summary paragraphs given in this chapter. Paragraphs 2, 3, and 4 should show how these ideas do or do not apply to your own life. Each paragraph should have a topic sentence that is an inference, and this inference should be supported by factual statements about your life. Paragraph 5 should be a well-written conclusion; it should contain your thesis sentence. Underline your topic sentences and this thesis sentence.

For the postwriting step, proofread your final draft carefully, being sure to correct the spelling and to eliminate any unmarked fragments, comma splices, run-on sentences, subject-verb agreement errors, errors in verb form, faulty tense shifts, or errors in use or omission of apostrophes.

Writing Assignment 7-3 You will begin this assignment by writing a summary of Charles Larson's "Competency Tests for Everyone," in this chapter. This paragraph will be the introduction to an essay that shows why you agree or disagree with Larson's main point.

For the prewriting step, brainstorm or use some other appropriate technique to come up with examples from your own life that will help you to support or attack Larson's ideas. You should also come up with a thesis sentence that explains your agreement or disagreement with the essay. (To be clear, this thesis will need to include either the name of the essay or the name of its author.)

For the writing step of this assignment, you need to compose a very structured five-paragraph essay. The first paragraph should be a summary of the main ideas in Larson's essay. It should follow the guidelines for summary paragraphs given in this chapter. Paragraphs 2, 3, and 4 should show how these ideas are right or wrong, according to your thinking and experience. Each paragraph should have a topic sentence that is an inference, and this inference should be supported by factual statements. Paragraph 5 should be a well-written conclusion; it should contain your thesis sentence. Underline your topic sentences and this thesis sentence.

For the postwriting step, proofread your final draft carefully, being sure to correct the spelling and to eliminate any unmarked fragments, comma splices, run-on sentences, subject-verb agreement errors, errors in verb form, faulty tense shifts, or errors in use or omission of apostrophes.

Writing Assignment 7-4 Your assignment is to write a dialogue illustrating a time when you felt emotion—anger, elation, good humor, anxiety, relief, jealousy, or some other emotion. (You may want to look back at "The Ticket" in Chapter 5 for some ideas.) The dialogue may be authentic or imaginary.

For the prewriting step, use whatever technique works best to help you generate ideas. You should decide what emotion you want to illustrate, and your thesis sentence should probably mention this emotion.

For the writing step, write the dialogue, making sure that it is always clear who is speaking. You will probably need some paragraphs of description and explanation to clarify the dialogue, but most of your paper should be conversation. For this assignment, do not state the thesis in the beginning. Your last paragraph should contain your underlined thesis sentence.

For the postwriting step, proofread your final draft carefully, being sure to correct the spelling and to eliminate any unmarked fragments, comma splices, run-on sentences, subject-verb agreement errors, errors in verb form, faulty tense shifts, or errors in use or omission of apostrophes.

CHAPTER 8

WRITING: THE MEDIUM (SOME WAYS TO PUT IT ALL TOGETHER)

In the writing you have been doing for this class so far, you have seldom used isolated sentences or isolated paragraphs. Instead, you have used the paragraphs as building blocks to create a larger structure—the essay. You have often done this without specific instruction on how to organize an essay, and yet you have generally been successful because you are already aware of the basic patterns. You've picked them up from reading as well as from past writing classes. Like other human beings, you have a need for structure and a tendency to see patterns in the things around you. Without this tendency, you would look at a picture composed of tiny dots of different colored paint and see just that—tiny dots of different colored paint. But you don't; you see the fruit, the bottles, the bowls, whatever pattern these tiny dots form. Because you need structure, you try to incorporate it in the papers you write, giving them at least a beginning, a middle, and an end. Because your readers need structure, they expect your writing to have some pattern to it. This pattern helps them to grasp your ideas and to remember them.

THE SIMPLEST PATTERN: CHRONOLOGY

Probably one of the earliest patterns of communication you learned as a small child was following the sequence of events. "First Jimmy called me a poo-poo head and then I called him a you-know-what and then he hit me—hard—right on the shoulder and then I socked him in the gut!" When you grew up enough to be assigned essays on what you did over summer vacation, you learned to call this pattern *time order* or *chronological order*. "We went to the amusement park. I ate three cotton candies. Then I ate two hotdogs and drank a root beer. Later I had ice cream on a stick, two bags of popcorn, and about half a pound of fudge. When we got home that night, I was really sick."

You can never outgrow the chronological pattern. No matter how sophisticated you are or how sophisticated you expect your readers to be, chronological order will still be the clearest, least confusing pattern to use for some kinds of papers. If you are retelling an event or a series of events, it just makes good sense to begin at the beginning and to follow through to the end. Creative writers may use other techniques—you are all familiar with the use of flashbacks in movies—but they always have some purpose in mind other than communicating as clearly as possible. They want to create an atmosphere, show the motivation for one of the characters, or draw parallels between past and present. If they wanted to narrate a story or to explain a process, they would use the same pattern of organization you use, the chronological pattern.

For an example of chronological order used effectively to relate an incident, look back at "The Ticket," the student essay in Chapter 5. It merits studying closely, for it illustrates one of the hardest principles to learn and apply in narrative writing—selection. Although using chronological order to tell a story does mean starting at the beginning and following straight through to the end, it is not quite as simple as it sounds. The process prescribes what order to use in assembling your details, but it does not dictate what details to assemble. Obviously, not all possible details will be included in any description, so the writer's job involves selecting the most appropriate details to make the desired point. For instance, Roberta Thompson, the student who wrote "The Ticket," included just a paragraph explanation of the scene before she introduced the meter-maid. Why? Another student might have followed the dictate to begin at the beginning by describing the preparations for the park outing in great detail, emphasizing the clothes both mother and son selected to wear, the frisbees they took along, and the lunch they packed (peanut butter and jelly sandwiches, corn chips, oatmeal cookies, and grape drink). Would this kind of introduction be wrong? Not really, but it would blur the focus of the account. Reading those details might make you think the story was going to be about how mother and son passed their time in the park; by the time you realized that they never even got to the park, you could feel slightly misled. Readers expect details to amount to something, so that when they finish reading and look back at particular descriptions, they can say, "Oh, now I see why that was there!" If the action of the tale focuses on the conflict with the meter-maid, grape drink and oatmeal cookies are irrelevant.

Thompson's essay shows that she understood the principle of selection: Choose details that emphasize the main point. Of course, you have to know what your main point is before you can follow this principle, and that is one reason why formulating a thesis sentence is such an important part of prewriting, even for a relatively straightforward narration like the description of an event. Once you have this thesis firmly in mind, it is not too difficult to make sure each detail you include earns its place in your paper by underscoring this point.

Another kind of writing assignment that almost always demands chronological order is a process paper. For any process you might describe—developing film, baking a soufflé, housebreaking your dog, filing for divorce—there will be definite steps, and these steps usually have to be taken in a set order. Unless you start with the first step and proceed through the steps in order until you get to the last, you will make it very difficult for your reader to follow your directions.

Think back to the most difficult directions you ever had to follow, perhaps the rules for playing some simulation game or the instructions for assembling a swing set. Suppose the instructions had been cut apart by steps and reassembled in some order that wasn't chronological—alphabetical order, perhaps. Do you think you ever could have succeeded in playing the game or building the swing set? Some people really enjoy a challenge, so perhaps you might have succeeded, but most people would have given up. When you describe the steps in the process, don't make them unduly challenging by changing their natural sequence.

When you write a process paper, it is especially important that you keep your readers and their knowledge of the subject in mind at all times, during the prewriting, writing, and postwriting steps. For an example of a process paper that does just that, look back at "A Good Cigar Is a Smoke," the student essay in Chapter 3.

OUTLINING FOR OTHER PATTERNS

When you follow chronological order, you probably do not need an outline to remind you about what comes next in your paper. However, when you write essays that are not narrations of events or descriptions of processes, you may need to work harder at organizing your thoughts into patterns that you can easily communicate to your reader. For a paper that is basically description, comparison/contrast, or argument, it may help you to have a brief outline.

For an example, look back at "The Swamp," the student essay in Chapter 6. As part of his prewriting, the writer may have made a list of ideas to cover that looked something like this:

Snakes in the swamp

Grandfather's stories

How big Hooper used to be

Indians on the knoll

The logging boom

Changes in the river

Thesis sentence: The fertile, tillable soil that is now Gun Plains was once a vast swamp, but it was unfortunately destroyed by man in the name of progress.

At this point he would have been able to see that he had plenty of material for a two-page paper, but unless he wanted to have it sound as meandering as the original river he was writing about, he would need to give it some organization. Some inspection of the list of ideas might have shown him that chronological order could be used for part of his organization. There are basically two time periods discussed in the essay: the time before the logging boom and the time after it. By dividing his ideas into these two blocks of time, he might have arrived at this outline:

Thesis sentence: The fertile, tillable soil that is now Gun Plains was once a vast swamp, but it was unfortunately destroyed by man in the name of progress.

I. The original swamp
   A. Grandfather's tales about the river
   B. The knoll, an Indian campground
   C. Snakes in the swamp
II. The effects of the logging boom
   A. On Hooper
   B. On the forests
   C. On the river
   D. On the swamp itself

For a fairly simple descriptive paper, such a brief outline should do nicely. It shows the two main divisions of the paper that will be used to support the thesis, and within each division it lists several points in the order in which they will be covered. Note that the thesis is not one of the Roman numeral sections of the outline. Students sometimes want to number the thesis point *I*, probably because they will be putting the thesis near the beginning of the paper. But an outline should be logical, and it stands to reason that the first section cannot be the only part of the paper that is about the thesis. If this were the case, what would the rest of the paper be about?

Another apparently arbitrary rule of outlining can be explained by logic. This is the "no one without a two, no *A* without a *B*" regulation you may have had dictated to you by your third- or fourth-grade teacher. When you think about the reason for this rule, remember that each division of your outline breaks down the larger division into parts. The Roman numerals break down the whole essay, the capital letters break down the Roman numeral section they are in, and the Arabic numerals—if you use them—break down the capital letter section they are in. Suppose you were to set up a division like this in the outline just given:

B. The knoll
   1. An Indian campground
C. Snakes in the swamp

Such an outline would be saying that you intended to break down the section on the knoll into just one part, a discussion of the Indian campground. Dividing a section into just one subsection is just as difficult as cutting a pie into just one piece. If you want to eat the whole pie, don't cut it first.

How about a comparison/contrast paper, a very common assignment in many college classes? Will the same simple outline form be useful for this more complex writing assignment? Basically, yes. Before you can outline a comparison/contrast paper, however, you have to make one decision: Will you use a *divided* or an *alternated* pattern? In a divided paper, you would cover all the points about your first topic before you discussed any of the points of comparison or contrast for the second topic. In a paper using the alternated pattern, you would go back and forth between the topics, discussing first one point about both topics and then a second point about the two topics.

Let's use the same assignment to illustrate both patterns—a comparison of the benefits of attending a large college with the benefits of attending a small one. Suppose you decided that the benefits of a small college were greater, and you chose the divided pattern to present your argument. You would say everything you wanted to say about large colleges first, and then you would present all of your ideas about small colleges. It would be possible to reverse the order, but it generally would not be wise. You want your strongest points for the side you favor to come at the end, where your readers will be most likely to remember them.

Thesis sentence: Although educators have put up a strong defense for colleges with over 10,000 students, the smaller school is more beneficial to the individual student.

I. Large colleges
   A. Academic activities
      1. Course offerings
      2. Grading
      3. Quality of instruction
   B. Extracurricular activities
      1. Clubs
      2. Social events
      3. Unstructured interactions
II. Small colleges
   A. Academic activities
      1. Course offerings
      2. Grading
      3. Quality of instruction
   B. Extracurricular activities
      1. Clubs
      2. Social events
      3. Unstructured interactions

A paper based on this outline would undoubtedly have an introduction and a conclusion, also. Unless these sections are fairly long (more than a paragraph or two), they do not need to be shown on the outline. Do not do what one student did and turn in a three-word outline:

I. Introduction
II. Body
III. Conclusion

The main problem with writing a divided-pattern paper should be evident from this outline. You may wind up with two mini-papers, one on large colleges and one on small colleges. To avoid such a result, be especially careful to provide at least a sentence of transition to help your reader get from section I to section II. Something like this will do the job: "Despite these apparent strong points of large colleges, those with fewer than 10,000 students actually provide more benefits in both academic activities and extracurricular opportunities."

The alternated pattern also has a built-in problem: It may be difficult to avoid repetition. If you do not always designate *small colleges* or *large colleges*, your reader can get lost. Also, it is especially important that you follow the same pattern in each section. If you discuss small colleges first when you talk about clubs, you cannot switch to large colleges for the first point about organized social events. You must establish a pattern of always discussing one topic first, and you must stick with it.

For the example of the alternated pattern, let's switch sides and argue for the larger colleges. This means we will want to discuss small colleges first under every point, so that our strong arguments for large colleges will come in the most memorable position.

Thesis sentence: Although educators have put up a strong defense for the small college, the college with over 10,000 students actually has more to offer the individual student.

I. Academic activities differ in the two types of college.
   A. Course offerings point up the distinction.
      1. Small colleges are forced to limit the curriculum.
      2. Large colleges can offer almost any class desired.
   B. Grading techniques differ.
      1. Small colleges often grade easy.
      2. Large colleges have more competition for grades.
   C. The quality of instruction often differs, also.
      1. Small colleges sometimes can't afford the best teachers.
      2. Large colleges can attract more scholarly professors.

II. Extracurricular activities are not the same in both types of colleges.
   A. The number and variety of clubs illustrate the difference.
      1. Small colleges generally have few clubs.
      2. Large colleges have clubs for every interest.
   B. Organized social events differ.
      1. Small colleges lack the money and personnel to sponsor many outings and dances.
      2. Large colleges have plenty of support for get-togethers.
   C. Unstructured interactions also differ.
      1. Small colleges tend to be cliquish.
      2. Large colleges are big enough that everyone can find some place to belong.

I am sure you will have noticed a difference between the two outlines other than just the patterns they use. The divided pattern outline is a *topic outline*; each number or letter has a noun or a noun phrase after it. The alternated pattern outline is a *sentence outline*; each number or letter has a full sentence after it. There is no connection between the pattern and the type of outline used. You can develop a topic outline for any kind of paper, and the same is true for a sentence outline. Both have their advantages and disadvantages, but to keep your instructor happy and to be logically consistent, you should be careful not to mix the two types. Don't begin with sentences and switch to topics or vice versa.

Some students think that writing a sentence outline is too much trouble, but they may not see the advantage this kind of outline has. Once you have written a good sentence outline, you already have topic sentences for your paragraphs, if you choose to use them this way. All you need to do is flesh out each sentence with personal anecdotes, detailed examples, and quotes from informed sources. In almost no time, your paper is finished!

It is true that you can jot down a topic outline more quickly than you can structure a sentence for each heading and subheading. Still, the topic outline has one pitfall the sentence outline does not have: All headings in a topic outline must be parallel in structure. This means that you can't start out choosing nouns for your headings and then suddenly switch to adjectives. You can't use this kind of division:

A. Academic activities
   1. Course offerings
   2. Tougher
   3. Quality of instruction

In that outline, no. 2 would not fit, because "tougher" is an adjective. "Course offerings" are a part of "academic activities," but "tougher" is not a part of them. Instead, it describes them. You can check your parallelism by reading the topic you have for A, followed by the topic you have for 1, and then repeating this process for A and 2, A and 3, and so forth. Each numeral topic should relate to its capital-letter topic in the same way; if one topic stands out as different, you will need to change it.

With a sentence outline, you can largely ignore parallelism. By virtue of being complete sentences, all the headings will be comparable.

PRACTICING DEVELOPING OUTLINES

1. To get a feel for the differences between topic outlines and sentence outlines, rewrite the sample outlines given for the comparison of large and small colleges, using a sentence outline for the argument for small colleges and a topic outline for the argument for large colleges.

2. Develop your outlining skills further by making an outline of either "A Growing Wealth of Words," the professional essay in Chapter 5, or "Men, Women and War," the professional essay in Chapter 6. It is up to you whether you make a sentence or a topic outline, but do not combine the two.

3. Choose two products that you have used as the basis for a comparison/contrast essay which you will outline. You might consider contrasting two brands of frozen dinners, two makes of automobiles, bicycles, tennis rackets, running shoes, television sets—anything that you have used and found to be both similar and dissimilar. Before you can develop an outline, you must have a thesis sentence that comments on the main differences or similarities you will be pointing out. Here are some sample thesis sentences to give you some ideas:

> Although Krispy Krunchees look appealing and have a fairly low price, they lack the nutritional benefits of Natural Nutties.
>
> Both Brand *X* and Brand *Y* aspirin will cure a headache, but *Y* is the better buy because of its speed and its lack of aftereffects.
>
> When you have a thesis, develop this into two outlines, one for a divided pattern paper and one for an alternated pattern paper. Make one of these a sentence outline and one a topic outline. You do not need to write the paper now, but you may have some use for the outlines in your next assignment.

RELATED READINGS

Student Essay

FIGHTERS
Mark Giles

Points to Consider

As you read the essay that follows, try to answer these questions:

1. What pattern of organization is used for this comparison/contrast essay?
2. At what point does the pattern change slightly? Is this change confusing, or can you find a reason for it?
3. Does the author make effective use of parallel structure at any point in the essay? Find sentences to support your answer.
4. The final paragraph includes several uses of figurative language. Are these effective for you? Why or why not?

Used with permission of Mark Giles.

In the sport of boxing there are two basic types of fighters. One is the slugger. He has short, muscular arms, slow hands and feet, and a heavy punch. The other has long arms, fast hands and feet, and a less-than-devastating punch. He is the boxer.

In my opinion there have been two fighters who epitomized these two styles. Rocky Marciano was the slugger, Muhammad Ali the boxer. Marciano fought with his head down, fists flailing, taking two punches for every one he delivered but winning anyway. Ali was slick, always moving.

The physiques of a puncher and a boxer are different. Marciano had a reach of 68 inches, while Ali had a reach of 81 inches. Marciano was five foot ten; Ali stood six foot three. Yet both men fought in the same division: heavyweight.

8 WRITING: THE MEDIUM (SOME WAYS TO PUT IT ALL TOGETHER)

Marciano was short, squat and relentless as a bulldog. Ali was tall, lean and fast. He was built like a panther.

The puncher by nature absorbs a lot of punishment. His style is to bull in, get his torso in between his opponent's arms, and pummel away. Rocky would take endless punishment. He had incredible stamina, and he never quit.

A boxer knows how to avoid punishment. He slides from right to left and back, flicking jabs, using his reflexes and speed to confuse the man in front of him. Ali was perhaps the greatest of all time at this art.

A prize fighter's style in the ring is often a reflection of his personality. A boxer tends to be glib and flashy. He is a talker. Ali loved the attention of the press. Marciano was reticent, more steady. Ali spent his money as quickly as he made it. Marciano was frugal, saving his money and investing it.

Marciano sometimes looked foolish, as terribly earnest men often do. But he could not be goaded into blind rage by the matadors he fought. Despite his simple methods, there was a dark cleverness in him. He was never a fool in the ring.

Ali was a bragger, a show-off. Such men are often accused of being cowards. Boxers are sometimes accused of having a "glass jaw." People feel they must fear being hit, for they surely go to great efforts to avoid it.

Ali proved to be a fighter of unparalleled will and courage. In the later stages of his career he took some shots and lost a lot of his reflexes. Ali fought such men as George Foreman, Ken Norton, and Joe Frazier—some of boxing's most destructive hitters. He survived and overcame these men by willpower alone. These are not the actions of a coward.

Rocky Marciano was a rock, an object. Ali was a flame, a catalyst. Marciano was strength; Ali was speed. These men were more than examples of prize fighters. They were examples of two sides of human nature—the tortoise and the hare.

Professional Essay

LABORS OF LOVE
Brian Friel

Points to Consider

As you read the essay that follows, try to answer these questions:

1. This essay uses chronological order to blend together three anecdotes, but it is almost a comparison/contrast essay as well. What is the main point? How is it related to the contrast between the writer and Marlon Brando? How is the Brando material used in the essay? Find references to the opening episode throughout the essay.

2. After reading the first two paragraphs, can you state the thesis idea? What is it?

3. What assumptions can you make about the audience for this essay? Since the essay was published in 1963, has it now become too dated for its audience? Why or why not?

4. Does the Irish setting cause any problems for an American audience? What details, if any, seemed particularly foreign to you? What details, if any, seemed universal?

Copyright © 1963 by The Atlantic Monthly Company, Boston, Mass. Reprinted with permission.

What I envy most in Marlon Brando, who is about the same age as myself, is his complete self-mastery in the presence of a beautiful woman. He just sits there at a table in Jabe's Joint, his legs crossed carelessly, his hands folded on his stomach, those saintly eyes of his lowered demurely. Not a tremor, not a twitch. And sooner or later the doxy always sidles up to him, sticks her shoulder into his back, rattles her castanets above her head, and then goes bashing about the place in what is ostensibly a dance, but what, even the holy Brando must know, is a spelling out of an invitation. Still he reveals no interest. And when the dance is over and the woman is panting for breath, he gets to his feet, tosses a coin to Jabe—who by this time is usually panting too—and saunters out to take a look around the corral. Every time I see a scene like that in the films I remember my own courting days and wonder, had I stood my ground like the bold Brando instead of prancing about as I did, if I would have fared any better. I don't believe I would. Indeed, I imagine that, apart from the redhead, none of the women I laid siege to was ever aware of the desperate purpose behind my acrobatics.

I have distinct memories of two thoroughly exhausting affairs before I was ten: one was with my teacher, Miss Blankly, and the other was with a young married woman whose husband was a sergeant in the British Army. Happily, both romances coincided with my acquisition of new skills, because in County Tyrone, where I grew up, it was the man who made all the play.

When I fell for Miss Blankly, I had just learned to cycle backward, and for at least a fortnight her evenings were disturbed by the sight of a dizzy lad careering up and down in front of her house on a bicycle without tubes or tires, and by his throaty yodeling, with which he hoped to embellish his act. This was a much more complicated and much more hazardous business than twiddling castanets and dancing, because I could yodel only when my eyes were shut tight, and to cycle backward at the same time called for a high degree of physical and mental concentration. However I managed it all is a mystery to me now. I must have been actuated by some sort of magnificent passion. Eventually, of course, I got a bad fall and was in the hospital for five weeks, the slowness of my recovery being due to my run-down condition: nothing is as weakening as cycling backward with your eyes shut tight. Now the only mementos I have of that affair are two scars on my left arm and two overdeveloped knots of muscle on the backs of my thin legs. And Miss Blankly? She never even visited me all the time I was laid up.

My "castanet-dance routine" with the married woman who could have been my mother took the form of handstands. Every time she opened her door I was upside-down on the step before her. If she went to the well for water, I was stationed at the flagstones like an inverted genie. If she put her washing out on the clothesline, I was there first, my nose in the earth, my feet in the clouds. Had her husband not returned before I was a week at this trick I might have burst a blood vessel. As it was, I suffered from severe headaches, and my eyes were constantly watering. I will never know how close I was to serious injury when he came home on leave, discovered me petrified in somersault in his garden, got down on his knees, and bawled into my blazing, streaming face, "Get 'ome to 'ell out o' this!" How I would have cherished even that recognition from his wife. But never once in all the time I blocked her path did she as much as bid the time of day to my shoes.

A third, and by far the most strenuous, romance occurred when I was eleven and fell for a huge, lumpy, redheaded girl who was in my own class and shared with me the distinction of being the best of the "slow group." The slow group, not having the same aptitude for higher things as the good group, amused itself by doing lines; and by a process of elimination Annie and I were left for one another. I accepted my fate and finally worked up courage to approach her. "Annie," I said, one evening after school, "will you go with me?" (That was the conventional opening. If the answer was yes, the second line, delivered aggressively, was, "Give me a kiss, then." If the answer was no, the suitor put out his tongue and said, "Go home to your pups" or "The only man you'll ever get is a lame dwarf, aul' watery face!", depending on the depth of his disappointment.)

"Why should I?" said Annie archly.

This response almost punctured me, but I stuck doggedly to my rehearsed part.

"Annie," I said again, more loudly this time, "will you go with me?"

"Paddy-one-tune!" she jeered.

A lesser man might have panicked. My assurance was undermined, but I was determined to see the act through.

"Give me a kiss, then!" I shouted, pretending to assume that her taunts implied a yes.

I gripped her and kissed her on the ear before she could run away. And that simple demonstration of my love, though I say it myself, transformed big Annie overnight. She became the most sought-after girl in the slow group; even the boys in the good group began looking at her. The explanation is much more simple and much less flattering than I like to believe. The truth is that, up to then, we had all been nervous of Annie's tremendous strength.

I will never know how I survived the weeks of that romance. In return for the purely technical title of going with her, Annie demanded that I fight all the new suitors who suddenly found her irresistible. Never a day passed but she slipped a note across the seats to me: "Billy Broderick wants to go with me.

Fight him after school"; "John Boyle wants to go with me. Fight him after school"; "Tom McGrath wants to go with me. Fight him after school." And every evening in the school yard I peeled off my jacket, handed it to her, closed my eyes, and went flailing into battle for a cause that meant little to me. I was always a puny child, but somehow I lasted through eighteen fights. I had teeth loosened and eyes closed and ribs bruised, but an obscure sense of gallantry kept me going. When a contest was over, Annie would hand me my coat, say in her broadest Tyrone accent, "You're not a bad fella," and waddle off home, leaving me to explore my battered face with gentle, trembling fingers.

I lost her to the nineteenth challenger—one of the McGuire twins. She accused me afterward of throwing the fight. But that was unfair. McGuire was the better man and would have killed me if I had not let him take me in the seventh round. Years later I heard that they had married and that she beats him up every Saturday.

My day of romancing is over; I am securely anchored to a woman who would scarcely raise an eyebrow if I were to leap across Everest or run a three-minute mile. But in my still ardent imagination I sometimes see myself strolling into Jabe's Joint and dropping easily into a seat. Jabe's hands hang poised above his hips. Doxy passes behind me and whispers, "Thank God you've come. It's Jabe—he's crazy jealous. Fix him, Hank! Fix him good!" I know I should ignore her. I know she is a tramp. I know that Jabe can break me with his little finger. I know, oh, so well, what Brando would do—sweet nothing. But old habits die hard. I kick over the table, reach for Jabe, and—if my wife were watching me many a night as I sit at the fire, she would see my face contract with pain and my head jerk back—he knocks me stiff with one straight right.

I'll wager that when Brando was young he never cycled backward with his eyes closed, or stood on his hands for hours at a stretch, or fought hopeless fights against boys who towered over him. But I'll wager that he slipped notes across the seats to his girl: "Mary Lou Grigg wants to go with me. Fight her after school"; "Stella Baptisti wants to go with me. Fight her after school." It is no credit to him that he looks so much better preserved than I.

WRITING ASSIGNMENTS

In doing any of the assignments for this chapter, you should strive to meet the following objectives. If you meet all six, you will get a satisfactory grade.

Objectives

1. Turn in your prewriting, showing that you used an appropriate technique.
2. Include and <u>underline</u> your thesis sentence.
3. Follow a pattern of organization appropriate to your topic. If the assignment requires an outline, one should be included with the prewriting, and the paper itself should follow the structure indicated in the outline.
4. Use details to clarify your major points.
5. Use standard American spelling.
6. Proofread to eliminate any unmarked sentence fragments, comma splices, run-on sentences, subject-verb agreement errors, errors in verb form, faulty

tense shifts, errors in use or omission of apostrophes, or incorrect uses of commas, semicolons, or colons.

Section 3 of the Handbook covers the most common punctuation problems, but here is a short summary of the problems you might have with commas, semicolons, or colons.

Aside from comma splices, the most common errors with commas come from putting them in where they don't belong—usually between the subject and the verb or between the verb and its object, as in these sentences:

The man who won her heart, was the one with money.

She thought, that he could support her in style.

Omitting the commas will correct these sentences.

Another place where commas don't belong is between an independent clause and a dependent clause if (1) the independent clause comes first, and (2) the dependent clause is closely related to it. When the dependent clause comes first, or when the dependent clause appears to be an afterthought, the comma is appropriate. All of these sentences are punctuated correctly:

As soon as he was paid, he squandered his money at the race track. (The independent clause comes second, so the comma is needed.)

He squandered his money at the race track because he had no sense. (The independent clause comes first, so the comma isn't needed.)

He squandered his money at the race track, although he never really had much to squander. (The independent clause comes first, but the dependent clause seems less important, not closely related to it. The comma is acceptable in this sentence.)

Semicolons are incorrectly used when they join dependent and independent clauses. Unless *both* clauses could be sentences, don't use a semicolon to join them. A comma is the correct punctuation for a sentence like this:

When he inherited a fortune; he suddenly became charming.

Colons are correctly used to join independent clauses when the second one illustrates or gives an example of what the first clause is saying. Generally, the first clause should sound complete before the colon.

His last advice was this: Never explain anything.

(Without "this," the first clause would not sound finished, and the colon would be misused.)

Colons can also be used to introduce lists.

He told her she lacked three things: brains, looks, and him.

Again, the sentence should sound complete before the colon. You should not write this:

He told her she lacked: brains, looks, and him.

This colon would be separating the verb, *lacked*, from its three objects. If you don't want to put a comma between the verb and the object, you certainly don't want to put any stronger punctuation—a colon or a semicolon—there.

Writing Assignment 8-1

For this assignment you will need to follow the form of the chronological narrative used by Brian Friel in "Labors of Love." You will need to select two or three reminiscences from your childhood to tie together in a unified essay. The anecdotes should be told in chronological order, and you should be particularly careful that the introduction and conclusion help to unify the anecdotes in some way.

For the prewriting step, use any of the techniques you have already learned to jog your memory for appropriate childhood happenings. You might consider episodes from your early days in school, stories that illustrate how you got along (or didn't get along) with your brothers and sisters, anecdotes involving family pets, or tales that show you learning to be a boy or to be a girl. As an important part of your prewriting, formulate a thesis sentence that will tie the various episodes together.

The writing step involves developing these episodes into a unified chronological narrative. The entire essay should support the thesis you have written, and each anecdote should be brief but detailed.

For the postwriting step, proofread your final draft carefully, being sure to correct the spelling and to eliminate any unmarked fragments, comma splices, run-on sentences, subject-verb agreement errors, errors in verb form, faulty tense shifts, errors in use or omission of apostrophes, or incorrect uses of commas, semicolons, or colons.

Writing Assignment 8-2

This assignment calls for a process paper, so you may want to look back at "A Good Cigar Is a Smoke," in Chapter 3. Also review the discussion in this chapter of using chronological order in the process paper.

For the prewriting step, decide on a process that you know well, using any of the techniques you have learned to come up with ideas. You should be able to write step-by-step directions without doing research. Be sure to do some thinking about your audience as part of the prewriting. You might select a process related to communications (how to win an argument with your father, how to overcome shyness, how to pick someone up in a bar) or some other kind of process (how to train your dog, how to give a blood transfusion, how to build your own atomic bomb). State the main idea about your process as a thesis sentence. Here are some examples:

Winning an argument with my father requires first that you make him think you agree with him; the rest is easy.

Behavior modification is the most effective system to use in housebreaking a puppy.

Giving a blood transfusion requires patience, professional attitude, and compassion.

The writing step requires that you develop your thesis into a clear description of the process, following chronological order and using sufficient details. Be sure to consider your intended audience's knowledge of the topic as you explain each step. Your explanation of how to build an atomic bomb, for instance, will depend on whether your readers are physicists, high-school students, or dental patients trying to distract themselves with *Reader's Digest* while they await root canal work.

For the postwriting step, proofread your final draft carefully, being sure to correct the spelling and to eliminate any unmarked fragments, comma splices, run-on sentences, subject-verb agreement errors, errors in verb form, faulty tense shifts, errors in use or omission of apostrophes, or incorrect uses of commas, semicolons, or colons.

Writing Assignment 8-3 For this assignment you will need to go back to the outlines you developed for the third activity under Practicing Developing Outlines. You will choose one of the outlines you wrote and develop it into a paper comparing and contrasting the two products you selected.

If you completed the activity carefully, you have already done the prewriting step. You did this when you decided on the products you would compare or contrast, the points you would make about them, and the thesis your outlines would support. The outlines themselves were also a part of the prewriting. The only part that remains is for you to decide which outline you will develop—the divided pattern outline or the alternated pattern outline. Before you begin writing, you should also check your selected outline carefully to be sure you have stuck to either a sentence outline or a topic outline.

For the writing step, develop your comparison and contrast of the two products in detail, following the order you have laid out in your outline. Be sure that everything in your outline is also in your paper and that the parts are in the same order in both the outline and the paper. Also, be sure that everything in your paper is in your outline. When you are finished, your outline should appear to be the skeleton of the paper, with only the details removed. Both should support your thesis.

For the postwriting step, proofread your final draft carefully, being sure to correct the spelling and to eliminate any unmarked fragments, comma splices, run-on sentences, subject-verb agreement errors, errors in verb form, faulty tense shifts, errors in use or omission of apostrophes, or incorrect uses of commas, semicolons, or colons.

Writing Assignment 8-4 This assignment calls for a comparison/contrast paper describing two people or two places. Consider people or places that might be expected to be alike but are really quite different, for instance, some twins you know, two math teachers, two apartment complexes, two amusement parks.

The prewriting step should include whatever idea-generating technique you use and should extend to stating a thesis sentence and formulating an outline.

You may use either a sentence outline or a topic outline, and you may follow either pattern—alternated or divided.

For the writing step, develop your comparison and contrast of the two people or two places in detail, following the order you have laid out in your outline. Be sure that everything in your outline is also in your paper and that the parts are in the same order in both the outline and the paper. Also, be sure that everything in your paper is in your outline. When you are finished, your outline should appear to be the skeleton of your paper, with only the details removed. Both should support your thesis.

For the postwriting step, proofread your final draft carefully, being sure to correct the spelling and to eliminate any unmarked fragments, comma splices, run-on sentences, subject-verb agreement errors, errors in verb form, faulty tense shifts, errors in use or omission of apostrophes, or incorrect uses of commas, semicolons, or colons.

CHAPTER 9

WRITING: THE MEDIUM (MORE WAYS TO PUT IT ALL TOGETHER)

Many of the ideas you may want to convey will be too complex to fit a simple chronological or comparison/contrast pattern of development. For these you will need to know more sophisticated essay patterns. Once you have mastered comparison/contrast, you should be ready to try your hand at classification and analysis, cause/effect, and argumentative papers.

CLASSIFYING AND ANALYZING

The skills you developed in writing comparison/contrast papers should stand you in good stead when you take the next step and write a classification or an analysis. Either assignment requires that you observe similarities and differences in order to organize the unorganized. If you are asked to break down one big subject into smaller parts and to explain how these parts are related and how they work together, you will write an *analysis*. *Classification* works in the other direction, grouping related items into categories to understand their importance better.

You have already used classification in one of your prewriting techniques. When you built a classification tree for the topic of Outdoor Dangers (Chapter 4), you categorized the dangers on the basis of their origin and created three groups: from the elements, from wildlife, and from humans. By studying the separate parts of each subclass, you discovered a possible significance to develop in a thesis sentence: The most dangerous creature we are likely to encounter outdoors is another human being. The act of classifying helped you to see relationships and to evaluate what might and what might not be significant.

Whether you are analyzing or classifying, you will need a *basis* for your divisions or categories. In the example of outdoor dangers, the basis for categorizing dangers was their origin. Generally, your basis will relate to your purpose. Let's look at two examples.

Suppose you were assigned to analyze the job of a firefighter. You might decide to use Required Skills as the basis of your division, and your subclasses might be Human Relations Skills (calming frightened people, training youngsters in fire prevention, for example), Technical Skills (driving the trucks, operating the equipment), and Physical Skills (climbing ladders, jumping into nets, and so forth). These subclasses might not cover all the skills required—that is why the *and so forth* is necessary in analysis or classification, as there should be a place for everything—but they would probably give you a good start on your analysis if your purpose were to prepare a training program for newly hired firefighters. Suppose you were a union organizer intent on analyzing the job in order to negotiate the first contract for a new firefighters' union? Then you might prefer an entirely different basis of division. One possibility you might choose is ranking the various tasks by Degree of Danger Involved, so that the Greatest Danger subclass would include jobs performed inside burning buildings, the Moderate Danger subclass would cover outside jobs like climbing ladders, and the Least Danger subclass would include waiting around the fire station for a call to come in. The basis for your divisions would be determined by the purpose for your analysis.

The same rule applies when you are classifying. Suppose you were planning a trip to California and wanted to appear as a contestant on a TV game show while you were there. You might want to classify the game shows to determine which would be your best choice. One basis for your categories would be Abilities Required of Winners, and you might group shows into Knowledge Required, Dexterity Required, Luck Required, and Combination Required. If you felt sufficiently confident to compete in any of these categories, you might prefer to group shows by the kinds of prizes offered, making your final decision to apply to the show with the most appealing prizes. If you won so much money as a game show contestant that you decided to start your own game show, you might classify the game shows for an entirely different purpose. Now you would probably be concerned about their popularity with different audiences, and Audience Appeal might be the basis for your classification.

Whether you are analyzing or classifying, when you begin to write your essay, there are several pitfalls to watch out for.

1. Avoid obvious groupings. Remember that the purpose behind either assignment is to help you see new relationships, so classifying your relatives into Men and Women would probably lead you nowhere. If you must classify the members of your family, any of these might be a more productive basis for division: Sense of Adventure, Social Status, Interest in Sports, Degree of Ambition, Attitude toward Cleanliness.

2. Do not have inconsistent categories. You would be making this mistake if, in the game show classification, you used *both* the Abilities Required of Winners and the Kinds of Prizes Offered divisions. Shows would fit in more than one category, both Knowledge Required and Financial Prizes, for instance. This leads to the next warning.

3. Do not have overlapping categories. You can't have a neat and meaningful analysis if there are several places you could put any one part and the final placement is determined by whim. Both analysis and classification should be logical.

Fall is a time of beginning—

Cat/Dog lovers

ns that result in just two categories, *A* and Not *A*. For
ets into Dogs and All Other Pets is not very meaningful
ne group that is much larger than the other. Grouping
erts and Introverts is even worse, for it omits a large
ne *ambiverts*, people who balance an interest in others
themselves. It is almost always a mistake in thinking to
e who is not at one extreme in something—intelligence,
liation, financial outlook—must be at the other extreme.
a genius or a moron, either gorgeous or hideous, either a
publican, either a spendthrift or a miser. Do not assume
are.

put your thesis in the very beginning of your essay. "There
rivers" does not make the catchiest beginning. If you can
etting, invent some dialogue, or even describe the first and
type before you introduce your thesis, you are more likely
der.

CING ANALYSIS AND CLASSIFICATION

of the following topics and do the prewriting for an
say on each. Try out at least two different bases of divi-
ch topic. When you have chosen the basis that would
e best essay, compose a thesis sentence for each topic.
ne topics:

hborhood	A Job You Have Had
lusic	A Cartoon Strip
drobe	The Popularity of Jogging
The Appeal of Your Favorite Actor or Actress	TV Violence

2. Choose two of the following topics and do the prewriting for a classification essay on each. Try out at least two different bases of grouping for each topic. When you have chosen the basis that would result in the best essay, compose a thesis sentence for each topic. Here are the topics:

Local Pizza Parlors	Ice-Cream Flavors
Cigarette Ads	Nursery Rhymes
Drinks	Cartoon Strips
Financial Aid at Your College	Problems You Had in Writing Your Last Essay

WRITING CAUSE-AND-EFFECT ESSAYS

Often you will be asked to analyze the reasons why—the South lost the Civil War, the Edsel went out of production so quickly, so many teachers are out of jobs, people are moving to the Southwest. Anything that has happened can be analyzed by examining its causes. This particular kind of analysis is a favorite of teachers who give essay exams, but it is sometimes given out as a writing assignment, too, and you may even find it as a job assignment. (Analyze the reasons why our toothpaste was outsold by brand *X* two-to-one last year in the Midwest.) When you do this kind of analysis, you will be writing a cause-and-effect essay.

Cause-and-effect papers are seldom equally balanced; if they emphasize the reasons why something occurred, they will be predominantly cause papers, but if they focus on the predicted results of an action, they will be predominantly effect papers. Either kind of paper may include only a short description of the other part, the effects or the causes.

Part of the confusion that exists about cause-and-effect papers comes from the different meanings that we give to the word *cause*. Scientists often talk about *necessary causes*, occurrences that have to exist before a result can occur, and *sufficient causes*, occurrences that can produce a result all by themselves, without assistance from other factors. For instance, an underground earthquake can produce a tidal wave all by itself, so it is a sufficient cause of a tidal wave. It is also a necessary cause of a tidal wave, for you won't have a tidal wave unless there has been an underground earthquake. Many sufficient causes are not necessary causes, however. You can see that arson would be a sufficient cause of a house fire, but it could hardly be a necessary cause, or fires could not be started by faulty wiring, kitchen accidents, and smoking in bed.

Many of the effects we try to analyze exist outside the world of the natural sciences, and their causes are usually less obvious than the examples just given. We usually must be satisfied with identifying *contributing causes*, events that were neither necessary for the result to occur nor sufficient to bring it about alone, but that added to other contributing causes to create the effect. For instance, what causes a person to commit suicide? Even when the person is a celebrity whose life is examined in detail, it is almost never possible to pinpoint a definite event that led directly to the overdose, the bullet in the temple, or the slashed wrists. Still, we can often identify contributing causes: financial losses, depression over career problems, romantic difficulties.

In order to write successfully about causes and effects, there are several problems you should know about before you begin.

1. Do not think that an event must be only a cause or only an effect; most happenings are both. You might make this mistake if you were studying a person's financial history and you noted a bankruptcy. "Aha," you might say, "this is the result of several credit-shopping sprees!" You could be right, but your thinking should go beyond this point. The bankruptcy could also be a cause. What could be its result? A poor credit rating. And could that also be a cause? Of course. It could cause our hypothetical creditaholic to pay cash for all his purchases. Our cause and effect analysis has now become a kind of chain:

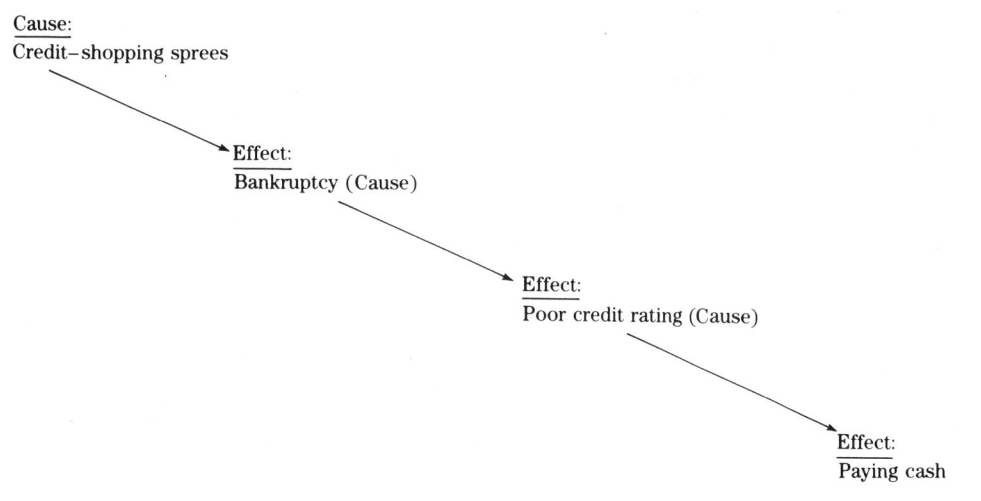

```
Cause:
Credit–shopping sprees
                    ↘
                     Effect:
                     Bankruptcy (Cause)
                                      ↘
                                       Effect:
                                       Poor credit rating (Cause)
                                                                ↘
                                                                 Effect:
                                                                 Paying cash
```

      Such chains of causes and effects are common in the real world; if you are on the lookout for them, you will avoid the next problem.

2. Do not oversimplify. Most effects that are worth writing about have more than one cause. You will not improve your credibility if you assert that divorces *cause* juvenile delinquency, that cigarette smoking is the *only cause* of cancer, or that the availability of handguns *causes* crime.

3. Try to avoid confusing causation with correlation. This statement needs some explanation. Two events are said to have a *high correlation* if they frequently occur together. For instance, you could say that the sale of hotdogs has a high correlation with the playing of ballgames. But could you say that hotdogs cause ballgames, or even that ballgames cause hotdogs? If you did, you would be mistaken.

      When two events frequently occur together like this, it is often hard to tell which is the cause and which is the effect. This chicken-or-egg dilemma usually comes about because neither one is the cause—both are effects of some other cause. I'll illustrate this with a personal example. As part of my graduate work, I studied the writings sent by college administrators to their faculties. I found a high correlation between accurate writing (grammatical and spelled correctly) and positive evaluations of the administrator by the faculty. The reverse was also true: Administrators whose writing displayed major flaws were likely to be rated as poor leaders by their faculty. Could I say that their poor writing caused them to be viewed as incompetent? Could I say that their general lack of competence caused them to write poorly? I couldn't say either. The likelihood is that some other consideration—a lackadaisical attitude, perhaps, or a lower intelligence than the other administrators—caused them to write poorly and caused them to be rated as poor leaders. If you are aware of the possibility that two related events may stem from the same cause, you will probably not confuse correlation with causation.

4. Finally, avoid sweeping generalizations by qualifying your statements. You can get in trouble if you say, "The proposal to build the new high school failed because all the senior citizens voted against it." Just one senior citizen who voted for it is enough to disprove your statement. You are more likely to be believed if you make a statement like this: "One of the major reasons the proposal to build the new high school was defeated was, according to voter surveys, the large 'no' vote among senior citizens."

PRACTICING CAUSE-AND-EFFECT ANALYSIS

1. Make a chain diagram similar to the one for credit-shopping sprees to show some of the possible effects of one of the following happenings:

   Your college increases tuition by 15 percent
   Credit cards entirely replace cash
   Students are allowed to quit school at age 12
   Federal law limits jobs to one per household
   Marriage licenses expire every five years
   The United States establishes a colony on Mars.

2. Choose some problem you have been faced with at work, school, or home recently. Analyze its probable causes. Do the prewriting as if you were going to write a cause-and-effect essay on the problem. Your last step should be to write at least one good thesis sentence for such an essay.

WRITING ARGUMENTATIVE PAPERS

The kinds of essays we have just been discussing—comparison/contrast, analysis and classification, and cause and effect—are really specialized kinds of argumentative papers. The thesis sentence for each is usually a judgment, and the details support that judgment, trying to get your readers to see the subject the same way you see it. Of course, not all argumentative papers fall into one of these specialized categories. Some argue about actions we should or should not take—passing a law, buying a small car, getting married young. Most arguments are fairly complicated and require many decisions in the prewriting step.

One of your first decisions in writing an argumentative paper should be whether you will argue directly or indirectly. You already have your topic and have decided what audience you will write for. Now you must ask yourself, "Which approach will work best with this audience, a direct statement of my thesis and the reasons I believe it is true, or an indirect, ironic reversal of my argument?" If you decide to be indirect, you will not include your thesis in your paper. Such an abrupt switch from tongue-in-cheek style would only confuse your readers. Instead, you will try to exaggerate the opposition to your thesis, hoping that your alert readers will read between the lines and decipher what you really mean to convey.

general conclusion about all similar cases. There is always the chance that they would change their minds about their conclusions if they were to see different cases, so the conclusion is, at best, an educated guess. Still, if the cases were well selected to be typical examples, the guess is most likely to be a good one.

How would you make your point about the inadequacy of club activities in small colleges, if you wanted to argue inductively? Well, you might choose four small colleges and examine their catalogs to determine what clubs exist in each place. You would want to choose the examples carefully, not limiting yourself to private colleges or to commuter colleges where students might lack both interest and time for extracurricular activities. If you chose the schools to be representative, your discovery that no school had fewer than four or more than six clubs might be significant. It would surely be significant if you contrasted it with a similar number of large colleges and found the numbers of clubs to range from nine to twenty-four. Your reasoning might look like this:

Merrycrest, Arbor View, Whittington, and St. Anthony's College, all colleges with enrollments under 10,000, offer their students from four to six clubs, with the average being five clubs.
Braxton, St. Paul's, Huron City College, and Poplar Bluffs, all colleges with enrollments over 10,000, offer their students from nine to twenty-four clubs, with the average being fifteen clubs.
Conclusion: Students in a large college are likely to have three times as many clubs to choose from as have students in a small college.

Of course, you can never be certain about this conclusion. If you looked at two more examples, they might reverse the trend. Perhaps the large college would list only six clubs, and the small one would list twenty. Possibilities like this keep you from stating the conclusion to an inductive argument more definitely. They account for the weasel word *likely* in the conclusion. Because of the inductive leap from the specific examples investigated to the broad hypothesis, the inductive argument will conclude with words like *most probably, generally, in a large number of cases*. These weasel words keep the argument from being more convincing than any statistical argument can be. Even if the conclusion is true in the overwhelming number of cases, it just might be false in the one case that interests you. (Many people depend on this possibility. Faced with evidence that their lifestyles can bring about early deaths in 99 percent of the cases, they still persist in counting themselves among the 1 percent that will live to be ninety.)

PRACTICING ARGUING INDUCTIVELY

Where would you look for evidence to use in inductive arguments supporting or attacking each of the following assertions? (If your instructor requests you to, choose one and actually find the evidence.)

1. More college students drop out of college for personal reasons than do so for dissatisfaction with their courses.
2. Alteration departments of large department stores discriminate against women who shop for clothing.
3. Mass murderers are no different mentally or physically from the rest of us.
4. American-made cars require twice as many repairs as do Japanese-made cars.
5. When a father participates in the birth of his child, the two are likely to form an especially strong bond.
6. Grocery stores in poor neighborhoods frequently charge higher prices than do their counterparts in middle-class neighborhoods.
7. Wearing a helmet when you drive your motorcycle may actually increase your chances of having an accident.
8. Television news coverage of local stories is seldom adequate.

USING DEDUCTIVE REASONING

How about deductive reasoning? In many ways it is the opposite of inductive reasoning. Instead of moving from the specific cases to the general conclusion, it reverses the process. It begins with a generally applicable statement, and it usually concludes with a specific case. In the large college argument, you might have used this deductive *syllogism*:

Premise: Any college that offers six or more foreign languages is a good school.
Premise: Braxton offers six foreign languages.
Conclusion: Braxton is a good school.

A syllogism is a three-statement argument that is structured in such a way that the conclusion cannot be false if the premises are true. This syllogism is a valid argument, a logically sound argument. If you accept the definition in the first premise and the factual statement in the second, there is no way for you to deny the conclusion. Of course, many people would argue with the first premise. A college might offer a dozen or more foreign languages but no math or physical education. Is that a good college? Perhaps, if your only interest is languages, but for many people it would be a very poor college.

A syllogism will only be as convincing as its premises, and many of the premises will need support in the form of personal anecdotes, statistics, quotes from experts, or even inductive reasoning.

Syllogisms can be tricky because little changes in the wording of the premises will invalidate them, making them no longer convincing. Is this syllogism still valid?

Premise: All good colleges offer six or more foreign languages.
Premise: Braxton offers six foreign languages.
Conclusion: Braxton is a good college.

You may need to study that for a few minutes before you decide that it is *not valid*. When you say that "all good colleges" do anything, you do not mean that *only* good colleges do it. All good colleges may do it, and 20 percent, 40 percent, or even 100 percent of the poor colleges may do it, too. After all, all good colleges have restrooms, but this does not prove that a college with restrooms is a good college!

This invalid syllogism is a poor argument because it commits a *fallacy*. A fallacy is an example of faulty reasoning, and you do not want to use it in any arguments you write. This particular fallacy is rather technical; it is called the *fallacy of the undistributed middle term*. In any syllogism the premises have to have a common term, or *middle term*, the idea that links them together and shows they belong in the same argument. In the valid syllogism the middle term was [*college that*] *offers six or more foreign languages*, and in this invalid syllogism it is the same. Now, in order to prove any connection between the other two terms (*good college* and *Braxton*), the argument must say something about all colleges that offer six or more foreign languages. It must say, "All colleges that offer six or more foreign languages are good colleges," or, "Any college that offers six or more foreign languages is a good college." The valid syllogism says this, but this is *not* what the invalid syllogism says. Because the argument says nothing about the entire category of the middle term, students of logic say that the term is *not distributed*. In this invalid argument, the distributed term is *good colleges*, because the first premise begins, "*All* good colleges." To make the syllogism valid, we would have to use *good colleges* as the middle term, using it in both premises so that it would link the two premises. Then our argument would read like this:

Premise: All good colleges offer six or more foreign languages.
Premise: Braxton is a good college.
Conclusion: Braxton offers six or more foreign languages.

This is a valid argument. Of course, it won't help you much if what you are trying to prove is that Braxton, a college with enrollment over 10,000, is a good college. In this case you need syllogisms that *conclude* that Braxton is a good college, not syllogisms that depend on this statement for a premise. Like the "given" in the geometry problem, a premise is something you start with, and you use it to get to your conclusion.

If you choose to use deductive reasoning, be careful how you word your arguments. Often it helps to work backwards. Suppose you want to prove that large colleges attract more professional teachers than do small colleges. This will be your conclusion, and you must do some thinking to dig out your premises. Perhaps the main reason you will discover is a difference in salary. If your research turns up the fact that large colleges have higher pay scales than small colleges have, you can use this as a premise. Now your argument looks like this:

Premise: Large colleges have the highest pay scales.
Premise: ? ? ?
Conclusion: Large colleges attract the most professional teachers.

Can you supply the appropriate second premise? It is this: All colleges with the highest pay scales attract the most professional teachers.

This is an argument you could use in your paper. You would need to give the facts you found to support the premises, and you might need to define the term *most professional teacher*. (Perhaps you could relate it to years of experience and prove that large colleges paid more for these years than their small counterparts did.)

Of course, you seldom see arguments written out in this premise-premise-conclusion form. In your paper, you might state the argument like this:

Because large colleges have the highest pay scales, and high pay attracts professional teachers, you will find the most professional teachers at the largest colleges.

Even more frequently, you will see or hear an abbreviated form of the syllogism, with the conclusion and one premise stated and the other premise implied. This is called an *enthymeme*, and it looks like this:

There are more professional teachers at large colleges because the large colleges have the highest pay. ("All colleges with the highest pay scales attract the most professional teachers" is the implied premise.)

Watch out for enthymemes! That implied premise may be one you would never accept if you saw it written out in black and white. Don't let a sneaky logician put something over on you.

I hope you can understand the *form* of these arguments whether or not you agree with their conclusions. When I say that some of them are valid arguments, I do not mean that I necessarily agree with them. An argument is valid if the form is logical, if anyone who agreed with its premises would have to agree with its conclusion. A valid argument is also a *good* argument when its premises are true and are given adequate support. Then—and only then—it becomes convincing.

PRACTICING ARGUING DEDUCTIVELY

Supply conclusions for each of the arguments below. Be sure that the syllogisms you create are valid.

1. *Premise:* Any college that does not offer financial aid cannot compete for students today.

   Premise: Pembrooke-Giddings College does not offer financial aid.

   Conclusion: ? ? ?

2. *Premise:* Colleges that offer men's sports but not women's sports violate federal guidelines.

   Premise: Muskrat U. offers men's sports but not women's sports.

   Conclusion: ? ? ?

3. *Premise:* Men who do the dishes are not macho.
   Premise: Florence's husband does the dishes.
   Conclusion: ? ? ?
4. *Premise:* All characters in soap operas are psychotic.
   Premise: Hilly Somerset is a character in a soap opera.
   Conclusion: ? ? ?
5. *Premise:* Only conservatives support the proposed amendment.
   Premise: Senator McGillicuddy supports the proposed amendment.
   Conclusion: ? ? ?

Supply the missing premises for each of the arguments below. Be sure that the syllogisms you create are valid.

1. *Premise:* All colleges that offer swimming must have pools.
   Premise: ? ? ?
   Conclusion: Pembrooke-Giddings College must have a pool.
2. *Premise:* ? ? ?
   Premise: Juanita J. opposes abortion.
   Conclusion: Juanita J. is a conservative.
3. *Premise:* ? ? ?
   Premise: Juanita J. is a conservative.
   Conclusion: Juanita J. opposes abortion.
4. *Premise:* ? ? ?
   Premise: The right to bear arms includes the right to own a handgun.
   Conclusion: The Constitution protects the right to own a handgun.
5. *Premise:* All business administration majors are practical people.
   Premise: ? ? ?
   Conclusion: Godfrey N. is not a business administration major.

Create your own syllogisms to support each of the conclusions below. Be sure that all the syllogisms are valid.

1. Your college is a good college.
2. Cats ought to be licensed.
3. Drunken drivers should automatically be jailed.
4. Alan Alda is a hero to women.
5. You are an excellent student.

USING ANALOGIES

If you choose a direct form of argument, you still have one other approach to consider—argument by analogy. Analogies are related to figurative language because they are based on comparisons of basically unrelated objects. When you compare your Chevette to another Chevette, you are not using an analogy, but when you compare it to the last dinosaur in its final days, you are.

Analogies are sometimes considered poor forms of argument because any comparison eventually breaks down. Two concepts may be similar in four or five dimensions, but when you compare them in a fifth or sixth, the comparison becomes ridiculous. Still, analogies can be especially effective arguments when the issue is an emotional one. Sometimes readers who are unable to see a point in one setting can recognize it easily in another setting and will then admit its fairness. One such example comes from Roger E. Greeley's "Busing: One More Time":

> Perhaps an analogy will help put the issue in its proper perspective. Because the issue of busing/integration is an emotional one, I believe we lose sight of the actual issue at stake. Think of this scene, a typical college football game. The air is crisp, the leaves turning, the crowd festive and enormous, the bands gaily parading and strutting their stuff, everything as usual except for one small detail. The two teams have not agreed upon any set rules by which the game will be played.
>
> One team, the Establishment team, is big, prestigious and from a relatively affluent segment of our society. The other school, from a relatively depressed and struggling community, is forced to play by the rules of the Establishment team. The officials really have no genuine judicial function to perform. They merely see to it that the Establishment team's concept of fair play is the *modus operandi* of the day.
>
> Now, obviously there is no justice in this ludicrous illustration. There must be rules that apply equally to all whether this changes the outcome of the contest or not. The big Establishment school may continue to dominate every game, but that is NOT the point—any more than quality education was the reason for integrating public education. What the Court struck down was the tyranny of the separate but equal doctrine which had resulted in two school systems, one vastly inferior to the other. Busing entered the picture when white flight and *de facto* segregation precluded integrated schools. Busing and integration may or may not result in a better educated populace, but this is truly irrelevant. What the court ordered is that we all play the same game by the same rules—period.*

DEALING WITH THE OPPOSITION

Whatever choices you have made about argumentative methods, there is one other question you need to ask yourself before you begin to write your argument: What opposing arguments are likely to occur to the audience?

Of course, if you are writing on a brand new topic, the audience's unfamiliarity with it may keep them from thinking of any responses to your reasoning, but how many new topics are there? Most topics for argumentative papers are

---

* Used with permission of Roger E. Greeley.

quite familiar controversies. Some are too familiar. Any reader who has been alive and conscious over the last few years will be able to supply a few arguments on either side of such controversies as abortion, the drinking age, and the Equal Rights Amendment. It is best to avoid these topics.

The reason you need to consider opposing arguments is that your readers will expect you to refute them. This does not mean that you devote equal time to both sides. Although some students have been taught to balance their papers in such a way, this fairness doctrine applies only to broadcast media. It is not expected of the essay writer, and it is certainly not a good way to support a thesis. You state opposing arguments in your paper for three reasons: (1) to keep your readers from supplying the arguments themselves, (2) to show that you are broad-minded enough to have considered both sides, and (3) to prove that these arguments are weaker than the arguments on the side you are supporting.

Let's see how Lee A. Iacocca, chairman of the board of Chrysler Corporation, handled the opposition's arguments in an article he wrote for *Newsweek*. Iacocca was arguing for temporary restrictions on Japanese auto imports, and his eighteen-paragraph essay contained these two paragraphs:

> Some people argue that restricting the number of Japanese cars sold in this country would hype the price of U.S. cars. That's just not so. We sell cars in a very tough market. We had competitive pricing over here long before the first boatload of Japanese cars docked in California. And we'll continue to have it in the future.
>
> Others argue that cutting down the flood of Japanese cars would help only the workers in Detroit. Do we still have to be reminded that the automobile industry accounts for one out of every six jobs across the country? Not just the jobs of autoworkers, but hundreds of thousands of jobs in America's basic industries: steel, iron, rubber, aluminum, glass, machine tools, plastics and electronics. Thousands of small companies—suppliers and dealers—depend on the auto industry.*

Never state an argument on the opposition's side unless you have an answer for it. If it really is a good argument, you can at least say something like this: "Although this argument clearly has its merits, it is outweighed by the fact that. . . ." (A comment like this may add to your credibility by making you sound objective.)

Where is the best place for this refutation section? It generally appears quite early in the essay, right after the topic has been introduced and the thesis has made clear which side you're taking. Paragraphs 2 and 3 will often take care of the refutation section, unless the opposing arguments are so strong that they need more to disprove them. Do not let refutation take up more than a third of your essay. ("It Is No Secret," the student essay in Chapter 7, contains three paragraphs of refutation among its twelve paragraphs.) Remember, simply proving that one side is wrong does not prove that the other side is right!

---

* Copyright 1981 by Newsweek, Inc. All rights reserved. Reprinted by permission.

As a part of your prewriting for any argumentative essay, an analysis of your audience (Are they likely to be in agreement, opposed, or neutral on your topic?) and a list of opposing arguments they are likely to know should be included. If you have all of this down on paper, you should be ready to develop a convincing case for your own beliefs.

ARGUMENTS TO AVOID

As you present your case, there are certain patterns of reasoning you should avoid. They are too easy for the opposition to refute because they contain errors in logic. They are known as *fallacies*, and you have already seen one in action—the fallacy of the undistributed middle term. Here is another example of this fallacy:

Premise: All male chauvinists oppose the ERA.
Premise: Phyllis Schlafly opposes the ERA.
Conclusion: Phyllis Schlafly is a male chauvinist.

Remember, the middle term is the one used in both premises, *opposes the ERA*. Since neither premise states anything about *everyone* who opposes the ERA, no conclusion can be logically drawn from this combination of premises. Although you probably see the absurdity of concluding that Phyllis Schlafly is a male chauvinist, would you see that the argument was equally invalid if it were about Joe Schmoe? You should.

Logic texts list dozens of other fallacies that illogical writers can commit, but you should be in pretty good shape if you know how to avoid a few of the most common. Here are some examples:

1. *Post hoc, ergo propter hoc* (after this, therefore, because of this—they all have Latin names, but this is the only one I really like): This argument states that event *A* caused event *B* because *A* came first. Causes do come before effects, but they also come before thousands of other unrelated occurrences. You need to show more than chronological connections to prove a statement like "The eruption of the Mount St. Helens volcano caused the breakup of the Mortimers' marriage the following week."

2. *Circular reasoning:* This is an argument that takes you back where you started. I used to use this fallacy, knowingly, when I drove a car that had no spare tire. I argued that I did not need a spare tire because I did not know how to change a tire anyway. But when a friend offered to teach me how to change a tire, I argued that I had no need for this knowledge, since I had no spare tire!

3. *Argument to ignorance:* This places the burden of proof on your opponent; it says, "If you can't *disprove* my point, my point must be true." If someone says, "Prove that you love me," and you reply, "You can't prove that I *don't* love you, so I must love you," you are arguing to ignorance.

4. *The bandwagon fallacy:* This argues that a statement is true because most people believe it. Until the discovery of the planet Pluto in 1930, most people believed that there were only eight planets in our solar system, but their belief did not make the statement true. "Most people" have been shown to be wrong over and over again.

5. *Argument about the person:* You would be committing this fallacy if you argued against an idea by stating that the person who believes it is a bad person, immoral, a communist, or undesirable for any personal reason that is unconnected with the idea itself. All causes, good as well as bad, have had some pretty kooky supporters. Vegetarianism was supported by Hitler. Christianity has been professed by a number of murderers. If you can argue against *any* idea by showing that a bad person has been in favor of it, you can argue against *all* ideas this way. Don't use this argument to attack views you dislike, or you may find it turned against your own favorite opinions.

RELATED READINGS

Student Essay

STARS AND DOLLARS: THE SPACE RESEARCH CONTROVERSY
Rick Chambers

Points to Consider

As you read the essay that follows, try to answer these questions:

1. At what point do you realize the essay's thesis?
2. Do the opening references to "Star Trek" serve any purpose? If so, what is it?
3. Is the "history of space exploration" needed? What transition does the author provide from this section to his actual argument?
4. How is the opposition dealt with? Do you think the refutation is adequate? Would the audience be likely to think of other arguments on the side of the opposition?

Used with permission of Rick Chambers.

Space—the final frontier. These are the voyages of the starship Enterprise. *Its five-year mission: To explore strange new worlds. To seek out new life and new civilizations. To boldly go where no man has gone before.*

For a span of about five years (4th to 8th grade) our family television set would dramatically speak these words every evening while a sleek spacecraft would flash across the video screen. I was one of the fanatical "Trekkies" who even today walk the earth and flash the Vulcan hand salute while murmuring the ultimate salutation: "Live long and prosper." Although my "Trekkie" days have passed away, I still watch "Star Trek" occasionally. (In fact, within 30 seconds of the start of any episode I can tell you the name and plot of the program and in what season it was produced.) "Star Trek" was, in my mind, the promise of man's conquest of space and the uniting of our planet. I have always supported space research despite arguments against it. The U.S. space program has been well worth the time, effort, and money invested in it, despite arguments to the contrary. Those arguments bear investigation, however, for they are not easily discarded or ignored. I intend to display both sides of the coin and yet show how important space research is to us.

Before presenting the pros and cons, let's refresh our memories with a brief history of space exploration. Much to the chagrin of the American people, the Russians won the first round of the "space race" when they launched the manmade satellite *Sputnik I* in October of 1957. The United States countered in January, 1958, with the launch of the satellite *Explorer I*. There was soon a flurry of space probe launches over the next several years as the two countries prepared for a more important project.

In April of 1961, the Russians again beat the United States by putting the first man into space: Cosmonaut Yuri Gagarin. In May, the United States again retaliated by launching Alan Shepard and *Freedom VII* on a short, suborbital space flight, thus beginning the program known as Project Mercury. Following this program was Project Gemini, which consisted of two-man spacecraft involved in rendezvous and docking procedures and various scientific experiments. The United States was reaching toward Earth's neighbor—the moon—in order to show up the Soviet Union, who had thus far dominated space exploration.

The American space program suffered a setback of tragic proportions on January 27, 1967. During a routine rehearsal for the launch of the first spacecraft in the new Apollo program, a fire broke out in the command module of *Apollo I*. Astronauts Virgil Grissom, Ed White, and Michigan-native Roger Chaffee burned to death before help arrived. It was then that people began to raise their eyebrows and wonder if this insane dash into space was really worth it. The United States continued the program, however, launching *Apollo VII* after months of intense research of the *Apollo I* tragedy.

On July 20, 1969, the United States and the entire world watched their televisions in fascination as the spacesuited figure of Neil Armstrong, commander of the *Apollo XI* mission, stepped off the landing pod of the lunar module and onto the surface of the moon, saying, "That's one small step for man, one giant leap for mankind." Success had been achieved; the United States had put the first man on the moon. Subsequent moon flights were made, even after an oxygen explosion in the service module of *Apollo XIII* almost doomed the three-man crew to death in space. After *Apollo XVII* came the launching of *Skylab*, America's first space station. In 1975, the space programs of the United States and the Soviet Union met in the Apollo-Soyuz Test Project, a joint rendezvous in Earth orbit of a three-man Apollo crew and a two-man Russian Soyuz team. It was also the last American-manned space mission of the 1970s. Work began on the development of the reusable Space Shuttle, the first of which has been named the *Enterprise* in honor of "Star Trek" and its symbol of universal peace and harmony. The first launch is slated for March of 1981.

Space exploration has not been idled since Apollo/Soyuz, however. The Viking Project put two remote landers on the surface of the planet Mars. Jupiter has been visited by the *Pioneer* space probe and by *Voyagers I* and *II*. In November of 1980, *Voyager I* flew by the ringed planet Saturn, with *Voyager II* due in August of 1981. In the planning stage is the Galileo Mission, which will consist of two space probes: one probe will establish orbit around Jupiter, and the other will plunge into the turbulent Jovian atmosphere as it transmits data back to Earth. Also being planned is a 1986 satellite rendezvous with Halley's Comet, which will be lighting up the sky when it returns to the inner solar system in that year. Still other missions are being discussed and planned.

There is a stumbling block in the path of the U.S. Space Program, however: opposition. While this opposition utilizes many arguments to downgrade space research, we will analyze only two of them. One of the arguments is also the most common. Isaac Asimov, in his article "Payoff in Outer Space" (*Space World*, June 1978), reported that the cost of sending man to the moon in the 1960s was about $24 billion. Even with today's inflation, that is a huge sum of money. And what good did it do, besides satisfy our American ego by beating the Soviets to the moon? Why, that money could have been put to use to solve problems on earth such as poverty and starvation. We should invest our money down here rather than shoot it off into space at 36,000 miles per hour.

Another argument against space research is somewhat connected to the cost opposition: Is space exploration really *necessary*? In his article "Looking for Life, Neglecting the Living" (*Space World*, June 1978), John Holt cites two examples of what he calls unnecessary space research. One example involved a statement by a space program spokesman on the research being done by an aerospace firm on the intensive raising of edible fish; he said that was one reason the space program needed support, so that we could raise food more effectively on earth. Holt showed great curiosity about how *space* research was necessary in order to learn how to replenish the food supply on *Earth*. Fish do not live long in the vacuum of space.

Holt's second example was drawn from another statement made by the same spokesman. The speaker bragged about how advanced our system of long-range weather forecasting had become due to the launching of space satellites to monitor Earth's weather conditions. However, Holt observed that most weather prediction is done by studying temperature, air pressure, humidity, and wind direction *here on Earth*. Besides, how advanced and accurate had weather prediction *really* become? Says Holt, "Much of the precision of modern weather forecasting is pure illusion; the statement 'Chance of precipitation: 50%' sounds very scientific, but what it adds up to is 'Well, it might rain, and then again it might not.'"

These are all strong arguments, but they don't stand up against the facts. Space research *has* accomplished much, and while it is by no means cheap, it is not as expensive as one might think. In "Payoff in Outer Space," Isaac Asimov divided the $24 billion figure mentioned earlier by the number of American people, arriving at a figure of $12 per person annually paid. He also reported that the American people spend $35 per person on alcoholic beverages and $17 per person on tobacco products. Asimov says, "It might be argued that alcohol and tobacco bring their addicts short-termed conviviality, satisfaction, and happiness, and that is worth all the cirrhosis and cancer they can get. Perhaps so. I won't argue. It may be that I don't understand and shouldn't be so short-sighted as to wish to deprive people of their fun diseases." To further this defense, Asimov reported that $500 per person annually is spent on war preparation. This is money spent for a war we cannot afford to fight, be it nuclear or non-nuclear. At best, a war would deplete our vanishing resources; at worst, a war could destroy the human race.

Rather than cost, Dr. Christopher Kraft cites the profits of the space program (*Space World*, April 1978). He reported an economic return of 33% from space research. Aerospace exports in the mid 1970s totaled $5.1 billion and achieved a favorable net balance of $1.7 billion, according to Dr. Kraft. These arguments shoot down the cost opposition undeniably.

Space research is a necessity. In "Payoff in Outer Space," Asimov shows several reasons why the space program must continue. Our world is rapidly running low on natural resources used to produce energy. With continued research, it is possible that huge relay stations could be built in space to collect solar energy and beam it by microwave to large receptor fields on earth for distribution to cities and homes. Also, with the problem of an escalating population growth on our planet, projects have been devised to establish large space colonies which would contain miniature cities, workable farmlands, and even blue sky, if the colony was large enough. Such structures could hold thousands, perhaps even millions, of Earthers in an artificial world. The most exciting part of all this is that these possibilities are likely to emerge within our lifetimes.

The most important reason for the continuation of space exploration is the ideal represented by "Star Trek." Mankind *can* unite and rise above the darkness of our time and say, as Captain Kirk of the starship *Enterprise* said, "I will not kill today." Together, hand in hand, we, the people of Earth, can unite, with the help of God, and strive toward a common goal: "To boldly go where no man has gone before."

Professional Essay

THE AGE OF INDIFFERENCE
Philip G. Zimbardo

Points to Consider

As you read the essay that follows, try to answer these questions:

1. What does the author mean by the *hacker mentality*? Can you diagram its causes, according to the essay? Are these causes necessary, sufficient, or contributing?

2. In addition to showing the causes of isolation, does this essay show its effects? What could some of these be?
3. Does the author substantiate the prediction that "tomorrow will be even worse"? What does he mean by this, specifically? Do you agree?
4. Do you think his concluding solution, admittedly "corny and unsophisticated," is a workable one? Why or why not?

Reprinted from *Psychology Today* Magazine. Copyright © 1980 Ziff-Davis Publishing Company. Used with permission.

In some schools where computers are used as tutors, children have reported developing a closer, friendlier relationship with their ever-reliable machine than with Ms. Dove and her sundry personal idiosyncrasies. As these kiddies mature, some of them are likely to become "hackers," members of a new subculture of grown-up electronic whiz kids obsessed by interacting with computers. Hackers spend long hours at night or early in the morning, when "downtime" is shorter, playing with their programs and sending messages via electronic bulletin boards to hacker associates seated at terminals a few feet away. Fascination with the computer becomes an addiction, and as with most addictions, the "substance" that gets abused is human relationships.

Not just in schools but in society as a whole, the hacker mentality is upon us, with or without the computer as a rationalization for putting other people at the bottom of our priority stack. There are forces at work in society increasing both the sense and the reality of our separateness from one another. It is as if we were suffering from a mysterious kind of "legionnaire's disease" of which the chief symptoms are isolation and a loss of naturalness in our relations with other people.

I used to believe that this separateness was the exclusive problem of the timid, introverted shys. For the past eight years I have been studying the personal and social dynamics of shyness, and I know that 40 percent of Americans quietly claim to be of that disposition. I also know that a surprising 25 percent of these sufferers became shy *after* leaving the universal self-concern and awkwardness of adolescence. I am aware, too, that self-help books for the shy are selling well; that shyness clinics are springing up; that social psychologists who used to be interested only in social affiliation are writing textbooks including chapters on loneliness, based on research and scientific meetings devoted to this fascinating phenomenon.

But shyness alone does not account for all of the isolation that marks contemporary society. My research team has surveyed, interviewed, observed, experimented upon, and done therapy with a vast number of shy people (reported in part in *Shyness: What It Is, What to Do about It*). While we were documenting their conversational awkwardness, passivity, reluctance to initiate social contact, and general social phobia, a curious discovery emerged—about a comparison group of nonshys. They do not show the same motivated avoidance and inhibition syndrome characteristic of their shy peers; theirs is an apparently unmotivated indifference. Unlike the shys, many of whom still *want* to connect, to have friends, date, marry, share intimate feelings, the nonshys often seem not to mind being isolated. Their conversations are rather banal and minimal, usually humorless, without signs of spontaneity, personal involvement, or joy in sharing ideas and feelings with friends. One gets the impression of watching a generation of clones of Mr. Spock from "Star Trek." Human speech is there, intelligence is evident, but the executive command programming does not include feeling or affection.

This fall, the class of 1984 will take its place in colleges and high schools, and it will be time to find out whether or not George Orwell's Big Brother prophecy of mind control comes true. By the time these students have graduated, I believe, the message they will have learned will prove to be not Orwellian but Garboesque: "Big Person is *not* watching you. He doesn't have time to care about you anymore. She'd rather be alone."

Don't get me wrong; I'm an optimist. I have always believed that people can control their destinies by work, self-discipline, humor, love of life, concern for other people, and a sensitivity to the tactics of manipulation by the authorities. But tonight is different from all previous nights in America, and tomorrow will be even worse. As the father of three children, it is with sadness that I make such an assertion, and with the hope it will be shown to be a false alarm.

I believe that the basic quality of our social lives is being diluted, distorted, and demeaned by a host of profound structural changes in society. Because these new forces are systemic and not just transient developmental stages, they won't simply be outgrown but are likely to become permanent fixtures in our daily existence. The consequences are serious. I know of no more potent killer than isolation. There is no more destructive influence on physical and mental health than the isolation of you from me and of us from them. It has been shown to be a central agent in the etiology of depression, paranoia, schizophrenia, rape, suicide, mass murder, and a wide variety of disease states.

There is no dearth of research, anecdotes, and observations demonstrating the pervasiveness of the disorder I am talking about. A recently published report by Ralph Larkin, a sociologist, on the crises facing suburban youth underscores some aspects of this new malaise of the spirit. The children of American affluence are depicted as passively accepting a way of life that they view as empty and meaningless. The syndrome includes a constricted expression of emotions, a low threshold of boredom, and an apparent absence of joy in anything that is not immediately consumable; hence the significance of music, drugs, alcohol, sex, and status-symbol possessions.

According to a high school guidance counselor, the current generation of students differs in at least one way from the young people of their parents' day: "Kids hate school much more now than they did then. I mean the word *hate* and underline it." But this hatred is among the few strong emotions they allow themselves to feel about anything.

Where do we witness displays of strong emotion anymore, except at sports events and rock concerts? And even when we witness them, how many of us will acknowledge as much or dare to share the emotion? On my way to visit my sister because she is dying of cancer, I explain the reason for my absence to student assistants. "Have a nice trip!" chortles one. "See you when you get back," says another. And that is all they say. They haven't learned to extend comfort to another in distress. Too heavy.

Another anecdote, different but just as telling: "I hate myself for having this daydream, but I can't help enjoying it every time it pops into my head," confides Denny, a sophomore in my introductory psychology class of 680 students. "Everyone else fails the final exam, all hundreds upon hundreds of them, the nerds, the jocks, the freaks, and I get an A. Mine is the only A, floating high and dry in a sea of failure. Then somebody, everybody, would have to notice me, because I'd be special."

Assuming that the narcissism of shyness was fueling this fantasy, I launched into my counseling spiel of "shyness-can-be-overcome-if-you-work-at-it-and . . ." "Hold on, don't get me wrong," he objected. "I'm outgoing, an extravert. I used to make friends easily, but it seems as if there's no value to that anymore. No one has time to go beyond the superficial level of 'How's it going?' 'Have a nice day!' 'See you around,' and stupid stuff like that. There must be something wrong with *me*, because I just can't seem to connect in any meaningful way to the people I live with. We are all working so hard to make it that maybe we don't have any energy left over for making it with each other."

The student health service at the university reassured this young man that his problem was a common psychiatric symptom of alienation and loneliness. In fact, it ranks near the top of the list of symptoms students present to this and similar clinics at other colleges when they seek professional help for their "attachment deficiencies."

Signs of alienation show up long before college. Visit the Serramonte Mall in San Francisco, the Smithtown Mall in Long Island, Florida's Broward County Mall, the Glendale Shopping Mall in Arizona. What you witness when school is out are mass minglings of kids too young to drive wandering about in the artificial air of a totally enclosed space amid artificial flowers, canned music, junk-food dispensers, and plastic twittering canaries. In smaller clusters are the elderly, keeping warm in winter and cool in summer, but never talking with the youngsters, except when the generations become adversaries over a particular piece of Astroturf. Neither side smiles, except when they detect that the mannequin in the window is a real woman pretending to be wooden—you see, she moves once every five minutes.

When the shopping-center kids get a little older, they escape the anxieties attendant on formal social dating (one-next-to-one) by dating in clusters. "We're all going for a pizza, wanna come along?" The tone seems to add, "No big deal if you say yes, no loss if you don't come."

Plenty of young adults who do date as couples find it less than satisfying. A handsome, successful television director tells me he has problems with women after the fifth date. He is concerned, wants help. For the first five innings, he has exciting, preprogrammed scripts for entertaining his dates. He strikes out when he runs out of scenarios and has to "be himself." Like many of his peers, he has never learned to be intimate, to relate closely to one other person, to make disclosures about his past, about his fears, frustrations, and future plans; in short, to reveal the private self behind the public facade. Disclosure presupposes trust, which in turn is nourished by sharing and gives substance and meaning to intimate contacts. But whom can you really trust these days?

If you yourself have switched from being a team player in life to going it alone more often, if you seek out your friends less often than you used to, it may be good for you, but it is a loss for the rest of us. Maybe you switched because we "weren't saying anything anyway," or because we "no longer turned you on," or because you had come to expect more of us while giving less of yourself. Or maybe, as a woman told me in Atlanta, "There's times peoples just be tired of peoples." Or then again, the message might be the one that the mother of one of my shy freshmen passed along to him: "Do you realize how boring you are?" Better not to play the game at all than to be seen as boring by the other players?

Yet another sign of how alienated people are: not one of a dozen students in my wife's college seminar on sex roles could realistically imagine making a long-term commitment to one partner. "It would be nice if it happened, but it's not very realistic to expect it," a student said.

What about short-term commitments simply to pass the time of day with people occupying common space with you? Our world is becoming like an elevator: "No talking, smiling, or eye contact allowed without written consent of the management." Next time you shop in a supermarket, do a study, make a word count of the conversations between shoppers in line or with the checkout person. Then try to use your data to prove that your subjects are not mute or deaf. The silence is not confined to America, either. Even the loquacious Italians, whose love for life persists despite daily reports of political disaster and economic uncertainty, look to me like automatons as I watch them in one of the new supermarkets in Florence or Rome. No time to say "Hello" or *"Ciao,"* to talk of zucchini or kings.

Our brave new world is one in which the basic social unit is the large, impersonal institution. In such institutions, authority is concentrated in the hands of a few remote power brokers. Decision making begins with concerns for cost-effectiveness, profitability margins, and efficient management of behavior, and ends with rules that must be followed—or else. If the rules are followed, everything runs smoothly, and the mark of impersonality is stamped on each product, each of us. Institutions can't do their thing unless they can count on the predictability and compliance of those they "serve." Thus there can be no spontaneity, impulsivity, strong emotion, dissent, opposition, time to think anything over, no time to be "just people." Today's young people are being forged into cogs in the corporate structure. And they are the ones who will eventually control our world.

Cult leaders and their management teams know all this. There they come, at least 2,000 strong, offering simple solutions to complex problems, love-bombing affection-starved youngsters. Cults attract a following not necessarily through political, religious, or economic ideology, but through offering the illusion of friendship, of non-contingent love. You exist, you are one of us, you get your fair share of our love and respect. (Wasn't that the message families once communicated?)

If there is a Devil, it is not through sin that he opposes God. The Devil's strategy for our times is to trivialize human existence in a number of ways: by isolating us from one another while creating the delusion that the reasons are time pressures, work demands, or anxieties created by economic uncertainty; by fostering narcissism and the fierce competition to be No. 1; by showing us the personal gains to be enjoyed from harboring prejudices and the losses from not moving out whenever the current situation is uncomfortable. Fostering in us the illusion of self-reliance, that sly Devil makes us mock the need for social responsibility and lets us forget how to go about being our brother's keeper—even if we were to want to.

Surely one cause of the growing sense of disengagement in our society is the rise in middle-class affluence since the 1950s, which has allowed an enormous number of people to buy space, privacy, and exclusive-use permits and services. The move to suburbia is a move away from too many people too close. The well-tended front lawn is the modern moat that keeps the barbarians at bay. Every occupant in a separate bedroom with private toilet, personal television, telephone, and hi-fi reduces hassles and conflicts. No need to share.

In the quest for upward mobility, the middle class sends its children away to colleges, moves to wherever its jobs demand, and does more and more of its business on the road. The consequence is a generation of children who have been uprooted time after time until, as one said to me, "I don't want to bother making friends. It's not worth the effort, because we'll be gone soon and it hurts more to leave good friends than casual acquaintances." The same is true of parents, who may find it even more difficult to make new friends in strange places. And as more of us take our paper-work jobs home or our jobs take us away from home, there is less time for family and neighborhood contacts.

Geographical mobility also strains the bonds of extended families. With relatives thousands of miles apart, ritual gatherings become rarer, and relatives become curious aliens to our children. The zero population growth movement has as one of its unintended consequences children with few siblings or cousins and eventually with few aunts or uncles. The paucity of relatives, coupled with the fact of delayed childbearing and the high divorce rate, mean there will be fewer of us with a sense of primal ties to many kin and of roots that run deep into one place, our "home."

By 1990, about one-third of all young people under 18 will have parents who have divorced at least once. Almost 60 percent of divorced couples have one or more children now under 18 years old. The number of children involved in divorce has risen from half a million in 1960 to 1.1 million now. Divorced mothers of children under 18 are increasingly likely to be in the labor force, which takes them away from home for long periods. I think a lasting legacy for the children of divorce is a deeply felt loss of trust in authorities (like parents, who have let them down) and in institutions (such as marriage, whose for-better-or-worse slogan won't sell even in Peoria).

Finally, youthful cynicism has been fed by watching, on the evening news, or in some cases, "up close and personal," almost everyone going out on strike for better bucks—teachers, police, fire departments—all, apparently, in it for the money, not love of a profession. Widespread cynicism about institutions seems to be evident across the board. How to trust anything, given the moral disgrace of Watergate, the vision of criminals being media-hyped to promote their best-selling exposes, and the weakening of national pride after Korea, Vietnam, OPEC control of economy, and the Bay of Pigs rerun in the desert of Iran?

As corny and unsophisticated as it sounds, the only escape from hackerdom is to think of people as our most cherished resource. We need to work hard at reestablishing family rituals, such as family meals without TV and with meaningful conversation. Parents and teachers should show more concern for the social-emotional development of children and put less emphasis on intellectual competition. We must oppose systems and procedures that deny our uniqueness while spreading depersonalization and anonymity in the guise of efficiency.

Social-support networks provide emotional sustenance, informative feedback, and validation of self-worth. They have been shown to buffer the adverse impact of change on physical and mental health, and it is important to create enough of them for everyone to have a chance to become a valued part of a life-support system.

Maybe the economic downturn the nation is facing is a blessing in disguise. Parents will not be able to afford divorce as readily and may eventually discover that they have something of value in common—as many of our parents did. More children may return home after college, and communal living and expanding, elastic family structures may become necessities. Sharing instead of hoarding, and caring instead of flaunting, may even become fashionable.

While waiting for all that to happen, it is well to reevaluate the survival strategies that many of the poor—immigrants, blacks, and other minorities—have used to advantage in the past when their money was soft and times were hard. Without a false sense of personal invulnerability, and with an accurate appraisal of the power of the "system" to overwhelm all in its path, they maintained their dignity by reaffirming family values and by tightening the bonds of friendship. Survival demands collective action; "alone" is for gravestones in hacker cemeteries.

WRITING ASSIGNMENTS

In doing any of the assignments for this chapter, you should strive to meet the following objectives. If you meet all six, you will get a satisfactory grade.

Objectives

1. Turn in your prewriting, showing the decisions made about your topic and your audience and including your thesis sentence and outline.
2. Develop your thesis into a detailed, well-organized essay that follows the outline.
3. Follow the pattern called for in the assignment (analysis or classification,

cause and effect, or a variety of argument), avoiding the common pitfalls listed in this chapter.

4. Write an introduction designed to interest your potential reader and a persuasive, polished conclusion.
5. Use standard American spelling.
6. Proofread to eliminate any unmarked sentence fragments, comma splices, run-on sentences, subject-verb agreement errors, errors in verb form, faulty tense shifts, errors in use or omission of apostrophes, incorrect uses of commas, semicolons, or colons, or pronoun agreement errors.

Problems with pronouns are covered in Section 4 of the Handbook. I'll cover only the most common errors here.

Remember that a pronoun is really a stand-in for a noun. If the original noun is plural, a singular pronoun can't take its place, and the opposite is also true. A singular noun requires a singular pronoun. Of course, sometimes it is hard to decide what noun a pronoun is actually replacing.

He changed the rules of the game so much that it was unrecognizable.

He changed the rules of the game so much that they were unrecognizable.

Which would you say? Either one is correct, depending on whether the game was unrecognizable or the rules were.

The most difficult agreement problems come from using the pronouns *anyone*, *everyone*, *someone*, and *everybody*. These words have traditionally been considered replacements for *singular* nouns, even though their idea applies to groups of people. Speakers of English have used the words as plurals for so long, however, that sentences like this one are generally becoming acceptable (except to many English teachers):

Anyone who cares about their country should see this film.

Accepting the plural *their* for *anyone* does get around the awkward decision between *his country* and *her country*. Still, many people object to this use. To be on the safe side, change the sentence to something obviously plural:

All people who care about their country should see this film.

One further warning: When you begin by talking about *the student* or *a student*, do not switch to *they* in your next sentence.

Writing Assignment 9-1 This assignment calls for an analysis or classification essay. You may write on one of the topics suggested in the Practicing Analysis and Classification exercise if you wish, or you may choose some other topic. It should be a topic you know sufficiently well that you can analyze it by breaking it down into its components and telling how these work together or classify it by dividing it into groups of related items so that the whole topic can be better understood.

The prewriting step should include whatever technique will work best to help you generate ideas (in this case, probably a classification tree), your decisions about your topic and your audience, your thesis sentence, and a brief outline—either a topic outline or a sentence outline.

For the writing step, develop this outline into a detailed, well-organized paper. As you write, watch for the five pitfalls discussed in the chapter—obvious groupings, inconsistent categories, overlapping categories, either-or categories, and dull introductions that place the thesis first. Make a special effort to write an effective introduction and conclusion.

For the postwriting step, proofread your final draft carefully, being sure to correct the spelling and to eliminate any unmarked fragments, comma splices, run-on sentences, subject-verb agreement errors, errors in verb form, faulty tense shifts, errors in use or omission of apostrophes, incorrect uses of commas, semicolons, or colons, or pronoun agreement errors.

Writing Assignment 9-2 For this assignment you will need to write a cause-and-effect essay. You may want to look back at the topics in the Practicing Cause-and-Effect Analysis exercise for some ideas, or perhaps Zimbardo's essay started you thinking about some contemporary phenomenon whose causes or effects you would like to analyze. Perhaps in one of your other classes you have been studying an event, a movement, or a relationship that would lend itself to cause-and-effect analysis. Any of these topics would be fine.

For the prewriting step, make the important decisions about your topic and audience and try out whatever techniques work best to help you come up with ideas. Develop these ideas into a thesis sentence and an outline to support it. Either a sentence outline or a topic outline will do.

In the writing step, you should develop this outline into a detailed, well-organized paper. Watch out for the four pitfalls cause-and-effect papers are prone to: forgetting that causes can also be effects, oversimplifying, confusing causation with correlation, and making sweeping generalizations. Avoid these in your essay. Make a special effort to write an effective introduction and conclusion.

For the postwriting step, proofread your final draft carefully, being sure to correct the spelling and to eliminate any unmarked fragments, comma splices, run-on sentences, subject-verb agreement errors, errors in verb form, faulty tense shifts, errors in use or omission of apostrophes, incorrect uses of commas, semicolons, or colons, or pronoun agreement errors.

Writing Assignment 9-3 An argumentative essay will fit this assignment if it includes *two* of the following kinds of argument: inductive reasoning, deductive reasoning, and argument by analogy. Any current controversy—personal, local, national, or universal—makes an appropriate topic. If you can take a stand (your thesis sentence) on the issue and support that stand logically, the topic should be suitable. If you need ideas, read newspapers and news magazines, listen to arguments in the cafeteria, think back over the arguments you've found yourself in during the last two or three months. There must be a topic just waiting for you, but be wise enough to avoid the really overworked topics that may put your bored reader to sleep. If you write on the legalization of marijuana, you'd better have something really striking to say!

Use any appropriate idea-generating technique for the prewriting step. When you have made up your mind about your audience, your topic, and your main idea, compose a thesis sentence. As part of the prewriting, write an outline—either topic or sentence—to support this thesis.

The writing step calls for developing this outline into a well-organized, detailed paper. Be sure to avoid the six kinds of fallacies discussed in this chapter: the undistributed middle term; *post hoc, ergo propter hoc*; circular reasoning; argument to ignorance; the bandwagon fallacy; and argument about the person. Instead of using these, use at least two kinds of reasoning—inductive argument, deductive argument, or argument by analogy. Where you have used these, mark the left margin with an abbreviation, *ded, ind,* or *an.* Make a special effort to write an effective introduction and conclusion.

For the postwriting step, proofread your final draft carefully, being sure to correct the spelling and to eliminate any unmarked fragments, comma splices, run-on sentences, subject-verb agreement errors, errors in verb form, faulty tense shifts, errors in use or omission of apostrophes, incorrect uses of commas, semicolons, or colons, or pronoun agreement errors.

Writing Assignment 9-4

For this assignment, you will need to find an argument to refute. There are many good places to look for these—editorials or letters columns in your local paper, syndicated columns in newspapers or news magazines, the *Congressional Record*, advertising that editorializes, books on controversial subjects, or pamphlets put out by various action groups. Your librarian can help you to find an appropriate argument to refute, if you get stuck.

The prewriting step calls for finding the argument and reading it carefully before you begin your prewriting technique to generate the ideas you will use in refuting it. You will actually be writing an analysis of the argument, breaking it down into its parts and showing where it went wrong. If you can find any of the six fallacies in it, be sure to point these out. Your thesis sentence should summarize your major criticism of the argument. You will also need to create an outline—either topic or sentence—showing how you intend to develop this thesis. Be sure to include a copy of the argument you are refuting as a part of your prewriting.

For the writing step, develop this outline into a detailed, well-organized paper that points out what is wrong with the argument you chose to refute. Keep in mind the suggestions in this chapter on dealing with the opposition. Show that your arguments are stronger and more reasonable than the ones you are refuting. Do not include any of the fallacies in your argument. Make a special effort to write an effective introduction and conclusion.

For the postwriting step, proofread your final draft carefully, being sure to correct the spelling and to eliminate any unmarked fragments, comma splices, run-on sentences, subject-verb agreement errors, errors in verb form, faulty tense shifts, errors in use or omission of apostrophes, incorrect uses of commas, semicolons, or colons, or pronoun agreement errors.

CHAPTER 10

POSTWRITING: REDUCING NOISE

I wanted to call this chapter "Postwriting: Eliminating Noise," but that would have been too idealistic. We can never *eliminate* noise in the communication process. Remember, noise is any distraction that interferes with the receiver's sensory receptors or with the process of interpretation. Think of the thousands of possible distractions which you, the writer, have no control over: Your reader is suffering from eyestrain, needs new glasses, has a migraine headache, has taken some medication or illegal drug that makes the letters on the page appear to be just a blur. Family problems, financial worries, or even some joyful event are uppermost in your reader's mind, and these thoughts keep interfering with the thoughts you are trying to put there. Actual noise—radio broadcasts, ringing telephones, fighting children—affects your reader's concentration on your message. It would be foolish to think that the writer could ever eliminate noise in the communication process.

Still, much of the noise in written communication is put there by the writer. Awkwardly worded sentences, poorly chosen words, ink blots, misspellings, misplaced or nonexistent punctuation marks—these are all distractions caused by the writer. They are worse than distractions that merely prevent the intended message from getting through, because they convey another, unintended message: The writer didn't care enough to send the very best.

There are two parts to the postwriting step, editing and proofreading. Although they overlap, editing usually comes first. You are editing when you go over your rough draft to make changes that improve it for presentation. Editing may include such large changes as moving one paragraph to an earlier position in the paper or such small changes as substituting the word *infer* for *imply*. Editing improves the sound of the paper. Proofreading concentrates more on the looks of the final draft, changes like spelling and punctuation that would not be evident to someone who merely heard the paper read aloud. These changes may seem minor to you, but they can make a big difference to your readers.

TESTING YOUR SKILLS

You've been editing and proofreading your papers for some time now, looking for specific errors listed in the assignment objectives as well as making other improvements that occurred to you to create smoother, clearer sentences. You should be pretty proficient at these skills by now. Why don't you test your abilities on the following passage, marking any changes you think are needed, and then comparing them with my suggested changes? (I have deliberately inserted twenty-four mistakes.)

Have you heard the old saying, "Kid's say the darnedest things?" Well, it seem to be particularly true of mine. There embarrassing comments, as if deliberately planned always emerge at a strategic moment. An episode from 1976 would be an example.

The occasion was important: My youngest brother Jay had just proposed to another WMU student and had been excepted. Since both sets of future in-laws lived at about equal distances from Kalamazoo, I decided to give a celebration dinner and providing them with a chance to get acquainted. Dinner went well, the food was delicious. The adults were on their best behavior, and I had hired a baby sitter to keep the kids out of the adult's hair. There were three kids: my sons, then four and eight, and the twelve-year old sister of the bride-to-be. Both the male baby sitter and my son, Greg, were tremendously impressed with her; because she was the most voluptuous twelve-year-old you could imagine. I could tell Greg was smitten, he wished he were older then not-quite-nine.

You also need to know that Greg had just recieved an entertaining sex education book, one of the Peter Mayle series, "Where Did I Come From?" Gregs' enthusiasm for his new book and his desire to impress the preteen bombshell burst out at just the wrong moment. When the polite, stilted conversation among the grownups had came to a momentary halt, we heard a loud voice from the next room: "Hey Lisa, do you want to know how to make a baby? Ive got this great book!"

How many changes did you make? Compare your list with mine; there are other possible wordings, but these are the spots that needed changing:

1. Kid's

    should be *Kids*
    (This isn't possessive.)

2. things?"

    should be *things*"?
    (The whole sentence—not the quoted part—is a question.)

3. it seem

    should be *it seems*
    (This corrects the subject-verb agreement problem.)

4. There

    should be *Their*
    (The comments belong to them, so this should be a possessive pronoun.)

5. planned always

    should be *planned, always*
    (Two commas are needed to set off "as if deliberately planned.")

6. 1976 would be an example.

    should be *1976 is an example*
    (What's keeping it from being an example? This use of *would be* is incorrect.)

7 and 8. youngest brother Jay

> should be *youngest brother, Jay,*
> (Two commas are needed to set off *Jay,* since the name is not needed to identify him. I can't have *two* youngest brothers.)

9. excepted

> should be *accepted*
> (His proposal had been agreed to, not omitted.)

10. providing

> should be *provide*
> ("To give . . . and providing" is not parallel structure.)

11. well, the food

> should be *well; the food*
> (This is a comma splice as written.)

12. adult's hair

> should be *adults' hair*
> (More than one of us had hair.)

13. twelve-year old sister

> should be *twelve-year-old sister*
> (Another hyphen is needed to make three words into one modifier.)

14 and 15. my son, Greg,

> should be *my son Greg*
> (Since I have two sons, the name is needed for identification and should not be set off with commas. This is the opposite of numbers 7 and 8.)

16. her; because

> should be *her, because*
> (The clause beginning with *because* is dependent, so a semicolon is not needed. Actually, it would be possible to have no punctuation at all.)

17. smitten, he

> should be *smitten; he*
> (This is another comma splice.)

18. older then

> should be *older than*
> (*Than* is needed for the comparison. It is not the same word as *then.*)

19. recieved

> should be *received*
> (*I* before *e* except after *c*, or when sounded like *a* as in *neighbor* and *weigh.*)

20. "Where Did I Come From?"

> should be <u>Where Did I Come From?</u>
> (Titles of books are underlined, indicating that they would be in italics if italic print were available.)

21. Gregs'

> should be *Greg's*
> (His name is Greg, and there is only one of him.)

22. had came

> should be *had come*
> (*Came* is simple past tense; it can't take a helping verb.)

23. "Hey Lisa,

> should be *"Hey, Lisa,*
> (The name of the person spoken to needs to be set off with commas.)

24. Ive

> should be *I've*
> (The apostrophe takes the place of the omitted *ha.*)

Although it is a little hard to tell which of these changes are editing corrections and which are proofreading corrections, I consider nos. 3, 6, 9, 10, and 22 errors that should be corrected in the editing process. They change the sound of the writing, and you should catch such mistakes before you write your final draft. Of course, you probably catch some spelling errors and problems like comma splices in the rough draft form, too. But if these manage to appear in the final draft, it is still not too late to correct them. By the final draft it is almost too late to rearrange the words, sentences, or paragraphs.

Here is a second passage for you to edit and proofread. This time I haven't included the answers. Rewrite the anecdote until it pleases you, and then compare your version with a version done by one of your classmates.

One of my mothers most embarassing moments came about indirectly because of Baby Sue, her dog. Although Baby Sue was a Saint Bernard with a pedigree my brother got her from the Humane Society. For $25 my brother got the dog, her papers, and the previous owners' name—Stanley Hubbard. He was also cautioned not to contact Mr. Hubbard about the dog; because Mrs. Hubbard, who didn't like Saint Bernards had told her husband that she had sold Baby Sue. He didn't know that the dog had went to the Human Society.

My mother had no intention of contacting Stanley Hubbard although she saw him frequently, he was a teacher in the same school where she was a counselor. That is, she had no intention until Baby Sue run away. My brother and her searched frantically all evening without finding the dog. She resolved to check with Hubbard the next morning to see if Baby Sue had returned to the Hubbard's house.

When she seen Hubbard in the cafeteria the next day; she wasn't sure how to bring up the subject of Baby Sue. She finally cleared her throat anxiously and plunged in: "Stanley, I'd like too speak to you for a moment about something personal. Its about Baby Sue."

"Baby Sue?" Hubbard cried his face showed alarm.

My mother finally understood the reason for his alarm when she found out that he and the Stanley Hubbard who had owned Baby Sue was two different people. Can you imagine his relief when he discovered that Baby Sue was a dog.

How many places did you make changes? There are nineteen intentional problems in the story, but you may have chosen to revise other parts as well.

10 POSTWRITING: REDUCING NOISE   **169**

A CHECKLIST FOR EDITING

Since you are editing to make your paper sound better, it really helps to read it aloud. Try to read naturally. If you stumble at any sentence, put a little mark in the margin to tell yourself that this spot needs reworking. After all, if you had trouble reading it—and you wrote it—think what trouble it might cause for someone who had never seen it before. There is almost always some simpler, clearer way to convey the same idea without forcing your reader to read the sentence twice. If you can't choose between two possible wordings, ask a friend's advice. This kind of assistance in editing is almost always considered legitimate help rather than cheating. Most teachers encourage students to read their papers to someone else who can judge whether or not they have communicated their intended ideas. Just remember that your friend is not being evaluated. The ultimate responsibility for the editing, like the grade, is yours.

As part of the editing process, you should ask yourself these questions about any paper you write:

1. Does everything in this paper support the thesis?
2. Have I given enough evidence to support the thesis?
3. Is the evidence arranged in a sensible, effective order?
4. Are all examples stated in enough detail that my readers can visualize what I mean?
5. Is the opening paragraph attention-getting without being misleading?
6. Does the conclusion sound finished?
7. Is the rest of the paper, the body, at least twice as long as the introduction and the conclusion put together?
8. Have I used a variety of sentence lengths and structures?
9. Do the paragraph divisions help my reader understand my meaning?
10. Are most paragraphs fully developed, running two-thirds of a page or so?
11. Have I provided adequate transitions from one idea to the next?
12. Is the tone of the paper consistent?
    (This can be difficult to answer. Abrupt shifts in tone may be evident when a paper written in general English includes brief snatches of formal English or nonstandard English. If your attitude toward your reader or subject seems suddenly different, you may have a problem with a shift in tone.)
13. Does this paper meet the requirements of the assignment?
14. Does it do what I set out to do?

If you can answer all of these questions positively, you are probably ready to write your final draft of the paper. If some of your answers are no, you may need to write another revised draft before the final one. How many drafts you will need depends upon your approach to writing and varies from one writer to another. Some writers may write as many as four or five rough drafts before they are ready to do the final version. You will usually find that a thorough job of prewriting, however, will reduce the number of drafts you will need. If you have sketched out the order of your points before you start the actual writing, you will probably not spend much time moving paragraphs around, drawing arrows, and writing "insert here." In addition, as you internalize more and more of the conventions of written English, you should find that your writing requires less editing than it once required. You need to develop the skill of writing an acceptable first draft, as there will be times—in-class assignments and essay examinations, for instance—when there will be absolutely no time for a second draft. However, you are expected to take the necessary time to compose more than one draft when you are writing outside class. Do not make the mistake of handing in a rough draft then; it will surely be recognized for what it is and graded accordingly.

A CHECKLIST FOR PROOF-READING

When you proofread your final copy, you do *not* want to be concerned with the ideas in the paper. You are reading for mechanics, not content, so you need to unlearn everything you know about speed reading and reading for comprehension. To keep from reading what you intended to write instead of what you actually did write, let as much time pass between the last writing and the final proofreading as you possibly can. If you can put the paper aside until the next day, you will have a better chance of coming to it cold and seeing what you have really written.

You may need to proofread two or three times, but you should try to answer these questions in the process:

1. Is each sentence really a sentence? (To answer this, try reading from capital letter to end punctuation mark. If your sentence is missing an independent clause and you don't want to add one, identify it as a fragment by putting an asterisk in front of it.)
2. Are the commas and semicolons in the right places? (Try reading from one mark of punctuation to the next.)
3. Whenever I have used a pronoun, is it clear what noun it replaces?
4. Are there any verb problems—inconsistent tenses or disagreement with subjects?
5. Is any dialogue clearly punctuated and labeled to indicate who is speaking?
6. Is everything spelled correctly?

Obviously, if you are going to answer all of these questions with confidence, you need to know the basic rules of grammar pretty thoroughly. Your experience at meeting the objectives in the assignments for Chapters 2 through 9 should mean that you're pretty familiar with these rules by now. The Handbook sections provide a review of the most important rules.

Even when you know the rules, it is easy to overlook mistakes in your own writing. You may need some gimmicks to force yourself to see what you have actually written. Here are some that have worked for other writers:

1. Try using a bookmark to force your eyes to focus on one line of words at a time. You may feel at first as if you've returned to second grade, but this technique will probably slow down your reading considerably. You can even go a step further and point your finger at each individual word. (This is

especially helpful if your problem is leaving out words or putting extra words in.)
2. Keep a list of errors you are prone to commit, and proofread one time just for these errors.
3. If your problem is spelling, try proofreading the paper backwards, from the last word to the first. Of course, this won't help you to catch errors like writing *then* for *than*, but it will force you to forget about the sense and to see each word individually.
4. Try reading the paper aloud in some very unnatural voice—perhaps singing it, using a peculiar accent, or pronouncing each syllable with equal stress, as-if-you-were-a-com-put-er. You may feel a trifle silly, but you will be forcing concentration on the *words* rather than the *meaning*.

Why should you put all of this effort into assuring accuracy? Does it really matter whether or not you have spelled everything correctly and put the punctuation marks in the best places? Can't you communicate in spite of a few mistakes? After all, nobody's perfect. Unfortunately, the answer is yes, it does matter. Punctuation marks are signaling devices; your reader expects you to use them in standard ways. Using them in some eccentric manner can be just as confusing to your reader as using Morse code with your own personal variations would be. If you use a semicolon, your reader expects to find a would-be sentence on either side of it, and if one of these clauses turns out to be dependent, you have put a stumbling block in the reader's path, forcing rereading. Even the most amusing of spelling errors is a distraction. When one of my students described an anxious teenage girl as "having breasts bigger than her pears," my mental response was an immediate return to the produce counter, where I searched among the Bartletts and Anjous for breast-sized fruit. Instead of inspecting pears, I should have been feeling sympathy for the teenager who didn't fit in with the other flat-chested girls, and that is what I would have been doing if the writer had proofread effectively and had written *peers*.

There are very few really excellent proofreaders in the world. Developing your skills to a high level will put you in a select group, give you additional confidence, and undoubtedly improve your grades. It takes work, but it's worth the effort.

WRITING ASSIGNMENT

In doing the assignment for this chapter, you should strive to meet the following objectives. If you meet all five, you will get a satisfactory grade.

Objectives

1. Turn in both versions of your answer, showing the difference between the prewriting and the final draft.
2. Comment on both your strengths and your weaknesses as a communicator, and illustrate your comments with detailed examples.
3. Make sure the final draft is significantly better than the prewriting.
4. Use standard American spelling in the final draft.
5. Proofread the final draft to eliminate any unmarked sentence fragments, comma splices, run-on sentences, subject-verb agreement errors, errors in

verb form, faulty tense shifts, errors in use or omission of apostrophes, incorrect uses of commas, semicolons, or colons, pronoun agreement errors, or dangling modifiers.

Dangling modifiers, the only addition to the proofreading requirement, are covered in Section 4 of the Handbook. I'll give a few examples here, but you should study the Handbook section for more details.

Whenever your sentence contains a cluster of descriptive words, you need to place these as close as possible to the word they describe. If the modified word is a long distance from the modifier, or if there is no modified word at all, the sentence has a *dangling modifier*. (Some texts distinguish between the two kinds, calling the first a *misplaced modifier*, since it can be corrected by merely moving the words around. The true dangling modifier requires that the sentence be reworded.)

Here are two examples with possible corrections in parentheses:

Using obscenities in the courtroom, the judge charged the witness with contempt of court.
(The judge charged the witness with contempt of court for using obscenities in the courtroom.)
(Because the witness used obscenities in the courtroom, the judge charged her with contempt of court.)
Growing an additional foot in three months, I was delighted with the plant.
(Growing an additional foot in three months, the plant delighted me.)
(The plant's growing an additional foot in three months delighted me.)

Writing Assignment 10-1

Note: There is no alternate assignment for this chapter.

For the prewriting step of this paper, spend twenty to twenty-five minutes writing an answer to this question: What are your strengths and weaknesses as a communicator? Write as fast as you can, and do not be concerned about correctness. Be specific. Cover both written and spoken communication. Discuss your plans for expanding your strengths and diminishing your weaknesses.

The writing and postwriting steps of this assignment will consist of producing a more polished version of your answer. You will need to edit and proofread, making your final draft more concise, more powerfully worded, better organized, and as error free as you can possibly make it. Proofread your final draft carefully, being sure to correct the spelling and to eliminate any unmarked fragments, comma splices, run-on sentences, subject-verb agreement errors, errors in verb form, faulty tense shifts, errors in use or omission of apostrophes, incorrect uses of commas, semicolons, or colons, pronoun agreement errors, or dangling modifiers.

CHAPTER 11
REWRITING: RESPONDING TO FEEDBACK

If you're a good conversationalist, you probably are constantly aware of little signals that tell you your listeners do or do not understand you. You watch their posture, hand movements, eyelids, eyebrows, and even mouths to get a reading on their reactions to your ideas. You may miss this ongoing feedback when you try to express your ideas in writing instead of in speech. Occasionally you write something for another person to read, and you get no feedback at all on it. You never know if your intended message was received. More often you do get some feedback—a response comes in the mail, your request is approved or denied, your paper receives a grade—but it is too late to use that feedback to improve your communication. Still, there are times when you get both the feedback and a second chance, the opportunity to rewrite, incorporating whatever lessons you have learned from the feedback to make your writing better.

INTERPRETING FEEDBACK

Feedback, like any communication, is open to misinterpretation. If you have ever worked on an election campaign to raise the tax rate for the schools, the voters provided you with feedback when they went to the polls. If the request passed, you probably interpreted this as positive feedback, and you planned to do more of the same in the next campaign. But what if the request failed? How did you interpret this feedback? Did your audience get some message other than the one you intended? Did they get the intended message, but it was outweighed by economic concerns you couldn't control? Was your communication totally ignored?

In a complex situation like that, you would need to do a thorough study before you could even begin to interpret the feedback. In the writing you will do for college assignments or for job requirements, the feedback is often more clear-cut. A poor grade is a pretty clear indication of some problem in transmitting your message, and almost all instructors will accompany the grade with a comment on the good and bad points of the writing. Even if you get a good grade, you will often be given suggestions for further improvement. If you submit a business report to your boss, you may get similar suggestions. How do you deal with these?

When you get negative feedback, your first problem is to decide exactly what it says. Is your reader disagreeing with the actual ideas you intended to convey, or is the disagreement with some other idea you never intended in the first place? If your paper contains marginal comments like "not clear," "ambiguous," "What do you mean?" and "vague," you can be quite sure that your intended message never came through. (English teachers are second only to doctors when it comes to illegible handwriting, so often their messages never get through, either. If you can't read the marginal comments, *ask*. Don't be like the student who was insulted by a note about her "vague language"; she thought she had been accused of using vulgar language!)

If you decide that your reader never quite understood your message, you can try again. Perhaps an additional example will make your point clearer. Now that you have been away from the paper for a time, you may be able to see some problems with the wording itself. Perhaps you can make some of your ideas more clearly connected by joining simple sentences with conjunctions like *since, because, although,* and *if.* If your thinking seems to jump around from one idea to the next, check out your transitions; perhaps adding a sentence at the beginning or end of some paragraphs will provide better thought bridges. Some of your sentences may just be too long; your reader may have become lost in the complications of your sentence structure. Find a shorter way to say the same thing. Look for simpler synonyms for too-technical words. Once again, take this opportunity to read the paper to a friend to get a second opinion on what might not be clear.

But suppose you decide that your reader understood your point perfectly and still didn't like it? What do you do then? Here, your personal ethics enter in. I would like to think that if you have written a defense of cannibalism and gotten a poor grade on it, the reason is not the instructor's disapproval of cannibalism but your own failure to organize, support, and state the defense well. I would like to think that a well-written defense of cannibalism would get a better grade than a poorly written attack on cannibalism. I would like to think these things, and about 80 percent of the time I can think them. Most instructors make a real effort to eliminate personal bias from their grading, and most succeed fairly well, I think.

Still, there will always be a few instructors who will grade a paper down because they disagree with its thesis. Not because of inadequate development, not because of confusing organization, not because of poor mechanics, but just because they don't like what the writer said. If your defense of cannibalism puts you in this predicament, you have two choices. You can succumb to pressure and write what you think the instructor wants you to say, or you can decide to write the most eloquent, flawless defense of cannibalism that was ever written. There's no guarantee that you will improve your grade with either approach, but you'll probably feel better about what you've written if you take the second.

HOW TO REWRITE

When you decide to attempt a second version of a paper that has already been evaluated, it is very important that you begin by getting a general impression of the evaluation. What was the main problem with the paper? What was its greatest strength? Never begin to rewrite a paper until you have read through the whole thing, noting marginal comments but paying special attention to any general comments—usually found at the end or by the grade. Some students will begin to rewrite almost as soon as they get the graded paper back. They may go through and correct all the errors noted in the margins, getting all the way to the end of the essay before they discover that they were told to reorganize their examples to put a more impressive one first. They have wasted their rewriting time.

Rewriting should be an organized procedure. You will not waste your time if you follow these steps:

1. Read any general comments first. These should give you an idea of how much changing you need to do. They should also warn you of things not to change; if your instructor has called something a "perceptive comment," make sure you don't omit this point in your final draft.

2. After you have read these general comments, begin a second prewriting sheet (actually, a pre-rewriting sheet). Jot down on this sheet any ideas you have about suggested improvements—clearer organization, smoother transitions, more varied sentence structures, more vivid details, a narrower thesis. This is a good time to look back at the Checklist for Editing on page 169. Keep this pre-rewriting sheet in front of you as you rewrite, and refer to it often.

3. Read your whole paper exactly as you wrote it, but stop at every correction or marginal note. Make sure you understand the reason for the note. If you're unsure about a correction, do *not* think you'll solve the problem by omitting the unclear sentence. Your instructor wants to know that you can fix the problem, not delete it. If you don't understand something, please ask. Very few teachers bite. Most enjoy the opportunity to explain themselves.

4. When you have read the whole paper and you're sure you understand all the feedback, you are ready to begin the rewriting. Be sure to take care of the big concerns—reasoning, organization, appropriate tone—while you're correcting the incidentals like spelling and punctuation. Try not to overlook any comments. If you don't want to incorporate some suggested change, you shouldn't have to. After all, it's your essay. Still, it would be polite to include a marginal note of your own to explain your reason and to let your instructor know you didn't ignore the suggestion.

5. As you rewrite, consider your sentence structure. This is your last chance to get your ideas across, so don't pass up an opportunity to say something a little more precisely than you did before. Don't settle for telling yourself that your reader can figure out what you mean. Clarity is the one virtue a rewritten paper absolutely must have.

6. Finally, you're ready to proofread. A rewritten paper should get two proofreadings. When you do the first one, you should put the graded paper and the new one side by side and check just for the problems that you had on

the first paper. You want to be especially sure that any spelling errors have been looked up in a dictionary and corrected. Nothing is a clearer indication of a don't-give-a-damn attitude than a rewritten paper with the same words misspelled as on the first paper, just misspelled differently this time! The second proofreading should come a little while after the first, if possible. This time you should regard the paper as if it were a brand new paper and read to catch new errors. Don't let two errors creep in while you're correcting one.

A final word of advice: Do not be afraid to make sweeping changes between the graded paper and the rewritten one. Some students seem to think that a rewritten paper should just be a cleaner copy of the paper that has just been graded. Your instructor knows you can write; another sample of your penmanship is not what is asked for. You rewrite to demonstrate that you can improve your work by writing a more effective essay—not just a neater one.

WRITING ASSIGNMENT

In doing the assignment for this chapter, you should strive to meet the following objectives. If you meet all five, you will get a satisfactory grade.

Objectives

1. Turn in your original paper, your partner's evaluation of it, and your rewritten version in response to this evaluation. Your partner should turn in the evaluation you wrote.
2. In the evaluation of your partner's paper, you should clearly state at least three concrete suggestions for improvements.
3. In the rewritten version of your own paper, you should show that you have considered the feedback provided by your partner and have tried to make the suggested improvements.
4. Use standard American spelling in both the evaluation and the rewritten paper.
5. Proofread both the evaluation and the rewritten paper to eliminate any unmarked sentence fragments, comma splices, run-on sentences, subject-verb agreement errors, errors in verb form, faulty tense shifts, errors in use or omission of apostrophes, incorrect uses of commas, semicolons, or colons, pronoun agreement errors, dangling modifiers, or faulty parallelism.

The new grammatical requirement for this assignment is that you eliminate faulty parallelism. You have already studied parallel structure in Chapter 6, and it is covered in Section 4 of the Handbook, too, so you should have no trouble with this requirement.

If you need to check your ability to correct problems in parallel structure, however, here is a sentence you can rewrite:

The twins were different in three ways: their appetites, they had completely opposite senses of humor, and snoring.

There are various ways to rewrite this, depending on what the sentence means. Here are a couple of versions that correct the parallelism problem:

The twins were different in three ways: They had different appetites, different senses of humor, and different habits of snoring.

The twins were different in three ways: Harry ate everything, laughed at the Three Stooges, and never snored, while Larry ate only peanut butter sandwiches and sardines, never laughed, and snored loudly every night.

Writing Assignment 11-1

Note: There is no alternate assignment for this chapter.

For this assignment the prewriting will consist of selecting some one of the papers you have already written for this class—preferably one of the weaker ones—copying it exactly as you wrote it but eliminating the instructor's comments, and exchanging this for another classmate's paper.

There are two parts to the writing step. First, write a one-page analysis of the paper your partner has given you. You may want to consider its readability, organization, level of language, and reasoning. Make at least three concrete suggestions on how the paper could be improved, and try to communicate these in such a way that your recommendations will be accepted. Second, when you receive the analysis that your partner has done of your own paper, rewrite the original paper in response to this feedback. You do not have to incorporate all of your partner's suggestions, but you should be ready to give reasons for rejecting any that you do not use.

For the postwriting step, proofread both your analysis of your partner's paper and your own rewritten paper. Make sure that you correct any spelling errors on both and that you eliminate any unmarked fragments, comma splices, run-on sentences, subject-verb agreement errors, errors in verb form, faulty tense shifts, errors in use or omission of apostrophes, incorrect uses of commas, semicolons, or colons, pronoun agreement errors, dangling modifiers, or faulty parallelism.

Turn in the copy of the original paper, your partner's evaluation of it, and your rewritten version of the paper. Your partner will turn in the evaluation you wrote. If the two of you can turn in all six papers together (two originals, two analyses, and two rewritten essays), your instructor's grading job can be simplified.

CHAPTER 12
SPECIAL ASSIGNMENTS: EXAMINATION WRITING

"Friday's test will be an hour-long essay exam covering Chapters 8 through 11 and your lecture notes for the last four weeks." Does such a pronouncement send you to bed with a migraine headache? Would you, given a choice, always opt for fifty multiple-choice or true-false questions rather than two essay questions? Or, do you see an essay test as a break, a chance to snow your prof and use your gift of gab to disguise the fact that you haven't actually read the assigned material?

If you revel in essay tests, you probably already know much of the material in this chapter. Still, you may be able to pick up a few pointers and benefit from someone else's test-taking experience. However, this chapter will probably not help you to get a good grade in a class without doing the assigned reading. Most test graders are experienced enough to recognize bull when they see it, and they seldom give credit just because you have demonstrated a flair for language. In fact, they may be especially hard on a paper whose well-written answer has absolutely nothing to do with the course content; they are angered by the fact that a student with such obvious potential didn't see their beloved subject as worthy of study.

If you'd rather go to the dentist for root-canal work than take an essay exam, this chapter may help you to change your attitude toward the ordeal and to be more successful the next time you have to go through it.

PREPARING FOR THE EXAM

Your preparation for an essay exam begins the minute you walk in the classroom door for the first time and ends five minutes after the exam has been handed to you. From the very first day, you should be taking notes on the course content and the instructor's expectations. Many students assume that nothing much will happen during the first week of class, and they sometimes don't even bring pens or paper to class with them until the third class meeting. This is a fatal error. Many instructors outline their whole courses the first day, giving very specific previews of what their grading system will be like and of the kinds of tests they give. (I have sometimes started a class by reading the past semester's final exam questions, giving the students some idea of what they should know by the time they have finished the course.) If you are not prepared to jot down these hints and suggestions the first day, you may never be able to get as specific a commitment from the instructor again.

Of course, the basic preparation for any test will occur as you read the assigned material and review it and your notes in the days just before the test. If you know that the test will contain essay questions, you should pay special attention to some of the big topics in the course, the ideas, movements, and terms that the instructor has stressed over and over again. Try to relate these to some of the details, events, names of people connected with various movements, and important dates. It will not be enough—at least if you want a good grade—that you can define the major terms and explain influential trends in the subject. The difference between an *A* answer and a *B* answer (or a *B* answer and a *C* answer) is often how effectively you are able to tie in the details—the who, what, when, where, why, and how—that any large movement must consist of.

Should you check with other students to get their impressions of Professor Whozit's exams? Sure, go ahead, but keep two reservations in mind. (1) Just because Whozit gave a certain kind of test last year, do not expect him to continue giving it for the rest of his teaching career. Instructors do change their testing methods; they even improve them occasionally. Do *not* assume that preparing to take last year's test will automatically qualify you to do well on this year's test. It may be altogether different. (2) Remember that a test that is a snap to one student may be torture to another. Whatever your friend tells you—good or bad—about last year's test, that is her judgment. Even if you had the same test she took, your reaction might be entirely different. Her opinion will be influenced by her knowledge of the subject, her attitude toward it, her previous experience with similar or different tests in the same subject, and perhaps whether or not she likes the curl in Professor Whozit's hair or the brand of running shoes he wears. Your judgments may be just the opposite.

Why did I say that your preparation ended five minutes *after* you were handed the exam? Because, no matter how much or how little time you have to write the exam, I think you should always spend five minutes surveying it, judging the length of time you should spend on each question, looking for questions in a later section that might help to refresh your memory about questions in an earlier section (Sometimes terms you must define in Part I will be used in Part III.), and planning your test-taking strategy. You do not always have to answer questions in a certain order. Answering the ones that seem easiest first can calm you down and provide the best mental set for the rest of the exam. You need to skim all the questions to see which will be the easiest ones. Five minutes spent getting the lay of the land will not be wasted. Do not panic when you see others begin to write; they are probably jotting down the first idea that comes into their heads, and it may be gibberish. Use your time to plan, and you will be ahead of them at grading time.

Here are some specific suggestions about steps you can take to come to an exam well prepared:

1. Always find out whether a test will be open-book or closed-book. Most tests are not open-book, but if yours turns out to be and you don't have your book with you, you will really be handicapped. If it is open-book, ask if this also means open-notes. If it does, make sure that yours are organized so that you can find answers quickly. (You might even want to stick tabs on the edges of particularly important pages.) If a test is open-book, do not assume that it will be easier than the traditional kind. Usually, your instructor will expect a much greater display of your knowledge than on a closed-book test. After all, you have access to all of the supporting data you might need right at your fingertips. So what if it takes ten minutes to find the answer to a five-point question? You should know the organization of your textbook very thoroughly for an open-book test. Anything you can't find in a minute or two is just as useless to you as is the name you can't quite recall when you are writing a closed-book exam.

2. As you study the text and your notes, try to look for obvious essay questions. Ask yourself, "What would I ask the class if I were designing a test over this material?" However, do not be so sure that you have second-guessed the instructor that you are only ready to answer your own questions. Sometimes students will write furiously for a whole hour answering questions they were never asked. I always assume that they prepared so thoroughly for those questions that they just couldn't believe I hadn't asked them, so they went ahead and answered them anyway. Often I give them a chance to answer these questions by asking this one: "What were you prepared to answer that I didn't ask on this test? Write a good question and a carefully worded answer worth ten points."

3. Try to be in good shape both mentally and physically for the exam. Often how well you do will be determined not so much by how much you remember but by how clearly your mind is working on the day of the test. Exam schedules can be horrendous, and pressures at home don't always help you either, but you should make every effort to be fairly rested and alert when a test begins. Eating something shortly before you take a test can also help to give you the energy you will need. A few relaxation techniques could stand you in good stead now, too. Take a workshop on dealing with stress to learn these, or check a book on relaxation out of the library.

4. Know how to spell the most important words in the course. Many teachers do not count off for spelling, but even if they don't, they can't help feeling a little negative toward the student of psychology who writes about "pyschology," the "buisness" major, or the future "dental higenist." This negative feeling toward you may be reflected in a lower grade even when spelling supposedly doesn't count. My own frustration is enormous when I have to grade a paper turned in for "Freshman Writting."

5. Read all of the assigned material.

6. Always take an accurate timepiece with you. Set it on the desk in front of you before the exam is handed out, and consult it often. As soon as you see the test, plan how you will spend your time. Know how many points there will be, and divide your time accordingly. If there are 100 points on the test, you should spend about a quarter of your time earning each 25 points. However, you should also allow that first 5 minutes for surveying the test

and at least as much time at the end for reading what you have written. (You might discover that you have omitted a word that would change your answer completely. Five minutes of checking your answer could mean as much as 15 or 20 points on your final grade.) For a 2-hour, 100-point exam, here is a good schedule:

- 5 minutes to survey the test
- 10 minutes at the end to read your answers
- (105 minutes left for writing answers to questions)
- 20 multiple-choice questions worth 1 point each
- 10 short-answer questions worth 5 points each
- 2 essay questions worth 15 points each

You can readily see that the short-answer questions account for half of your points, so you should spend about 50 minutes on them. Each question deserves a 2- or 3-sentence answer. In the remaining 55 minutes, you should answer the multiple-choice questions and the 2 essays. You can probably handle the 1-point questions in less than a minute apiece; let's say 15 minutes for the 20 questions. This leaves you with 20 minutes each for the 2 essay questions—enough to write about a 2-page answer for each, if you write and think fast.

WRITING THE EXAM

Generally, the wording of an essay exam question will give you many clues as to what is expected of you. But not always. Here is a true story from my career as a test-taker.

I was taking a Shakespeare course at the University of Michigan. In the semester we had studied about a dozen of Shakespeare's plays. The three-hour final was to determine the entire course grade. The test, written on the blackboard by the professor, consisted of one word—*Iago*. The question was not "Analyze Iago's character," or "Contrast Iago with five other Shakespearean villains," or "Trace the development of Iago's villainy." It was just "Iago." If you get a question like this, you must make several assumptions, which I did. First, I assumed that the professor expected us to take close to the full time—three hours—with our answers. Who could think of three hours' worth of information about one character? Obviously, he wanted us to discuss more than just one character, even though there was only one name on the board. This was my second assumption: We were supposed to demonstrate our knowledge of several plays, not just *Othello*, the play containing Iago. I assumed that he really wanted a comparison/contrast essay, even though he didn't come right out and ask for it. (He was also testing our ability to infer what the real question was. I'm sure if anyone had written entirely about Iago, the resulting grade would not have been good.) Finally, I assumed that most of the other thirty students in the class would begin immediately to write comparisons of Iago and some of the other villains we had studied that semester. I wanted to be different. After all, the professor would have to suffer through thirty essays that all sounded pretty much alike; how could I be sure he would be impressed enough with mine to give it the *A* I wanted in the course? Instead of writing immediately, I started to plot out some way of describing Iago that would enable me to bring in at least a half-dozen plays and that would be unique—or nearly so. After a few minutes, I came up with a thesis like this: Iago has most of the virtues of a Shakespearean hero, but he carries them to such extremes that they act as vices. In supporting this, I was able to discuss several plays other than *Othello*, and the contrasts with their heroes were at least sufficiently interesting to earn me the *A* I thought I deserved.

If you ever have a similar experience, you will have to make assumptions similar to mine. Keep in mind that most tests are supposed to fill the time allotted for them. Most of the time, however, your instructor will indicate her expectations much more clearly by the wording of the questions. Always read each question slowly and carefully, paying special attention to the verbs, which tell you what actions you are expected to perform.

Some of the most general questions will ask you to *discuss, explain, review,* or *comment on*. These might seem to be easy, anything-goes questions. After all, if you are told to "Discuss the importance of the Beatles in modern music," how can anything you say about the Beatles be wrong? Don't make the mistake of assuming that a general question calls for a general answer. The instructor can afford to be vague; you cannot. If you are asked to *discuss*, you had better be ready with details about the topic, and all the details should be leading somewhere, to some opinion you can use them to support. Sound like the old thesis sentence again? It should. Perhaps you can use your details to show that "The Beatles were more influential in America than they were at home in England," or that "The Beatles' influence on our dress and social customs at first disguised the fact that their music was truly revolutionary." Whatever idea you come up with, it is bound to be better than a laundry list of facts about Beatles records and Beatles concerts. Similarly, if you are asked to *review* some event or phenomenon, you will need to have details at your fingertips to present, generally in chronological order. *Explain* or *comment on* may really be calling for a cause-and-effect essay. This is what you would write if you were asked to "Explain the stock market crash of 1929," or to "Comment on the significance of the development of cloning procedures."

Analyze, describe, and *interpret* are only slightly less general directions. The first calls for an analysis essay, of course. You will need to break down whatever the topic is into the parts that make it up, and you will try to explain how they work together. This kind of answer also begins best with a thesis: Four kinds of people joined together to work on the Abolitionist Movement. A question asking you to "Describe the formation of basalt rock" calls for descriptive details, but even these will need some organizing principle, probably chronological or spatial. If you are asked to write an interpretation of something, you may need to define it before you clarify why it is or is not important.

Other common verbs in essay questions fall into three categories: those that do not involve opinion, those that provide the opinion and ask you to defend it, and those that ask for your opinion. In the opinionless group are *define, illus-*

trate, summarize, and *trace*. The first asks for a detailed definition or explanation, with synonyms, contrasting words, and probably examples. You need to give an example or two when you are asked to "Illustrate the process of photosynthesis," too. When you summarize something, you are listing important ideas or events connected with it. If you trace its development, you are taking a historical approach to this summary.

When you are given an opinion to defend, you may be asked to *demonstrate* or *show that*. For instance, "Show that the lost continent of Atlantis could not possibly be at the bottom of Lake Erie." Now, if you are really convinced that Atlantis *is* at the bottom of Lake Erie, you're in trouble. Most instructors will not ask you to defend ideas that go against your own beliefs. I still remember a question from my historical geology final: "Give ten proofs or ten disproofs for the theory of evolution. You may use the Bible once." I don't know how many students chose to give disproofs, but I respect the instructor enough to believe that he graded them fairly. Another term used when the opinion is given to you is *substantiate*, as in "Substantiate Goodman's statement that a draft should include women as well as men." Here, you would need to recall Goodman's arguments and summarize them in support of her opinion.

If you are asked to *compare* and/or *contrast*, your own opinions will be needed, as will the factual observations on which they are based. Some of the material you include may just be a repeat of information given you—in your text or in a lecture—but you will probably be expected to include your own reactions, too. If you are asked to *evaluate* some happening or the contributions of some individual or group, your own judgments will be essential.

The reason you need to pay special attention to the verb in the essay question is that many students get into trouble for following a direction other than the one they are given. They are asked to *evaluate*, and they just *explain;* they are told to *contrast*, and they *describe* two ideas; they are requested to *demonstrate*, and they merely *discuss*. Whenever you finish writing an essay answer, you should make it a habit to read the question one more time, asking yourself, "Does this answer do what the question asks?"

As you're reading over your answer, here are some other points to check for:

1. Did you write on the correct topic? To determine this, you need to look at the *nouns* in the question. I remember totally missing one question because I wrote about *Theodore* Roosevelt's Secretary of State when the question asked about *Franklin D.* Roosevelt's. Don't be too nervous to read the question.

2. Did you use some of the specific terms stressed in the course? If the instructor has said "ethnocentrism" at least once per lecture, you won't make a very good impression if you talk about "that idea or feeling, you know, when you think that whatever your own group does is OK and whatever anyone else does is weird." Use the language of your subject, and you will probably get more points for your ideas.

3. Have you used examples? Concreteness is just as valuable in an essay exam as it is in an essay. For many subjects a hypothetical illustration will be just

fine, if you can't remember an actual example. It at least demonstrates that you understand the concept. If the instructor's examples of ethnocentrism made no impression on you, you can invent an American traveler who took his own silverware to China because he refused to "stoop to the barbarism of using chopsticks."

4. Is your answer long enough for the points allotted to the question? Only a short-answer question (no more than five points) should be answered in two sentences. This does not mean that you should pad your answer; twelve pages of repetitious nonsense will earn you no more points than a two-sentence answer would. State your answer, and then give plenty of details to support it. When you've done this, quit. It is time to proofread.

5. Have you made the answer easy for your instructor to grade? I think underlining is a particularly useful technique here. If the question asks for five reasons, it wouldn't hurt to underline each of the five. Reasons can get lost in a long essay, and you wouldn't want to lose 20 percent of your points just because the grader, hurriedly reading your answer, missed your fifth point.

A good essay test should be a learning experience. You should find when you're finished that you have put some ideas together in new ways and had some different insights than you had before you started writing. If you have followed the suggestions in this chapter, you should leave the testing room with a feeling of satisfaction and pleasant anticipation of the day when you will find out your grade.

PRACTICING EVALUATING ESSAY ANSWERS

Here is a twenty-point question from a European history exam:

What effect did Darwinism have on social and economic attitudes?

The following answers, one actual and one hypothetical, were written in about fifteen minutes. Evaluate the answers, showing how each student did or did not follow the suggestions for preparation and writing given in this chapter.

1. Surprisingly enough, Darwinism had a great effect on social and economic attitudes despite the fact that Darwin's theories were only meant to affect science.

Several schools of thought developed. The wealthy quite often adopted the ideas called *social Darwinism.* They used the argument of survival of the fittest to prove that they were rich because they were superior. Their criterion for judging superiority was success in business. Of course their ideas were the result of only surface study of Darwin's theories.

Opposed to these were the Reform Darwinists, who were more humanitarian and did not feel that change was only in the remote past and future. They hoped that by making changes for the better in a humanitarian way, they could improve society now. Extreme advocates of Darwinism were the Racists and Eugenicists. The former used the argument of survival of the fittest to support their prejudiced attitude toward other races. Eugenicists believed man should be bred.

On the economic level, Darwinism was used as an argument for imperialism, saying that imperialistic nations were strongest, best able to survive, and therefore superior to the smaller nations. Also, this was used as an argument for a policy of *laissez-faire*. The idea behind this was that controlling business would interfere with survival of the fittest companies.

2. Charles Darwin died in 1882. Before he died, he wrote a book called *On the Origin of Species*. This book shook up the scientific community and got a lot of people mad to think that perhaps men used to be monkeys a long time ago. Some schools are still having battles about whether their science classes will teach Darwin's theories or the Bible's version of creation.

Many people objected to the man-from-monkey ideas, and they turned against people who agreed with Darwin. This caused a lot of trouble socially. Each side of the argument felt that it was the fittest to survive. Sometimes the battle lines were drawn along economic lines, too. The rich people were on one side, and the poor people on the other. The rich said that if the poor were more fit, they would be rich, too. If they were poor, it was their own fault.

WRITING ASSIGNMENTS

In doing the assignments for this chapter, you should strive to meet the following objectives. If you meet all four, you will get a satisfactory grade.

Objectives

1. Turn in your prewriting: This should consist of (1) a time schedule showing how you planned to spend your time answering the questions, and (2) notes you jotted down before answering each question.
2. Answer each question appropriately, giving fuller, more detailed answers to the questions with many points and shorter answers to the questions with few points.
3. Be sure to pay attention to the verb in each question and perform whatever action it calls for.
4. Proofread your answers to be sure you have not omitted any words and that you have expressed your ideas clearly.

Special Assignment 12-1

Spend 60 minutes taking the following essay exam. It is designed to give you practice in responding to the *form*, so it is not based on any specific content. Answers will be graded on their reasoning and their appropriateness to the question.

(100 points)

1. (40 points) Analyze the results—good and bad—you could expect if you decided to organize your grocery store alphabetically.
2. (20 points) Compare and contrast any 2 of the following brands of pen: Bic, Expresso, Flair, Papermate, Scripto, Write Bros.
3. (40 points) Illustrate what is meant by any 4 of the following sayings:
   a. He who hesitates is lost.
   b. A rolling stone gathers no moss.
   c. What's sauce for the goose is sauce for the gander.
   d. The grass is always greener on the other side of the street.
   e. The difference between men and boys is the cost of their toys.
   f. As the twig is bent, so grows the tree.

Special Assignment 12-2

Spend 60 minutes taking the following essay exam. It is based on readings from earlier chapters: "The Many Me's of the Self-Monitor," "A Growing Wealth of Words," "Competency Tests for Everyone," and "The Age of Indifference."

(100 points)

1. (20 points) Describe the major differences between a low self-monitor and a high self-monitor.
2. (30 points) Use words mentioned by Cousins to substantiate the following comment: Most of the words added to the English language in the twentieth century serve only to emphasize what a sorry state the English-speaking world is in currently.
3. (15 points) Explain Larson's reasons for putting the initial blame for the current incompetence he sees around him on the universities.
4. (15 points) Evaluate Zimbardo's concluding solution for dealing with the age of indifference.
5. (20 points) Compare and contrast the views of modern society expressed by Larson and Zimbardo.

CHAPTER 13
SPECIAL ASSIGNMENTS: EMPLOYMENT WRITING

Perhaps you are already working at the job you expect to have for the rest of your life. Chances are, however, that if you are taking a class using this textbook, you are likely to be job hunting again—or perhaps for the first time—at least two or three times between today and the day you retire. Whether or not you land the best job for you may depend at least in part on your writing ability. The suggestions in this chapter are designed to assure your success.

PRESENTING YOURSELF ON PAPER

Before a potential employer ever sees you in the flesh, she is likely to evaluate a "paper image" of you, a summary of your past experiences, current abilities, and future ambitions. This sheet of paper is usually referred to as your *résumé*, but Richard Lathrop (*Who's Hiring Who*) makes a good case for calling it a "qualifications brief." It doesn't really matter what you call it, as you won't need to put a title on it, anyway. What matters are its content and its appearance. There are many possible formats you can follow. If you want to see a variety of these, check your library for a recent book on résumé writing. (Lathrop's book has some excellent examples.) The sample on the next page contains all the essentials. Look it over carefully, but before you prepare your own qualifications brief, read the discussions of each section.

Although the material at the top, sometimes called the personal section, appears very cut and dried, it is really a very controversial section. What should it contain? In the past, résumés often gave physical details (height, weight, hair color—a possible indication of race), marital history, birthdate, and a commentary on the applicant's health; most of this is generally not included now. The main reason for this change is the change in questions that potential employers are legally allowed to ask of applicants. Federal guidelines are quite limiting on employers, and most of this information is considered not pertinent to many jobs. Some employment counselors still recommend including a few details, such as your birthdate. However, since federal guidelines become more stringent all the time, and it is pretty hard to establish that much of this information is really relevant for most job openings, I prefer a minimum of personal details on the qualifications brief. Unless including a particular detail will help you to

JILL HAMILTON
4322 CRAVEN HILL
KALAMAZOO, MI 49008
386-9999

OBJECTIVE

TO WORK AS ACTIVITIES DIRECTOR in a nursing home or drop-in center for senior citizens where there is a chance to develop new programs, to work with clients individually, and to find innovative solutions to boredom.

EDUCATION

AAS DEGREE IN RECREATION SUPERVISION expected from Kalamazoo Valley Community College in May of 1983; specialization in therapeutic recreation; 3.4 grade point average (4.0 possible).

GRADUATE, PLAINWELL HIGH SCHOOL, 1981; major—history; minors—math, French, physical education; 3.8 grade point average (4.0 possible).

RELATED EXPERIENCE

ASSISTED ACTIVITIES DIRECTOR AT THE JUNEDALE NURSING HOME, Otsego, Michigan, August to December, 1982, as an experience-based education placement (through Kalamazoo Valley Community College); taught craft workshops; served as square dance caller; designed special program of activities for six women confined to wheelchairs.

SERVED AS CANDY-STRIPER AT PLAINWELL GENERAL HOSPITAL June 1979 to August 1981; assisted nurses on the terminally ill ward; helped with daily care, feeding, and morale boosting of 14 terminally ill patients.

ACCOMPLISHMENTS

RECEIVED KALAMAZOO VALLEY COMMUNITY COLLEGE TRUSTEE ACHIEVEMENT AWARD for 1981–1982.

GRADUATED AS SALUTATORIAN, PLAINWELL HIGH-SCHOOL CLASS OF 1981.

NAMED "CANDY-STRIPER OF THE YEAR" at Plainwell General Hospital in 1981.

EARNED 72 MERIT BADGES AS A MEMBER OF GIRL SCOUT TROOP 321, Plainwell Methodist Church, between 1975 and 1981.

REFERENCES

Ms. Ann Liggett Activities Director Junedale Nursing Home 1785 W. 103rd Street Otsego, MI 49078	Frank Wright Director of Volunteers Plainwell General Hospital 950 Morrissey Plainwell, MI 49080	Mrs. Bertha Zee 10 N. Frederick Plainwell, MI 49080 (Girl Scout Troop Leader)

get a job—the fact that your hobby is weightlifting, for instance, when you apply for a job as a boxcar loader—leave it out. Include only what an employer needs to know to reach you: name, address, and phone number.

The Objective section is a very important one. You will want to state your desires as clearly as possible without making them sound limited to one and only one job. After all, you want to send your brief to several potential employers, so the description should fit jobs that each has to offer. On the other hand, don't describe your ideal job in such broad terms that the employer will think you really haven't decided what you want to do. "A job working with people," for instance, is no good as a job objective statement. If you are applying for two or three different types of jobs—as a dancing instructor, as a proofreader, and as an executive secretary, for instance—create a qualifications brief for each one. You can't possibly combine all the objectives sensibly or stress all the qualifications you have for all the jobs on one unified brief, so don't try. Your objective statement should not be more than three or four lines, but it should give some indication of what you feel your strong points are. The sample does this in these words: "where there is a chance to develop new programs, to work with clients individually, and to find innovative solutions to boredom." Remember that this statement may determine the employer's first impression of you. If she is not impressed, she may read no further.

The Education and Related Experience sections are interchangeable. Put whichever one you consider to be most impressive first. If you have been in the working world for years, your experience is likely to merit first place, unless it is entirely unrelated to the job you are looking for now. If you are trained for some job you have never done, you will list your training before your experience. Of course, if your experience is unrelated, drop the *Related* from the category heading.

In the Education section, as in other sections, work backwards. This means list current schools or jobs first, followed by the immediately previous school or job, and so on back to your high school or your first job. Of course, if you have had numerous jobs—more than six or seven—you may decide to eliminate those that go back fifteen years or more, or those that were very brief and unrelated to your current plans. Keep the brief brief—not over two pages.

Should you mention your grades in the education section? If you have a *B* average or better, why not? If your average is below this, it is probably wisest not to be specific about it. However, you can mention grades in related courses. For instance, if you are applying for a math-related position, and your overall average is only 2.5, you can neglect to mention it; but point out that you had a 3.8 average in your math courses (if you really did).

Notice that the Experience section is not limited to jobs for which you were paid. In the sample brief, the first job listed may or may not have been for pay. (Some experience-based education placements are for credit only, although most combine credit with pay.) The second job was strictly volunteer, but it provided experience that would certainly be relevant to the job in a nursing home. Do not forget experiences you have had that might help you get the job, even if they didn't pay a cent.

Must you have an Accomplishments section? No. Do not say, as one of my students actually did, "Accomplishments—none." That is entirely too negative. Besides, how could you live long enough to be applying for a job and have absolutely *no* accomplishments? If you honestly feel that your successes are unimpressive, omit the section altogether, but before you decide to do this, discuss your achievements with a relative or a close friend. Perhaps you are just being too modest and reluctant to blow your own horn. You are expected to blow your own horn on the qualifications brief even if you never do it again, so throw away modesty for once. Your father may be able to remember some achievement you have forgotten—getting the Most Improved Camper Award at summer camp, winning the sixth-grade spelling bee (If you're over forty-five, think twice before including this one.), or designing the winning float for your college homecoming. Job-related achievements can be included here, too: setting a sales record, planning a particularly effective advertising campaign. However, if you find you have only one accomplishment to list, you might prefer to include it in the education or experience sections, by the school or job where it fits appropriately. The Accomplishments section will look most impressive if it contains at least two items.

The last section in the sample is References. More and more résumés today say something like "References available on request from Western Michigan University Placement Office." There are reasons for and against listing specific people as your references. You don't want to do this unless you have checked with these people, gotten their permission, and are sure they will give a glowing report of you. If you are sending out hundreds of qualifications briefs, you might decide not to name names, as your references could conceivably grow tired of responding to requests for information about you. Still, an "available on request" statement could be read as "I really can't think of anybody right now who could put in a good word for me, but if you insist, I'll try to come up with somebody." To avoid making this impression, I would list at least two references, including their business addresses (if they have these), and indicating their connection with you when the address doesn't make this obvious. Note the parenthetical comment on the third reference in the sample.

Now you're finished. You have a qualifications brief ready to send out—or almost ready. You must double-check the final product for neatness and accuracy. If you don't type, this is one time when it pays to hire a good typist. Even if you find the world's best, be sure that *you* proofread. After all, this is your life you're summarizing, and your typist can't be expected to be as familiar with it as you are. Any mistakes will keep you from getting a job; they won't hurt your typist at all. Take responsibility for the finished product yourself. Perfection should be your goal. It can be achieved. (Perfection is actually *required* of you if you're a community college student in Michigan. State guidelines require that students in all programs demonstrate that they can write résumés that are "accurate, legible, and spelled correctly.")

If you are actually using this qualifications brief to apply for jobs—and not just doing it for a college assignment—you will want to have at least two dozen or so copies made. Check around at small printing firms; you can probably find several where you can make neat copies on a good-quality paper for minimal

WRITING THE COVER LETTER

cost. Consider this a necessary expense connected to job hunting, and don't forget to make a note of your expense. You'll want to report it on your tax forms after you have gotten that job.

Preparing your qualifications brief is really only half of the writing you will need to do to get a good job. You can't just slip a copy of the brief in an envelope, include an address and a stamp, and drop it in a mailbox, hoping for an interview appointment by return mail. The brief must always be accompanied by a letter of application, also called a "cover letter," because it covers or accompanies the qualifications brief. This letter is different from the brief in two important ways: (1) It is an individual letter, so you should never have duplicate copies run off; and (2) because it is written individually, it provides an opportunity for you to stress certain strengths that might make you especially suited to that one employer's needs.

The prewriting that you do before you write a cover letter is especially important. You will need to know as much as possible about the job situation, the company, and even the specific person who is likely to read your letter. Always try to address an individual; never write a letter "to whom it may concern." You will sound old-fashioned and stuffy. If it is absolutely impossible to find the name of an individual to write to, you can settle for "Dear Personnel Director," but it is a very poor second choice. Today it is just plain foolish to address an unknown person, who could be either sex, as "Dear Sir." "Dear Sir or Madam" is at least inoffensive, but it lacks the appeal that a personal letter addressed to *you* always has. The only time you should settle for an impersonal greeting is when you are answering an advertisement for a job opening and the address is just a box number. Your references are likely to have a similar problem if they write letters to be included in your placement file. The letters may be sent to dozens of individuals, so how can they be appropriately addressed? If you ever have to write a reference for a friend, you might try a solution I once used. I began my letter this way—"Dear Person Considering Hiring Judy Foy: Do it!" Of course, I had to go on to back up my advice with detailed praises of Judy Foy. The letter was an attention getter; one employer commented that he certainly wanted to meet the person that letter was written about! That is the reaction you hope your letters will receive.

The prewriting that you do should go beyond discovering a name to put at the top of the letter—after your address and date, of course. (See the sample on p. 192.) You should try to find out as much as possible about the potential employer so that you can demonstrate that your qualifications will satisfy the employer's needs. (Of course, if there is no match between qualifications and needs, you probably shouldn't apply; don't fake it.) Make sure that the skills you are offering for sale will be useful to the employer. This seems like an obvious point, but it is one ignored by job seekers at all levels. You would be surprised by the numbers of applicants for teaching positions at community colleges who emphasize their strengths in teaching Literature of the Italian Renaissance—as if we had such a course!

4322 Craven Hill
Kalamazoo, MI 49008
April 10, 1983

Mrs. Alicia Ferris
Director
Green Haven Nursing Facility
240 Salisbury NW
Grand Rapids, MI 49090

Dear Mrs. Ferris:

Do your patients in wheel chairs need some special activities designed just for them? As your Activities Director, I could put my past experience in planning programs for similar patients at the Junedale Nursing Home to work to add some fun to their days.

I will be completing an AAS degree in Recreation Supervision next month. My course work at Kalamazoo Valley Community College has included a specialization in therapeutic recreation, making me ideally trained to be Activities Director at a facility such as yours. When I visited Green Haven last semester in connection with one of my classes, I was very favorably impressed with its spick-and-span appearance and with the obviously caring attitude of the staff. I would like to become a part of that staff.

When you have had a chance to study my enclosed qualifications brief, I hope we can get together to discuss the job opening in greater detail. Please call me at 386-9999 to let me know when this would be convenient.

Sincerely,

Jill Hamilton

Jill Hamilton

The sample cover letter reveals that the writer did quite a bit of homework before applying for the job. She visited the facility (see the comment in the second paragraph) and determined that a group of patients had special needs that her experience qualified her to meet. That was what she stressed in her most important sentence—the first one. If you were Mrs. Ferris, whom would you interview—Jill, or an applicant whose first sentence was this one: "I am responding to your advertisement in the *Kalamazoo Gazette* about an opening for Activities Director"? There is nothing *wrong* with that sentence, but it tells the potential employer nothing she doesn't already know. Mrs. Ferris is busy; she may have received seventy-five applications for that one position in this morning's mail, and she has to divide these quickly into two piles, probably sixty-nine or so who won't even get interviews, and perhaps a half-dozen who will. The second writer may be qualified, but she has shown no concern for Green Haven's needs in her opening sentence. For this reason, Jill's letter stands a better chance of making the short stack. Give your cover letter an equal chance by writing a superlative opening sentence that will show that you've considered something other than your own need for the job.

Once you get beyond your opening sentence, summarize your most outstanding qualification very briefly. You may also refer to other related experience, but remember, you will be including a qualifications brief, so don't try to put it all in your letter as well. The brief should contain a few surprises. Close your letter with the suggestion that you would like to meet the interviewer. (Some job counselors suggest you avoid the actual word *interview*.) If you are hardly ever home and therefore prefer not to wait for a call, you may close with a sentence like this one: "I will be in the Grand Rapids area next week and will be happy to call your office for an appointment at your convenience so we can discuss the job opening in greater detail."

Will a letter like this one really improve your chances for getting that all-important interview? Well, a study conducted in the 1970s showed that companies averaged one interview for every 245 résumés received!) You know that *all* of the other applicants can't have lacked qualifications, yet for some reason they weren't chosen. Perhaps some of the reasons were arbitrary: The personnel manager used to date a girl with the same last name, and he never hires Hamiltons for that reason; the candidate attended a college that refused to admit the personnel manager. There are some obstacles that you can't possibly predict or avoid, but you might as well do your best to see that your cover letter isn't one of them.

One final caution about the cover letter: Proofreading is as important as it is in preparing your qualifications brief. Be sure your letter is neat and your spelling is perfect. You wouldn't go to a job interview with a spot of last night's pizza on your tie or your slip hanging two inches below your hem; a mistake in your cover letter is an equally serious blot on your "paper image." Be sure to double-check the spelling of the job title as well as these frequently misspelled words: *personnel*, *experience*, *receive*, and *sincerely*.

WHAT NEXT? Your qualifications brief and your cover letter have made a hit with the person doing the hiring. You have an interview for next Tuesday. Can you stop worrying about your writing and start working on getting the job? Not quite. The interview itself is not too likely to require you to write, although you might make out an application. For some jobs, there may even be written examinations, usually scheduled for some time after the initial interview. The suggestions about essay exams in Chapter 12 should help you in this situation. For the interview itself, your major concerns should be with your spoken communication and with what your appearance communicates about you. (For help in answering the questions of the interviewer, see the Related Reading section in this chapter.) But after the interview, you will write at least one more letter, if you are wise.

Job counselors almost always advise applicants to write a thank-you letter to the person interviewing them. After all, the interviewer is a busy person who gave them a chunk of time from an appointment-filled day. It is only polite to drop a very brief note of appreciation in the mail. It is only polite—and it is very impressive. The reason it is impressive is that so many people fail to do it. If you remember, the interviewer is bound to be impressed. Be sure to send the note immediately; two weeks after the interview it will appear to be a nagging reminder (Haven't you made up your mind about me yet?), but the very next day it will just be an indication of your very good manners.

RELATED READING

Professional Essay

Q: WHY DO YOU WANT TO WORK HERE?
Theodore Pettus

Points to Consider

As you read the following essay, try to answer these questions:

1. If you were the interviewer, which of these questions would you want to ask? Would all the suggested answers satisfy you? Why or why not?
2. If you were being interviewed, which of these questions would call for some of the information your prewriting for the cover letter should have turned up?
3. Have you ever been asked any of these questions when you applied for a job? If so, was your answer similar to the one Pettus suggested?
4. Which of the twenty-one questions would you find personally the most difficult to answer? Why?

From *One On One: Win The Interview, Win The Job* by Theodore Pettus. Copyright © 1979 by Focus Press. Reprinted by permission of Random House, Inc.

Most job-hunters make two devastating mistakes when they are being questioned in an interview. First, they fail to *listen to the question.* They proceed to annoy the interviewer either by answering a question that wasn't asked or by giving out a lot of superfluous information.

Second, and more important, they attempt to answer questions with virtually *no preparation.* The glibbest person on earth, even the most skilled debater, cannot answer questions off the cuff without damaging his or her chances of success.

What follows are a number of questions that various surveys have indicated are asked most often, regardless of the job classification. Study them carefully, develop strong responses, and your candidacy will receive prime consideration.

1. *"Why do you want to work here?"*

Because you have done your homework on the company, you know exactly why you want to work there. All you must do is organize your reasons into several short, hard-hitting sentences. "You make the best product on the market today." "Your management is farsighted enough to reinvest the company's profits so that soon you will be the leader in the category."

2. *"Why should I hire you?"*

The interviewer asking this question does not want a lengthy regurgitation of your résumé. She is not yet asking for a barrage of facts and figures. She is interested in testing your poise and confidence. Give her a *short, generalized summary.* "I have the qualifications to do the job that has to be done and my track record proves it," or, "I know that this is the job for me and that I will be successful."

3. *"What interests you most about this position?"*

Give a truthful, one- or two-word answer like, "The future." "The challenge." "The competitiveness." "The environment." This response will force the employer to ask you to explain, giving you yet another opportunity to demonstrate your profound knowledge of the company.

4. *"Would you like to have your boss's job?"*

By all means, "Yes!" Ambitious, hungry people are always preferred over those willing to settle for a safe routine. If you sense this answer threatens your interviewer's security, you might add, "when I am judged qualified," or, "should an opening develop in several years."

5. *"Are you willing to go where the company sends you?"*

Obviously this is being asked because they have every intention of shipping you off. If you answer "no," you will probably not be hired. If you answer "yes," understand that once you are a trusted employee you may be able to exert the necessary leverage to avoid the less desirable out-of-town assignments.

6. *"What kind of decisions are most difficult for you?"*

Be human and admit that not everything comes easily. But be careful what you do admit. "I find it difficult to decide which of two good men (women) must be let go." "It is difficult for me to tell a client that he is running his business badly."

7. *"How do you feel about your progress to date?"*

Never apologize for yourself. "I think I've done well, but I need new challenges and opportunities." This is a good time to drop hero stories. "No one in my company has advanced as fast as I have." "I think you'll agree, I've accomplished quite a bit in the last five years."

8. *"How long will you stay with the company?"*

A reasonable response might be, "as long as I continue to learn and grow in my field."

9. *"Have you done the best work of which you are capable?"*

This is best answered with some degree of self-effacement. "I would be lying to you if I told you I was perfect, but I have tackled every assignment with all my energy and talents." Or: "I'm sure there were times when I could have worked harder or longer, but over the years I've tried to do my best and I believe I have succeeded."

10. *"What would you like to be doing five years from now?"*

To answer this question, make sure you know exactly what can and cannot be achieved by the ideal candidate in your shoes. Too many job-hunters butcher this question because they have not done their homework and have no idea where their career will lead them. If you see yourself at another company, or in another department of the company you are interviewing, tread lightly. You can't afford to tell your interviewer that you believe you'll be more successful than she is.

11. *"What training/qualifications do you have for a job like this?"*

Deliver a short, fact-filled summary of the two or three most important qualifications you have. "I have a background in accounting. I've demonstrated proven selling skills. I'm capable of handling several projects simultaneously."

12. *"Why do you want to change jobs?"*

This is one of the first questions interviewers ask. Be sure you are ready to answer it satisfactorily. If you're currently in a dead-end position, locked out of advancement opportunities, explain this. The interviewer will understand. If your job has become a routine, void of learning experiences, she'll accept that. If you feel your present employer is losing ground to competition, through no fault of your own, she'll accept that too.

However, if you say that your salary is too low she'll become suspicious. If you say you hate your boss, she'll wonder if soon you'll be hating her. If you say you are bored, she'll suspect that you're just another job-hopper.

13. *"Why do you want to change your field of work?"*

Before your interview spend one hour and organize these reasons into a written statement. Memorize this explanation and be prepared to deliver it, because you will certainly be asked. Your explanation should include:

a. How your previous work experience will contribute to your new career.

b. What excites you most about this new field.

c. How you came to make this career change decision.

14. *"Why were you out of work for so long?"*

If there is a gap in your résumé you must be prepared to explain what you were doing in that period. Until you have satisfied your interviewer's curiosity, you will not get hired. If you were fired and have spent the last year looking for a job without success, you will understand an employer's reluctance to hire you. If, on the other hand, you explain what you have learned or accomplished during this hiatus, she will warm to your candidacy. For example, "I have taken several courses to strengthen my skills in . . ." Or, "I used this period to re-examine my goals and have reached this conclusion: . . ." The interviewer must have a positive explanation.

15. *"Why have you changed jobs so frequently?"*

This question is crucial. In fact, an unsatisfactory answer to this one is among the top reasons why applicants fail to get the jobs they want. You must convince your interviewer that your job-hopping days are over. If you feel you made a mistake leaving previous jobs tell her so, while at the same time reminding her that your job performance was never in question. She'll appreciate your candor. If something in your personal or business life has recently changed and would affect your stability in the future, come right out with the facts. She'll be anxious to hear.

16. *"Have you ever hired or fired anyone?"*

You are being asked this question for two important reasons. First, to determine whether you are capable of performing these duties. Second, to determine if the previous experience you have described was at a high enough level to include hiring/firing responsibility. If you have had no experience in hiring/firing, you must make a considerable effort to convince the interviewer that you are capable of performing in this area.

17. *"How have you helped sales/profits/cost reductions?"*

Have your hero stories ready and be willing to prove that you have made significant contributions in one or more of these basic areas. Again, keep your explanations short and try to include specific dollar amounts.

18. *"Why aren't you earning more at your age?"*

This question, a current favorite, can frighten the wits out of an unsuspecting applicant. One of the following suggested responses should cover your situation: "I have been willing to sacrifice short-term earnings because I felt that I was gaining valuable experience." "I have received (been promised) company stock (or other benefits) in lieu of an increase in salary." "I have been reluctant to gain a reputation as a job-hopper, preferring instead to build my career on solid, long-term achievement."

19. *"How many people have you supervised?"*

Similar to the "hired or fired" question, the interviewer is trying to determine the depth of your experience. Be careful not to exaggerate.

20. *"What are the reasons for your success?"*

It is best to keep this answer very general, permitting your interviewer to probe more deeply if she wishes. Offer a short list of positive character traits that describe you. "I like to work hard." Or, "I get along with all kinds of people and I know how to listen." Or, "I pay close attention to details, I know how to watch costs and I can keep difficult customers smiling."

21. *"What kind of experience do you have for this job?"*

Summarize four or five key areas of experience which you can bring to your new job. Demonstrate to the interviewer specifically how each one helps solve her problems. For example, "My experience in new-product introductions will be very helpful to your entire marketing effort." "My industrial design background will strengthen your sales-force capability in dealing with large clients."

WRITING ASSIGNMENT

In doing the assignment for this chapter, you should strive to meet the following objectives. If you meet all five, you will get a satisfactory grade.

Objectives

1. Turn in your prewriting, including the advertisement or other description of the job opening for which you are applying.
2. Be sure that the qualifications brief is organized appropriately, following the suggestions in the chapter, and contains all the necessary information.
3. Write a cover letter that is suitable for the selected job and that follows the model in the chapter.
4. Begin your cover letter with an opening that is designed to show that you have considered the needs of your potential employer.
5. Proofread both your qualifications brief and your cover letter to eliminate spelling errors or errors in sentence structure.

Special Assignment 13-1

After you have studied this chapter carefully, you should be ready to prepare your own qualifications brief and write a cover letter to go along with it when you are applying for a specific job. These are the two tasks required of you for this special assignment.

Begin your prewriting by looking through ads for jobs in your daily paper or employment listings in your college's placement office. Find an opening that you are already qualified for or one that you will be qualified for in no more than a year. Make a copy of this description to turn in with your prewriting. The rest of your prewriting will consist of jotting down notes for the listing of your qualifications and for the cover letter.

Next, prepare your qualifications brief. Follow the categories given in the sample brief, and give accurate information about your background. Be sure to list schools and jobs in reverse chronological order, starting with today and working backwards. Take special pains with the wording of your objective statement; be sure that it is specific enough to make a good impression but not so limiting that it would eliminate jobs that might really interest you. When you are satisfied that no employer would be likely to toss your brief into the rejection pile, make one neat, perfect copy of it.

The second part of the writing step will consist of writing the cover letter to accompany the brief when you send it to apply for the job opening you have found. (You are not required to send it, of course, but you can if you are actually interested in the job.) Try to address your letter to a specific person, and consider the qualifications that person will be looking for when you frame your first sentence. Show interest in something other than your own need for the job. Write a letter that will be such a good "paper image" of you that the interviewer will be eager to meet you. Again, when you are totally satisfied with the wording of the letter, make one neat, perfect copy of it.

The postwriting should consist of proofreading both the qualifications brief and the cover letter very carefully at least twice. Both should be letter-perfect and flawless as to legibility. If at all possible, both should be typed on good quality paper without visible corrections. Make sure that anyone judging you entirely by these two sheets of paper would have a very favorable impression.

CHAPTER 14
SPECIAL ASSIGNMENTS: RESEARCH WRITING

So you've finally gotten the assignment, the one so many students dread: Write a research paper. Why should this one assignment be greeted with universal fear and trembling? What, after all, is a research paper?

The term itself is controversial. For some instructors, the assignment calls for the collection of a large number of facts, all of which are to be set out in a kind of museum display for the final paper. The "best papers," those rewarded with the top grades, will be those with the largest collection of facts, the least intrusion of authorial opinion, and the most impressive bibliographies. Is it obvious that I don't prefer this kind of paper? I don't see fact collecting and assembling as particularly valuable skills worth teaching in English classes.

The more justifiable kind of research paper is actually a kind of dressed-up version of the argumentative paper. It develops a thesis that is the opinion of its author, and it does this in much the same ways that the assignments covered in Chapter 9 use. It may differ from these essays in length—although some research papers may be as short as five typewritten pages—and in the source of the proof offered. Instead of supporting your ideas solely from your own experiences or those of your friends, you will need to find supporting evidence from other sources, primarily material written by authorities. When you write a research paper, you must document these sources, providing notes and bibliography entries to show where you were able to find this information. After all, your reader might want to do an in-depth study of the same subject, and your sources could provide a good place to start. Since this documentation is the main difference between a research paper and any other argumentative paper, I prefer to call the assignment a "documented paper." As far as I am concerned, that is what you will be studying in this chapter—how to write a documented paper. Does that sound less formidable?

A SAMPLE PAPER

There are two reasons this assignment is often greeted less than joyfully in my classes. The first is related to boredom. There can be few things more boring than reading page after page on a subject that really leaves you cold. (The Empire State Building, The Growth of Truck Farming—I remember these two topics from my year of teaching high school in a system where the School Board had to approve a list of acceptable topics for the senior research papers. Do I need to say I threw out the list?) Unless the topic is selected for you, you should be able to avoid this problem. Pick a topic that you really are burning to know more about, and you will get more from your reading than just a collection of note cards. The second reason for the groans that greet the assignment of a documented paper is probably lack of experience. Many students have somehow gotten to college without ever having to do one (The teachers always assumed it had been covered the semester before, probably.), and the fear of the unknown overwhelms them. They have only the vaguest notion of what is expected of them. If you are fortunate enough not to have this problem—you wrote term papers in every high-school class, perhaps—you can probably skim the rest of this chapter, just looking for places where my advice might differ from what earlier teachers have said. If you are one of the uncertain students, wondering what a documented paper should look like, anyway, the suggestions in this chapter should help to get you through your first research experience with your sanity intact.

On the next pages is one answer to the question of what a documented paper should look like. It is an essay written in a first-semester English class at Kalamazoo Valley Community College. Please look it over carefully before we go through the specific details of the assignment.

You will notice that the paper looks slightly more formal than the average paper done for this class. It has a title page and a topic outline. (A sentence outline would be okay, too, but this writer settled on a topic outline.) The beginning doesn't look any different from your average paper. If you look, you can find a modified version of the thesis sentence at the end of the first paragraph. Only when you get to paragraph 3 will you notice a difference: The paragraph ends with the number one, slightly raised above the period. This is the first sign that the paper is documented. The number tells you that the source of this information—in this case, the example illustrating the difference between obedience and conformity—will be listed somewhere in the paper. Where will you find this source? Well, if the paper were older than it is, you would undoubtedly find the source given at the bottom of the page, in a *footnote*. In recent years instructors have been sympathetic with the plight of the student-turned-typist who struggles to fit all of the footnotes in that little bitty space at the bottom of the page, and they have modified the required form of the documented paper. Most papers today will have notes, but these will be at the end of the paper, on the last page after the text. Because they are no longer at the foot, they should not be labeled "footnotes." In this paper they are called "endnotes," but you can just as easily call them "notes." Just don't call them "footnotes" unless you want to put them at the foot of each page.

What other differences will you find between your papers written for this course so far and Linda Asmus's paper? Very few. The content of her paper is based largely on her reading, as you can tell. The reading she did for the paper is listed on the very last page, in the bibliography. How is this different from the page of endnotes? Well, the format is different, as we will discuss when we get

BLIND OBEDIENCE TO AUTHORITY

It Could Happen to You

Linda Asmus
English 101
December, 1978

Used with permission of Linda Asmus.

BLIND OBEDIENCE TO AUTHORITY

It Could Happen to You

Thesis: Most ordinary people will blindly obey authority even when that authority directs them to unlawful or immoral action.

I. Definition of obedience

II. Examples of instances of obedience to authority

    A. To political leaders

        1. Lt. William Calley

        2. Hitler's Germany

    B. To religious leaders

        1. Abraham

        2. Rev. James Jones' cult members

III. Dr. Stanley Milgram's experiment

    A. Description of experiment

    B. Results of experiment

BLIND OBEDIENCE TO AUTHORITY

It Could Happen to You

Imagine for a moment you are a nurse working in a hospital. A doctor has left an order for medication for one of his patients. You believe the dosage to be dangerously high. Do you administer the medication in the strength indicated? Perhaps not. Perhaps first you check with your supervisor, who supports your belief. You then check with the doctor involved. The doctor confirms the order as written and directs you to administer the medication immediately. You are, by now, more than ever convinced that this is a potentially lethal dosage. What will you do? The horrifying fact is that if you are an average, ordinary person you will obey authority. History, both modern and ancient, has demonstrated that people will obey authority, even when that authority directs them to unlawful or immoral action.

Blind obedience to authority is the sublimation of one's own will to the will of a supposedly higher being. Blind obedience can become so inbred that one no longer recognizes right from wrong, lawful from unlawful, moral from immoral. All that remains of free will is the will to obey.

Obedience needs to be differentiated from conformity. Conformity is going along with the actions of people who have no special right to direct one's actions. Obedience is complying with the orders of a superior figure. Obedience and conformity can be differentiated further by the example of a soldier who scrupulously carries out the orders of his superior (obedience) and adopts the habits and language of his peers (conformity).[1]

Obedience is required of men in war. Soldiers are trained to obey orders immediately and without question. This is the kind of indoctrination that has led to some well-known atrocities committed in the name of obedience. The Japanese kamikaze pilots were not chosen for their assignments because they were suicidal maniacs. They were highly trained men, obedient even to taking their own lives in the name of country and honor.

Lieutenant William Calley was not a depraved, bloodthirsty monster. He was trained "to find, to close with, and to destroy or capture the enemy."[2] After being charged with the murder of 100 people at My Lai, many of them civilians, women and children, he said, "Could it be I did something wrong? . . . I had found, I had closed with, I had destroyed. . . ."[3]

The worst holocaust in human history, Hitler's destruction of more than 6 million people, is a further example of the consequences of blind obedience to authority. This obedience does not refer solely to Hitler's SS men or even to those who worked at the extermination camps. Every civilian who stood by while these atrocities were taking place displayed passive obedience as they accepted the actions of their government's authorities.

Obedience to religious authorities is documented as far back as the Old Testament of the Bible. In Genesis 22:1–12, God commanded Abraham to sacrifice his only son, Isaac. Obeying God's command, Abraham built an altar, bound Isaac, laid him on the altar and raised his knife to kill him. Here, the Bible tells us, an angel intervened, telling Abraham not to kill his son; the command from God to kill Isaac was a test and Abraham had successfully passed the test.

To this day people still obey religious authorities. Most recent were the well-publicized events at Guyana. The Reverend James Jones was a self-proclaimed messiah. He led 900 devotees to a mass suicide.

> While this tragedy was not entirely voluntary, this was a case where the disciples of Jones lacked the will to resist orders backed by a few armed guards. And perhaps the greatest horror in the scene lay in the realization that more or less ordinary people had been so indoctrinated . . . that nearly anybody might be manipulated in the same way.[4]

Some cults of this kind seek out misfits, the poor, social outcasts and drug addicts; people needing a place to belong, someone to love. But other religious groups, such as the Moonies, Children of God and the Hare Krishnas, prefer college students of above average intelligence. They depend on recruiting these young people at a time in their lives when they are at a crossroads, a time of indecision or confusion. According to UCLA law professor Richard Delgado, who has been studying cults for years, "Everybody is vulnerable. You and I could be Hare Krishnas if they approached us at the right time."[5]

Stanley Milgram, Ph.D., is a professor of psychology at the Graduate Center of the City University of New York. During the years 1960–1963 Dr. Milgram conducted an experiment to determine what a person would do when asked to carry out orders that conflict with conscience. The experiment was conducted at Yale University.

3

The "subject" of the experiment was deceived into believing that he was taking part in an experiment to determine the effects of punishment on learning. A man who was an actor and conspirator in the experiment played the part of the "learner." He was strapped into a chair and an electrode was attached to his wrist. The subject was seated before a shock generator with 30 control switches indicating 15 to 450 volts. The subject was told to read a list of word pairs, then to question the learner about the words read. The subject was then told to administer a shock, and to increase the voltage of the shock, each time the learner made a mistake. As the voltage increased the learner began to protest, then to cry out in pain. He demanded to be released from the experiment. His protests increased to the point of agonized screaming. Let it be said here that the learner was not being shocked at all but was, as previously mentioned, an actor, playing a part.

Whenever the subject indicated that he wished to terminate the experiment, the "authority figure" (the experimenter) responded with a sequence of "prods" to bring the subject into line:

Prod 1: Please continue. Or, please go on.
Prod 2: The experiment requires that you continue.
Prod 3: It is absolutely essential that you continue.
Prod 4: You have no other choice; you <u>must</u> go on.[6]

If the subject still resisted after prod 4, the experiment was concluded.

The purpose of the experiment was to determine how high a voltage the subject would administer before he would refuse to obey authority. The results of the experiment overwhelmingly support the theory that most people will blindly obey authority. Almost two-thirds (65%) of the subjects continued to the last shock on the generator, 450 volts. The mean maximum shock level administered was 405 volts.

Dr. Milgram says:

> This is, perhaps, the most fundamental lesson of our study: ordinary people, simply doing their jobs, and without any particular hostility on their part, can become agents in a terrible destructive process. Moreover, even when the destructive effects of their work become patently clear, and they are asked to carry out actions incompatible with fundamental standards of morality, relatively few people have the resources needed to resist authority.[7]

So here is the frightening, very real possibility: that any one of us could have obeyed orders in My Lai, at Auschwitz, in Guyana. . . .

ENDNOTES

[1] Stanley Milgram, *Obedience to Authority* (New York: Harper & Row, Publishers, 1974), p. 113.

[2] John Sack, *Lieutenant Calley—His Own Story* (New York: The Viking Press, 1971), p. 7.

[3] Sack, p. 8.

[4] Kenneth L. Woodward and others, "How They Bend Minds," *Newsweek*, December 4, 1978, p. 72.

[5] Woodward, p. 72.

[6] Milgram, p. 21.

[7] Milgram, p. 6.

BIBLIOGRAPHY

The Bible, Confraternity-Douay Version. New York: Catholic Book Publishing Company, 1962.

Milgram, Stanley. _Obedience to Authority._ New York: Harper & Row, Publishers, 1974.

Sack, John. _Lieutenant Calley—His Own Story._ New York: The Viking Press, 1971.

Woodward, Kenneth L., Mary Hager, Janet Huck, Michael Reese, Rachel Mark, and William D. Marbach. "How They Bend Minds." _Newsweek_, December 4, 1978, pp. 72-77.

around to format, but the main difference is that the bibliography lists all the reading she did to prepare for writing the paper. The endnotes page lists only sources for the quotes, specific details, or opinions she actually *used* in the paper. (Some instructors prefer that the bibliography omit books read for background information and list only those cited in the paper; if you are supposed to prepare this type of bibliography, you should change its title: Selected Bibliography or Works Cited.) Seeing this example of a successful documented paper should convince you that you can write one, too.

PREWRITING THE DOCUMENTED PAPER

What is the very first step in writing a paper based on research? Buying a stack of four-by-six-inch note cards! You can do this even before you decide on a topic, for whatever your topic turns out to be, you will surely need them. Do not ever make the mistake of taking your notes on sheets of tablet paper; they will be very hard to organize, and you will run the risk of neglecting some vital piece of information altogether, thinking that you had already included everything on that page. The smaller three-by-five-inch cards will often not provide enough room for you to complete a quote or a summary of some important point. There are cards larger than four by six, but they could encourage you to write more than one point on a card. If you limit your notes to one point per card, you will find that organizing them to fit your outline should be easy—even fun!

Once you have your cards, you should be ready to decide on a tentative topic. I am assuming that the choice is yours; if it isn't, you can skip this section. If you are handed a topic, I sympathize with you. Still, I suppose there is something interesting to know about any subject in the world. After all, some people find worms fascinating and make their livings from their knowledge of worms. What may appear to be a dull subject at first may turn out to surprise you. I hope so, for your sake. If you do get a dreadful topic, try to approach it with a sense of humor. Remember, we have all had them. My own worst topic was Glue, and I lived to tell about it.

The most common topics fall into three categories: (1) literary topics, (2) occupational topics, and (3) other controversial topics. In English classes you are often limited to literary topics. Perhaps that is another reason the documented paper is not a popular assignment. Students seldom get worked up about a topic like Thomas Hardy's Use of the Passive Voice in Three Early Novels. Don't get stuck with a topic like this just because it is on a suggested list and you can't think of anything else. Even if the teacher has passed out a list of suggested topics, you can usually get special permission to research a related topic, if you check far enough in advance of the due date. (Don't wait until the class period before the paper is due to suggest a new topic; this looks suspiciously as if your cousin just arrived in town with a paper he had written for a similar course at the state university.)

So how can you find a literary topic that really interests you? Start by thinking about what you like, even if the only literature that comes to mind is a TV show. You like "Star Trek"? Okay, how about working with science fiction? You might compare the work of Jules Verne to that of one of today's science fiction writers, Ray Bradbury or Isaac Asimov, for instance. You might ask yourself this question: How do science fiction writers treat their female characters? I'm sure you could do some fascinating reading before you arrived at the answer that would eventually be your thesis! Maybe you would really rather read *Playboy* than your literature text. Does that suggest any topics to you? How about taking some book that was banned at one time as pornographic and evaluating it? Is *Lady Chatterley's Lover* really pornographic? The answer to that question should be a thesis to satisfy any English prof. Literature is such a broad category, including every aspect of the human condition, that you surely can find a way to relate it to your own interests. Whatever your interests are—cars, money, religion, music—somebody has written about them in novels, poetry, and plays. Find some of this writing, with the help of your librarian, and use it as the basis for a paper that interests *you*.

If your assigned paper has to be in the second category, you will be writing about your current or future occupation, so there should be no problem of lack of interest. However, if you are expected to write an argumentative paper, you may have to give some hard thought to the topic. Imagine a convention of people from the career you are considering. What topics would these people be arguing about in the hotel's cocktail lounges? Some of these ideas might make good questions to begin your research. Suppose you want to be a banker; a good topic for you might be the disappearance of money. Will the change from cash to plastic and to automatic deposit really be as trouble free as some bankers are telling us now? If you set out to answer this, you might come across some information that would be useful to you long before you begin your career. In health careers, controversies are abundant. Every new drug creates a conflict because of possible side effects. Every laboratory discovery opens up possibilities that some would prefer remain closed. Look through a few issues of a professional journal for your specialty; you will surely see some articles on current controversies that might make interesting subjects of research for you.

You're really in luck if your documented paper falls into the third category—other controversial topics. The sky is the limit in this category. Absolutely anything that interests you—well, almost anything; it's hard to turn your new boyfriend or girlfriend into a documented paper—can become a good topic for a paper. The sample paper fits into this category. It was written shortly after the mass suicide at Jonestown, so I imagine the writer got the idea for the topic from that. She probably asked herself, "Why would people obey the Reverend James Jones even to the point of killing themselves and their children?" This led to a broader question: "Is it human nature to obey authority no matter what the consequences?" The reading she did to answer that question convinced her of her thesis: Most ordinary people will blindly obey authority even when that authority directs them to unlawful or immoral action.

What was the last really interesting article you read? Perhaps the topic of that could be turned into a documented paper topic. What about that argument you got into last week? Couldn't you defend your point a little better if you did some reading on the topic? The paper this reading enables you to write may be just incidental. Have there been any crises in your life? Perhaps finding out how other people handled similar problems could lead to a good documented paper. On the other hand, fantasy or the supernatural may be more appealing to you than calamity. Could you argue about the existence of ghosts, the reliability of astrological predictions, or the power of ESP? By now you're probably brimming with ideas, and your only problem is that you can write only one paper! Jot down any ideas you don't use this time in case you ever get a similar assignment.

You don't want to begin your research with a carved-in-stone thesis sentence. After all, your reading might not support your original idea, and you shouldn't force the research into a preexisting mold. Beginning with a question is probably the best way to make sure that the reading you do will be sufficiently related to lead to a paper. Just keep in mind that the *answer* to that question, not the question itself, will be your thesis.

Deciding on a topic is only part of the prewriting, of course. You need to determine your audience and the role you will take in relation to them, too. For most documented papers, however, the choice is quite clear. You write as the expert (your research has made you one) addressing a group of people who are not as informed on the subject as you are. Part of your job may be to clarify certain terms for your audience, as the sample paper did in the second and third paragraphs. Keep in mind that your audience will not be experts, and you should be able to judge how many definitions and explanations they will need.

PREWRITING AT THE LIBRARY

As soon as your paper is assigned, you have your cards, and you've thought of a possible subject, go to the library where you will be doing most of your research. You can't go too soon, so don't tell yourself that it's silly to start four, five, or six weeks before the paper is due. There is a reason that the paper was assigned so far in advance, and that reason is that it will probably take much longer than you expect it to take. Give yourself some leeway by starting early.

Once you are inside the library doors, where do you begin? You probably know that the books are listed in the card catalog (or card catalogs—there may be separate files for author cards, title cards, and subject cards) and that many of the magazine articles are listed in the *Readers' Guide to Periodical Literature*. But where will the information for *your* subject be? Probably in both books and magazines, unless the topic is a really recent controversy. If the discussion is likely to be less than two or three years old, books will not help you very much, and you will have to depend on articles in magazines or newspapers. Do not depend entirely on books, in any case. The most recent information will always be in periodicals. Students who expect to walk into the library and walk out with an armload of books all devoted to their exact topic are almost always disappointed. Even if several books do exist, and even if your library owns most of these books, it is always possible that some other student is writing a paper on a related topic and has beaten you to the books. Even if the shelves have no books on your topic, never say that there isn't any material on that subject. There is always material on any subject you can imagine, and a truly diligent librarian will be delighted to accept the challenge of helping you find it.

You should probably begin your hunt for material with a three-pronged approach: (1) the card catalog, (2) the encyclopedia, and (3) the indexes of magazines. Unless you already know of an author who has written on your subject, you won't get much help from the author-card section of the card catalog; begin with the subject-card section. If you can't find your exact topic, look for related ones. For instance, if you decided on a topic related to pornography, but you couldn't find useful books under this heading, you should check the heading for *censorship*. It might have just what you need. A general encyclopedia is another good place to start, although it won't look particularly impressive in your bibliography. It will provide an overview of the topic and usually suggest some places to go for a more in-depth study of the subject. Don't use it as a major source, but it makes a good jumping-off place. You can get a more intensive discussion of your topic if you can find it in one of the more limited encyclopedias—*Encyclopedia of Religion and Ethics, Encyclopædia of the Social Sciences, Encyclopedia of Social Work, Concise Encyclopedia of Living Faiths,* and *Larousse Encyclopedia of Mythology* are only a few.

Of course, you will already have thought of looking up your topic in the *Readers' Guide*. If you get results that are less than exciting, don't give up on magazines, however. The *Readers' Guide* lists articles printed in the general magazines, the kind you buy at the grocery store or the magazine stand. More specialized magazines—sometimes called quarterlies (because they come out four times a year) or journals—are not indexed in the *Readers' Guide* although they may contain just what you are looking for. Try to decide what kind of magazine might contain articles related to your topic, and then ask your librarian if the library has an index for that kind of magazine. Four especially helpful indexes are the *Education Index* (education magazines have articles on every subject taught in the schools), the *Essay and General Literature Index*, the *Humanities Index*, and the *Social Sciences Index*.

Your forays into the card catalog, the encyclopedias, and the magazine indexes should have produced a few titles, names of books or articles that might be useful to you. Here is where your cards begin to come in handy. For each title that really appears to hold promise, you should make out a bibliography card. On this one card, get down all the information you will need later when you construct the bibliography for your paper. You can save time by putting it down in the same form you will use later; then your final bibliography can be typed right from your cards—alphabetized, of course. If you have all the details you need on these bibliography cards, you can get by on your note cards with only the author's name and the page number (plus a short form of the title, if you have more than one source by the same person). If you have all the details, you also will be saving yourself a late-night trip to the library just before it closes to check the date of publication or the page numbers you will need before you can turn in your paper the next day. This is a lesson most of us have learned the hard way; you shouldn't have to. Your bibliography card should look like this:

```
Milgram, Stanley. Obedience to Authority.
    New York: Harper & Row, Publishers,
    1974.
Call #— (Optional)
```

When you actually find this book, if it is as useful as you expected, you should begin to take notes. Each note card should contain just one idea, and it should be labeled with the source (author and page number). Some of these cards will contain exact quotes. If you are making note of a controversial opinion or you have found an important point worded in an impressive or catchy way, you will want to write down *exactly* what was said. Pay attention to details, even spelling. If a word is misspelled in a passage you want to quote, write the word as the other writer has it, but follow it with [*sic*]. This notation is a Latin abbreviation that tells your reader that you, too, noticed the error, but that you were not at liberty to change it. When you do copy down exact words, be *sure* to put the quotation marks down, too. If you mistake someone else's words for your own and insert them into the paper, you will have made a very unscholarly booboo called "plagiarism." Punishment has been known to range from a poor grade to expulsion from college.

When you take notes on points that you do not quote exactly, you will probably be summarizing the ideas of others in your own words. Accuracy is still very important; you do not want to mistake an author's intent. Leave your speed reading skills at home. If you read too rapidly, it is easy to mistake a minor point for a major one, or to think that a writer is presenting his own ideas when he is actually making note of points he intends to refute. Remember Chapter 9's quotes from Lee A. Iacocca, the head of Chrysler Corporation? Suppose you saw the opening of his rebuttal section—"Some people argue that restricting the number of Japanese cars sold in this country would hype the price of U. S. cars"—and ignored his refutation of this point. If your note card on this section said that Iacocca opposed restrictions on Japanese cars because they would lead to higher prices on American-made cars, you would be dead wrong. Read carefully enough that you can be sure you're getting the author's point.

DEVELOPING YOUR OUTLINE

The research has been going well, you've found several books and magazine articles on both sides of your issue, and you have a stack of note cards that is threatening to break the rubber band that confines it. You should be ready to create your outline. You may want to look over parts of Chapter 8 again to refresh your memory about outlines. The outline for the sample paper is a good example to follow. Perhaps you will find, as I do, that this step of the documented paper is the most fun.

Let's work through the process as Linda Asmus might have done to create her outline. She probably had noticed certain groupings of ideas as she made her note cards. She may have noticed a difference right away between her notes on the Reverend James Jones and her notes on Hitler: The first was a religious leader, the second a political one. When she started making notes on Lieutenant Calley, his obedience in a battle situation was clearly political rather than religious, so she knew he belonged with the followers of Hitler. This distinction eventually turned up in her outline as II. A. "To political leaders" and II. B. "To religious leaders."

Each outline heading or subheading should be put on a separate card. This means Linda had eleven cards for her outline. Now the business of organization becomes very much like a game of solitaire—Round the Clock, I think it's called. Every card from the note-card pile must find an outline card to fit under; if it can't, it goes in the rejection pile. Linda was probably lucky and didn't have too many rejected note cards, as she had a pretty good idea of her topic right from the start. Still, almost every writer finds at least one or two tidbits of information that seem worth writing down when they're discovered but never really fit into the scheme of things later. Don't cry over these; they are a sign that you now have tight control over your subject.

What happens when you have distributed all of your cards if the piles for certain sections of your outline are almost nonexistent? That is a good sign that you need to do more research on that limited area. I hope you have allowed some time for this possibility and not waited to organize your cards until the night before the paper is due. Of course, an outline can be revised, but don't change it unless you are sure you are making it better.

After the cards are in the right piles, your job is to arrange them into sensible order within the piles. Here, too, you may find gaps to fill in with more research. When each outline section appears to have adequate material for development, you are well on your way to having a completed paper. Congratulations!

WRITING THE PAPER

You really don't need a lot of help in writing this documented paper, for it isn't very different in this step from any other argumentative paper you have written. Probably the main problem you will have is fitting in quotations, so pay special attention to any you plan to include.

Look at the first page of Linda's paper. Notes 2 and 3 show two different ways of incorporating quotations. Both are in the paragraph beginning "Lieutenant William Calley." The quote in the second sentence is the kind I call a "silent quote." If you heard the sentence read aloud, you would be unaware that it contained a quote; only part of the sentence is quoted, and it fits right into the grammar of Linda's sentence. The second quote, the conclusion of the third sentence, is obviously a quote and would be recognized as such even if you were listening to the sentence being read aloud. Two clues tell the listener this: the words *he said*, and the use of the first person—*I*—in what he said. If Linda had chosen to use an indirect quote here, she would have had to rewrite the sentence something like this: "He asked if he had done something wrong."

Now look at the quote that goes with note number 4. It is a long quotation, so it is treated the same way any quoted passage over three lines of type should be treated: typed without quotation marks, single-spaced, and indented. These visual clues tell the reader that the material contains someone else's words. It is often good to use introductory words as a clue, too. Linda might have used any of these:

"According to Kenneth L. Woodward,"

"A recent <u>Newsweek</u> article had this comment:"

"As <u>Newsweek's</u> writers observed,"

"Kenneth L. Woodward, writing in <u>Newsweek</u>, points out that this was also a case of obedience to authority."

Any one of these verbal clues would have gone on the line before the indented paragraph and would have been double-spaced, as it was not a part of the quote.

You should note one other point about this indented quotation before we leave it. The last sentence has three spaced points between the word *indoctrinated* and the word *that*. These indicate that the original passage in *Newsweek* contained additional words here that Linda was able to omit without changing the meaning. She did this to achieve conciseness, and it is a good idea to do this so long as you are sure that the meaning is not altered. Some words absolutely could not be treated this way, however. Suppose Linda had decided to put ellipsis points (the official name for the spaced points) in place of the words *not entirely* in the quote's first line? Her quotation would now begin this way: "While this tragedy was . . . voluntary." This would have a very different meaning from what the writer intended; making a change like this one would indicate very poor scholarship.

One other kind of change can be made in quoted material, and although Linda did not use it, you should know about it. Words can be inserted to clarify some point explained in another part of the passage that you do not plan to quote. Suppose, for instance, that Linda had worried that her reader would not know the reference for the words *this tragedy* in the quotation's first line? She could have inserted an explanation in brackets: "While this tragedy [the massacre at Jonestown] was not entirely voluntary. . . ." I ended this quote with *four* spaced points, and if you are enough of a stickler for details to be counting and wondering why, I'll explain. The fourth ellipsis point is actually the period at the end of the sentence. When a sentence does not end in the omitted part of the passage, you need only three spaced points, but if a sentence ends, add a fourth one for the period.

Any quotation that you put in your paper should *sound* as if it fits in. This means matching the grammar of the quotation to the grammar of your sentence. When in doubt, read the whole thing aloud. If you stumble, reword your part of the sentence, or quote less (or more) of the original. This example should show you how you can correct such a problem:

The poet's drug problem had grown to mammoth proportions; according to Holliday, "they were living on borrowed time."[3] (Since the sentence refers to only one poet, the reference to *they* is confusing. Quoting a shorter section would do away with the problem.)

The poet's drug problem had grown to mammoth proportions; according to Holliday, he was "living on borrowed time."[3]

If this documented paper is a little longer than the essays you are accustomed to writing, you may have one other difficulty to watch out for—the introduction. Some students, accustomed to writing very short papers, will leap in with both feet in their first sentence, often starting with their thesis sentence and creating an introduction that is just too abrupt for this slightly-longer essay. Remember that you have a little more time to get to the point in this paper than you often have, and make use of this added freedom. Do not wander all over the place, but make use of your first paragraph or two to attract your reader's attention. Linda's essay is again a good example of using this technique. Note her dramatized hospital scene. Doesn't it get you involved in the conflict right away? What *would* you do if you were the nurse? That's a good introduction, I think.

POSTWRITING CONCERN: THE FORMAT

The postwriting step will be harder for this assignment than it has been for any other you have had to do. You might as well face it: One of the reasons instructors assign documented papers is to give students the experience of following a detailed format. Accuracy to the point of nit-picking is expected. This is not time to protest the conformity demanded by lock-step education. Write your paper against conformity if you must, but be sure its outline, bibliography, and endnotes conform. Creativity does not belong in the form of a note or in a bibliography entry.

It could all be so simple if there were just *one* format to learn and everyone would use it. That's not the case, unfortunately. There are several standard formats, and most disciplines have one that they prefer. However, a department of a college or even an individual professor may have a slightly different set of rules to follow. The most important lesson you should learn in writing a documented paper is this: Always find out what format is the one preferred for the assignment and follow it to the letter. I could write that last sentence ten times, and I still would not be overemphasizing it. It does not mean follow the format pretty closely; it does not mean get the gist of it and improvise the rest; it does not mean make your paper look something like the one given as an example. It means follow it to the letter, right down to the placement of periods.

A big part of the postwriting for this assignment will consist of (1) checking to make sure you have documented what needs to be documented, and (2) checking the form of this documentation to be sure it follows the format given you. Both parts can be difficult.

What needs to have an endnote to tell where you got the idea? To answer this question, consider your reasons for including endnotes. You tell your readers the source of your supporting material in order to provide them with additional material if they want to track it down, to avoid plagiarism and possible lawsuits over stolen ideas, and to establish your own credibility. After all, if you can show that your ideas are based on a thorough reading of a number of reputable sources, your readers will be impressed and will at least give your views some careful thought. This means you need to include endnotes for at least three kinds of material. The first and most obvious kind is the *quotation* or *paraphrase*. Where you have used someone's exact words, or a restatement that comes close to exact words, you must give the source. Second, give the source for people's *opinions* even if they are not included as exact quotes. For instance, if you tell me that Robert Redford is opposed to a bill currently before Congress, I want to have some way of verifying his opposition without calling him up and asking him about it. An endnote will tell me where you found out that he was opposed. Also to be noted are any pieces of factual information that cannot be found easily by consulting a general encyclopedia. Such facts as percentages, costs, population figures or numbers of people involved in various movements or experiments should generally be noted. Dates are readily available in encyclopedias and should not need notes unless there is some doubt about what the actual date was. In general, if you had to look in some special source to find the fact, save your readers' time by telling them what that source was.

Now comes the hard part—what the notes and bibliography entries should *look* like. If you flip back to the page of endnotes in the sample paper, you will see three different kinds of notes: first references to books, first references to articles, and second references to either one. The second references are the easy ones, as they generally need only the author's last name and the page number. Notes 3, 5, 6, and 7 are all of this type. There are times, however, when your second reference is a little more complicated. What do you do when your article has no author? Then a shortened version of the title is used, followed by the page number. Note that the Latin abbreviation *Ibid.* is out-of-date and is no longer commonly used. It should have been given decent burial years and years ago, as it caused more problems than it ever solved. Do not use it.

Books are relatively easy to create notes for, but there can be complications that did not occur in the sample paper. Here are a few examples:

A book with two authors
[1] Carol J. Boltz and Merle O'R. Thompson, Language and Reality: A Rhetoric and Reader (Sherman Oaks, California: Alfred Publishing Co., 1979), p. 24.

(The word *California* is included here because Sherman Oaks is not as well known as New York is.)

An essay that is included in a book written by someone else
   ² Philip G. Zimbardo, "The Age of Indifference," in <u>Writing to Communicate: Rhetoric, Reader, and Handbook for College Writing,</u> ed. Maureen P. Taylor (Belmont, California: Wadsworth Publishing Co., 1983), p. 155.

A book translated from another language
   ³ Paul Valéry, <u>The Art of Poetry,</u> trans. Denise Folliot (New York: Random House, 1958), p. 220.

The sample paper has a note for only one kind of article, a magazine article whose authors are known. Often article notes can be more complicated. Study these examples:

An anonymous article in a magazine
   ⁴ "Affirmative Action," <u>Today's Education,</u> March-April, 1975, p. 91.

(Note that the form is just the same as for the signed article, but the author's name is removed because it isn't known.)

An article in a newspaper
   ⁵ "Athletic Success Starts Early," <u>The Kalamazoo Gazette,</u> May 11, 1983, p. C-1.
   ⁶ Roger Kullenberg, "Election Shows Public Concern," <u>The Kalamazoo Gazette,</u> June 10, 1983, p. A-9.

A pamphlet put out by a group
   ⁷ Michigan Civil Rights Commission, <u>Affirmative Action: Assuring the Right to Equal Job Opportunity</u> (Lansing, Michigan: Michigan Civil Rights Commission, n.d.), p. 2.

(The abbreviation "n.d." stands for no date.)

An article in an encyclopedia
   ⁸ "Alhambra," <u>Funk & Wagnalls New Encyclopedia,</u> 1979 ed., I, 417.

(The Roman numeral is the volume number, and the Arabic numeral is the page number. Usually, when both volume and page numbers are given, the "p." is omitted.)

   ⁹ W[illiam] E. W[elmers], "African Languages," <u>Funk & Wagnalls New Encyclopedia,</u> 1979 ed., I, 250.

(The difference here is that the article ended with the writer's initials. By consulting the Key to Signed Articles in the front of the encyclopedia, you could determine whose initials they were.)

There are other types of articles or pamphlets you could encounter, but these examples should give you an idea of how to handle most problems you may run across. If you have an especially difficult source to note, ask your instructor how to do the note.

When you assemble these items on your endnotes page, you have two choices: double-spacing everything or single-spacing each note and leaving a double space between one note and the next. Both methods are used and recommended by reliable books on how to do a documented paper. You can make your decision based on how many notes you have, if your instructor leaves the choice up to you. If you have too many notes to fit on one page if you double-spaced everything, choose to single-space the notes. If you have only a few notes, double-space everything (as the sample paper does) so that the page won't look so empty.

When you have gotten this far, you have only one more section of your paper to do—the bibliography. Your bibliography cards should be in such good shape that you can just alphabetize them and type right from them. Here are some special points to notice about the bibliography entries:

1. The first difference you should note between the endnotes page and this one is that there is only one entry for each source used, no matter how many references you made to that source.

2. Unlike notes, the bibliography entries are not numbered. They should be easy to count, however, because their indentation is the reverse of that of a note: The first line is the only one that comes to the margin; all other lines are indented five spaces.

3. The order of the bibliography entries is determined alphabetically, by the first author's last name, unless there is no author. In this case, the first significant word in the title (not counting *a*, *an*, or *the*) is used to determine the order. Because of this alphabetical listing, the first author's name—or the only author's name—is inverted, the last name coming before the first name and separated from it with a comma.

4. The punctuation of a bibliography item is also different from that of an endnote. Periods go after the authors' names, after the book or article title, after the date of publication for books, and after the page numbers for articles. Books do not have page numbers given for them, and the numbers given for articles indicate the whole length of the article. (See the fourth entry in the sample paper's bibliography.) Parentheses are not used around the publication information for books, as they were on the endnotes page.

Why don't you see if you can put all this into practice by creating a bibliography for the nine items used as sample notes in this part of this chapter? You may not be able to work out all the details, but try your hand at it, anyway. The bibliography would have to be for an incredible paper to include such dissimilar readings, but forget reality for the moment. After you have constructed your own bibliography from these items, check it against mine on page 221.

WRITING ASSIGNMENT

In doing the assignment for this chapter, you should strive to meet the following objectives. If you meet all seven, you will get a satisfactory grade.

Objectives

1. Turn in your prewriting, including all of your note cards arranged in the order you used them in the final paper.

2. Include an outline, following the standard format, as the page after your title page. This outline should include your thesis sentence.

3. As a major part of the support for your thesis, include references to the reading that you have done. These references should be in the form of summaries (in your own words) and exact quotes.

4. After the text of your paper, include a page of endnotes keyed to the references in your paper.
5. After the endnotes page, include a complete bibliography of the works you read in preparing this paper.
6. Make sure that all of these sections of your paper follow the format of the sample paper given in this chapter and the other recommendations in the chapter.
7. Use standard American spelling, grammar, and punctuation.

BIBLIOGRAPHY

"Affirmative Action." Today's Education, March-April, 1975, pp. 89–94.

"Alhambra." Funk & Wagnalls New Encyclopedia. 1979 ed.

"Athletic Success Starts Early." The Kalamazoo Gazette, May 11, 1983, p. C-1.

Boltz, Carol J., and Merle O'R. Thompson. Language and Reality: A Rhetoric and Reader. Sherman Oaks, California: Alfred Publishing Co., 1979.

Kullenberg, Roger. "Election Shows Public Concern." The Kalamazoo Gazette, June 10, 1983, p. A-9.

Michigan Civil Rights Commission. Affirmative Action: Assuring the Right to Equal Job Opportunity. Lansing, Michigan: Michigan Civil Rights Commission, n.d.

Valéry, Paul. The Art of Poetry. Translated by Denise Folliot. New York: Random House, 1958.

W[elmers], W[illiam] E. "African Languages." Funk & Wagnalls New Encyclopedia. 1979 ed.

Zimbardo, Philip G. "The Age of Indifference." In Writing to Communicate: Rhetoric, Reader and Handbook for College Writing. Edited by Maureen P. Taylor. Belmont, California: Wadsworth Publishing Co., 1983.

Special Assignment 14-1

For this assignment you may choose a topic from any of the three categories for argumentative papers mentioned in this chapter: (1) literary topics, (2) occupational topics, and (3) other controversial topics. Proceed with the prewriting as the chapter directs, preparing bibliography cards, taking notes on cards, creating an outline, organizing your note cards to follow the outline.

For the writing step you will need to develop the support for your thesis so as to make the best use of the material you found through your research. Incorporate some quotations into your paper, being sure that they fit smoothly into your own writing. Some of the material you have found should be incorporated in the form of summaries, stated in your own words but still identified with a note.

Take special care in your postwriting with matters of format. Be sure that the outline, the endnotes, and the bibliography all follow the format you are given. Provide a title page to identify your paper. Proofread everything at least twice, checking spelling, grammatical details, and punctuation. Be especially attentive to these matters in any passages you have quoted. Fasten the whole essay together with a paper clip, and turn it in with a feeling of pride in your work.

PART TWO
READER

FOCUS
SELF

FOCUS
AUDIENCE

FOCUS
THESIS

FOCUS
WORDS

FOCUS
SENTENCES

FOCUS
PARAGRAPHS

FOCUS
ORGANIZATION I
(CHRONOLOGY, PROCESS,
COMPARISON/CONTRAST)

FOCUS
ORGANIZATION II
(ANALYSIS, CAUSE AND EFFECT,
ARGUMENT)

F o c u s

SELF

Here are three very personal essays, all about calamities of sorts. Each describes a very emotional time for the author, and yet each involves a lesson that has significance far beyond the individual. Reading these statements, two by professional writers and one by a student, should give you some insights into ways that personal writing can be used in a universal cause.

Professional Essay

MOMMY GOES TO JAIL
Judith Viorst

Judith Viorst's *Redbook* columns usually offer humorous commentary on some of the ironies of modern life. Although this column contains traces of humor, too, its seriousness was a departure from the norm. In this dramatic narrative, appearing the year before the American withdrawal from Vietnam, Viorst used a very personal experience to make a statement that went beyond the personal: withdrawal from the war was essential for American self-respect. As you read her essay, consider the following points:

1. What is the purpose of Viorst's detailed description of her antiwar activities for almost ten years before the incident of her arrest? Do you think this passage achieves its purpose?
2. What notes of humor do you find in this essay? Do these add to or detract from the generally serious tone of the piece?
3. Do you have a sense of "being there" as you read the narrative of these events? Why or why not?
4. Like Ellen Goodman's "Men, Women and War," this essay appeared in *Redbook*, written by a woman, on a topic related to war. Do you see any other similarities between this essay and the reading in Chapter 6?

Copyright © 1972 by Judith Viorst. Originally appeared in *Redbook* Magazine. Reprinted by permission.

It was the day after I'd been arrested in a peace demonstration and our whole family was sitting around the breakfast table in our home in Washington, D.C.

"Well, Mommy," my five-year-old said, "did you do it?"

I didn't understand. "Do what, baby?" I asked him.

"Did you," he inquired, "end the war?"

Well, no, I'm afraid I didn't. I'm afraid I didn't end the war at all. But then, that wasn't really what I'd expected to accomplish when I made the scary—and for me quite staggering—decision to commit an act of civil disobedience.

For it was, indeed, a staggering decision.

Until that time, you see, my entire criminal history had consisted of one traffic ticket, which had to do, I believe, with parking 24 feet instead of 25 feet from a fireplug. I'd never even swiped a towel from a hotel room. In my personal experience a policeman wasn't a pig but Officer Friendly, a man who, when one of my sons was lost, not only helped me to find him but lent me his hanky to mop up my tears of relief.

You'd certainly call me a law-abiding citizen.

At any rate, that's what you'd have called me until Wednesday, May 24, 1972, when 94 highly proper, respectable war protesters—I among them—sat down in the marble corridor of the Capitol building and chose to be put under arrest.

Actually I'd been preparing to be arrested—should it come to that—well before I'd climbed the steps of the Capitol. It had taken me almost a decade to reach that point.

Yes, for almost ten years I had been marching—in ladylike dresses, sometimes with gloves and a hat—in well-bred protest against the Vietnam War as 5,000, then 15,000, then 50,000, young Americans lost their lives.

For almost ten years I had been picketing the White House or assembling at the Mall or crossing the Potomac to the Pentagon with one child, then two, then three, as I clutched contour diapers and bottles of orange juice—a not very menacing lady.

For almost ten years I had marched—and sung songs and signed petitions and sent telegrams and written letters. But never, not once, had I ever stepped over the line, that line between dissent and disobedience.

Last May I was ready to.

Last May the man who had run for President of the United States on the promise that he would get us out of this war was engaged in dropping bombs up and down North Vietnam and in mining the harbor of Haiphong.

Day after day, flesh-and-blood people like us, flesh-and-blood children like ours, were dying under the assault of American warplanes.

Our President had explained that it was his right and duty as commander-in-chief of the nation's armed forces to protect our boys abroad. But it seemed to many of us, louder and clearer than ever, that there was a far, far better way to protect our boys:

Stop the war.

Stop it now.

Bring them home.

A protest was scheduled.

Milton and I sat down with the kids the evening before. We had already talked it over and decided that only one parent should risk going to jail.

"I might get arrested tomorrow," I began, "in an antiwar demonstration."

Now, let me tell you, it's very hard to capture the rapt attention of three small boys, but I finally succeeded. So before I could lose them to a rerun of *I Dream of Jeannie*, I tried to explain what this protest was all about.

It was the Constitutional right of every American, we told the kids, to petition Congress for a redress of grievances—for the making right of a wrong.

The wrong in this case—our grievance—was the waging of a war we believed unlawful, a war that Congress never had declared.

An emergency-action project, known as Redress, had recruited some 150 solid citizens, many of them distinguished and honored citizens, to petition the United States Congress to end this war.

It was our intention to march to the Capitol, where Congress meets, to present our petition to Carl Albert, the Speaker of the House, and then to wait for Congress to interrupt its business-as-usual business and consider this urgent matter.

It was our intention to wait inside our nation's Capitol for redress.

We might, some of us, wait for a couple of hours. And some of us might wait till asked to leave. And others of us might decide to continue waiting, to sit down on the floor and keep on waiting, even if we were told such an act was unlawful, even if the penalty was arrest.

Needless to say, the children had plenty of questions.

Anthony, my ten-year-old, was cynical. "What's the use of another demonstration?" he said. "None of the others ever helped at all."

Nicholas, my eight-year-old, was bewildered. "But good guys," he insisted, "obey the law. Bad guys break it."

Alexander, my five-year-old, was alarmed. "Will you be taken to jail?" he asked. "And who will tuck me in when I go to sleep?"

Now, I'm not, God knows, cavalier about the fears of a five-year-old child. If anything, I'm considered overprotective. But by the time we'd finished talking about the details ("I'll be home the very next day at the very latest," I told him, "and you're going to have your dad to tuck you in"), he seemed assured that he would be okay.

And after we'd finished explaining that an act of passive civil disobedience had little to do with his gaudy TV notions of break-ins and holdups and shoot-outs and getaway cars, he seemed assured that I'd be okay too.

The other boys were not so easy to answer.

For what could I say that would justify breaking the law to a child I had recently punished for snitching a nickel? I deeply do not believe in the snitching of nickels. I deeply do not believe in the breaking of laws.

And that's what I said.

"I'm doing something I think is a sad thing to do. Something I've always thought I shouldn't do. Something that, for me, is terribly hard to do."

"So how come," Nick interrupted, "you want to do it?"

As best I could I spoke of how I didn't *want* to do it, but felt I must. I said that the reluctance with which I'd commit an act of civil disobedience and the sorrow with which I would consciously break a law were a crucial part of the protest I was making. For I would, in effect, be saying to my Government: My horror of the war, my revulsion toward it, has pushed me finally to this desperate act.

"And it won't," said Anthony, "do a bit of good."

I told my son that maybe he was right, that maybe it wouldn't do a bit of good. And yet, I said, it seemed to me that we had to keep on trying. How awful if nobody cared enough to try!

Then it was time to be going to sleep, for I planned on rising early the following morning. I might be willing to get myself arrested, but not before I'd made the beds, dusted the whole downstairs and waxed the front hall.

Which is what I found myself doing at 6 A.M.

It would be nice to say that at 8:15, when my children kissed me good-by and left for school, we shared a touching and rather beautiful moment. But rather beautiful moments are hard to come by with my exceedingly unsentimental boys.

"Bring us a present from jail," hollered Nick as he galloped out the door.

"Make it a police dog," yelled Alexander.

And Anthony added, tossing a baseball into his well-oiled glove, "Behave, or else they'll put you on bread and water."

I had, of course, no real concern about diets of bread and water, but it struck me that my dinner might be delayed. And so before I went to the demonstration I stuffed my canvas tote with survival rations: 30 Hershey bars, a big box of crackers and several packs of sliced American cheese.

Furthermore, as long as I was preparing I threw in a murder mystery, my toothbrush, my jar of aspirins in case I got a headache and my cystitis pills in case I got cystitis.

On a more sobering note, in my wallet there were $50 for bail money and a dime for the just one call I'd be able to make.

My husband gave me a hug and told me he loved me. I was on my way.

My first stop was a meeting of the people who would join the Redress action, where we reviewed the petitioning procedure and the possibility for some of us of arrest. The discussion was led by an earnest and gracious man, Robert Lifton, professor of psychiatry at Yale. He was among the well-dressed, not terribly young, middle-class men and women in that room who would later be taken to jail, along with Nobel-prizewinning biochemist George Wald; Felicia (Mrs. Leonard) Bernstein; educator Jonathan Kozol, author of *Death at an Early Age;* folk singer Judy Collins; actress Barbara Harris; Richard Falk, professor of international law at Princeton; and Dr. Benjamin Spock.

At one point in the meeting, the elderly, balding, gentle Dr. Wald, who, like most of us, had never before been arrested, asked if someone could say what it would be like.

Dr. Spock, impeccable in his somber business suit, stood up and explained, in a tone and style right out of *Baby and Child Care,* precisely what to expect in the course of arrest. As always, he was very reassuring.

At the end of the meeting we signed the giant scroll upon which the grievance petition had been lettered. And then, two by two, in solemn and silent procession, we marched through the heat of early afternoon across the Capitol Plaza . . . up the Capitol steps . . . into the corridors of the Capitol.

Before we entered the building we were offered greetings and support by several members of Congress, and inside the Capitol, House Speaker Carl Albert courteously accepted our petition. It would, he told us, be sent to the proper committee right away. "Nice to see you," he said. "Thank you for coming."

At this stage, of course, the mannerly thing to do would have been to leave. And all of us who were there were mannerly people. But this time we would stay where we were, and thereby press beyond the point of politeness. Most of us—a group of 32 women and 62 men—would stay where we were when, at the end of that long afternoon, we were ordered out by the Capitol police.

"This wing of the building is now closed," came the announcement over the bullhorn.

We sat down.

I did not feel in myself as I sat there, or in those around me, anything either frivolous or enraged. My companions seemed to be serious, rational people who, when they spoke of how they had come to this moment in their lives, said things like this:

"It isn't fair that it's always the kids who take the risks for peace. Their elders must too."

And, "I will not behave like a Second World War 'good German.'"

And, "I want my son to respect me."

And, "I'm here today because I love my country."

And that was the theme—not "Ho-ho-ho Chi Minh" but "America the Beautiful"—of the songs we sang as police came to take us away. One at a time, first women, then men, we were led unresisting down the Capitol stairway, sustained by the applause of those still there. The hand of the young policeman who held me trembled as he guided me to the paddy wagon. Don't be nervous, I thought, and neither will I.

But just as the good Dr. Spock had promised earlier, there was nothing to be nervous about.

The paddy wagons drove us to police stations (the men to one, the women to another) where in groups of five we were locked into tiny, quite grubby-looking cells, each with a metal bunk and an open toilet. My cell mates, ranging in age from their 20s to 40s, were women with jobs and credit cards and kids, the kind of women you meet for lunch at Schrafft's or share car pools with. Sitting side by side on our bunk, we traded names and histories and Hersheys—and waited for the "processing" to proceed.

Processing meant being fingerprinted and photographed and questioned and searched. My belt was taken away from me, and so were my glasses, my wedding ring, my pills and my purse.

"She's a walking lunch bag!" one astounded policeman exclaimed as he plowed through the food supplies in my canvas tote. But they let me keep it.

And they treated me, for the most part—despite the official procedures—much more like a neighbor than a crook. I even discovered that one of them was helping to coach my ten-year-old's neighborhood ball team. Were we really on opposite sides?

I was let out of jail at 10:30 P.M., though some of the others weren't released until morning, and my husband and oldest boy came to pick me up. Friends were waiting back at my house to show that they would still be glad to know me.

It was good to be home.

The following Wednesday I appeared at a hearing, with several other defendants, on a misdemeanor charge, illegal entry. (This charge apparently also includes not going when ordered to leave.) Some pleaded not guilty on the grounds that the right of a citizen to petition his Government should not so abruptly be abridged. In other words, why *couldn't* they sit and wait? A future trial date was set for them.

Like most of the others, I pleaded *nolo contendere*, which means no contest, a by-and-large guilty plea. The judge, a kindly gentleman, fined me $25 and asked if I would like to make a statement.

I told him I would.

The words I chose were those of Congressman James Abourezk, who comes from a state in our nation's heartland, South Dakota. Many eloquent men, both in and out of Congress, have spoken against the war, but few, I think, as movingly as he.

"Mr. Speaker," he said, addressing House Speaker Carl Albert this past April, "it is a dirty war.

"It is a hateful war.

"It is a war which has hurt us at home more than we will ever know.

"It is murder.

"It is folly.

"It is the second-worst enterprise of which mankind has been capable in the twentieth century.

"Those are human beings, Mr. Speaker, on our side, on their side. When a bullet rips the flesh, when a midnight explosion scatters the parts of the body and when the blood runs on the ground, whether on our side or theirs, it is part of the family of man that has been destroyed.

"Are we cannibals? Do we propose to tame political passions in Vietnam by killing or crippling everyone there?

"When does it stop, Mr. Speaker? When?

"When our own children will no longer look us in the eye, is that when?"

I have a police record now, and I'll have it as long as I live. I am now a convicted offender and a crime statistic. My kids are aware of this, but I don't believe they're ashamed of me. They might even be proud.

"Did your mother really go to jail?" one of Nick's classmates, appalled and enchanted, asked him.

"Yes, she did," Nick answered. "Why didn't yours?"

SELF 231

Professional Essay

MEMORIES OF A SMALL BOMB
Morton Sontheimer

In this "My Turn" column, Sontheimer relates a personal experience from World War II to make a commentary on the possibilities of nuclear warfare today. Like Viorst, he uses a very personal approach to draw attention to a universal problem. As you read his essay, consider the following points:

1. The opening paragraph is a real attention-grabber. Does he also use this to unify the essay? Is the promise of this opening carried out?
2. Much of this essay is descriptive, and many of the descriptions are sentence fragments. Do you see any reason for these? Are they effective for you? Why or why not?
3. Does this essay have a real thesis sentence? Where is it? If there is none, could you formulate one to summarize the obvious point of the essay?
4. Which of the many descriptive images is the most powerful for you? Why?
5. Do you think Sontheimer would have described his Nagasaki experiences in basically the same way if he had written this in 1945, or have the intervening years affected the self he is presenting in this essay?

Copyright 1981 by Newsweek, Inc. All rights reserved. Reprinted by permission.

Did you ever sit home alone at night reading, and suddenly have the feeling that something ominous lay crouched and waiting for you?

It happened to me the other night. No ghost story, no fiction did it. I was reading a solid analysis of Israel's sudden bombing of the Iraqi nuclear plant and the Israelis' explanation that they were afraid of the nuclear bombs they expected to come from the plant. Such an incident, said the article, could presage a nuclear war. . . .

My mind went back to a clear day in August, 36 years ago this summer.

On that day an American airplane appeared over Nagasaki, released a single bomb and wisely hastened off, all throttles open. Three days earlier the same thing had happened over Hiroshima, but then the Japanese Government reacted only with stunned confusion.

Nagasaki shook them out of it. Within six days—quite fast for a muddled government—the Japanese surrendered unconditionally, bringing the end of World War II, and the beginning of God knows what.

There are people today who may not remember that Nagasaki was the last city to sample nuclear warfare.

Sample? Yes, that bomb was a peewee compared to the bombs and missiles in the hands of Russia and America and England and France and China and maybe Israel and South Africa and perhaps soon Pakistan and other countries.

Blast: I was among the first small detachment of Americans to enter Nagasaki after the bomb. I got to see a little bit of what that peewee did. Only a little because the devastation stretched for miles and from where I stood, all transportation had dissolved, literally.

I was at Point Zero, the designation for the exact center of the blast. Not where the bomb hit. It never did. It was set to explode *above* the city and that's what happened, precisely where intended. Precisely above where I was standing.

How could we tell? Easy. The only things that withstood the blast were metal poles. Not trees. They had vanished totally, as had whatever the poles once carried. But at this particular spot, you could turn in a complete circle and every pole leaned precariously away from you. Point Zero.

The destructive power of modern war was not new to me. I had been through the battered walls and buildings of old Manila. I had just come from trudging through the debris of acres and acres of Tokyo, where thousands of our bombs had blasted buildings and bodies into jigsaw junk.

Nagasaki was different. An open field. Occasional low humps of stone, bricks, mortar. No wood. No bodies. It was, in a ghastly way, neat. Clean even.

It was different in another, more subtle way, too. In Tokyo curious crowds had gathered around us, craning to see those tall foes in khaki who had defeated them. In Tokyo they were not unfriendly. Those who could speak English were generally helpful. But in Nagasaki the Japanese we saw avoided us. There was no mistaking the fear in their eyes. And the hatred. Nobody lifted a hand against us. Their Emperor had told them not to, and the Japanese were a most obedient people. But they could shoot glances of pure dread and enmity. There was no mistaking that.

One building, a university about a mile away on a hill, had its walls intact. I don't know why. The distance probably helped but it had to have been a remarkably solid structure. Somebody told me everything inside had vanished in the blast.

I tried to grasp that one plane with one bomb in one instant had done all this. Was it really possible? Still, I had been grateful for that bomb. Yes, many of us, perhaps most of us who expected to go in on the invasion of Japan, were grateful for the abrupt end of the war. We didn't talk about it much but I'm sure many of us thought the bomb had saved our lives. Up until that time, though, it had seemed a newfangled invention that did a necessary job quicker. How quicker? One of the team of scientists whose entry had provided my excuse for being there was speaking to me.

"Hey, Captain," he said. "You know you're standing on a corpse?"

What the hell was he talking about? He was pointing at my feet. I looked down. My feet were in a circle of fine white ash, not thick enough to feel through my boot soles.

I can't tell you my reaction. I felt confused, embarrassed, as though some sort of apology was called for. I stepped outside the ashen circle. I resisted a temptation to take off my cap.

Strange: Had that spot been a man? A woman? A child? An oldster? Beautiful? Ugly? What color? No answer. All human ashes look alike. Nothing left to bury.

I had seen many of those spots on my way to Point Zero. There was so much strange emptiness to engage my vision that I had hardly noticed them or been curious.

Later I learned to distinguish the small irregular oblong spots, many fewer, that had been animals—dogs or cats, I guess.

Altogether there were thousands of spots. It occurred to me that they marked the most instantaneous deaths in the history of the world.

They never knew. Never felt a thing. They lucked out, they really did. Miles away, the maimed and the blinded, the mindless and the limbless took longer to die. Some of them took years. Many were disfigured and grotesque. The kind of people who may be left to repopulate the world someday.

It would be fitting to say I've never stopped thinking about it, never been able to get it out of my mind. But that's not true.

Funny how the mind works. I had erased it completely from my thoughts. To this day, what I've written here is absolutely all I really can remember about the several days (can't recall how many) I spent in Nagasaki. And dredging up that much was difficult.

If an experience is awful enough, I guess the mind kindly expels it or covers it up.

Then suddenly one peaceful night it comes back to haunt you. And makes you realize what lies crouched and waiting—unless the whole world is quickly blessed with wisdom. God grant.

Student Essay

PREPARING FOR THE JOB
Mary Jo Volosky

Here is a third example, this one by a student, of a very personal essay with far-reaching implications. Although the focus is on the self, the lesson to be learned applies in one way or another to us all. As you read this essay, consider the following points:

1. Is Miss Scott's lecture a good beginning for this piece? Why or why not? Could its counterpart be found in high schools today, more than twenty years after she delivered it?
2. What purpose do the two dialogues serve in this essay? Are they effective for you?
3. Has Volosky included a direct statement of this essay's thesis anywhere? If so, where is it? If not, could you state one for her?
4. It would be easy to write an essay on this personal topic and to make it a real tear-jerker, an appeal for pity. Has Volosky added any touches to lighten the topic, to keep it from becoming a sob story?
5. What does the conclusion accomplish?

Used with permission of Mary Jo Volosky.

"Now, girls," began Miss Scott, "in choosing your curriculum for next semester, be mindful of the job for which you are preparing." As she spoke, I sat attentively beside my friend Ruthie, in the old U-shaped building known as St. Luke High. Later, as we walked our usual route home, past Grosso's Corner Market, where we frequently stopped for a nickel bag of Snyder's potato chips, we discussed Miss Scott's lecture.

"Okay, Merje, what are you taking?"

"Well, Rue, I'm thinking about taking trig."

"Oh, Merje, that's for boys! Geez, you going to be an old maid, or what?"

The year this conversation and many others like it took place was 1959. Girls were encouraged to learn to cook, sew, raise children and keep house. The boys would take care of everything else. Then you simply met Mr. Right and married. Oh yes, there would be problems, but nothing that couldn't be handled with an extra fancy dinner prepared for that special man of yours.

Two years ago, the man I had married 17 years before announced that he no longer wished to remain married to me. In addition to the emotional consequences were the practical ones. I scanned the want ads of our local newspaper, looking for a job for which I was "prepared."

"Let's see, Housewife, Mommy, Pantspatcher, Cook?" Yes, there was an ad for a cook. Hopefully, I dialed the number. The voice on the other end of the phone inquired as to my qualifications.

"Well, Sir, I have cooked for my family for 17 years and was at the top of my cooking class in high school."

"I'm sorry, Ma'am, but we need someone with experience. Thank you for calling."

Today, I had a long distance call from my friend Ruth. Her husband of 15 years had left and was living with another woman, leaving Ruth and their two children alone. She is struggling to take care of them and at the same time hold her minimum-wage job as a nurse's aide at the local nursing home.

My mind darts back to the dinner we shared at Ruthie's nearly a year ago. She was a wonder. She had a happy husband, two lovely children, and that cucumber salad—where did she get that recipe? She had a beautiful, well cared for home and plans to move into a new one soon.

Before you begin to think of me as a cynic, let me stop to clarify a point. I am not saying that all women of my generation evolved in this manner, but rather that all of us were trained for one job which many of us no longer hold. The women's movement has helped so, at least, I don't feel like a rejected freak. I can say simply that I'm "doing my own thing," or whatever.

But I did my job so well. Everyone says I'm a marvelous cook, even my ex-husband. So why, at the age of 36, am I taking trigonometry?

F O C U S

AUDIENCE

All three writers of the following essays had to give particular thought to their audiences before they started to write. The two professional authors were both writing for quite similar audiences, but their indictments of television are based on very different details. Study the ways they addressed their audiences, and determine the effectiveness of their appeals. Although the student essay is less argumentative, it represents a particular problem in the author-audience relationship: writing as an expert without turning off the uninformed reader. If you ever have to write a process paper, you should read this one for clues in handling the problem.

Professional Essay

DECODING TV COMMERCIALS
Hal Kome

This former advertising writer has really thought about his audience and what they should know about TV advertising. He provides them with a behind-the-scenes view of the commercial industry, which should make them more effective and informed consumers. As you read his essay, consider the following points:

1. Kome starts his article with a lengthy illustration before he gets to his main point. Does the example of Fresh Start make a good introduction? Why or why not?
2. Which of the various coding devices mentioned by Kome do you notice most frequently on TV?
3. Which of the coding devices seems most dishonest, or are they all honest business tactics?
4. Does Kome try any special techniques to keep this article from sounding like a string of illustrations, one after the other, with no continuity?
5. Do you think that advertisers in recent months have made any attempt to be less misleading than they were in the commercials quoted here? Give some examples of recent commercials that either continued the practices discussed in this essay or gave more honest views of their products.

Copyright 1980. Reprinted with permission of *Consumers Digest* Magazine.

You're watching TV and a detergent commercial comes on. It shows you "concentrated detergent granules that contain the best cleaning ingredients of powders and the best grease dissolving ingredients of liquids." The detergent is called Fresh Start.

Does Fresh Start do a better job than other detergents? No. It may be as good as other detergents, but it's not better.

How can you tell? The commercial itself tells you, because the last words in the commercial are, "No leading detergent does *more* for your wash."

Looked at another way, those words mean that at least one leading detergent, and possibly more than one, can claim to do as much as Fresh Start. If this weren't the case, Fresh Start would be eager to say, "No leading detergent does as much as Fresh Start can do."

This is an example of what advertising people call a *strong parity claim.* It's one of the many coding devices ad people use to try and make you believe their products are better, newer, healthier, or more effective than their competitors—whether they are or not.

If you understand the coding devices, you can decode TV commercials and end up with a pretty accurate idea of any advertised product's worth. The key is to expect some hidden messages and half-truths. All sophisticated advertisers have their ways of conveying positive impressions without venturing into the area of outright lies or fraudulent advertising—and it's up to you to recognize these.

The strong parity claim is one of the most often used coding devices. A Hertz commercial uses this device, but combines it with another. Hertz, according to the commercial, gets you "from the plane seat to the driver's seat fast." This is noncomparative, or what's known in the ad business as a *monadic claim.*

Hertz will get you in a car fast—according to their own definition, which may not be yours. You have no way of knowing, from the commercial, whether Hertz's service is the fastest, or even whether it's faster than Avis or National or Budget, or anybody.

The Hertz commercial does, however, make one thing clear. It confirms Hertz's lack of superiority in the number of ways to provide fast service. The commercial's final line is a typically rendered strong parity claim. When it comes to fast service, according to the commercial, "Nobody's figured out more ways than Hertz."

From a decoder's point of view it's clear that the other fellows have probably figured out just as many.

Champion spark plugs has used a strong parity claim for years, because they are not superior to other spark plugs. The Champion claim, delivered with great conviction and sometimes even in a song, is "You can't buy a better plug." Obviously, you can buy one that's just as good. And if it's cheaper, it's a better buy.

Rolaids likewise relies on a strong parity claim. A stentorian announcer tells you that "Rolaids gives relief that Tums can't beat; yes, relief that Tums can't beat." He seems to be saying that Rolaids is better than Tums. In fact, he's saying that Rolaids is just as good as Tums, but not better.

Strictly Speaking

The strong parity claim has a number of ad coding relatives, all designed to make you believe that products are better than they are. Fortunately, with a few decoding lessons, you can read the commercials like a good pro quarterback can read the opposition's defenses.

Palmolive Dishwashing Liquid is a fascinating commercial to decode. The commercial is strictly truthful, but so artfully done that you probably get the impression of a much bigger promise than the commercial in fact makes.

Madge the manicurist, played by actress Jan Miner, has been featured in Palmolive Liquid commercials for fifteen years. She has a succession of clients with rough skin on their hands. Palmolive Liquid appears to be the answer.

Two decoding devices are used in these commercials. The first device is *literal truth,* otherwise known as *strict construction.* The second device is that of *casual candor.* It is very similar to the way a card trick artist forces a card on you, without your realizing it.

The literal truth device comes at the turning point of the commercial. Madge tells each client that Palmolive Liquid "softens your hands while you do the dishes." This is literally true. Any noncorrosive liquid, combined with water, will moisturize, or soften, hands for the time they are in it. But not after. The statement is literally true, but appears to be promising much more.

Now let's look at casual candor. Madge's client asks Madge, "What'll I try?" Madge answers, "Everything. And use Palmolive Dishwashing Liquid." That word, "Everything," is a prime example of coding by casual candor. Most viewers undoubtedly miss it, and not by accident. It's placed in the dialogue in a highly missable position, and delivered by the actress as a deliberate throwaway.

What the word tells a decoder is that the results shown at the end of the commercial come from good, comprehensive hand care, not merely from the use of Palmolive Liquid. A decoder's reading makes it easy to learn that Palmolive Liquid is no world beater when it comes to softening the skin on your hands.

So What?

Moisture Wear by Cover Girl spends almost an entire commercial trying to convince the viewer of its moisturizing magic. Then, in the last line, a good decoder learns the truth. The model on camera says, "Imagine, with the right makeup, I can look years younger."

The code device might be termed the *connected irrelevancy*—a form of false syllogism. It isn't relevant to Moisture Wear's moisturizing ability that the right makeup can make a person look years younger. But it seems to be, because moist, unlined skin can also make a person look years younger.

The two things are connected, but not in a relevant way. The commercial is actually telling you that good makeup can make you look years younger, but Moisture Wear probably can't, or they would have said so.

Raintree uses an irrelevant fact in a different way. Raintree claims to be different because "every drop's got real natural protein." This is probably true, but it's also entirely beside the point. Protein has no moisturizing effect whatsoever. If it did, many women would go to bed every night with their faces packed in hamburger.

Helpful Hints

Tone, another skin care claimant, uses two code devices to make a promise seem bigger than it is. The first is the commonest of all ad writers' cliches, the *helps device*. In the Tone promise it reads like this: "Tone can help you start your day with your skin the best it can be."

The word "help" is everywhere in advertising. It means, first of all, that the product can't really do what it claims to do, it can only help do it. Secondly, it does not stand for any specific degree of help. It may be 50 percent help, or 10 percent help, or 1 percent help. Or less.

In general, when a TV commercial decoder sees the word "helps" in a commercial, it means to him or her that the product is ineffective or, at best, only partially effective.

Did you catch the other Tone device? It's a variation of the strong parity claim. A variation that places the burden not on the product, but on you, the user.

It's the part about getting your skin "the best it can be." That may not be very good, but it's not Tone's fault. Tone bows out of responsibility with that phrase. If your skin looks lousy after using Tone, it's because it just can't be made to look any better. And that's that.

Apples and Oranges

What about commercials that actually dare to compare? Some commercials appear to be revealing the true state of things. And sometimes they are what they appear to be, but only if you're adept at decoding.

Take the case of Duracell, a product that has dared to compare for many years. "Duracell," the commercial ends, "no regular battery looks like it, or lasts like it."

That's the truth. But it's also true that both Eveready and Ray-O-Vac have premium batteries that do perform as well as Duracell. The key to understanding this kind of advertising is in understanding the code device of *carefully chosen comparison*.

"After four hours of use," the Duracell commercial says, "regular carbon batteries wear out." But Duracell is not a regular carbon battery, nor is Eveready's best battery, nor is Ray-O-Vac's. A top of the line item is being compared to a run-of-the-mill item.

Excedrin uses the same device, claiming that Excedrin "works better than ordinary strength pain relievers."

Ban roll-on uses the carefully chosen comparison in a very sophisticated way. A woman in the commercial says that "A friend lent me her Sure aerosol." This same woman learns that her Ban roll-on works better, and the commercial claims that Ban "keeps you drier than any leading spray."

It's true. But it's also true that roll-ons, in general, contain about twice the concentration of antiperspirant found in sprays. Any decent roll-on will be a more effective antiperspirant than any spray. Ban, significantly, avoids comparisons with other roll-ons.

Which brings us to Right Guard, purportedly made for men, "because men perspire more." Does this mean that Right Guard is a superior antiperspirant? Decoding says no.

Here's the Right Guard claim: "So strong, so effective, it helps stop a man's perspiration all day long—strong, effective Right Guard." The "helps" device is at work here, as is the strong parity claim. But nothing in the commercial should lead you to believe that Right Guard is a superior product.

Not So Unique Features

Preemption is another favorite coding device of TV commercial writers. The writer takes a fact which is common to all products in a particular category and makes it seem exclusive only to one product.

The Pillsbury Frosting Supreme paper knife is an example. It's true that Pillsbury Frosting Supreme can be spread with a paper knife, but so can Betty Crocker frosting.

Miss Breck hair spray ads also use a preemptive device. The young lady in the commercial says, "Miss Breck hair spray weighs less on my hair than this feather." Undoubtedly true, not only of Miss Breck, but of many hair sprays.

Doan's pills have preempted an entire category—backache. Doan's claims to have a "medically proven pain killing ingredient" that "takes the ache out of backache." Aspirin, the ingredient, is hardly unique to Doan's.

But Doan's isn't the only product that plays games with aspirin. Many products do it. Perhaps the most widely known is the Anacin claim for having the "pain killer that doctors recommend most." The ingredient, of course, is aspirin.

Grammatical Games

Hookups were once a very popular coding device for ad writers. Certain regulatory changes have made them less common, but they still exist.

In using a hookup, an ad writer will take a desirable quality of a product and hook it up with a less desirable quality. Then the commercial will claim overall superiority, implying that the product is better in all respects, not just in one.

A recent example involves two cereals aimed at the "kiddie market," Frankenberry and Count Chocula. Frankenberry claims to have "strawberry flavor and real marshmallow." Count Chocula claims to have "chocolatey flavor and real marshmallows."

A good ad decoder sees that the only thing "real" in either cereal is the marshmallows. The word "real" seems to hook up with "strawberry flavor" and with "chocolatey flavor," but in fact it doesn't. The careful grammatical construction is a clear sign that these products use artificial strawberry flavoring and artificial chocolate.

Viva towels use a hookup device somewhat differently. Viva claims to be "unbelievably strong, unbelievably absorbent." They then show two towels in use, side by side. The Viva towel is shown to be stronger, but not necessarily more absorbent. You are being helped to think, however, that Viva is both stronger and more absorbent, through the device of a hookup.

Colonial Penn Life runs a commercial that borders on deception, because the decoding device is *deliberate withholding of information*. The company offers life insurance at only $6.95 a month to anyone between the ages of fifty and eighty. What the commercial neglects to mention—one rather important thing—is the amount of the coverage.

Comet Cleanser falls back on an old bugaboo of grammar teachers to make its claim seem important. The claim is that Comet is "the cleanser more hospitals use to disinfect bathrooms." The coding device here is the *dangling comparison*, and the decoder's question is "Compared to what?" Again, information is being withheld.

Feeble Promises

One more coding device might be called *softening the promise*. This is related to the "helps" device, but is usually reserved for products with a clear difference that, somehow, don't deliver as well as you might think.

Soft Scrub is a good example. Soft Scrub is a liquid cleanser that calls itself a mild abrasive. Soft Scrub says that it "doesn't scratch like powder cleansers."

This seems very reasonable, considering that Soft Scrub is a liquid. But the product claims less than one might think, promising only "cleanser scrub without all that cleanser scratch." Obviously Soft Scrub does scratch, though to a lesser degree, and that's the decoding of it.

Liquid Dentrol, a denture adhesive, uses the same device to soften its promise. Liquid Dentrol says it's for people who "hate the grit, hate the mess, hate the taste."

The product promises to seal dentures "without all the gummy, gritty, gooey mess you hate." An ad decoder has to conclude that Liquid Dentrol still involves some gum, grit, and goo.

Decoding Exercises

Now let's see if you can decode a couple of commercials on your own.

Close-Up toothpaste "gets your teeth as white as they can be." Is Close-Up a superior tooth whitener?

A Carolina diaper service offers "the most absorbent cloth diapers you can get." Are the diapers more absorbent than Pampers?

If you decided that Close-Up is not a superior tooth whitener, you were a good decoder. "As white as they can be" may not be very white at all.

If you decided that the diaper service diapers are less absorbent than Pampers, you were a good decoder. Obviously the comparison was limited to cloth diapers, probably because the diaper service diapers are inferior in absorbency to products like Pampers.

Here's a tougher one. The commercial says "No little cinnamon gum freshens breath longer than Big Red. Give your breath long-lasting freshness with Big Red."

If you think that Big Red freshens breath longer than Dentyne, you're wrong. The words quoted above are a very artful use of our first code device, the strong parity claim. No little cinnamon gum freshens breath longer than Big Red. But, clearly, it freshens breath just as long.

Finally, let's try to decode a pair of commercials that seem to be contradicting each other.

Mazola Corn Oil, "one hundred percent corn oil and nothing else," says that "Mazola tastes lighter." Sunlite, a sunflower oil, claims that "no oil makes fried foods taste lighter."

These two commercials seem to be contradicting each other, but maybe not. When Mazola says "Mazola tastes lighter," they may mean that Mazola tastes lighter when you sip it from a spoon, not when you taste it on fried foods. Or they may mean that Mazola tastes lighter than lard, or mutton fat.

In fact, the Mazola claim is a dangling comparison, with no antecedent. It doesn't mean, or promise, anything and should be discounted.

Sunlite, on the other hand, is probably understating its case. In the real world, not the world of decoded TV commercials, sunflower oil contains significantly more polyunsaturates than corn oil. And since polyunsaturates are the lightest oils, it follows that a sunflower oil should be, and should taste, lighter.

The Sunlite ad writer's inability to deliver the product's promise is exasperating. Still more exasperating is the willingness of Mazola to imply that corn oil is the standard of lightness. Even if you're good at decoding commercials, you can't learn the truth from this pair.

And that is the ultimate limitation of decoding. Even once you have succeeded in decoding a commercial, you will probably still lack enough hard information to judge the product's merits.

After all, when you've sorted out all the dangling comparisons, softened promises, connected irrelevancies, and parity claims, what remains? Unfortunately for the consumer, very little. Stripped to their essentials, most 30- and 60-second TV commercials are little more than "sound and fury, signifying nothing"—though they imply and suggest much more.

Professional Essay

THE ARAB STEREOTYPE ON TELEVISION
Jack G. Shaheen

Shaheen, professor of mass communications at Southern Illinois University, is writing here for the same audience as the previous essayist—television viewers. His concern is to educate his readers about a kind of discrimination in television programming that they may not have considered, and he uses numerous examples of shows and commercials—only about half reproduced here—to make his point. As you read his essay, consider the following points:

1. What does Shaheen tell you about himself to establish his credibility for you? Do you accept his credentials?
2. What is the television image of the Arab, according to the description in this article?
3. Which example seems the most discriminatory to you?
4. Have Arabs been depicted any more even-handedly in programs or commercials aired in the most recent television season? Think of some examples to back up your opinion.
5. What other groups are still shown in a bad light in current television programming?

Copyright 1980. Reprinted with permission of Americans for Middle East Understanding.

In recent years the mass media have exploited to an excessive degree the stereotype of the Arab, in spite of the known detrimental effects of such exploitation. Stereotyping is not only a crime against Arabs and Arab nations, but also against the human spirit.

"Without mass media," writes Jacques Ellul in *Propaganda*, "there can be no modern propaganda." Ellul says that propaganda operates on many false assumptions: "half-truth, limited truth, and truth out of context." Propaganda, in my opinion, does more than change opinions; it leads men to action. One cannot deny the powerful conditioning of the media on behavior and thought. . . .

The negative portrayal of Arabs prompted syndicated columnist Nicholas Von Hoffman to write, "no religious, national or cultural group . . . has been so massively and consistently vilified." Because of such stereotyping, most Americans do not view Arabs objectively.

"Arab is a word that people learn to hate when they hear it on television," said a young Jordanian to writer Jonathan Raban. "They never connect it with you," he said. "The English people perceive Arabs as being terrorists or millionaires; it means you are not a human being."

There is within our nation an absence of understanding of who the Arabs are and where they have been. How many Americans are aware that Arabs were world pioneers in introducing hospitals and traveling clinics and, like every minority, have made positive contributions to our society? Television has failed to offer such positive portrayals. There is never a human Arab, never a good Arab. I have never seen an Arab hero.

When I use the word "Arab," I think of 100 million people in the great expanse of the Arab world. They are city dwellers, suburbanites, villagers, farmers. Some dress in robes, others in trousers, coats and ties. Some Arab girls go veiled in the streets, others in the latest European fashions. There are white-, brown-, and black-skinned Arabs; Arab Christians, Arab Muslims and Arab Jews. Television, however, ignores this reality.

The medium has failed to show what Arabs have contributed to civilization. Arab scholars, for example, preserved the ancient Greek theory that the world is round. They wrote commentaries on ancient philosophical and medical texts such as the works of Plato and Aristotle. Omar Khayyam was a mathematician-astronomer-poet. Arab scholars developed algebra, geometry and trigonometry. They contributed to the theory of music, being the first to give a specific time value to musical tones. The guitar was an Arab instrument. Arab architecture inspired the Gothic style. Crusaders learned how to build military fortifications from their Arab antagonists. Arabs introduced oranges, the cotton shrub, the mulberry bush, sugar cane and date palms. And, the Arabs gave the West chivalry and the idea of romantic love.

This report is based on five years of television viewing. Since returning from the American University of Beirut in 1975, I have attempted to document those programs which falsely portray Arabs. At times, members of my immediate family and several university associates assisted, by calling my attention to programs that I did not view. The findings, therefore, are limited in scope and direction, and do not reflect any organized attempt to monitor all programs. Although this report primarily focuses on prime-time entertainment shows, it also contains some information on news documentaries. . . .

Nearly every other week for the past five years an entertainment show projecting an anti-Arab image has appeared in prime time.

As an American, I am sensitive to the stereotyping of minorities. But because of my Arab heritage I am particularly sensitive to any form of Arab stereotyping. . . .

Why does this Arab image persist? Understandably, wartime generates stereotypes of the enemy. The Japanese became devious, sadistic creatures, while Italians seemed cowardly. During the cold war, America had its hate-image of Communist China. Today, the People's Republic of China is considered almost an ally. Yet we are not at war, nor have we ever been at war, with Arabs.

I think the ugly Arab image exists in part because few Arab-Americans are members of the creative force in Hollywood where the programs are written and produced.

Ben Stein, in *The View from Sunset Boulevard*, says that writers and producers are the real creative force in television. "They are all white males," he writes. "Almost never younger than thirty-five, the writer tends generally to be Jewish or Italian or Irish."

There are, according to Stein, eight major TV show contractors: Universal, Mary Tyler Moore (MTM), Tandem (TAT), 20th Century Fox, Paramount, Quinn Martin, Spelling/Goldberg and MGM. They provide the three networks with "almost all the creative content of prime-time TV shows."

Yet, Stein contends that television represents the views of only a few hundred people in the western section of Los Angeles who "believe all the things that are being illustrated on television. It is a highly parochial, idiosyncratic view of the world that comes out on TV screens," he believes.

It appears that TV producers and writers perceive Arabs in an adversary role. As a result, prime-time TV shows fail to project any benevolent feeling about the Arabs. From children's shows to commercials, to prime-time adventure dramas, news documentaries and situation comedies, television proclaims there are only bad Arabs. Hollywood repeatedly shows Arab men as primitive rulers buying up America and opposing equal rights for women. The entertainment capital also perpetuates the myth that the modern Arab has harems and operates white slavery rings.

To me, this anti-Arab entertainment image influences a great deal. The contempt felt by many Hollywood writers and producers toward Arabs and their culture affects the attitudes of Americans and their political representatives. As the world's leading exporter of television programs, America transmits those sentiments far beyond its borders. The impact of Hollywood's Arab reaches Europe, the Third World, and particularly the Arab states where viewers see the Arab in all his and her stereotyped humanity.

As we look more closely at examples of improper characterizations within the last five years, we need to remember certain guidelines for what constitutes responsible handling of the Arabs and their culture. Stereotyping is a human problem which merits a human approach. Perhaps such guidelines are found in the words of former United States Senator James Abourezk, "When I say Arab, think of another minority, think of a Jew, think of a black, think of an Irishman, or an Italian." Perhaps then we can better understand the significance of stereotyping that occurred in television's more recent days.

During the 1978–79 season of "Vegas," a sinister sheik was in a hotel with bodyguards who were as inept as they were ugly. Tony Curtis, one of the "Vegas" regulars, threatened to fight with the sheik. Curtis said to his friend, "The last war took only seven days; this one won't last more than a few hours."

In another "Vegas" episode, Cesar Romero told a showgirl, "You as a person mean nothing. But your body and your looks are worth $25,000 to anybody who likes blonde hair and straight teeth." Romero informed his associate that, "We'll take this girl and the others and leave for the Middle East in our chartered plane." In a "Fantasy Island" episode, Romero played an Arab sheik with several wives. His problem: deciding which one to spend the night with.

In another "Fantasy Island" episode, a meek schoolteacher wanted to become an Arab sheik with a harem. Giggling, scatter-brained Arab girls began to grant him all his wishes—but not his college heartthrob who posed as a belly dancer. She was in the harem to save his life because the "real sheik" planned to murder the schoolteacher. The teacher and his sweetheart easily managed to elude the bloodthirsty Arabs, portrayed as unsavory, inept assassins.

Three short-lived series in 1979 were "Whodunnit," "The American Girls" and "Sweepstakes."

Sheik against sheik described the "Whodunnit" episode, "A High Price for Oil," featuring a host of Arab schemers and ruthless oil developers. The good character was a police officer, Lt. Horowitz, who was "unimpressed by Arab royalty." When one Arab character drew his sword, Horowitz said, "Tell fatso to put the toothpick away. This is Beverly Hills, not the desert."

Wealth and sexual appetites were exaggerated. Sheik Khalim, ruler of Mammoonia, struggled to decide which of his four wives to spend the night with. He was anxious; the chosen one must "be prepared and bathed."

He had difficulty obtaining land. "Are you thinking of buying property in

Palm Springs?" his aide asked. "No," said the sheik, "I'm thinking of buying Palm Springs."

Khalim purchased five jets: four white ones for his wives, a blue one for his brother. But there was no brotherly love in the mythical kingdom of Mammoonia. His brother, Prince Zaid, killed Sheik Khalim.

In "The American Girls," a group of wealthy, international businessmen bid on young women at an auction. They planned to take them God-knows-where. Only one was identified: the Arab.

In "Sweepstakes" the stereotyping was more subtle. On learning that someone was willing to pay nearly a half million dollars for a piece of property in the United States, the show's hero said, "Who, Arabs?" As we know, the Arabs are always being charged by the media with buying up America, when in fact the leading investors in the United States, according to columnist Nick Thimmesch, are: the Dutch, $9 billion; the British, $7.4 billion; the Canadians, $6.5 billion; the Germans, $3.2 billion; the Swiss, $2.7 billion; the Japanese, $2.6 billion; and the French, $1.9 billion. "While there are highly publicized cases of individual Arabs flaunting their oil wealth," added Thimmesch, "the vast majority of the 100 million Arabs are a poor but emerging people."

The top-rated television series "Charlie's Angels" began the 1977–78 season with two 2-hour specials. One, "Angels on Ice," pitted Arab against Arab. Six dissidents attempted to assassinate their countrymen in a crowded auditorium—a familiar theme. What distinguished this episode from others were the table manners. A group of Arab assassins watched an exotic dance while eating a meal. They used no utensils or napkins, but instead sloppily shoved food into their mouths with their hands and sucked food scraps from their fingers.

"Angels on Ice" also showed the dissidents preparing to use weapons that would kill scores of innocent people in less than two seconds. In the end, actor Phil Silvers menacingly uttered to one of the captured dissidents, portrayed as bungling fighters: "You ain't so tough . . . you camel eater!"

In a 1979 "Angels" episode, a star-struck "Arabian" Princess entered an all-women's marathon race. Her father, backward but rich, had just bought Rodeo Drive in Beverly Hills. The princess was progressive, competitive and highly protected, while her father and his bodyguards shed a less-than-favorable light. It was the Angels, not the Arab bodyguards, who rescued the princess from would-be abductors.

Arab women seldom have a television role, usually restricted to bowing and fetching food and drink. They do not even perform an occasional belly dance, provided instead by the show's American heroine. In "Charlie's Angels" and "Bionic Woman" episodes, the stars commanded the attention of the camera and the burning lust of evil-eyed Arabs.

In a two-part story of "The Six Million Dollar Man," Mahmoud, an Arab diplomat, conducted blackmail of the highest order. An indestructible machine called Deathprobe was on its way to an American city where thousands, perhaps millions, of innocent people would be killed. Mahmoud refused to stop Deathprobe unless Steve gave him two nuclear bombs for his small Mideast country.

"The Bionic Woman" also featured a two-part episode on the nuclear theme. All nations were urged not to test atomic weapons because an explosion would set off a bomb that would destroy the world. They all complied with the warning and curtailed testing, except an Arab leader, who proceeded with an atomic test, thus reinforcing the notion of social irresponsibility and human insensitivity.

In another episode of "Bionic Woman," Jamie became a harem girl. She then berated a young Arab boy about the status of women in his country, falsely implying that harem life was a normative experience for young, attractive Arab females. . . .

Another episode of the mid-seventies was "Medical Center," produced by Frank Glicksman, also responsible for the new 1979 series, "Trapper John, M.D." In one "Medical Center" program, the wealthy son of an Arab potentate fell in love with Esther, a Jewish widow. Esther, imbued with courage, struggled to support her young son by running a kosher deli. In contrast, Pete Rashid was TV's rich, spoiled Arab who acted irresponsibly.

When Rashid was in the hospital, Dr. Gannon jokingly said, "When you're on your feet you can buy me a hospital." Soon afterwards Gannon's associate observed, "Some lunatic wants to buy the Medical Center so he can give it away as a gift." Unable to buy the hospital, Rashid purchased Gannon's apartment building and had the doctor's apartment refurnished. Dr. Gannon was not impressed. "While you're at it why don't you hit me with my own private gas pump?" Rashid responded: "They told you? It was supposed to be a surprise."

Rashid's father appeared on the scene; he was obnoxious and prejudiced. When he learned that his son wished to marry Esther, he said, "Love? With a Jewess? What does love have to do with honor, duty, Allah?" He turned away from Rashid, telling his bodyguards, "My son is a fool; we will take the necessary steps." Eventually, love conquered hate and the program ended on a happy note. This same theme about Arab riches and backward behavior reappeared in a "Trapper John, M.D." episode. . . .

In a M*A*S*H episode, the treatment was more subtle. An Arab word meaning love took on a unique meaning. As actor Jamie Farr led an imaginary camel around the base, he kept referring to the animal as habebe (loved one). When Farr went to the mess hall, he returned with two plates. At one point, Farr abruptly stopped, scolded his habebe, and began cleaning up imaginary camel dung. . . .

Stereotyping also occurred in television commercials. A recent TV ad for *Life* magazine featured a number of slick photographs, including a group of uniformed Palestinians grasping automatic weapons. *Life* promised to "show Palestinian terrorists" to its readers.

In a TV spot for Frigidaire, a fat, robed sheik casually ordered 150 new refrigerators for his 75 wives. The script was provocative:

Sheik: Your finest refrigerator, please.

Salesman: (walks over to some Frigidaire refrigerators and describes their excellent features)

Sheik: (enthusiastically) I'll take 150 for my wives.

Salesman: You have 150 wives?

Sheik: Only 75, but they get very thirsty.

Although this commercial received initial approval by the three networks, former Vice President of Program Practices at CBS-TV, Van Gordon Sauter, refused to allow additional airings of the Frigidaire spot. At his direction, CBS yanked the commercial. Frigidaire executives, however, did not respond to my letter requesting an explanation for their sheik/harem commercial.

Some companies are more sensitive to the stereotyping problem. When I wrote to Volkswagen of America, Inc. to express my concern about VW's "sheik" commercial which showed Arabs in an unethical and prejudicial manner, I received a prompt reply from John Slaven, Manager of Advertising. Slaven said, "It is our intention to sell cars through advertising and hopefully not to offend people in the process, as we have obviously done in your case. Please accept my personal apologies for having done so, and I hope that our response will be viewed by you in a positive way."

Telecast by the three major networks, the "sheik" commercial showed bearded, robed and mysterious-looking Arabs with dark glasses snapping their fingers at veiled women. The sheiks were very upset because of the Rabbit Diesel; it did not use gas so their "entire community is in jeopardy." . . .

The J. Walter Thompson Agency produces nutritional ads for "Captain Kangaroo," a show with millions of regular young viewers. The Thompson Agency created a spot for tooth care by developing an animated Arab rascal who acts as tooth decay. Fortunately, Donn O'Brien, Vice President of Program Practices at CBS-TV, rejected the Thompson spot.

Young people age 12 to 18 spend one-fifth of their waking hours watching TV; by the time of graduation the average high school senior will have spent 12,000 hours in the classroom and 15,000 hours in front of the TV set. "Many children develop well-formed attitudes about ethnic groups," writes Dr. Carlos Cortes, "including prejudices and stereotypes by the time they reach school."

Several cartoon series slandered the Arabs: "Woody Woodpecker," "Bullwinkle," "Johnny Quest," "The Little Drummer Boy," and Public Television's "Electric Company."

"Woody" included an Arab dancing girl, pursued by an Arab sheik who appeared from the hump of a camel. Sheik El Rauncho snatched the dancer, but Woody came to the rescue, gave the sheik a good beating, and marched off with the heroine.

In "Bullwinkle," Sheik Faraut handed out wristwatches to his friends. His generosity was deceptive. The watches, warned Bullwinkle, will explode. Not so, said his buddies, who tossed the watches in the air. They exploded, failing, fortunately, to hurt anyone—only the credibility of the sheik.

In "Johnny Quest," a modern, urbanized Arab dignitary made friends with Johnny and his pals. All was well until the dignitary decided to doublecross his American friends in the name of Arab unity. He viciously attempted to dispose of them with several poisonous snakes. Due to his own ineptness, he failed.

"The Little Drummer Boy," a Christmas special televised each year, featured an oversized, unsympathetic scoundrel in typical Arab clothing, who continually exploited the show's protagonist, a poor innocent drummer boy wearing a yarmulke.

The vigorous hero of "Electric Company," Letterman, constantly righted the wrongs of Spellbinder, a short, grubby-looking character resembling an Arab with Indian features. The music was middle eastern and the costuming and animation suggested that Spellbinder was an Oriental troublemaker. Although his mischievous deeds appeared harmless (he was always doing the *wrong* thing), his constant teasing and naughty behavior served to perpetuate a racist notion for millions of children.

My initial letter to the Children's Television Workshop, written a few years ago, was not answered. Dr. Edward Palmer, CTW's Vice President for Research, recently responded to my current note saying, "I believe I understand the basis for your criticism, but, after screening a couple of segments that contain Spellbinder, have come to a somewhat different conclusion."

Palmer continued, wondering "how this character as you interpreted him could have survived this long the scrutiny of our own ethnically diverse staff and advisers." Palmer contended that Spellbinder is simply a magician. "I do not say your observations should be ignored," he added. "The series is in its third year of reruns, however, and no review or renewal of its elements is planned within the foreseeable future . . . the stations in the Public Broadcast System have purchased the rights for continued airing of the series."

Even though "Electric Company" is in reruns, some positive steps should be immediately taken. CTW should proceed to conduct research on the character of Spellbinder. Discussions with staff members should be supplemented by selected sampling of viewers. Should the data and discussions indicate that there is racism, Spellbinder's segments could then be edited out of the series. . . .

The situation comedy series "Alice" reflected the range of false images on entertainment programs. One episode depicted an Arab oil baron who:

1. Had three wives but sought to make Flo, an American waitress, his fourth, because "in my country red hair is considered hot stuff."
2. Would take his bride-to-be and all her friends to his country in his modest 747.
3. "Is one of those Arabs who is buying up the whole country."
4. Complained that he had a terrible experience at the gas station; he filled up his tank and had to pay too much for the gas.
5. Quoted his wise father who, among other things, said: "A man with no friends must dance with his camel."

When Flo discovered the Arab had other wives, she abruptly threw his $100,000 engagement ring into a bowl of couscous, after boasting "I'm rich enough to eat with my fingers." . . .

The December 8, 1979, telecast of "Saturday Night Live" presented a sitcom spoof on Arabs, based on the 1960's series "The Beverly Hillbillies." The original hillbillies were lovable, innocent country folk, while in "Saturday Night," "The Bel-Airabs" were paranoid, treacherous camel drivers.

The segment began with the "Hillbillies" theme music; the words are changed:

> Come and listen to my story 'bout a man named Abdul,
> A poor Bedouin barely kept his family fed.
> And then one day he was shootin' at some Jews,
> And up through the sand came a bubblin' crude.
> Oil that is.
> Persian Perrier,
> Kuwait Kool-aid,
> Saudi Sodie.

The spoof centered on an Arab family living in the exclusive Bel-Aire area. Despite their new-found wealth, Abdul, the father, and Mudhat, the son, held fast to TV's view of Islamic customs. Two unscrupulous Americans, who wouldn't fool a ten-year-old, attempted to swindle Abdul and Mudhat.

Another American arrived, denounced the culprits, and wanted to call the police. The Arabs refused, however. They delivered the justice of the desert: one hand was removed from each swindler.

An Arab Granny, present throughout, wore a chador and jumped and jabbered meaningless syllables.

I wrote Bettye King Hoffman, Vice President, Program Information Resources, NBC, expressing my concern about the "Bel-Airabs." Ms. Hoffman promptly responded explaining:

> I hope you will bear in mind that during the years this program has been on the air, just about everyone and everything has been satirized. If you have watched the program, you know that the satire and humor, while irreverent, is not malicious. . . .

In spite of the distorted TV image, I hope for more accuracy in the future. As stated in NBC's Broadcast Standards for television:

> Television is a home medium designed to appeal to audiences of diverse tastes and interests. Television programs should reflect a wide range of roles for all people and should endeavor to depict men, women and children in a positive manner, keeping in mind always the importance of dignity to every human being. . . .

Student Essay

BRASS RUBBINGS
Tonia Mekemson

The audience for this paper consists of people who know absolutely nothing about the subject, so Mekemson is writing here as the expert. She had to consider her readers carefully before she began, finding ways to interest them in the unknown and to give them all the necessary details without talking down to them. As you read her essay, consider the following points:

1. The directions do not actually start until the fourth paragraph. What do the first three paragraphs accomplish? Are they an effective beginning for you? Why or why not?
2. What little details establish Mekemson's credibility on this topic?
3. Are the steps described in enough detail that you could follow them? Do any of the hints seem particularly helpful?
4. Can you find any sentences where Mekemson seems concerned with giving her reader encouragement?
5. Mekemson made a conscious effort to personalize this subject to keep it from being a dry, technical process paper, as it easily could have become. Do you think she succeeded? Why or why not?

Used with permission of Tonia Mekemson.

When I was living in England, I didn't feel a need to have mementos and reminders of her history in my home. I was surrounded by buildings that were centuries old, by traditions that were also centuries old, and knew that references to the past could mean anything dating from the Roman Empire to World War I. I took rose windows and gargoyles for granted, as I did those picturesque thatched cottages and those old country inns that were havens for weary travelers. And yet, I had always appreciated her fine Gothic architecture, the devotion and skills of her early artisans, and the foundations that her earlier citizens had laid. However, when I returned after a long absence, I knew that I had to capture something of England's past that I could bring back to the U. S. with me and keep in my home.

I discovered that nothing could be more fitting than brass rubbings! They are inexpensive to make, they are portable, and they provide that much-needed sense of history. I also discovered that making rubbings is an activity that is absolutely fascinating, is fun for the whole family and at the same time can provide some very personal souvenirs for the visitor to England. If you've ever enjoyed making replicas of coins by slipping them under a paper and gently rubbing that paper with a lead pencil, then you'll most certainly enjoy rubbing brasses.

You may wonder what these "brasses" are. They are memorial plates that were engraved by skilled craftsmen sometime between the 13th and 17th centuries, in memory of the dead. They come in all sizes. Some are just small rectangles measuring 18" × 24", and some are huge, measuring as long as 78". Every one that I have seen has been extremely ornate and detailed. They depict the deceased but do not necessarily resemble that particular person. The depiction is achieved by the information that is etched on the brass. If the person was of military standing, he would be shown in a suit of armor; and if he had died in battle there would probably be a picture of a lion curling around his feet to indicate valor. The brass would certainly bear his Coat of Arms. Ecclesiastical brasses can be especially ornate, as the engraver would even show the embroidery detail of the deceased's vestments. Often, a decorated border, called a canopy, would frame the brass. Some of these canopies would have elaborate arches, and their designs would change according to the era. It seems that the details in brasses are infinite, and that's one of the reasons for making copies of them—so that you can look at them time and time again.

There are two ways to go about this fascinating task. You can either wait until you get to England and hope that you stumble across some of these plates, or, you can learn their whereabouts ahead of time and make the necessary arrangements to rub them.

Almost any book on brasses will give a listing of locations of the more outstanding ones, along with their condition, type, and age. Once you have discovered where they are, you then have to get permission to rub them, and this is obtained from the priest of the church where they are located. This address can be found in a directory called *Crockford's Clerical Directory*, which is on file at most English libraries. It's a good idea to write to the priest, enclosing a stamped, self-addressed envelope, and stating the day that you would like to reserve for your rubbing.

Next, you should buy your materials, and these can be found at any good art shop. You will need a special wax-carved heelball, lining paper, masking tape, a plastic eraser, a soft brush and a rag. The heelball and paper come in a variety of colors, and one of the most stunning combinations is a silver heelball on black paper. I have seen rubbings made in black heelball on finely embossed wallpaper, too, and they have been particularly attractive.

The priest will give you information on where to find the brasses that are in the church. More often than not they are protected by rugs and are situated in awkward positions. Be prepared to move pews and to search around the back of the organ. The priest will also inform you whether any fee is payable. The most I was ever asked for was $2.00; more often than not I was just asked for a donation that could be put in the church's restoration fund.

With all these arrangements made, you are now ready to make your brass rubbing. The first thing you must do is clean the brass plate very carefully with the brush, and make sure that you remove as much dust as possible from the incising. Then really study the plate hard and make notes on what you see. For example, if there is a long sword, note which way it hangs. If there is an animal curling around the feet of the person, make a point of remembering how it is positioned. This is necessary because once the paper has been taped on the brass, and you have begun rubbing, you cannot peek underneath to see what those strange shapes are that are beginning to appear.

Next, cut your paper larger than the brass and stick it with masking tape to the surrounding stone. Run your fingers round the edge of the brass to get an indication of outlines, and then, while holding the paper firmly in place with one hand, take the heelball in the other hand and begin to rub over the brass with short, hard strokes. You will be absolutely elated as the detail of the brass is inch-by-inch revealed. I always like to start rubbing in the middle of the plate and work my way to the edges. A lot of books suggest that you start at the top and work down to the bottom. Either way, you must exercise a lot of care to make sure that you don't go outside the outline. Rub in all directions as you work over the brass, so that you avoid having strokes show. When the rubbing is complete, polish it with a silk-like rag before removing it from the plate.

You will be delighted with the finished product. It will show the detail of the plate so much finer than on the actual brass, and you will feel extremely pleased with yourself for having made such a terrific copy of one of England's finer relics.

Once you have removed the rubbing from the plate, roll it up and keep it in a cardboard mailing tube until you are ready to mount it. Be sure to write down details pertinent to that specific plate; and if you wish, find out more about the deceased by checking into local history and chatting with the local people.

I can guarantee that when you get your brass rubbings home, they will be great conversation pieces and will give you all kinds of pleasant memories of your trip through England.

FOCUS

THESIS

The authors of the following three essays all found interesting ways to develop their thesis sentences, and they all placed them in different parts of their essays. The two professional essays are both critical, but only one is serious. For a change of pace, the student essay is the least personal of the group, as it is based on much technical information and supported by a bibliography of sources consulted. These three papers should give you some ideas about leading up to and supporting your own thesis sentences.

Professional Essay

THE SPORTING SPIRIT
George Orwell

A British journalist and novelist, George Orwell is probably most famous for the novel *1984*. If you have heard someone say, "Big Brother is watching you," you have heard that novel quoted. Both in his books and in his columns, Orwell often took unpopular stands, as he does here. Consider the following points as you read his essay:

1. How soon do you know what the thesis of his essay will be? Does it make you want to continue reading? Why or why not?
2. Does his discussion seem to be limited to football? What other sports does he mention?
3. Orwell's examples to show that "international sporting contests lead to orgies of hatred" all occurred in 1945 or earlier. Would more recent examples support or refute this point? Try to think of two or three specific events to illustrate your answer.
4. Do you agree with his contention that sport in the Middle Ages was not political? How would you explain a jousting tournament?
5. Do Orwell's criticisms of international competitions apply equally to local rivalries (high-school basketball tournaments, for instance)?
6. If you disagree with Orwell's thesis, what evidence could you use to refute his claims? Be specific.

Note: The spelling and punctuation used in this essay follow British conventions. Do not model your own spelling and punctuation after them!

From *The Collected Essays, Journalism, and Letters of George Orwell*, Vol. 4, copyright © 1968 by Sonia Brownell Orwell. Copyright the estate of the late George Orwell and Martin Secker & Warburg Ltd. Reprinted with permission of Harcourt Brace Jovanovich, Inc. and A. M. Heath & Company Ltd.

Now that the brief visit of the Dynamo football team[1] has come to an end, it is possible to say publicly what many thinking people were saying privately before the Dynamos ever arrived. That is, that sport is an unfailing cause of ill-will, and that if such a visit as this had any effect at all on Anglo-Soviet relations, it could only be to make them slightly worse than before.

Even the newspapers have been unable to conceal the fact that at least two of the four matches played led to much bad feeling. At the Arsenal match, I am told by someone who was there, a British and a Russian player came to blows and the crowd booed the referee. The Glasgow match, someone else informs me, was simply a free-for-all from the start. And then there was the controversy, typical of our nationalistic age, about the composition of the Arsenal team. Was it really an all-England team, as claimed by the Russians, or merely a league team, as claimed by the British? And did the Dynamos end their tour abruptly in order to avoid playing an all-England team? As usual, everyone answers these questions according to his political predilections. Not quite everyone, however. I noted with interest, as an instance of the vicious passions that football provokes, that the sporting correspondent of the russophile *News Chronicle* took the anti-Russian line and maintained that Arsenal was not an all-England team. No doubt the controversy will continue to echo for years in the footnotes of history books. Meanwhile the result of the Dynamos' tour, in so far as it has had any result, will have been to create fresh animosity on both sides.

And how could it be otherwise? I am always amazed when I hear people saying that sport creates goodwill between the nations, and that if only the common peoples of the world could meet one another at football or cricket, they would have no inclination to meet on the battlefield. Even if one didn't know from concrete examples (the 1936 Olympic Games, for instance) that international sporting contests lead to orgies of hatred, one could deduce it from general principles.

Nearly all the sports practised nowadays are competitive. You play to win, and the game has little meaning unless you do your utmost to win. On the village green, where you pick up sides and no feeling of local patriotism is involved, it is possible to play simply for the fun and exercise: but as soon as the question of prestige arises, as soon as you feel that you and some larger unit will be disgraced if you lose, the most savage combative instincts are aroused. Anyone

---

[1] The Moscow Dynamos, a Russian football team, toured Britain in the autumn of 1945, playing against leading British clubs.

who has played even in a school football match knows this. At the international level sport is frankly mimic warfare. But the significant thing is not the behaviour of the players but the attitude of the spectators: and, behind the spectators, of the nations who work themselves into furies over these absurd contests, and seriously believe—at any rate for short periods—that running, jumping and kicking a ball are tests of national virtue.

Even a leisurely game like cricket, demanding grace rather than strength, can cause much ill-will, as we saw in the controversy over body-line bowling and over the rough tactics of the Australian team that visited England in 1921. Football, a game in which everyone gets hurt and every nation has its own style of play which seems unfair to foreigners, is far worse. Worst of all is boxing. One of the most horrible sights in the world is a fight between white and coloured boxers before a mixed audience. But a boxing audience is always disgusting, and the behaviour of the women, in particular, is such that the army, I believe, does not allow them to attend its contests. At any rate, two or three years ago, when Home Guards and regular troops were holding a boxing tournament, I was placed on guard at the door of the hall, with orders to keep the women out.

In England, the obsession with sport is bad enough, but even fiercer passions are aroused in young countries where games playing and nationalism are both recent developments. In countries like India or Burma, it is necessary at football matches to have strong cordons of police to keep the crowd from invading the field. In Burma, I have seen the supporters of one side break through the police and disable the goalkeeper of the opposing side at a critical moment. The first big football match that was played in Spain about fifteen years ago led to an uncontrollable riot. As soon as strong feelings of rivalry are aroused, the notion of playing the game according to the rules always vanishes. People want to see one side on top and the other side humiliated, and they forget that victory gained through cheating or through the intervention of the crowd is meaningless. Even when the spectators don't intervene physically they try to influence the game by cheering their own side and "rattling" opposing players with boos and insults. Serious sport has nothing to do with fair play. It is bound up with hatred, jealousy, boastfulness, disregard of all rules and sadistic pleasure in witnessing violence: in other words it is war minus the shooting.

Instead of blah-blahing about the clean, healthy rivalry of the football field and the great part played by the Olympic Games in bringing nations together, it is more useful to inquire how and why this modern cult of sport arose. Most of the games we now play are of ancient origin, but sports does not seem to have been taken very seriously between Roman times and the nineteenth century. Even in the English public schools the games cult did not start till the later part of the last century. Dr Arnold, generally regarded as the founder of the modern public school, looked on games as simply a waste of time. Then, chiefly in England and the United States, games were built up into a heavily-financed activity, capable of attracting vast crowds and rousing savage passions, and the infection spread from country to country. It is the most violently combative sports, football and boxing, that have spread the widest. There cannot be much doubt that the whole thing is bound up with the rise of nationalism—that is, with the lunatic modern habit of identifying oneself with large power units and seeing everything in terms of competitive prestige. Also, organised games are more likely to flourish in urban communities where the average human being lives a sedentary or at least a confined life, and does not get much opportunity for creative labour. In a rustic community a boy or young man works off a good deal of his surplus energy by walking, swimming, snowballing, climbing trees, riding horses, and by various sports involving cruelty to animals, such as fishing, cock-fighting, and ferreting for rats. In a big town one must indulge in group activities if one wants an outlet for one's physical strength or for one's sadistic impulses. Games are taken seriously in London and New York, and they were taken seriously in Rome and Byzantium: in the Middle Ages they were played and probably played with much physical brutality, but they were not mixed up with politics nor a cause of group hatreds.

If you wanted to add to the vast fund of ill-will existing in the world at this moment, you could hardly do it better than by a series of football matches between Jews and Arabs, Germans and Czechs, Indians and British, Russians and Poles, and Italians and Yugoslavs, each match to be watched by a mixed audience of 100,000 spectators. I do not, of course, suggest that sport is one of the main causes of international rivalry; big-scale sport is itself, I think, merely another effect of the causes that have produced nationalism. Still, you do make things worse by sending forth a team of eleven men, labelled as national champions, to do battle against some rival team, and allowing it to be felt on all sides that whichever nation is defeated will "lose face."

I hope, therefore, that we shan't follow up the visit of the Dynamos by sending a British team to the USSR. If we must do so, then let us send a second-rate team which is sure to be beaten and cannot claim to represent Britain as a whole. There are quite enough real causes of trouble already, and we need not add to them by encouraging young men to kick each other on the shins amid the roars of infuriated spectators.

Professional Essay

NEW DEAL FOR THE ACADEMIC SHUFFLE
Stephen Crites

This "Accent on Living" column was written by an assistant professor of religion. Knowing this about him may help you decide how you should take his thesis. As you read his essay, consider the following points:

1. The essay begins with a long summary of the research process, as you may have used it in writing documented papers. There is no thesis in these first two paragraphs, so what is the point of the introduction? Is it effective?
2. Where is the first indication that Crites is not really serious about what would appear to be his thesis?
3. What does Crites's opinion of textbooks appear to be? Find evidence in the essay for your answer.

4. What do you think was his purpose in writing this apparent attack on scholarly writing? Do you believe that many readers would be inclined to see this as a straightforward appeal to turn the research process over to IBM machines? What clues does Crites give that this was not his purpose?

Copyright © 1963 by The Atlantic Monthly Company, Boston, Mass. Reprinted with permission.

It is well known that current scholarly writing requires the use of note cards, which are blank in their original state and can be purchased in three different sizes. A prospective author buys a quantity of these cards, the size being left to personal taste, and as he reads books in his field of interest, he transfers the contents of these books onto the note cards. As the collection of note cards grows, he shuffles and sorts them out into convenient classifications by means of index cards. These divisions are further subdivided, appropriate titles and subtitles are chosen, and from the chaos of ink and cardboard with which one began an orderly-looking table of contents starts to emerge, complete with parts, chapters, sections, and subsections. Further toil is required to blend the note cards in each microdivision into a more or less continuous text, and then the rest is up to the publisher.

So a new book comes into existence. The book is read by scholars and students who are engaged in producing papers, books, articles of their own. These scholars and students, of course, also possess clean note cards of one size or another. By use of these cards, the book is dismantled and reduced once again to its elements. The cards, now carefully inscribed, are shuffled together with those gleaned from other documents, are annotated and indexed, and new scholarly writings are underway.

The waste involved in this process is obvious, and also shocking in a land whose people pride themselves on efficiency. It is evident that scholarship would be enormously facilitated and accelerated by the elimination of one step in the process described above, a step for which no rational defense can be made. I mean, of course, the blending of the notes into the appearance of a continuous text—the production of the book or article as such. This step not only involves the writer in such tedious business as constructing transitions and copying his notes into the text, but also obliges the reader to copy it all out again on his own note cards. The solution is clear. Instead of collecting their material into books and articles, scholars should simply publish their note-card collections.

Traditionalists will doubtless object that such a streamlining of scholarly publication, however sensible it may be, would remove the originality from the scholar's task. But each author would be free to organize and index his collection in such fashion as to indicate what he takes to be its rationale, in case anyone is interested. In fact, the cards could be arranged and rearranged in all manner of clever ways. Witty titles and marginal notations could be added, and the author could even include special cards, indexed under "Grand Design" or something of the sort, which would suggest the generalizations which he supposes he has established by a particular card arrangement. Readers opposed to metaphysical pretension could simply drop these cards out of their sets. On the other hand, a suitable substitute for the textbook could be created by publishing collections composed entirely of these generalization cards.

Documentation would be both simplified and exquisitely refined, since each card would bear the name of the person who originally wrote it up, and perhaps also the collection in which it first appeared. Of course, a card bearing some particularly seminal material would keep turning up in any number of the published collections. Scholars could exchange such duplicates among themselves and vie with one another in accumulating complete collections of the most popular cards, as youngsters do with the pictures of baseball heroes cut from cereal and bubble-gum wrappers. Card games could be devised beyond the wildest dreams of present practitioners of solitaire and bridge. A player might, for example, lead Freud on the Oedipus Complex, only to be trumped by a Jungian Archetype.

Creative writing could be similarly revolutionized, to the great benefit of critics, reviewers, and other serious students of literature. Imagine the toil and needless speculation which these busy people would have been spared if, say, Mann had simply published a collection of leitmotiv cards, and perhaps another on Obstacles to the Bourgeois Prussian as Artist; or if Melville had produced a collection on Religious Symbols from Nautical Life; or if a committee of recent American writers had collaborated on Forms of Decadence in the Southern Part of the United States.

Other committee projects come to mind, such as an Existentialist Encyclopedia from "Anguish" to "Zarathustra," or a collection on Sexuality, subdivided into all those interesting hyphenated forms. Writers need no longer labor coquettishly to obscure their insights under a cloud of rhetoric. Let them actually lay their cards on the table, so that critics, reviewers, and other serious students of literature can see at a glance what it is they wish to say.

Revolutionary as this new departure in publishing may seem, it can be seen to be a natural development if viewed in large enough historical perspective. The movement toward greater flexibility in the handling of written material had already begun when the contents of stone tablets and wall inscriptions were transferred to scrolls, and still a more decisive step was taken when the scrolls were cut into pages and bound into books. The further transition to cards may seem strange to the older generations; after all, traditionalists no doubt held on to scrolls long after books were in existence. But the new form will seem natural enough to a new generation being nurtured on teaching machines and machine-graded tests. The wave of the future is constituted by droplets.

The next step beyond the note-card form will be considerably less drastic. The proper pattern of nicks and holes can very easily be punched in the cards, and the whole scholarly enterprise turned over to IBM machines. Homo sapiens can then devote himself to television—or card games of the old-fashioned sort—with a good conscience, confident that the production and assimilation of written matter, so necessary to civilization, is being carried on with the highest possible efficiency.

THESIS

Student Essay

SAFER AT ANY SPEED
John Kison

This student found a way to develop a hobby—tinkering with automotive design—into a thesis for a good argumentative paper about the source of many of the new safety devices on passenger cars. As you read his essay, consider the following points:

1. The first three paragraphs dramatize a wreck at an auto race. Do you think it is an actual wreck being described? Does its reality or unreality affect the power of the introduction?
2. After the introduction, does Kison seem to follow any plan in presenting the various safety devices? If so, what is it? If not, can you think of one he might have chosen?
3. Generally, he writes as the expert addressing less-informed readers. What details show that he considered his readers' lack of information when he wrote the explanations? What details, if any, could use a clearer explanation?
4. Where do you find this paper's thesis? Is this an effective place for it, in your opinion? Why or why not?

Used with permission of John Kison.

You hear the roar as the engine fires and comes to life. The car rolls down pit row and onto the track. The 700 horsepower engine soon has the car moving at nearly 200 mph. Many laps later a tire blows. The car slews sideways into the wall, tearing off the nose section and front wheels. The car flips end over end, tearing loose the rear section and engine. The driver's compartment, now looking much like a bathtub, comes to rest on the track surface. The rescue crews are there instantly, ready with firefighting and medical equipment. The crews help the driver from the car; he waves to the crowd.

There are bits and pieces of race car strewn all over the place. It looks as though no one could survive an accident of this magnitude. Many fatal accidents leave better-looking cars than this.

This man survived because he was in a USAC (United States Auto Club) approved and inspected championship-type car. This is the type of car that runs in the Indy 500. This is one of the safest cars in the world.

Let's first define what we mean by "safety." The ability to avoid an accident in the first place will be referred to as "active safety." The ability to survive an accident that is already happening will be referred to as "passive safety."

Once the accident occurs, it is the passive safety mechanisms that become paramount. The above car was designed to sacrifice the framework of the car for the benefit of the driver.

Older passenger cars were designed with two frame rails with a body set on top; this design afforded the passengers no real protection. Racing cars, on the other hand, have adopted new ways of absorbing the energy of a collision.

One of these is the space frame design, and the other is the monocoque design. The chassis must be designed to collapse progressively in a collision, thus reducing the driver's rate of deceleration. A space frame gets its strength from the space it surrounds, and its diagonal cross bracing. If you took four soda straws, ran a string through them and tied the ends together, you would have a square shape. Take hold of two opposite corners and push them together or pull them apart; you can see the square *deform*. Now put a straw diagonally across the form. It will resist deformation. You have now made a simple space frame.

Monocoque construction is an altogether different means to the same end. In monocoque construction, the body is the frame of the car. The body panels accept all the loads and stresses upon the vehicle. Due to the collapse characteristics of the front end, a monocoque is better at absorbing frontal impact. In a side impact, the space frame will provide better resistance to intrusion than will the monocoque.

Features of these two frame construction techniques have been combined in unit-body construction. In unit-body construction, there really is no frame on the car. The car is made from sections of sheet metal stamped into shape and spot welded together. They are supported by braces at stress points. This method also allows for increased rollover protection. If the support panels are stronger, more support can be built into the roof of the car. All of Chrysler Corporation's new cars are of the unit-body construction. Many manufacturers construct cars using this method. This type of construction also has the positive side-effect of having fewer squeaks and rattles.

What kept the driver inside his protective cockpit? That small miracle was accomplished by the use of a six-point seat harness. This harness is similar to a seatbelt, the only difference being that the harness anchors to the car at six points. This consists of a lap belt, two shoulder straps, and two straps that bolt to the floor between the driver's legs. The harness controls the lateral as well as the vertical movement of the occupant.

Some people think that seatbelts will trap them in a burning or submerged vehicle. Investigators are finding that you have a much greater chance of survival in any crash if some restraint holds you in the car. Even in a rollover situation when the cars land upside-down, people in belts survive without serious injury simply because they are held in their seats. Even in a fire or submerged situation, seatbelts can actually speed your escape because they lessen the chance of other injuries that could hamper escape.

The auto manufacturers have adopted the above measures in their newer cars. There are some other technological advances available to the racing world that the auto industry hasn't adopted for use in passenger cars.

The fuel cell hasn't been used in passenger cars. The fuel cell is a fuel or gasoline tank designed to resist an explosion. This type of fuel tank considerably reduces the fire hazard, and the foam filling in them is a further help; it only reduces tank capacity by about five percent. A fuel cell could have eliminated the Ford Pinto tragedy. USAC, NASCAR (National Association for Stock Car Auto Racing), and CART (Champion Auto Racing Teams) all require fuel cells and full roll protection.

We also try to *prevent* accidents. This attempt is called "active safety." We must be in control of the vehicle. We must be able to put the vehicle where we want it. These methods were originally designed to make racing cars handle well at high speeds and go through the corners more quickly.

The radial tire, now commonplace, was originally developed as a high-speed racing tire. The radial-ply design is subject to less internal heat buildup than the bias-ply type of tire, thus making it less likely to blow out at higher speeds, as well as capable of greater cornering loads. The radial tire has much better traction qualities. Nearly all tire manufacturers are now in the radial tire market.

Another way of improving the control of the car is to use more efficient steering methods. Rack and pinion steering has been used on racing cars for many years. Why rack and pinion? It's fast, simple to work on, and lightweight because it eliminates some of the usual linkage. Rack and pinion steering is now becoming accepted by the automotive industry and is used on more cars each day.

We can keep the car stable on the road by the use of aerodynamic improvements. Streamlining can reduce the car's tendency to lift or pitch, thereby keeping the tires on the ground where they do the most good. Streamlining can also make improvements in driver visibility.

Some items are designed for safety rather than sheer performance. The disc brake is a good example. It was designed so the car could go faster and slow down just in time to make the turn. It was developed to increase reliability in competition. The brake is one part of the car that must work every time. Disc brakes resist fade better than drum brakes. Drums lose their grip at about 1200 degrees Fahrenheit, whereas discs are coming on strong at 1500 degrees.

While I have already mentioned seatbelts, they also add to active safety by keeping the driver behind the wheel of the car and in control. This could very well prevent an accident.

Auto racing has increased levels of technology in the automotive field. This ever-increasing drive to go faster has bred efficiency attainable only through competition. The car, now more efficient in many ways than its predecessors, does not have to be doomed to extinction. Today's automobile is safer than those of the past largely because of racing's influence.

Sources Consulted

Edmonds, I. G. *Hot Rodding for Beginners*. Philadelphia: Macrae Smith Company, 1970.

Fales, Edward D., Jr. *Belts on Buttons Down*. New York: Delacorte Press, 1971.

Murray, Spencer, ed. *Basic Chassis, Suspension & Brakes No. 3*. Los Angeles: Peterson Publishing Company, 1974.

Norbye, Jan P. *Streamlining and Car Aerodynamics*. Blue Ridge Summit: TAB Books, 1977.

Schofield, Miles, ed. *Basic Chassis, Suspension & Brakes No. 2*. Los Angeles: Peterson Publishing Company, 1971.

Terry, Len, and Alan Baker. *Racing Car Design and Development*. Cambridge: Robert Bentley, Inc., 1973.

FOCUS

WORDS

All of the essays in this book really could be included in this section, as words are vitally important to them all. Still, words are of special significance in the following three writings. One professional essay is about words, while the other one and the student essay both concentrate on the descriptive power of words. The two descriptive essays, however, use their well-chosen words to create radically different effects. One may turn your stomach, while the other may send you back to pleasant memories of your childhood. Both will demonstrate the power of words to create images in your mind.

Professional Essay

DEFINING A FEW TERMS
Sydney J. Harris

Sydney Hárris writes a syndicated column that often probes the meaning of words. In the four columns excerpted here from a collection of his columns, he analyzes the meanings of *intelligence, jerk, culture,* and *discipline.* As you read his essays, consider the following points:

1. What are the five kinds of intelligence that Harris differentiates? Which kind is most abundant in your own personality? Can you think of any kind he omitted?

2. Can you find any figurative language used in the definition of a jerk? Is the description an effective one? Does it remind you of anyone?

3. Describe the kind of person Harris calls a "culture-vulture." How is this person different from a culture-hater? How are the two extremes alike?

4. How do you respond to the quotation about spanking in the definition of *discipline?* Would the view of discipline that Harris expresses here be useful in modern public schools?

From *Last Things First* by Sydney J. Harris. Copyright © 1957, 1958, 1959, 1960 by the Chicago Daily News and General Features Corporation. Copyright © 1961 by Sydney J. Harris. Reprinted by permission of Houghton Mifflin Company.

A couple dropped in while I was playing chess the other evening, and the woman made the customary remark that she wasn't "intelligent" enough to take up the game.

Yet, although I have been playing since I was ten, with duffers and experts alike, I have not seen the slightest relation between chess ability and general intelligence. Indeed, I have seen some Masters who barely knew enough to tie their shoelaces properly away from the chessboard. They can beat me blindfolded every game, but their non-chess intelligence is scarcely visible to the naked eye.

I suggest that the word "intelligence" is not a single unitary thing, but is rather a composite made up of many strands. There are different *kinds* of intelligence, and one is not necessarily better than the other.

There is social intelligence, for instance, which few intellectuals possess—the ability to understand how other people feel and to live and work with them in reasonable peace.

There is mechanical intelligence, which I don't possess an iota of—the ability to manipulate and conquer physical objects, to make, to repair, to take apart and put together.

There is mathematical intelligence, of which chess is a part—the ability to visualize abstractions in space. This is a rare gift which has sometimes been given to men who are otherwise idiots.

There is verbal intelligence—the ability to use words with force and clarity; but some of the writers who are best at this (Hemingway comes to mind) are appallingly poor thinkers and have evolved a philosophy of life that would scarcely do credit to a high school sophomore.

And there is a deep intelligence of the blood and the bone, which is not articulate, which cannot express itself verbally, but which knows what to do in practical situations where a genius might find himself helpless or hysterical.

We must not be bluffed or intimidated by a word. "Intelligence" can cover a wide spectrum of human aptitudes; and, besides, this spectrum is so colored with our emotional lives that many people seem dumb (to themselves as well as to others) because they are merely fearful and confused.

No real gauge of intelligence has yet been devised; the I.Q. test is a makeshift device, heavily weighted in favor of those who can express themselves deftly and swiftly. But millions of others have simply not learned to use more than a fraction of the intelligence they have.

I don't know whether history repeats itself, but biography certainly does. The other day, Michael came in and asked me what a "jerk" was—the same question Carolyn put to me a dozen years ago.

At that time, I fluffed her off with some inane answer, such as "A jerk isn't a very nice person," but both of us knew it was an unsatisfactory reply. When she went to bed, I began trying to work up a suitable definition.

It's a marvelously apt word, of course. Until it was coined, no more than twenty-five years ago, there was really no single word in English to describe the kind of person who is a jerk—"boob" and "simp" were too old hat, and besides they really didn't fit, for they could be lovable, and a jerk never is.

Thinking it over, I decided that a jerk is basically a person without insight. He is not necessarily a fool or a dope, because some extremely clever persons can be jerks. In fact, it has little to do with intelligence as we commonly think of it; it is, rather, a kind of subtle but pervasive aroma emanating from the inner part of the personality.

I know a college president who can be described only as a jerk. He is not an unintelligent man, nor unlearned, nor even unschooled in the social amenities. Yet he is a jerk *cum laude*, because of a fatal flaw in his nature—he is totally incapable of looking into the mirror of his soul and shuddering at what he sees there.

A jerk, then, is a man (or woman) who is utterly unable to see himself as he appears to others. He has no grace, he is tactless without meaning to be, he is a bore even to his best friends, he is an egotist without charm. All of us are egotists to some extent, but most of us—unlike the jerk—are perfectly and horribly aware of it when we make asses of ourselves. The jerk never knows.

Nor does he feel the common pangs of remorse and humility. He is locked snugly in his tight little shell and looks out at the world with smug, uncomprehending eyes. He has no real sense of humor, because he thinks the only things that are funny are the things he laughs at, and he has no real sense of values, because he thinks the only things that are true are the things he believes in.

The most serious indictment against the jerk is that he is always trying too hard to get people to like or respect him, without trying to like or respect them at all. It can't be done, but it's impossible to explain this to a jerk. That is what makes him one.

The word "culture" takes an awful beating in our society—from its friends as much as from its enemies.

To its friends, "culture" is something lofty and spiritual and almost sacred; to its enemies, "culture" is a mess of hifalutin nonsense that is spouted by people who think they are superior to the ordinary run.

Yet the clearest, as well as the shortest, description of the word was given a century ago by Thomas Carlyle, when he said: "The great law of culture is this—Let each become all that we were created capable of being."

The culture-vultures try to be more than they were created capable of being, and so they often sound pretentious and absurd. The culture-haters are content to remain less than they can be, and so they sound barbarous and bigoted. Both, in different ways, are untrue to themselves.

A truly cultured person is one who appreciates Beethoven as well as jazz, who relishes a well-written mystery book as well as a literary masterpiece, who knows that a human being is made up of varying and contradictory tastes and desires, and wants to expand his personality to the widest range.

Most people, I am convinced, were created capable of being much more than they are in everyday life. When they allow themselves to be touched, by a play or a piece of music, you can see how a part of them, beneath the surface, has a deep hunger for something beyond the banalities of their ordinary existence.

But the culture-vultures, and the intellectual snobs, and the self-appointed guardians of the Muses often frighten off the average person from the free development of this appetite.

There is a need for more tolerance on both sides. The barbarian who rejects the unfamiliar just because it is unfamiliar is no worse than the snob who embraces the difficult and obscure simply because it makes him feel superior to the mass. Each attitude, in turn, perpetuates the vicious circle of contempt.

Every human being of average intelligence was created capable of being more than he is. He can appreciate Shakespeare because Shakespeare wrote for him, not for scholars; he can glory in Beethoven, because Beethoven expresses the deepest passions and perplexities of the spirit.

Americans are tremendously interested in "personal development"—and this is all that Carlyle meant by "culture." The term needs to be rescued from the prissy-lipped promoters of afternoon teas and given back to the people, who are looking for greatness, but do not know it.

The study of words is useless unless it leads to the study of the ideas that the words stand for. When I am concerned about the proper use of words it is not because of snobbism or superiority, but because their improper use leads to poor ways of thinking.

Take the word "discipline" that we hear so much about nowadays in connection with the rearing of children. If you know something about word derivations, you know that "discipline" and "disciple" come from the same Latin root—*discipulus*, which means "to learn, to follow."

The disciples of Jesus were those who followed his teachings and adopted the discipline of Christianity. There was no idea of punishment or chastisement connected with the word "discipline."

When we forget this, or do not know this, then we use the word "discipline" in a wholly misleading sense. We think of discipline for the child as consisting of a strict set of rules, followed by punishment for their infraction.

But genuine discipline means leading the child by example, giving him a firm pattern of conduct to follow, as Jesus gave the disciples. It means bringing out the best in them, not hammering down the worst in them.

In connection with this distorted view of discipline, it is interesting to note that we speak of "old-fashioned" discipline, meaning the severity of the nineteenth-century family. But this was very new-fashioned, if we take a long view of human history.

As George Sheviakov recently observed, spanking as a means of discipline is unknown among the so-called primitive peoples. "It is the civilized man's method," he tells us, and goes on to say, "Perhaps we civilized people resort to spanking because we are too much in a hurry about many little things. And hurry is not a child's way of living."

I am not rigidly against spanking, so long as we recognize that it is a poor substitute for real discipline, and reveals a weakness on the part of the parent more than a willfulness on the part of the child. We may do it for exasperation, but not as a matter of principle.

Our task is to make our children into disciples of the good life, by our own actions toward them and toward other people. This is the only effective discipline in the long run. But it is more arduous, and takes longer, than simply "laying down the law." Before a child (or a nation) can accept the law, it has to learn why the law has been created for its own welfare.

Professional Essay

MEMORIES OF THE CHAMPIONSHIP
Ed Vital

Carefully-chosen words make this reminiscence of a sandlot ballgame from the writer's youth stand out above sports writing on more prominent games. Notice the picturesque language and the suspense-creating detail. As you read the essay, consider the following points:

1. Except for the first and last paragraphs, this essay is told in the present tense, as if the game were being played right at this moment. What effect does this unusual choice of tense have on the narration?
2. Where can you find figures of speech used in the description? Which ones are the most effective for you?
3. Vital obviously tried to create suspense in certain parts of the story. Where is this most noticeable, and how does he manage to achieve this effect?
4. Who has the only speaking part in this essay? Do you think that this is a significant choice?
5. What can you say about Vital's choice of verbs in this essay, especially in the last third of the episode?

Copyright © 1980. Reprinted by permission of Ed Vital.

I had a chance to be a hero once, when I was only 14 years old. I was just an average kid, and opportunities for heroics didn't come often. Oh, I had dreamed of being a hero lots of times, but I never really knew how I would act when my big chance finally came.

It's the summer of 1947 on a hot, sticky day in Detroit. August in the city is when the air hangs heavy with humidity, and heat waves simmer up from the pavement. But today, the heat doesn't matter—it's the day of the Championship Game.

The playing field isn't fancy, an island of green and brown grass surrounded by wire fence and concrete. It's bordered on all sides by busy main streets jammed with noisy city traffic. Out toward left field, beyond the fence, is the massive Ford River Rouge factory. Its towering chimneys are belching ominous clouds of black smoke mixed with an occasional puff of white steam.

This is the deciding game in a league sponsored by the Detroit Department of Parks and Recreation. The winners will receive a championship emblem which will advertise them as city champions to all.

Just an average player on a good team, I feel lucky to be here. A scrappy, "never say die" team, we are the West Side Champs. Our opponents are champs of the East Side.

They are just one pitch away from winning that precious emblem. The situation looks as black as the water in the Detroit River at midnight. We are losing by three runs with two out in the ninth inning. The count is three balls and two strikes on me, the batter. We trail 4–1, but the bases are loaded.

A grand slam homer could win it!

I call time-out to scoop up some soft brown dirt and rub it on my sweaty palms and slippery bat handle.

Taking one last look around, I struggle to control my nervousness. Out in center field patches of brown grass, seared by the summer sun, lie dying. In left, the isolated tufts of green grass contrast sharply with the white of the third base foul line and the red, rocky infield.

I notice the left fielder playing me deep and away from the line. He pounds his fist into the pocket of his glove, ready for the final pitch.

The din of the traffic fades as I step back into the batter's box and dig in. Crouching slightly, I reach out and tap the center of the plate with my 33-ounce Louisville Slugger.

I check my distance from the plate carefully. Too close to the plate and I'll hit the ball weakly on the handle; too far, and the outside corner looms unprotected, inviting that final strike.

The pitcher towers over me like the Penobscot Building—only 60 feet, 6 inches away. He glares in at the plate while I take a few practice swings. The building bends in the middle as the pitcher leans forward, shakes off the catcher's first two signs, then nods his head in agreement. Smiling confidently, he knows he has selected the right pitch.

A second ago my body was as taut as an overwound clock, but now I feel strangely relaxed. The silence is deafening and my concentration almost audible as the pitcher starts his wind up. My eyes locked onto his motion, I wait for the deciding pitch.

The pitcher kicks his leg high as he strides towards the plate. His face a mask of fierce determination, he lets the ball fly.

Sweat drips down my forehead stinging my eyes with salt as I stand there hypnotized by the balloon-sized ball floating toward me.

I see only the ball bearing in on me, then suddenly breaking sharply away.

I almost smile with confidence, knowing I have guessed right. It's a curve, not his fastball.

Viciously, I whip my bat around as the ball continues to break right over the center of the plate.

The solid smack of wood against leather sends my spirits soaring. The stung ball screams out towards the left field line.

A shadow of despair quickly replaces my temporary elation. For the first time, I see the left fielder racing towards the ball. My only hope is that he will never reach it in time. But wait! It looks like it's curving foul.

Eyes transfixed by the ball, I snap out of my trance and spring towards first. White chalk flies as the ball hits right on the line.

Time seems impaled and unmoving, awaiting the umpire's decision. The players are frozen in mid-air as suspense stretches like a rubber band to the breaking point. "Fair ball," he yells, setting the players back in motion.

Heart pounding, adrenalin pumping, I'm running full speed. Shouts of encouragement from teammates spur me on faster than I could ever run.

It's as I'm rounding second that I see their shortstop go out into left field and get ready for the relay.

My teammates have gone mad, jumping and screaming wildly as I steam towards third. Arms whirling like a windmill, the third base coach is frantically waving me home.

Rounding third my legs begin to feel leaden. Am I slowing down, or is it my imagination? Now only 90 feet away from home, I will my body to move faster, but my brain dares it to try. Robot-like I continue running, unaware of what is happening behind me.

The catcher sprouts up in front of me in perfect position to take the shortstop's throw. The home plate umpire peers over the catcher's shoulder ready to call the play. Is that pity I read on his face?

Home plate taunts me, promising glory as I start my slide. The dust swirls up around us, and I know it's going to be close. I see my feet cross the plate through the misty red cloud as the ball smacks into the catcher's mitt. I can't believe my ears when the umpire screams out his decision.

The chance to be a hero doesn't come often for an average guy like me. Determination alone can't make you a hero. You have to have either an ounce of luck or a smile of divine assistance. You'll have to decide which for yourself, when your turn comes.

"Safe," the umpire roars, as the ball bounces out of the catcher's glove and dribbles to the backstop. "West wins 5 to 4."

Bedlam erupts around me as I am hauled to my feet by my deliriously happy teammates and screaming fans. Now the opposing players are shaking my hand and offering congratulations. Never having been a hero before, I feel embarrassed and tongue-tied. I guess I surprised myself along with everyone else, but I can't help feeling proud.

The celebrating has long since subsided, and the excitement has been replaced by the warm glow of a happy memory. Over 30 years have flown by and Detroit has changed dramatically, but I still remember my big chance on the day of the championship game.

| **Student Essay** | **SPARE ME THE DETAILS**
Kathy Marsh |

This descriptive essay may repel you with its vivid detail, but you won't be able to deny the power of its words. You will see here that all well-chosen words are not necessarily pretty. As you read the essay, consider the following points:

1. Much of the detail in this description is very concrete. Find some of the words that created a particularly realistic picture of the man for you. Where would you place these words on the ladder of abstraction?
2. What one detail strikes you as most repulsive? Why?
3. Do you think this man was a suitable subject for an essay? Why or why not?
4. What figures of speech can you find in this essay? Do they add to the over-all effect?
5. Is the conclusion effective for you? Does it make the paper seem complete?

Used with permission of Kathy Marsh.

I was sitting in a corner of the restaurant when a movement at the entrance area caught my attention. Coming into the restaurant was the ugliest and most obese person I had ever seen. He sauntered to the table across from me and, after a slight struggle, managed to arrange his body to fit the chair. The grotesqueness of his features was deepened by the dimness of the area.

His small, beady eyes reminded me of a rat that roams the room wildly. He had a broad nose that lay flat against his face and large lips that on another might seem sensuous but on him only looked disgusting. He had a habit of wetting his lips with a small red tongue that slipped in and out of his mouth like a serpent's. His greased-back hair swept away from his forehead, from which small beads of sweat were sliding. He was sitting slouched in his chair, his stomach hanging over his belt and the buttons of his shirt straining in protest, when the waiter appeared. As he was placing his order, his fat, hairy hands were constantly moving in a nervous gesture.

I forced myself to concentrate on my dinner until the aroma of barbecue directed my senses to his table. Being placed before him were two platters overflowing with steaming mounds of barbecued spareribs and another plate of fluffy white spuds with pools of butter. A basket of rolls and a decanter of wine were also brought to the table before the waiter left.

The man reached across the table to the decanter and filled his glass to the rim. After placing the napkin under his chin, he arranged the platter of food in front of him. He picked up his spoon and, without hesitation, plunged it into the center of the steaming potatoes. Moistening his lips, his eyes full of anticipation, he opened his mouth and, placing the food in it, closed his jaw as a captor does to its prey. I could almost see the way he was anticipating the initial appeasement of his hunger by the way he slid the potatoes around in his mouth, and with one final swallow the entire mass was transported to his stomach. He then lifted the wine glass, swished the liquid around, stuck his nose to the rim and professionally sniffed at the aroma. Satisfied that the quality was above average, he placed the glass to his lips and unceremoniously drained it of its contents.

After repeating these acts until the platter of potatoes was left practically barren, he focused his attention on the mounds of ribs. By this time, the sight of this man had definitely ruined any chances I had of enjoying my meal. My eyes were glued to his hands as they greedily reached down to pick up the first sparerib and bring it to his mouth. His mouth opened, showing yellow, cavity-filled teeth, and then closed as the juicy pieces of meat were ripped from the bone. In two bites, he managed to clean the bone of any edible material.

What happened next is to remain forever imprinted upon my memory. After setting the bone back on the platter, the man lifted his hand to his mouth. With a gleam in his eye, as if relishing each moment, he pursed his lips and slowly placed his forefinger in his mouth. Closing his lips, he cautiously retracted his finger, dripping with spittle. He went through this process with each finger and when finished sat back in his chair, wiped his mouth with the sleeve of his jacket, patted his stomach, and let out a slow, passion-filled belch.

The entire time he was devouring the spareribs, the above process was being repeated. By the time the platter of ribs was gone, my stomach was churning and my face had gone pale. I could no longer watch him eat, but I could see him in my mind each time I heard a bone being placed on the plate.

Later I felt my eyes being pulled, as if by a magnet, back to the table where this man was struggling to get up. Once standing, he took a final gulp of the wine, placed his napkin on the table and began staggering to the door. My eyes were glued to his retreating form, and when I thought I was having my final look at him, he turned around. I watched as he ran a hand through his hair and his tongue moistened his lips. Feeling his penetrating gaze on me, my eyes hesitantly rose to meet his. I felt my body shiver at the light I saw in his eyes and sat stunned as he provocatively winked. I watched the door close silently behind him.

FOCUS

SENTENCES

Humor is a common link in the three short essays in this section. The subjects are diverse—rubber bands, dogs, and car keys—but the authors all play with words, creating some amusing scenes through the use of a variety of sentence structures and rhythms. You'll want to notice how they use parallelism, dialogue, very short sentences, and even sentence fragments when they suit the writer's purpose. Enjoy!

Professional Essay

THE BAND PLAYS ON
Melvin Maddocks

This tribute to the hardiness of the rubber band gave Maddocks a chance to assemble a variety of sentences. As you read his essay, consider the following points:

1. Look at the variety of sentence lengths. Some are complete paragraphs, while the shortest are only six words. Do you see any reason for the shortness of the sentence that ends the fifth paragraph?
2. Where do you find examples of parallel structure in Maddocks' sentences?
3. According to Maddocks, "the durable rubber band connects—loosely, of course—our present to our past." Is this true for you? Does the smell of rubber bands take you back in time? If so, what memories surface for you?
4. The concluding sentence emphasizes the casualness of the rubber band. Is this point made elsewhere in the essay? Look for examples.
5. Do you think rubber bands make a suitable topic for an essay? Why or why not?

Reprinted by permission from *The Christian Science Monitor*. © 1981 The Christian Science Publishing Society. All rights reserved.

It is a pleasure to report that the good old rubber band seems to be stretching resiliently into the '80s. Nobody has invented a plastic substitute yet. The rubber band is still the simplest and cheapest way to roll a newsboy's paper, keep a lobster's claws closed, color-code different grades of scallions, rig an orthodontist's braces, or maybe hold onto your party hat when you hear astounding statistics like these, relayed by the *New York Times* from Akron, Ohio, the Rubber Band Capital of the World:

> Some 25 million pounds of rubber bands are sold each year in the United States, at a going price of around $1 a pound. Since there are about 4,000 rubber bands of the newsboy's size in each pound, we're talking about 100 billion rubber bands.

Why is the rubber band so popular, you ask. We suggest that, like chicken wire, friction tape, and the bobby pin, the rubber band stands in the honorable American tradition of make-do. Seldom does a rubber band represent the ideal bit of equipment for the job. A rubber band is the get-me-home-on-a-dark-night device that holds a wiring harness in place—just barely—on a 12-year-old car. Wound and rewound, a rubber band can stabilize a record player arm that has lost one of those tiny but irreplaceable screws.

The rubber band is a plucky defensive effort, designed to keep the center from falling apart and chaos from taking over.

You cannot imagine a rubber band staying in place forever, like a paper clip. The paper clip is a rigid gadget—the tool of the orderly mind at its most inflexible. A paper clip even has its position prescribed: upper left-hand corner. A paper clip is the army.

Stretch a rubber band and it comes alive. Stretch a paper clip and you get a broken metal pretzel.

A rubber band doesn't have the confidence to clamp or shackle. It just sort of tentatively gathers in.

A rubber band is a reluctant leash that allows things to wander but not quite get lost.

A rubber band is not sure neatness is worth the price. On the other hand, it believes that real messes should be controlled, or at least disguised.

A rubber band is less a command than a question: *Shape up?*

There are rather pleasant rituals associated with the rubber band. Some people like to smooth out any twists—make the band lie flat. For others, the game is to choose the right size of band, or even the wrong size. Nothing in the line of desk work is more thrilling than taking a small band and carefully expanding it to a larger diameter than it was ever intended for. One knows the delicious terror of a bomb squad.

Children like to chew rubber bands. Most adults, if not being observed, enjoy sniffing rubber bands now and then. Rubber bands and gum erasers are the last organic smells in an office desk. For the rest, it's chemicals—type cleaner and white-out fluids.

One manufacturer claims the rubber band has 2,000 uses. We don't want to hear anybody say: "Isn't that stretching it?" On the other hand, we don't want to hear about probably 1,978 of those uses.

Maybe the important news is that the durable rubber band connects—loosely, of course—our present to our past.

The Proustian scent of a rubber band is enough to bring back second grade.

In a certain attic a rubber band holds together a stack of family letters over 30 years old. The band is red and thick. One knows what the letters say. One can almost hear the voices. The band is red and cracked, like drying clay. Some hot, dry summer day it will break from its own tension. Or perhaps, some fresh spring morning, while taking winter clothes up and summer clothes down, one will risk all and tenderly stretch the band, releasing the letters and everything that's in them. In the meantime, the rubber band makes the perfect retainer—as casual as an arm around a shoulder.

Professional Essay

SNAPSHOT OF A DOG
James Thurber

Cartoons, essays, and fables, many of them published in the *New Yorker*, made Thurber one of the best-known humorists of this century. This recollection of one of his dogs exhibits the gentler side of his humor. As you read his essay, consider the following points:

1. Why do you suppose he selected the word *snapshot* instead of *portrait* for the title? Is there a difference in the connotations of the words?
2. What effect does the introduction create by referring to Rex as *him* in the first line?
3. The fight described in the second and third paragraphs is called *Homeric*. If you don't know the meaning of this adjective, look it up before deciding whether or not it is appropriate for this particular dogfight. Why would Thurber choose it?
4. What is significant about the sentence lengths and structures in the concluding paragraph? Do you think Thurber manages to avoid sentimentality in this death scene? Find specific details to support your answer.

From *The Middle-Aged Man on the Flying Trapeze*, published by Harper & Row. Copyright © 1935 by James Thurber. Copyright © 1963 by Helen W. Thurber and Rosemary T. Sauers. Reprinted by permission of Mrs. James Thurber.

I ran across a dim photograph of him the other day, going through some old things. He's been dead twenty-five years. His name was Rex (my two brothers and I named him when we were in our early teens) and he was a bull terrier. "An American bull terrier," we used to say, proudly; none of your English bulls. He had one brindle eye that sometimes made him look like a clown and sometimes reminded you of a politician with derby hat and cigar. The rest of him was white except for a brindle saddle that always seemed to be slipping off and a brindle stocking on a hind leg. Nevertheless, there was a nobility about him. He was big and muscular and beautifully made. He never lost his dignity even when trying to accomplish the extravagant tasks my brothers and [I] used to set for him. One of these was the bringing of a ten-foot wooden rail into the yard through the back gate. We would throw it out into the alley and tell him to go get it. Rex was as powerful as a wrestler, and there were not many things that he couldn't manage somehow to get hold of with his great jaws and lift or drag to wherever he wanted to put them, or wherever we wanted them put. He could catch the rail at the balance and lift it clear of the ground and trot with great confidence toward the gate. Of course, since the gate was only four feet wide or so, he couldn't bring the rail in broadside. He found that out when he got a few terrific jolts, but he wouldn't give up. He finally figured out how to do it, by dragging the rail, holding onto one end, growling. He got a great, wagging satisfaction out of his work. We used to bet kids who had never seen Rex in action that he could catch a baseball thrown as high as they could throw it. He almost never let us down. Rex could hold a baseball with ease in his mouth, in one cheek, as if it were a chew of tobacco.

He was a tremendous fighter, but he never started fights. I don't believe he liked to get into them, despite the fact that he came from a line of fighters. He never went for another dog's throat but for one of its ears (that teaches a dog a lesson), and he would get his grip, close his eyes, and hold on. He could hold on for hours. His longest fight lasted from dusk until almost pitch-dark, one Sunday. It was fought in East Main Street in Columbus with a large, snarly nondescript that belonged to a big colored man. When Rex finally got his ear grip, the brief whirlwind of snarling turned to screeching. It was frightening to listen to and to watch. The Negro boldly picked the dogs up somehow and began swinging them around his head, and finally let them fly like a hammer in a hammer throw, but although they landed ten feet away with a great plump, Rex still held on.

The two dogs eventually worked their way to the middle of the car tracks, and after a while two or three streetcars were held up by the fight. A motorman tried to pry Rex's jaws open with a switch rod; somebody lighted a fire and made a torch of a stick and held that to Rex's tail, but he paid no attention. In the end, all the residents and storekeepers in the neighborhood were on hand, shouting this, suggesting that. Rex's joy of battle, when battle was joined, was almost tranquil. He had a kind of pleasant expression during fights, not a vicious one, his eyes closed in what would have seemed to be sleep had it not been for the turmoil of the struggle. The Oak Street Fire Department finally had to be sent for—I don't know why nobody thought of it sooner. Five or six pieces of apparatus arrived, followed by a battalion chief. A hose was attached, and a powerful stream of water was turned on the dogs. Rex held on for several moments more while the torrent buffeted him about like a log in a freshet. He was a hundred yards away from where the fight started when he finally let go.

The story of that Homeric fight got around town, and some of our relatives looked upon the incident as a blot upon the family name. They insisted that we get rid of Rex, but we were very happy with him, and nobody could have made us give him up. We would have left town with him first, along any road there was to go. It would have been different, perhaps, if he'd ever started fights, or looked for trouble. But he had a gentle disposition. He never bit a person in the ten strenuous years that he lived, nor ever growled at anyone except prowlers. He killed cats, that is true, but quickly and neatly and without especial malice, the way men kill certain animals. It was the only thing he did that we could never cure him of doing. He never killed, or even chased, a squirrel. I don't know why. He had his own philosophy about such things. He never ran barking after wagons or automobiles. He didn't seem to see the idea in pursuing something you couldn't catch, or something you couldn't do anything with, even if you did catch it. A wagon was one of the things he couldn't tug along with his mighty jaws, and he knew it. Wagons, therefore, were not a part of his world.

Swimming was his favorite recreation. The first time he ever saw a body of water (Alum Creek), he trotted nervously along the steep bank for a while, fell to barking wildly, and finally plunged in from a height of eight feet or more. I shall always remember that shining, virgin dive. Then he swam upstream and back, just for the pleasure of it, like a man. It was fun to see him battle upstream against a stiff current, struggling and growling every foot of the way. He had as much fun in the water as any person I have known. You didn't have to throw a stick in the water to get him to go in. Of course, he would bring back a stick to you if you did throw one in. He would even have brought back a piano if you had thrown one in.

That reminds me of the night, way after midnight, when he went a-roving in the light of the moon and brought back a small chest of drawers that he found somewhere—how far from the house nobody ever knew; since it was Rex, it could easily have been half a mile. There were no drawers in the chest when he got it home, and it wasn't a good one—he hadn't taken it out of anybody's house; it was just an old cheap piece that somebody had abandoned on a trash heap. Still, it was something he wanted, probably because it presented a nice problem in transportation. It tested his mettle. We first knew about his achievement when, deep in the night, we heard him trying to get the chest up onto the porch. It sounded as if two or three people were trying to tear the house down. We came downstairs and turned on the porch light. Rex was on the top step trying to pull the thing up, but it had caught somehow and he was just holding his own. I suppose he would have held his own till dawn if we hadn't helped him. The next day we carted the chest miles away and threw it out. If we had thrown it out in a nearby alley, he would have brought it home again, as a small token of his integrity in such matters. After all, he had been taught to carry heavy wooden objects about, and he was proud of his prowess.

I am glad Rex never saw a trained police dog jump. He was just an amateur jumper himself, but the most daring and tenacious I have ever seen. He would take on any fence we pointed out to him. Six feet was easy for him, and he could do eight by making a tremendous leap and hauling himself over finally by his paws, grunting and straining; but he lived and died without knowing that twelve-

and sixteen-foot walls were too much for him. Frequently, after letting him try to go over one for a while, we would have to carry him home. He would never have given up trying.

There was in his world no such thing as the impossible. Even death couldn't beat him down. He died, it is true, but only, as one of his admirers said, after "straight-arming the death angel" for more than an hour. Late one afternoon he wandered home, too slowly and too uncertainly to be the Rex that had trotted briskly homeward up our avenue for ten years. I think we all knew when he came through the gate that he was dying. He had apparently taken a terrible beating, probably from the owner of some dog that he had got into a fight with. His head and body were scarred. His heavy collar with the teeth marks of many a battle on it was awry; some of the big brass studs in it were sprung loose from the leather. He licked at our hands and, staggering, fell, but got up again. We could see that he was looking for someone. One of his three masters was not home. He did not get home for an hour. During that hour the bull terrier fought against death as he had fought against the cold, strong current of Alum Creek, as he had fought to climb twelve-foot walls. When the person he was waiting for did come through the gate, whistling, ceasing to whistle, Rex walked a few wabbly paces toward him, touched his hand with his muzzle, and fell down again. This time he didn't get up.

Student Essay

KEYS AND ME
Julie Allen-Avery

This writer made a humorous essay out of an experience common to many of us—being locked out of her car. Her narrative has some unusual touches, however, including a talking gourd. The sentence variety in this essay is worth noticing, too, especially the dialogue. As you read the essay, consider the following points:

1. The opening paragraph tells of an event that happened apparently some time before the episode of the essay. Does this make a good introduction? What is the effect of its two-word final sentence?
2. How do the various bits of dialogue—the self-talk, the gourd's imagined advice, and the comments from the crowd—affect the atmosphere created in this episode?
3. What figures of speech are used in the passage describing her struggle with the coat hanger? Do these create the scene for you?
4. Some of the sentences in this essay are really fragments. Can these be justified by the style of the writing? Find one to illustrate your answer.
5. How do you respond to the conclusion of this paper?

Used with permission of Julie Allen-Avery.

No one else has as many problems with car keys as I do. One lunch hour I sped to the corner drugstore, jumped out of the car with my keys in one hand, my mail in the other, and quite casually threw my keys into the big red and blue mailbox. There I was with a handful of bills to start my car instead of keys. The mailman's next pickup was scheduled three hours later. I thought this would be the epitome of my experience with car keys. It wasn't.

When my new 1980 X-car arrived, nothing seemed more fitting than to drive down to Brown County, Indiana, to the resort town of Nashville for the Fourth of July weekend. Little did I know how much I would find out about my new car on this trip.

Nashville is unique: like a Saugatuck, but friendlier. There are hundreds of quaint shops in the Brown County area. I found the largest gourd you have ever seen in your life at one of these shops. I asked the shopkeeper to hold it while I went to get my car. I didn't want to walk through the crowded streets carrying that huge, dried vegetable. I just knew someone would say, "Wow, look at that gourd!"

My shopping spree was near an end. Time to go get the gourd. I double parked, ran in, grabbed it, ran back outside, and guess what? The keys were in the ignition! My extra set was in my purse, and that was locked in the car. "No problem here," I said. "Just use the old coat hanger trick." I was an expert at this; years of the very same thing had made me quite an engineer at bending hangers to fit assorted cars.

A shopkeeper gave me a hanger and while untwisting it (and motioning traffic to move on by) I noticed there weren't any lock buttons on the doors. That's right! Electric door locks!

I frantically shoved the hanger in through the door edge. Out of the corner of my eye I could see the gourd swaying back and forth on the hood of my car. It would lean forward, watching me, then move back and sort of sway from side to side, as if saying, "No, no, that's not right." The hanger bobbed around inside the car. I did what I could to direct it toward the far-down armrest where the door lock was located. The distance was just too great—I had no control. The hanger twisted and turned and resembled Leonard Bernstein's baton during his direction of "Flight of the Bumblebee." I glanced at my reflection in the window. I even looked like Leonard Bernstein! The temperature was in the 90's, my hair was a mess, and my perspiration had drawn two buzzing deer flies from the crowd to encircle my head. The gourd kept watching, almost knowingly, and the crowd started gathering.

"Let me help."

"Wow, look at that gourd."

"Here, try my Jeep key."

"Did you ever see a gourd like that?"

"That's GM designing for you."

I was close to tears when the police arrived. The "police" in Nashville was a force of one, a big woman named Darlene, her pin told me. She surveyed the situation, got out her tool kit, and shortly thereafter informed the crowd that her tools weren't made for electric door locks. But I was lucky. She had an unofficial sidekick who suggested going through the trunk. He revealed a type of punch used to remove the entire cylinder from the locks of trunks in accidents where victims have to be removed through the rear of the car. He placed it in the eyelid keyhole of the trunk, hit it with the heel of his cowboy boot and—nothing. Just a hole in the trunk lock big enough to insert the jailer's key from the Bastille!

By now my car was covered with nose prints, pop and beer cans adorned the roof, and someone was holding my gourd above the crowd. Several good people had inserted their own devices, hangers or whatever, and I felt a little sick from the sun. An hour had passed. Why not just call a locksmith or a Pontiac dealer? My friend had done that, to no avail—not on a holiday weekend.

Soon a young man with one arm approached me. He said the reason the power door locks would not move was because there was not enough pressure from the long-reaching coat hanger to trigger the electronic mechanism. He suggested simultaneously touching both front door locks, that perhaps double pressure might be just enough to do the trick. The crowd quieted down as two young men lined up their hangers. Bingo! It worked! The crowd cheered and applauded. A shopkeeper rang an old dinner bell. The gourd appeared, relieved from the spectator's grip, to rest once more on the hood. It moved forward and backward, as if to say, "Yes, that's how I'd have done it."

The entire damage done to my car exceeded whatever replacement glass might have cost had I broken a window. Next time, that's what I'll do. And I won't have a gourd with me ever again. It hangs in my yard, feeding winter birds. Occasionally, someone says, "Wow, look at that gourd," and I hear it whisper, "Got your keys?"

F O C U S
PARAGRAPHS

All three essays in this section are worth studying because of their paragraph organization and development, but they all have a theme in common, too: the relationship between the sexes. Two approach this seriously—the professional essay from a fairly impersonal point of view, using statistics from recent surveys, and the student essay from the standpoint of personal experience—and one takes a humorous approach with a satirical commentary.

Professional Essay

SOME CHEERFUL WORDS ABOUT MEN
Gloria Steinem

One of the cofounders of the magazine *Ms.*, Steinem writes in this essay of some major changes that have taken place in American society recently. Her thoughts are well organized, and her paragraphs are most often models of paragraph development. As you read her essay, consider the following points:

1. The essay uses a two-paragraph introduction. How is this tied in to the third paragraph? Is the introduction attention-getting for you?
2. Does the third paragraph have a topic sentence? How is the topic developed?
3. Can you find any transitional paragraphs? What are the ideas that they serve as bridges between, if you find any?
4. Are you convinced by the discussion of the People's Choice Awards?
5. The six changes in attitude reported by Daniel Yankelovich are worth some study. Do they seem to reflect American society as you know it? Which of the new attitudes, if any, reflect your own views?

From *Ms.* Magazine, June 1981, pp. 43–45. Reprinted by permission.

If you've been reading and watching the same media that most of the country sees, you may be feeling depressed, even embittered, by the masculinist backlash. Ever since Reagan and other antifeminist politicians were sent to Washington by the most disproportionately male voter turnout (not to mention the oldest, richest, and whitest) in United States election history, the media landscape has been littered with articles on the New Macho and the mandate for a retreat from equality.

Not only is last year's election used to support this theory of a conservative and antiwoman tide. So is anything from the male supremacism of the Moral Majority to men's return to shorter hair, women's to shorter skirts, and the popcultural rebirth of the fifties.

Obviously, there are big factual flaws in that majority claim. Most eligible Americans chose not to vote at all, and even among that 25 percent who *did* vote for Reagan, the majority made clear in postelection surveys that they were voting *against* inflation and the status quo, not *for* his right-wing positions. The American obsession with Who Won and Who Lost has served to obscure those two truths about where most Americans are (and are not). Just 60 days after he entered the White House, a Gallup poll reported a record-breaking 24-percent public disapproval rating for Reagan.

As for pop culture, there is no evidence that men with shorter hair are any less likely to share child care or housework, or that women returning to shorter skirts are any more likely to give up legal rights. On the other hand, the fifties revival probably *is* an escape from current change, just as increased pornography and the sexualization of little girls is certainly a backlash against demands for equality by adult women.

Nonetheless, the majority of men are *not* reverting, as some of the media would have us believe, to a vision of an ideal man who is some amalgam of Ronald Reagan and John Wayne.

On the contrary, the world of entertainment has produced a media idol who tells us something very different about ourselves. It is no longer even Burt Reynolds, himself a transitional figure who wasn't afraid to campaign for the Equal Rights Amendment in spite of his image as Good Ol' Boy, and who certainly had more sense of humor about his own "macho" style than John Wayne ever did. Now, the national favorite is one of our own.

In the People's Choice Awards, the only multiple entertainment awards determined directly by the public, Alan Alda has won both top positions for the second year in a row: both Favorite Male Performer on Television, the entertainment form that most Americans see, and Favorite All-Around Male Entertainer in all media.

To assess the shift, think of John Wayne, Bob Hope, and other traditionalists who have won these awards in the past. Now contrast these public images with that of Alan Alda, whose much-acclaimed role in M*A*S*H is antiwar, sensitive, skeptical of authority (and frequently written by Alda himself): who explains on talk shows that his top political priority is the passage of the Equal Rights Amendment, and who also campaigns and endorses fund appeals for candidates who support women's right to reproductive freedom; who turns down and protests roles in major films that are biased against women; who, as both a writer and an actor, has dramatized many men's need to lessen their drive toward public success in order to be good parents and whole people in private; who limited his own career by leaving California and other movie locations in order to be home in New Jersey each weekend; whose musician/photographer wife and three grown daughters are clearly regarded by him as equals, not ornaments; whose long-running marriage and lack of even rumored affairs give him an "antimasculine" image of constancy and faithfulness; and, perhaps most unusual of all, who refers to himself publicly and often as a feminist.

"Aha," you say, "*women* voters must have made Alan Alda a national favorite." In fact, he won Favorite Male TV Performer by an overwhelming margin and his supporters were slightly more men than women. (And there were differences elsewhere. For instance, Carol Burnett won Favorite Female TV Performer with a big margin of women's votes.) For Favorite All-Around Male Entertainer, Alda's supporters were only slightly more women.

Even in the limited world of People's Choice Awards, however, all the news is not good. This year, Clint Eastwood won the award for Favorite Motion Picture Actor for his very violent roles in a series of similar Westerns—beating out *both* Burt Reynolds and Robert Redford. Of course, the movie audience is overwhelmingly younger, as well as much smaller, than the television one. Florence Skelly, partner in the social research firm of Yankelovich, Skelly, and White, notes that the male 14- to 21-year-old moviegoer is the main support for the current wave of "kill-the-woman" movies; films in which independent women are sadistically murdered. Perhaps that fact, like the higher margin of male votes for Eastwood, underlines the greater insecurity of some young men, and their discomfort with female equals, or with any women at all.

Nonetheless, the ascent of Alan Alda, Male Feminist, to two top spots on the national favorite list should remind us that the backlash is a minority response. There has been a majority change in values, of which many men are a part. In fact, the backlash is against them as well as us.

For instance, Daniel Yankelovich cites these areas of basic change among both women and men:

- By 1978, fewer than 30 percent of Americans disapproved of "a married woman earning money if she has a husband capable of supporting her." In 1938, the disapproval rate was more than 75 percent. (Even through the 1960s, a majority felt that a wife's work showed that the husband was incapable of providing for his family, and was therefore not a "real man.")
- By 1980, a majority of Americans agreed that "both sexes have responsibility to care for small children." In 1970, agreement had been only about 30 percent; a big change in a decade. Prefeminist polls hadn't even bothered to ask the question.
- For the first time in history, a majority now rejects the double-standard idea that a woman should be a virgin when she marries, or that it's more excusable for a husband to have affairs.
- By 1980, nearly 80 percent of Americans were willing to vote for a woman President. In 1937, only about 30 percent would have agreed.
- At the beginning of the 1970s, only a 42-percent minority of Americans wanted to strengthen women's status in society. By the end of the decade, a

64-percent majority agreed. (Among males, black men moved faster and farther; from a 47-percent approval rate in 1972 to 67 percent just two years later.)

- By the late 1970s, 75 percent of Americans agreed that remaining unmarried or choosing not to have children could be a valid and positive choice. Only one generation earlier, in the late 1950s, 80 percent believed that being unmarried was an unnatural state for a man or a woman, and that those who chose not to have children were selfish and wrong.

Obviously, this support for new lifestyles and new equality is high in ambivalence, and depends on how much disruption and sacrifice is required of men. In *Psychological Effects of Motherhood* (Praeger), Dr. Myra Leifer, a behavioral scientist, reports that even men who played an active role in childbirth classes and the birth itself were unlikely to share equally after the baby was born. A survey by Doyle Dane Bernbach, a New York advertising agency, found that less than a third of men liked the changes in women's traditional role. Why? Because they had to do more household chores. On the other hand, 78 percent of men whose wives worked outside the home approved of that fact, and so did a majority of men whose wives did not. Why? Because work brought money and, they had to admit, made their partners "more interesting." However reluctant the change might be, Doyle Dane Bernbach came to the conclusion that it was permanent. Creators of ads were advised that they had better start thinking about men in the supermarket, and other new trends.

Since the male role is supposed to be the superior one, the setter of norms, the desirable standard, its changes may have even more seismic effects than the female role changes that forced and encouraged it.

Underneath the current landscape of backlash, transitional ills, and confusion, there is an earthquake of changed hopes—and some of them belong to men.

Professional Essay

BODY LANGUAGE SPOKEN HERE
Art Buchwald

Art Buchwald often writes his syndicated commentaries on recent news in the form of dialogues. You can learn a great deal about writing conversations—and enjoy his original outlook on life—from studying a column of his. As you read this essay, consider the following points:

1. Four people are speaking at various points in this essay. How does Buchwald arrange his paragraphs so you can always tell who the speaker is?
2. Do the quotations—made-up, except for the opening one by Phyllis Schlafly—sound like real conversation? Why or why not?
3. It is difficult to work in a thesis sentence when the essay is almost all dialogue. Do you think Buchwald has overcome this problem, or are you left wondering what the point of the essay is?

4. The woman at the water cooler and Schlafly seem to represent opposite views on the body-language issue. With which do you agree? Can you tell from this essay whether Buchwald agrees with either one?

Copyright © 1981. Reprinted by permission of Art Buchwald.

Phyllis Schlafly testifying in front of the Senate Labor Committee on sexual harassment in the workplace: "When a woman walks across the room, she speaks with a universal body language that most men intuitively understand. Men hardly ever ask sexual favors of women from whom the certain answer is 'No.' Virtuous women are seldom accosted by unwelcome sexual propositions or familiarities, obscene talk or profane language."

I never accept a statement from a Senate witness without first checking it out. So I went to a government agency the other day run by a friend of mine and showed him Mrs. Schlafly's statement.

"What do you want to do?" he asked.

"I would like to observe the universal body language of your female employees, to see if they're saying anything."

"Be my guest," he said.

I went out into a large office and stationed myself near the water cooler.

In a few moments I noticed a woman walk across the room with a folder in her hands. Intuition told me she was trying to tell me something.

When she got to the cooler, I said, "What were you saying with your body when you were coming over here?" I asked her.

"I was thirsty and wanted a drink of water."

"There was more to it than that," I challenged her. "I got the feeling you were going to say 'Yes.'"

"Yes, what?"

"Yes, please."

"Get out of my way, buster, before I kick you in the shins."

"Please don't get upset. I'm just doing a study on sexual harassment in the office, and I felt that because of the way you were swinging your hips as you crossed the room, you were sending me a message."

"What kind of message?"

"Well, if it wasn't clearly a 'yes,' it certainly wasn't a definite 'no.'"

"No what?"

"No, like in 'what kind of a girl do you think I am?'"

"What department in the government did you say you were from?"

"I'm not in any department. You see, Phyllis Schlafly, who is an expert on sexual harassment, testified that you can tell a loose woman from a virtuous woman just by the way she walks. There are certain women who men know instinctively are asking for it all the time."

"She sounds sick."

"On the contrary. She's a very distinguished member of the far right, and because of her walk she's never been propositioned in her life."

"Maybe it's her face."

"Oh, no, she's a very presentable woman, but there is something about her that would keep any man from wanting to accost her. She exudes virtue and has never been pinched once."

"That's because she's never run into Sammy."

"Who's Sammy?"

"That creep over there. He's got more tentacles than an octopus."

"Maybe he's a student of body language, and he can tell when a woman wants to be harassed and when she doesn't," I suggested. "I'll bet he wouldn't lay a hand on Phyllis Schlafly."

"You don't know Sammy. He doesn't care how women walk as long as they are wearing a skirt."

"But if what you say is true, that means that Mrs. Schlafly's theory about women is all wet."

"I don't know about that. But if she worked next to Sammy she'd be black and blue by the end of the day."

"Even if everything about Mrs. Schlafly's body language says, 'No'?"

"Sammy says those are the easiest kind."

Student Essay

MALE ATTITUDES IN THE ARMY
Laurie Wardell

This essay links together several incidents from Wardell's tour in the Army to prove her point about sexual harassment in the service. Pay special attention to her paragraph development as you study her paper. As you read the essay, consider the following points:

1. Does this essay have a thesis in the introduction?
2. How many of the paragraphs have topic sentences? Where are these sentences located in the paragraphs?
3. How are the topic sentences developed? Do any of them seem to need further development than they get in the essay?
4. Which incident of sexual harassment do you consider the most significant? Is it positioned in the essay where it can be most effective?
5. Some feminists would object to Wardell's use of *ladies* and *girls* to describe women in the Army. Do these terms bother you? If they do, can you suggest substitutes that would sound better to you?
6. Does the concluding paragraph give the essay a finished sound?

Used with permission of Laurie Wardell.

When my best girlfriend told me she was considering joining the Army, I desperately tried to talk her out of it. Instead, I talked myself into it. Better put, my recruiter talked me into it. He spoke of "seeing the world," being in great physical condition, and the G.I. Bill. Little did I imagine what was in store for me.

Basics, being predominantly female, was tough, but bearable. It was when I went to AIT (Advanced Individual Training) that my problems began. Sexual harassment is a problem encountered by many females in the military, as I found out. I was no exception.

Numbers have always been my friends, so it was fitting that I went into the finance field. One of my instructors at school gave me my first experience with sexual harassment. I was at the top of my class academically and was somewhat of a teacher's pet. I was friendly with Sgt. Brown; everyone was. After classes we all usually met at the bowling alley. One night, Sgt. Brown took me aside and plainly stated that if I slept with him, I could expect to be first in the class. The sound of my hand slapping his face caught the attention of everyone present. I was so insulted by his remark I guess my reflexes took over. Instead of being first with help, I was second, on my own merit.

In my unit in Germany, I encountered another form of sexual harassment. My company clerk had the attitude of "you scratch my back and I'll scratch yours." Literally. He made up the CQ rosters and thought of himself as God. I think the power went to his head. Besides being company clerk, Feldstein was our company photographer. He fancied himself a real professional. I posed for him once, and he gave me several photos to keep. I didn't realize that it was the come-on. He made me an offer next that if I would pose for him topless, he would arrange for me to be off the CQ roster for the next six months. I didn't fall for his line, but unfortunately several girls did. What a joke on them! After the photos were taken, Feldstein had a sudden lapse of memory. Since juggling the roster was illegal, they couldn't even complain.

I was discriminated against once when it came time for me to be promoted. I was seven months pregnant when I became eligible to go before the promotion board. Since the Army did not have a maternity uniform, I had to wear civilian clothes during my pregnancy. To go before the board, though, you had to be in uniform. Therefore, I had to wait four extra months before I was back in uniform and could be reviewed. The way the promotion points were based, that four-month delay held my promotion back seven months.

Sometimes, we were unintentionally harassed. Our first sergeant made up the extra duty detail rosters. He was under the impression that women were unable to do hard work. If painting had to be done, or any heavy lifting or strenuous work, only men could have that detail. Naturally, we received a lot of negative comments from the guys about our "special treatment." In my unit we had formed a grievance committee. We discussed our differences and tried to come up with possible solutions. In this instance, we were able to convince our first sergeant to give the ladies a try. It surprised him when the girls finished before the guys did at the next paint-in.

Sometimes, when a female received an award for something, there were snide remarks made. A lot of males wondered whom she slept with. It was hard for some of them to admit that women were capable on their own merit.

The Army is doing its best to stop sexual harassment. It has an organization called Human Relations. It deals with harassment of all kinds. It's not perfect, but it is a start. In the not too distant future, sexual harassment could be eliminated entirely from the military. Maybe then, more women would choose to make the Army their careers, instead of just a four-year stint.

FOCUS

ORGANIZATION I (CHRONOLOGY, PROCESS, COMPARISON/CONTRAST)

Fairly simple patterns of development are followed in each of the three essays here. The simplest, chronological order, can be seen in the student essay about an unforgettable teacher. The professional essays are only slightly more complicated. They demonstrate a process paper—nine steps to take in dealing with the government—and a comparison/contrast commentary on sex and food. Each can give you ideas for your own papers.

Professional Essay

HOW TO OUTSMART THE BUREAUCRATS
Jack Anderson

The well-known investigative reporter explains here how to deal successfully with a government agency—a process we all might need to know some day. As you read his essay, consider the following points:

1. Anderson's introduction tries to convince the readers that their daily lives are controlled by government edicts. Do you think he succeeds? Is this true in your own life? Can you give examples?
2. Which of the nine steps he suggests do you think is the most important? Do the steps seem to be arranged to emphasize this one?
3. Notice the imagery used in step 4. Does this create an effective picture for you?
4. Have you had any experiences with bureaucrats that support the points made in Anderson's essay? Do you have any other suggestions to add?
5. Are all nine of the steps stated clearly?
6. Do you think the final paragraph would be encouraging or discouraging to the reader who wanted to battle the government on some issue? Why?

From *Parade* Magazine, July 27, 1980. Reprinted by permission.

In the year ahead, Americans will be inundated with more election advice than they really want. The choosing of a President will inspire millions of newspaper editorials, television commentaries and other political guides to assist the voters. Yet the man in the Oval Office will have less impact on our daily frustrations than the government clerk in his cubicle. The greater need is for a guide to help citizens cope with the bureaucracy.

Taken in the aggregate, the bureaucracy is a marvel to contemplate. Consider its metronome-like delivery of millions of benefit checks, its irrigation of thousands of agri-farms, its moon shots and space shuttles, its highways extending to every horizon, its inexhaustible catalogue of services.

But its ultimate achievement is the finesse, the unobtrusiveness, by which it rules. So gently, prosaically, gradually and invisibly does it tighten its bonds that we never appreciate the extent to which we are in its grip. Not too long ago, we Americans were distinctive throughout the world as a breed of self-starters, innovators, doers. Now we are becoming bound up in red tape—reduced to a nation of paper-shuffling petitioners, forever waiting permission from some government office for our next step, continually putting aside the work of the world in order to fill out forms.

Many regulations are necessary, and many bureaucrats are effective public servants. Few question that. But the aggregate picture produced by regulations-run-wild is of a government whose pace is hobbled, whose progress is dribbling to a halt, yet whose growth is exploding beyond control or even comprehension.

Citizens caught in the benevolent toils of the bureaucracy come to feel powerless and quickly succumb to the nothing-can-be-done-anyway syndrome. Yet something can be done; there is a way through the dark tunnels of the bureaucracy. Here is my own guide. It might be called "How to Succeed with the Government—but Only after Trying."

1. *Remember who the sovereign is.* The people are the source of the power that the bureaucrats wield. So in any encounter with a bureaucrat, you are the sovereign and he is the servant. You would do well to be pleasant and patient. But you don't have to take "no" for an answer. Find out and follow the appeal procedure.

2. *Don't let the bureaucrat hide behind his anonymity.* Bureaucrats are skilled at evading issues, shifting responsibility and diverting decisions to someone else. The more committees and conferences there are to share the burden of decision, the less chance there is that any single bureaucrat will be blamed. So try to identify and isolate the civil servant responsible for your case. Deal with him person-to-person rather than citizen-to-government. Perhaps you can reduce his feeling of splendid insulation from the populace. If he mishandles your case, name him, complain about him; proceed against him.

3. *Fight paper with paper.* Many a faceless bureaucrat finds his *raison d'être* in the regulation books, developing a mastery of them with which he confounds the real world. He buttresses every move with paperwork. You can beat him at his own game if you, too, keep detailed records—letters, forms,

receipts, memos. Put into writing any verbal promises you extract from a bureaucrat.

4. *Don't start at the top.* It's useless to go over the heads of the bureaucrats to their political chief. The typical high appointee quickly discovers during the honeymoon that he is in bed with an octopus, smothered in its loving embrace, the undulating arms simultaneously caressing him and keeping him occupied. With too many arms to outmaneuver, the incoming administrative head usually becomes the pampered captive of the octopus he is supposed to control. So you may as well start with the lower official and work your way up.

5. *Keep it cool.* The maligned government clerk, after all, is human. Try to deal with him face-to-face. Then you become a real person with a problem, not just a case number. Bring all essential documents with you, state your problem concisely. Don't spout, shout or threaten. The wrong approach can turn him off; the right one can persuade him to be helpful.

6. *A word on paper is worth two on the phone.* If you cannot confront the official, don't telephone him. Write him a letter. Make it businesslike. State your problem; give the facts; explain what you think should be done. Enclose copies of all documents involved and ask for a response within a reasonable time.

7. *If at once you don't succeed . . .* Try, try again; then raise hell. You see, the hardcore bureaucrat in his heart of hearts is at odds with democracy. He dislikes controversy, which disrupts the smooth implementation of plans and procedures. He embraces secrecy because what is not known cannot be disrupted. His craving for small certainties also discourages dissent. So if all other approaches fail, you may get a rise out of him by rocking his bureaucratic boat. Complain to his superiors; write to your Congressman; raise a howl.

8. *Seek legal help.* Abraham Lincoln's idea of government of, by and for the people has turned, in the bureaucratic age, into government of, by and for the lawyers. You will be better off, therefore, if you can afford the services of a lawyer.

9. *Yes, it does help to write your Congessman.* Most members of Congress, given the need for votes on Election Day, will help constituents with their federal problems. Congressional inquiries get top priority at most government agencies. You should seek the assistance of the Congressman from your home district or the Senators from your home state.

It is often less painful to submit to the unjust government edict than to fight it, less expensive to pay the unfair tax assessment than to oppose it. But each generation must proclaim anew its Declaration of Independence, and the ascendant danger of our day is the government bureaucrat. The average American just wants the government to leave him alone—all the more reason why he must stand up to the bureaucrats and oppose their encroachments, lest they forget they are servants, not masters, of the nation.

Professional Essay

THE PLACE OF SEX AMONG HUMAN VALUES
Bertrand Russell

Russell, the British philosopher and mathematician, published this commentary during the Prohibition era in America. Ten years later, he had been hired to teach mathematics at the College of the City of New York when his appointment was abruptly withdrawn. His "immoral teachings"—apparently not in mathematics—were given as the reason for the firing. This excerpt may give you an inkling of what was considered immoral in the thirties. As you read the essay, consider the following points:

1. Russell compared the human need for food and drink to the need for sex. Do his examples convince you that the two drives are similar? He does admit that they are different in one way. What is that?
2. You may need to check some of his terms for extremists, such as *gormandizer*, *dipsomaniac*, *voluptuary*, and *ascetic*. What do these mean? Are the words good choices to make his points?
3. What does Russell say will be true of the first generation that "ceases to believe in the conventional teaching"? Do you see any signs that his prediction was true?
4. He compares the restraints we should have regarding sex to the three restraints we have regarding food. What are they? He discusses only two of the sexual restraints. What would the third one be? Would society be able to get along with only these three types of restraint on the sex drive? Why or why not?

From *The Basic Writings of Bertrand Russell* by Robert E. Egner and Lester E. Denonn, eds. Copyright © 1961 by Allen & Unwin. Reprinted by permission of Simon & Schuster, a Division of Gulf & Western Corporation, and George Allen & Unwin Ltd.

. . . Sex is a natural need, like food and drink. We blame the gormandizer and the dipsomaniac, because in the case of each an interest which has a certain legitimate place in life has usurped too large a share of his thoughts and emotions. But we do not blame a man for a normal and healthy enjoyment of a reasonable quantity of food. Ascetics, it is true, have done so, and have considered that a man should cut down his nutriment to the lowest point compatible with survival, but this view is not now common, and may be ignored. The Puritans, in their determination to avoid the pleasure of sex, became somewhat more conscious than people had been before of the pleasures of the table. As a seventeenth-century critic of Puritanism says:

> Would you enjoy gay nights and pleasant dinners?
> Then must you board with saints and bed with sinners.

It would seem, therefore, that the Puritans did not succeed in subduing the purely corporeal part of our human nature, since what they took away from sex they added to gluttony. Gluttony is regarded by the Catholic Church as one of the seven deadly sins, and those who practise it are placed by Dante in one of the deeper circles of hell; but it is a somewhat vague sin, since it is hard to say where legitimate interest in food ceases and guilt begins to be incurred. Is it wicked to eat anything that is not nourishing? If so, with every salted almond we risk damnation. Such views, however, are out of date. We all know a glutton when we see one, and although he may be somewhat despised, he is not severely reprobated. In spite of this fact, undue obsession with food is rare among those who have never suffered want. Most people eat their meals and then think about other things until the next meal. Those, on the other hand, who, having adopted an ascetic philosophy, have deprived themselves of all but the minimum of food, become obsessed by visions of banquets and dreams of demons bearing luscious fruits. And marooned Antarctic explorers, reduced to a diet of whale's blubber, spend their days planning the dinner they will have at the Carlton when they get home.

Such facts suggest that, if sex is not to be an obsession, it should be regarded by the moralists as food has come to be regarded, and not as food was regarded by the hermits of the Thebaid. Sex is a natural human need like food and drink. It is true that men can survive without it, whereas they cannot survive without food and drink, but from a psychological standpoint the desire for sex is precisely analogous to the desire for food and drink. It is enormously enhanced by abstinence, and temporarily allayed by satisfaction. While it is urgent, it shuts out the rest of the world from the mental purview. All other interests fade for the moment, and actions may be performed which will subsequently appear insane to the man who has been guilty of them. Moreover, as in the case of food and drink, the desire is enormously stimulated by prohibition. I have known children refuse apples at breakfast and go straight out into the orchard and steal them, although the breakfast apples were ripe and the stolen apples unripe. I do not think it can be denied that the desire for alcohol among well-to-do Americans is much stronger than it was twenty years ago. In like manner, Christian teaching and Christian authority have immensely stimulated interest in sex. The generation which first ceases to believe in the conventional teaching is bound, therefore, to indulge in sexual freedom to a degree far beyond what is to be expected of those whose views on sex are unaffected by superstitious teaching, whether positively or negatively. Nothing but freedom will prevent undue obsession with sex, but even freedom will not have this effect unless it has been associated with a wise education as regards sexual matters. I wish to repeat, however, as emphatically as I can, that I regard an undue preoccupation with this topic as an evil, and that I think this evil widespread at the present day, especially in America, where I find it particularly pronounced among the sterner moralists, who display it markedly by their readiness to believe falsehoods concerning those whom they regard as their opponents. The glutton, the voluptuary, and the ascetic are all self-absorbed persons whose horizon is limited by their own desires, either by way of satisfaction or by way of renunciation. A man who is healthy in mind and body will not have his interests thus concentrated upon himself. He will look out upon the world and find in it objects that seem to him worthy of his attention. Absorption in self is not, as some have supposed, the natural condition of unregenerate man. It is a disease brought on, almost always, by some thwarting of natural impulses. The voluptuary who gloats over thoughts of sexual gratification is in general the result of some kind of deprivation, just as the man who hoards food is usually a man who has lived through a famine or a period of destitution. Healthy, outward-looking men and women are not to be produced by the thwarting of natural impulse, but by the equal and balanced development of all the impulses essential to a happy life.

I am not suggesting that there should be no morality and no self-restraint in regard to sex, any more than in regard to food. In regard to food we have restraints of three kinds, those of law, those of manners, and those of health. We regard it as wrong to steal food, to take more than our share at a common meal, and to eat in ways that are likely to make us ill. Restraints of a similar kind are essential where sex is concerned, but in this case they are much more complex and involve much more self-control. Moreover, since one human being ought not to have property in another, the analogue of stealing is not adultery, but rape, which obviously must be forbidden by law. The questions that arise in regard to health are concerned almost entirely with venereal disease, a subject which we have already touched upon in connection with prostitution. Clearly, the diminution of professional prostitution can be best effected by that greater freedom among young people which has been growing up in recent years.

Student Essay

THE BEST TEACHINGS
Michelle M. Marlett

This chronological narrative tells the story of a very special fifth-grade teacher. As you read the essay, consider the following points:

1. The organization of this essay is simple, and the sentences are direct and straightforward in style. Can you think of any reasons why this approach was particularly appropriate for this topic?
2. Which of the episodes related here has the most effect on you? Why?
3. To cover a whole school year in a short paper, Marlett had to pay special attention to the principle of selection, leaving out many details of events that didn't suit her purpose. Can you think of some actions that must have occurred but that she decided to leave out? Was omitting them a wise decision?
4. Is the last paragraph necessary to give the paper a feeling of completion?

Used with permission of Michelle M. Marlett.

When I reflect upon my days in school, one year stands out in my memory: fifth grade. I don't remember much about the subjects I studied, or the other scholastic lessons I learned. What I do remember is a wonderful man who took our class and created a family. His name was Mr. Rice.

Mr. Rice was a little round man, no taller than most of us. He always smiled and had a laugh that was contagious. He helped us all to experience new and wonderful things, from dealing with death to watching life be created.

The year began as any other with a handful of strangers thrown together learning to be friends. By the end of September we were bound together by the tragedy which struck our class. Mr. Rice started class one morning with tears in his eyes. Chris had died the night before. As he told us, we were left silent, but the silence soon was filled with questions. He tried to explain why an 11-year-old child had been taken from us, but there was no reasoning. Most of us had never experienced death before, and as I think back, I believe his words said it as best he could: "God needed her for a very special reason."

Within a week the cloud which hung suspended over our class had lifted, and we were excitedly forming plans for the class trip to Mr. Rice's farm. He had horses and cows, animals which the majority of us had only seen on TV. He also had an apple orchard, which we descended upon and ate our fill of until we were sick. We milked the cows (or at least attempted to) and petted the horses. We ran wild in the meadows and explored the barn until we were ready to drop. When the sun began to set, Mr. Rice produced a surprise—a wagon filled with hay. We all piled on and went for a long ride nestled in the sweet-smelling hay.

The trip to the farm was the topic of conversation for weeks to follow, until Mr. Rice announced to our class the next adventure on which we were going to embark. We were going to choose, cast and produce a play which we would give in two performances, one for the school and one for our parents and friends. It all began simply enough; he read us scripts until we chose the two plays we wanted to do. Then the work started. We tried out for parts. There was one for everyone (though some were played by two people). We rehearsed every other day during lunch, and those who weren't rehearsing were kept busy building the sets and painting the scenery. Finally the work was done and the time for performance had come. It was wonderful; nothing major went wrong, and when the curtain call came and everyone clapped and cheered, it sparked within us all a delightful sense of accomplishment.

Then spring came, and Mr. Rice brought our class a present, two baby guinea pigs. We got to name them, feed them, clean their cage and watch them grow. One day we witnessed a miracle of life. We all stood in awe as they came together and mated. When his cat was almost ready to give birth to her kittens, Mr. Rice brought her into school, and one warm May day we speechlessly watched six tiny lives come into the world. The boys laughed, but many of us girls cried; it was so beautiful. It was life.

A few days later, he brought us another animal, a snake. The boys loved it, and they took turns letting it wrap itself around their necks. Most of us girls didn't want anything to do with it until one day when the snake began to change, and we watched it shed its skin. Within a few short months we had witnessed three miracles of nature, and none of us would ever forget what wondrous things animals really were.

As I look back, I realize what a brilliant man Mr. Rice is. He taught me more through the experiences he gave me than most of my studies could ever teach me. I have much love and respect in my heart for that man, and I hope he can continue for years to come to touch and change the lives of children.

FOCUS

ORGANIZATION II (ANALYSIS, CAUSE AND EFFECT, ARGUMENT)

The three essays here follow quite complicated patterns of development. The first professional essay deals with the causes of teenage pregnancies (or is it a spoof of cause-and-effect essays?), and the second is a personal analysis of the qualities of life that give it meaning. The student writer developed a very comprehensive response to one of the earlier professional essays on the drafting of women.

Professional Essay

MUSIC TO GET PREGNANT BY
Mike Royko

This column, reprinted in *Stereo Review*, purports to be a cause-and-effect essay. Is it? You decide. As you read the essay, consider the following points:

1. After the news item—which is authentic—the essay consists almost entirely of dialogue. Can you always tell who is speaking? What devices of punctuation does Royko use to keep from confusing the reader and at the same time avoid repeating *I said* and *he said*?
2. Can you identify Benny Goodman, Glenn Miller, Lawrence Welk, and Bach? If you need to look them up, try a music encyclopedia.
3. Would you accept the cause-and-effect link made in the news article between rock music and teen pregnancy? Are the statistics convincing? How could you check out the possible relationship?
4. Does this essay have an effective conclusion? What is suggested by the last line?
5. Do you think the interview really took place? Give reasons for your answer.

Reprinted by permission of Mike Royko.

Because of my interest in rock music, the following news item out of Tallahassee, Fla., caught my eye:

> Damning rock music for its "appeal to the flesh," a Baptist church has begun a campaign to put the torch to records by Elton John, the Rolling Stones, and other rock stars. Some $2,200 worth of records were tossed into a bonfire this week after church officials labeled the music immoral.
>
> The Rev. Charles Boykin, associate pastor and youth director at the Lakewood Baptist Church, said he had seen statistics that "of 1,000 girls who became pregnant out of wedlock, 986 committed fornication while rock music was being played."

It was the last part—the amazing statistic—that intrigued me. I considered getting a portable radio and blasting rock music at the first 1,000 women I met.

But first I decided to get further details from Mr. Boykin. I phoned him and we had the following interview:

Where did that statistic come from, the one about all those girls getting pregnant while listening to rock music?

"I want to be accurate, so let me correct you. They didn't all listen to it *during* the sex act. I was speaking of listening to it as a prelude to fornication, as well as during."

I see. But rock music was involved in all but 14 pregnancies out of 1,000 cases?

"That's right. It was sort of like a Gallup Poll of unwed mothers."

And who provided the statistics?

"This man. He's from West Virginia. Or maybe Virginia. He stopped in our church one day and gave us the statistics."

He's a professional poll taker?

"Uh, no. He's an evangelist. He travels all the time."

And you believe his statistics?

"Oh, yes. There's a definite relationship between illicit sex and any music with a syncopated beat. That covers rock and country music and even some gospel music."

Goodness, a decent girl has got to walk around with earmuffs on. Tell me more.

"Well, the low bass tones of the bass drum and the bass guitar make people respond sexually."

(They make me put my fingers in my ears. Am I strange?)

But the syncopated beat has been around a lot longer than rock music, hasn't it?

"That's right. And the debauchery began when Benny Goodman introduced swing music."

Benny Goodman caused debauchery?

"That's right. His music had a syncopated beat."

Then why weren't lots of girls getting pregnant because of his music?

"They were, but it was covered up. When Goodman had a concert in Los Angeles in 1938, there was open sex."

In 1938?

"That's right. The syncopated beat did it."

How about Glenn Miller, Lawrence Welk?

"When they used the syncopated beat, yes."

Remarkable. I wouldn't have thought Lawrence Welk capable of such rascality. It makes me wonder what really goes on in all those nursing homes.

"It doesn't matter whether a song is slow or fast. It is the syncopated beat. You can trace it all the way back to the jungle, where the beat was introduced. It is primitive, pulsating, hypnotic."

How alarming! Then what kind of music should a nice girl listen to if she doesn't want to be swept up by a jungle, animal instinct?

"Well, the syncopated beat is not predominant in patriotic songs or in most gospel music."

How about classical music?

"I'm not advocating all classical music. In his later music, Bach introduced some syncopated beats."

Aha! I suspected as much of Bach. The old hipster fathered twenty children.

Have you conducted any other scientific research, besides the Traveling Evangelist Poll?

"Well, we made some tests with plants. We played classical music for one group of plants, and rock music for another group, and we didn't play any music for a third group.

"The plants that were exposed to classical music grew in the direction of the speakers. The plants that weren't exposed to any music grew straight up."

And—let me guess—the plants that listened to rock music fornicated and all but 14 plants became pregnant, right?

"No, the plants that were exposed to rock music just grew away from the speakers. Then they died."

Well, that's better than breaking your daddy's heart.

Professional Essay

ON THE MEANING OF LIFE
H. L. Mencken

Mencken was a journalist and literary critic known for his writing of satire. If you saw the movie *Inherit the Wind,* you will remember the part played by Gene Kelly; it was modeled on Mencken. This statement of his personal beliefs will show you why he was considered outspoken. As you read it, consider the following points:

1. What is Mencken analyzing here? Can you tell what question he is addressing in the first paragraph?
2. In Mencken's view, what components go to make up a rewarding life? Which of these, if any, would you include in your own analysis?

3. Mencken says he became a writer because he "was born with rather more than the average facility" for expressing ideas. Do you accept this view that writers are born, not made? If this is true, is there any reason for the existence of classes such as the one you are in right now?

4. Although Mencken is not presenting an argument for or against religion, he does summarize the reasons for his own views. Evaluate these reasons. Are any of them convincing? Why or why not?

From *On the Meaning of Life* by Will Durant, ed. Copyright © 1932 by Will Durant. Reprinted by permission of Simon & Schuster, a Division of Gulf & Western Corporation.

You ask me, in brief, what satisfaction I get out of life, and why I go on working. I go on working for the same reason that a hen goes on laying eggs. There is in every living creature an obscure but powerful impulse to active functioning. Life demands to be lived. Inaction, save as a measure of recuperation between bursts of activity, is painful and dangerous to the healthy organism—in fact, it is almost impossible. Only the dying can be really idle.

The precise form of an individual's activity is determined, of course, by the equipment with which he came into the world. In other words, it is determined by his heredity. I do not lay eggs, as a hen does, because I was born without any equipment for it. For the same reason I do not get myself elected to Congress, or play the violoncello, or teach metaphysics in a college, or work in a steel mill. What I do is simply what lies easiest to my hand. It happens that I was born with an intense and insatiable interest in ideas, and thus like to play with them. It happens also that I was born with rather more than the average facility for putting them into words. In consequence, I am a writer and editor, which is to say, a dealer in them and a concocter of them.

There is very little conscious volition in all this. What I do was ordained by the inscrutable fates, not chosen by me. In my boyhood, yielding to a powerful but still subordinate interest in exact facts, I wanted to be a chemist, and at the same time my poor father tried to make me a business man. At other times, like any other relatively poor man, I have longed to make a lot of money by some easy swindle. But I became a writer all the same, and shall remain one until the end of the chapter, just as a cow goes on giving milk all her life, even though what appears to be her self-interest urges her to give gin.

I am far luckier than most men, for I have been able since boyhood to make a good living doing precisely what I have wanted to do—what I would have done for nothing, and very gladly, if there had been no reward for it. Not many men, I believe, are so fortunate. Millions of them have to make their livings at tasks which really do not interest them. As for me, I have had an extraordinarily pleasant life, despite the fact that I have had the usual share of woes. For in the midst of those woes I still enjoyed the immense satisfaction which goes with free activity. I have done, in the main, exactly what I wanted to do. Its possible effects upon other people have interested me very little. I have not written and published to please other people, but to satisfy myself, just as a cow gives milk, not to profit the dairyman, but to satisfy herself. I like to think that most of my ideas have been sound ones, but I really don't care. The world may take them or leave them. I have had my fun watching them.

Next to agreeable work as a means of attaining happiness I put what Huxley called the domestic affections—the day to day intercourse with family and friends. My home has seen bitter sorrow, but it has never seen any serious disputes, and it has never seen poverty. I was completely happy with my mother and sister, and I am completely happy with my wife. Most of the men I commonly associate with are friends of very old standing. I have known some of them for more than thirty years. I seldom see anyone, intimately, whom I have known for less than ten years. These friends delight me. I turn to them when work is done with unfailing eagerness. We have the same general tastes, and see the world much alike. Most of them are interested in music, as I am. It has given me more pleasure in this life than any other external thing. I love it more every year.

As for religion, I am quite devoid of it. Never in my adult life have I experienced anything that could be plausibly called a religious impulse. My father and grandfather were agnostics before me, and though I was sent to Sunday-school as a boy and exposed to the Christian theology I was never taught to believe it. My father thought that I should learn what it was, but it apparently never occurred to him that I would accept it. He was a good psychologist. What I got in Sunday school—beside a wide acquaintance with Christian hymnology—was simply a firm conviction that the Christian faith was full of palpable absurdities, and the Christian God preposterous. Since that time I have read a great deal in theology—perhaps much more than the average clergyman—but I have never discovered any reason to change my mind.

The act of worship, as carried on by Christians, seems to me to be debasing rather than ennobling. It involves grovelling before a Being, who, if He really exists, deserves to be renounced instead of respected. I see little evidence in this world of the so-called goodness of God. On the contrary, it seems to me that, on the strength of His daily acts, He must be set down a most stupid, cruel and villainous fellow. I can say this with a clear conscience, for He has treated me very well—in fact, with vast politeness. But I can't help thinking of his barbaric torture of most of the rest of humanity. I simply can't imagine revering the God of war and politics, theology and cancer.

I do not believe in immortality, and have no desire for it. The belief in it issues from the puerile egos of inferior men. In its Christian form it is little more than a device for getting revenge upon those who are having a better time on this earth. What the meaning of human life may be I don't know: I incline to suspect that it has none. All I know about it is that, to me at least, it is very amusing while it lasts. Even its troubles, indeed, can be amusing. Moreover, they tend to foster the human qualities that I admire most—courage and its analogues. The noblest man, I think, is that one who fights God, and triumphs over him. I have had little of this to do. When I die I shall be content to vanish into nothingness. No show, however good, could conceivably be good forever.

| Student Essay | **THE CASE AGAINST THE DRAFTING OF WOMEN**
John Holler |

Holler wrote this essay in response to the professional essay in Chapter 6. It demonstrates that well-written arguments can be created to support any side of an issue—and that you don't have to agree with the English instructor to get a good grade! As you read his essay, consider the following points:

1. The first two paragraphs present the introductory material to the argument. Do these include any attempt to get the reader to see the writer as fair-minded, rather than just anti-women's rights?
2. What are the "practical" arguments that the writer discusses? Could these be refuted? If so, how?
3. How does our "international prestige" enter into the argument? Do you rate this point as a strong one? Why, or why not?
4. How are you affected by the imaginary scene on the railway platform? Is this one of the stronger or weaker points for the all-male draft?
5. In the Goodman-Holler debate, who wins? Could you give the contestants a score?

Used with permission of John Holler.

There is a question in America today concerning the legality and practicality of drafting women into the Armed Forces. There is a possibility that this matter will shortly be laid to rest by an intelligent Supreme Court ruling, a ruling that will take into account the harmful consequences of conscripting women to fight our country's wars. This matter offers concepts that do not easily fit into the relatively simple categories of "women's rights" or "equality," but rather force us to deal with cultural institutions, the inherent value of which defy easy articulation.

Ellen Goodman has written an article, "Men, Women and War," which appeared in *Redbook* in May of 1980. Her article is an opinion which embodies a great many of the arguments that proponents of a male-female draft put forward. By examining these arguments in the light of the practical needs of the military and the cultural values of the American people, we shall shed new light on the question of a male-female draft and expose its pitfalls and dangers.

Ms. Goodman writes, "There are simply no reasonable grounds for a male-only draft today." Ms. Goodman is wrong; there are grounds for a male-only draft. Examining males and females comparatively, we see that men are much better prepared to bear the burden of combat. While women are capable of great physical stamina and perseverance, they simply do not possess the upper-body strength that men do. To be sure, carrying a machine gun or a mortar tube or a litter with a wounded 200-pound soldier are no easy tasks and require raw-boned, muscular men. Many have argued that women are great achievers in swimming, marathon running and bicycling, but these are athletic events which require stamina rather than great strength. To compare the physically demanding tasks which are required on the battlefield with athletic events is to make an unfair comparison.

One aspect of ground combat is ignored by Ms. Goodman: that is the fact that ground combat is a particularly filthy undertaking. This would put women at a distinct disadvantage, especially during their menstrual cycle. This is a problem men do not have, simply because they are not women.

Ms. Goodman suggests that women be assigned to jobs as "noncombat soldiers," presumably to free more men for the combat roles. This type of thinking seems to be common among the social experimenters who would sacrifice the combat readiness of our army upon the altar of "women's rights." Why? There simply isn't any such thing as a "noncombat soldier." All soldiers in the Army need to be able to fight and should expect to be called upon to do so should the need arise. As a matter of fact, combat readiness problems already exist in the Army because there are too many women in some outfits. Under the law, women cannot be sent into combat; thus, their presence in some units renders these units unqualified for combat. If certain units in the Army are unqualified for combat due to the makeup of their personnel roster, one might wonder what the purpose for having an army actually is. The Navy is experiencing difficulties of a similar nature. Many Waves fill various shore-duty assignments quite competently, but in so doing, they complicate the sea-shore rotation plan. Sailors spend several years (usually four) on sea duty before they are eligible for a shore duty assignment. During their sea duty rotation, they spend the greater part of each year on deployment aboard their ship, and in the case of married men, away from their families. With a preponderance of females filling shore duty assignments, there are fewer billets (assignments) available for the men when they are eligible to rotate to shore duty. It is then argued by some supporters of a female draft (although not Ms. Goodman in this particular article) that women, too, could be assigned to sea duty; then the sea-shore rotation problem would be solved. But do we really want that? Consider the enormous problems that would arise if this proposal were put into practice. A fighting ship in the U. S. Navy is not a luxury liner. The men live, work, eat, and sleep in close proximity to one another. Space and privacy are both at a premium. Bunks are stacked one on another so closely that the sailors cannot turn over in bed in many cases. There simply is not enough room, in most cases, to give the women the privacy from the men that they would need and that discretion would call for. Beyond that, the romantic situations that would inevitably develop would hopelessly complicate the command structure and threaten morale and discipline, as petty jealousy and competition for affection spread through the ship. This is not conjecture, but a real problem which presently exists on several ships in the Navy which have some women assigned to their complement as an experiment. It is obvious from the examination of these areas that integrating women on a massive scale into the military infrastructure would create enormous problems and lower combat readiness.

There is also the possibility of damage to our international prestige should our country draft women into the Armed Forces. The only other countries which have followed this practice of conscripting women are some Communist nations whose social policy is to create a society that is unisexual and makes little if any distinction between men and women. Other countries which have followed this policy found themselves compelled to do so as a result of being locked into a desperate battle for their very survival, as was the case in the Soviet Union during World War II and Israel in 1948. These nations did not have the luxury of choice as we do.

Ms. Goodman writes that, in her opinion, women should be included with men in any future registration and/or draft ". . . because society demands it." Ms. Goodman could not possibly be more in error. Society not only does not demand this practice but is strongly set against it. Perhaps the greatest argument against the female draft is that it runs counter to our national values and customs. America has simply not shown that it is willing to permit, much less "demand," that women be drafted out of their homes or be sent into combat where a portion of them would undoubtedly suffer grisly and violent deaths. Americans have never laid this mantle of responsibility upon the shoulders of women, but we have expected it of our men. This is a question of values, not a question of equality. When a ship is torpedoed or bombed, the result is not very pretty. Sailors are killed in the explosions, scalded to death by bursting steam lines, burned to death in fires, or trapped in compartments to suffer the horrible fate of drowning. Combat injuries and deaths are no less gruesome when they take place on land. Americans have never proposed sending their women to suffer these fates, but we have placed this mantle of responsibility on men simply because we did not want our women to fight. This is a concept that has served us well in past wars and will serve us just as well in the future.

One who is aware of our country's drafting policies in World War II and Korea might be led to ask: Would young mothers be drafted as were young fathers during these past conflicts? Such a situation would have disastrous impact upon our families. Yet another question looms: What of the resultant gender confusion that would come from a reversal of traditional male and female roles? A queer picture comes to mind, one in which a young man with flat feet (and therefore unqualified for military service) is standing on a railway platform waving goodbye to his sweetheart as she boards a train that will take her to an army induction center.

It becomes obvious that the idea of drafting women is a social experiment, and we all are the guinea pigs.

Ms. Goodman attempts to tie the Equal Rights Amendment to the concept of a female draft in her article. She writes, "I am sure the anti-ERA people know that drafting women would eliminate the very last argument against passing the ERA." Ms. Goodman has gotten her reasoning reversed in this emotional issue. It is the possibility of the drafting of females (under the ERA) that has led so many states to oppose ratification, rather than the states' opposing the draft (of females) in order to cause the defeat of the ERA. The ERA has not been ratified because it is not a good law. It is too comprehensive and dangerously vague, giving the Congress in Washington too much influence over the affairs of states.

Many laws have been passed in all states dealing with discrimination against women with regards to hiring practices and obtaining credit, as well as more equitable alimony and social security laws. These laws are a legitimate progress towards extending full civil rights to women, and need not find their ultimate fruition in a female draft. The two simply do not have to be linked together, as we would be led to believe by Ms. Goodman. Americans are an enlightened, progressive people living on the forefront of human rights, and we have the ability to discern what we want and don't want, what would be good for our society and what would not. We should not sacrifice our culture in a misguided attempt at women's rights.

It becomes obvious, after some of these problems are examined, that the case against drafting women is a matter of cultural values and practicality, and not a question of equality. No matter which viewpoint is used to approach this topic, the problems that arise from having a preponderance of women in the Armed Forces are readily apparent to those who are knowledgeable in military affairs or appreciative of our cultural institutions.

PART THREE
HANDBOOK

SECTION 1
PROBLEMS WITH CLAUSES

SECTION 2
PROBLEMS WITH VERBS

SECTION 3
PROBLEMS WITH PUNCTUATION

SECTION 4
SOME OTHER GRAMMATICAL PROBLEMS

SECTION 5
SPELLING PROBLEMS

SECTION 6
USAGE PROBLEMS

SECTION 1

PROBLEMS WITH CLAUSES

FRAGMENTS Although you often speak in fragments, you are expected to write in complete sentences. Everything you start with a capital letter and end with a period, question mark, or exclamation point should be an *independent clause*. If it isn't an independent clause and you know it isn't, you can still get away with using it as a sentence if you have some reason for using it and you'll mark it with an asterisk to show that it is intentionally a fragment. It will look like this:

She wanted to be by herself. *Completely alone.

But how do you know that what you have written as a sentence is an independent clause? Well, first, to be a clause it must have a *verb* and a *subject*. If your sentence is giving your reader an order or an instruction, you can omit the subject, as in these sentences:

Wait!

Peel the onions first.

Don't do that!

Please give me a kiss.

The subject in sentences like these is assumed to be *you*, and we sometimes say that the subject is *implied*.

The verb can never be implied. It is the word or words that name the action in the sentence or declare the existence of something, the subject. In the sentences above, the verbs are *wait, peel, do(n't) do*, and *give*. The *n't* or *not* that makes the verb negative is *not* a part of the verb, so I put it in parentheses.

The most common verb is *is* (and its other forms, *am, are, was, were, be, being,* and *been*), so if you're having trouble finding the verb, look for one of these words.

One peculiarity of a verb will always help you find it: A verb changes its form to indicate the time of the action. Look at this sentence:

Speed causes accidents.

How would you change it to indicate that it will be true in the future?

Speed will cause accidents.

And suppose you wanted to indicate that it had been true in the past?

Speed caused accidents.

To make these changes in time, we have changed *causes* to *will cause* and *caused*. These must be the verbs in the sentences.

Once you have located the verb, *causes*, you can just ask yourself, "What causes?" The answer, *speed*, will be the subject.

Every group of words with a subject-verb combination is a *clause*, but not every clause is an *independent clause*. See if you can tell what the difference is in these pairs of clauses:

Speed causes accidents.
Because speed causes accidents.

The horse kicked him.
After the horse kicked him.

He had better pay.
That he had better pay.

I hate his guts.
Although I hate his guts.

You probably noted that the second clause sounded as if something were missing in each case. You needed another idea to complete the thought.

Because speed causes accidents, *we ought to stick to the fifty-five-miles-per-hour speed limit.*
After the horse kicked him, *he was never the same.*
This is the bill that he had better pay.
Although I hate his guts, *I will admit that he is gorgeous.*

These incomplete-sounding clauses are *dependent clauses*. Like dependent children, they need another clause to support them. The clauses that I have supplied for them make them into complete sentences.

**An independent clause can be a complete sentence by itself.
A dependent clause cannot be a complete sentence by itself.**

If you write a dependent clause as if it were a sentence, you will have written a fragment. In the sentences above, note the words that turned the clauses into dependent clauses: *because, after, which, although*. These are *subordinating conjunctions*, as are *if, since, unless, when, while,* and a few others. You can begin a complete sentence with one of these words, but if you do, make sure that you are joining the opening dependent clause to another clause which is independent.

Many fragments are really dependent clauses that ought to be joined to the sentence just before or the sentence just after them. But there is another kind of fragment that can cause trouble—the fragment that isn't really a clause at all because it has no verb:

1 PROBLEMS WITH CLAUSES

His being a millionaire.
The girl hitchhiking to Chicago.
The car abandoned in front of my house.

Wait a minute, you say. Aren't *being, hitchhiking,* and *abandoned* verbs? Almost, but not quite. They are *verbals,* nouns or modifiers made out of verbs by adding *-ing* or *-ed* endings to the verb. Each of these verbal phrases could be used as the subject in a longer sentence:

His being a millionaire may cost him votes.
The girl hitchhiking to Chicago never got there.
The car abandoned in front of my house started to smell.

Another way to correct these fragments is to insert a verb in place of the verbal:

He *was* a millionaire. (You couldn't say, "His was.")
The girl *was hitchhiking* to Chicago.
The car *was abandoned* in front of my house.

You may still be puzzled about *abandoned,* as it can certainly be used as the verb in some sentences. How about this one?

The police abandoned the car in front of my house.

That sounds fine, but note that the subject, *police,* is doing the abandoning here. In other words, *abandoned* is an active verb. In the fragment above, the subject, *car,* was not doing the abandoning. When the subject does not do the verb but has the verb done to it instead, you need a passive verb. You need to add *was* to convey this message:

The car *was abandoned* in front of my house.

Now, test your ability to find and correct fragments.

Exercise 1-1 Identify the following items as either fragments (*F*) or sentences (*S*). Rewrite the *F*'s to make them *S*s.

1. One of the most fattening foods is the cookie.
2. Whenever I start eating them.
3. I just keep eating and eating as if I didn't know when to stop.
4. Although cookies fresh from the oven are best.
5. Some of my favorites coming from Pepperidge Farm.
6. If I could live on Bordeaux and Cappucino cookies.
7. My happiness would be assured.
8. However, I would weigh 210 pounds.
9. Which would keep me from being happy.
10. Obesity being difficult to feel good about.

Exercise 1-2 Now rewrite the following story so that it will not contain any fragments.

(1) Have you heard the family anecdote about the coalman and the fleas? (2) Since we had two large, pampered dogs. (3) My grandmother's favorite summer pastime was "picking fleas." (4) The chosen dog lying on its back across Grandma's lap. (5) Fleas that didn't hide quickly enough were either cracked between thumbnails or left to drown slowly in a glass of water. (6) The humorous incident occurring one early September day. (7) When we were getting our annual coal delivery. (8) Hot, tired, and thirsty, the coalman took a break and came in for a glass of water. (9) Although my mother offered to pour him a glass. (10) He was an independent soul and insisted on helping himself. (11) If you can guess what he drank.

COMMA SPLICES AND RUN-ON SENTENCES

Comma splices and run-on sentences are related to fragments because both problems are caused by not recognizing clauses or knowing how to punctuate them. When you create a fragment accidentally, you punctuate something as if it were an independent clause when it is really a dependent clause or not a clause at all. When you punctuate two independent clauses as if the first clause were dependent, you have a comma splice. When you run the two together with no punctuation, you have a run-on sentence.

Although this explanation may sound juvenile, it sometimes helps my students to visualize the problem:

Think of each independent clause as a cement block. Now, how do you stick cement blocks together? You use mortar, or you use a mixture of concrete mix and water. You do not use the water or the dry concrete mix by themselves, and you certainly do not press the cement blocks together and try to use the power of positive thinking to keep them from falling apart.

When you join two independent clauses, you also have to use the right stickum. You need punctuation strong enough to hold them together. The grammatical equivalent of the mortar is a *semicolon*. It works like this:

Semicolons are handy; they join independent clauses.

The grammatical equivalent of the concrete mix and water is a comma followed by a coordinating conjunction: *and, but,* or *or* (sometimes *nor, for,* and *yet*).

Commas can join independent clauses, *but* they can't be used alone.

If you try to use the comma without the additional word, you are creating a *comma splice*, the grammatical equivalent of putting cement blocks together with water. If you use the *and, but,* or *or* without the comma, you also have an error, but since no one has thought of a fancy name for it, your English instructor will probably not be as upset by this error. Joining two independent clauses with no punctuation is the grammatical equivalent of putting the cement blocks together with the power of positive thinking. It doesn't work, and it creates a run-on sentence.

If that explanation made sense, you should be able to identify the errors in the following sentences. Some of them are comma splices, and some are run-on sentences.

1 PROBLEMS WITH CLAUSES

I don't have the money, I probably will next week.
I get paid every other Friday this isn't the Friday.
Count me out I won't be there.
I'd like to come, however, I can't afford it.

I hope you identified the first and last sentences as comma splices and the middle two as run-on sentences. Now, here are some ways to correct them:

1. Separating the sentences:

I don't have the money. I probably will next week.
I get paid every other Friday. This isn't the Friday.
Count me out. I won't be there.
I'd like to come. However, I can't afford it.

2. Using semicolons:

I don't have the money; I probably will next week.
I get paid every other Friday; this isn't the Friday.
Count me out; I won't be there.
I'd like to come; however, I can't afford it.

(In this last sentence, *however* is a *conjunctive adverb*. When conjunctive adverbs start independent clauses in the middles of sentences, they have commas after them and semicolons before them. Other conjunctive adverbs are *moreover, besides, nevertheless, consequently,* and *therefore.*)

3. Using commas and coordinating conjunctions:

I don't have the money, but I probably will next week.
I get paid every other Friday, but this isn't the Friday.
Count me out, for I won't be there.
I'd like to come, but I can't afford it.

4. Turning one of the clauses into a dependent clause (called *subordinating* it to the independent clause):

Although I don't have the money, I probably will next week.
While I get paid every other Friday, this isn't the Friday.
Count me out since I won't be there. (Why no comma here? Well, when the dependent clause is the second of the two clauses, a comma is not usually required.)
I'd like to come even though I can't afford it.
or
Even though I'd like to come, I can't afford it.

Remember, it takes a comma to have a comma splice. (*Splice* means *join together,* as you do when you splice film.) The comma is insufficient punctuation in this case, so use stronger punctuation; don't omit punctuation altogether.

Sometimes a student gets back a paper with "comma splice" written on it, and he isn't sure what the mistake is. Knowing that something is wrong with the comma, he may try to correct it by simply removing the comma. You know what this causes, of course—a run-on sentence! It also causes frustration on the part of the English teacher. Don't do it! (Your instructor may see this as a deliberate attempt to increase the stress of his job.) Now you should be ready to try your hand at identifying and correcting comma splices and run-on sentences.

Exercise 1-3   Identify the following items as either comma splices (*CS*), run-on sentences (*RO*), or correct sentences (*S*). Rewrite the *CS*s and *RO*s to make them *S*s.

1. Our college has a metal annex to its first building it is called the Tin Hut.
2. When the Tin Hut was built, a terrible mistake was made.
3. The workman connecting the plumbing was inexperienced he had to be to do what he did.
4. Crawling on his belly under the building, he hooked something up incorrectly.
5. He was supposed to be connecting the sewer pipes, instead he connected the toilets to the rain spout.
6. The first day the building opened was registration day.
7. Registration took place in the Tin Hut, thousands of people were there.
8. Many of them used the bathrooms, and you can guess what happened.
9. Finally, the president called the contractor, the contractor blamed the mess at first on "some dog you've had around here."
10. He believed the story only when he saw the mess with his own eyes it was fixed in a hurry, then.

Exercise 1-4   In the following story, some of the sentences are correct (*S*), while others are run-on sentences (*RO*) or have comma splices (*CS*) in them. First, identify each sentence as *S*, *RO*, or *CS*. Next, correct the sentences with errors. When you rewrite the comma splices, be sure that you do not create run-on sentences!

(1) It is important that we try to understand children's language, we need to know what words mean to them. (2) Regardless of what words mean to adults, they may mean something different to children. (3) To understand your child better, listen carefully to the child's explanations and questions. (4) You should remember some of the confusion you had when you were a child then you might understand your own children better. (5) Here is one example of a childhood misunderstanding about language, it happened when my brother was about four years old. (6) He and my mother were lying on the bed, they were having a pleasant bedtime conversation. (7) Then the conversation turned to a program at my school, a program that Dan was not going to attend. (8) Dan began to protest being left at home with a babysitter my mother became annoyed. (9) She explained several times that the program was for *grown* people, finally she asked why he wanted to go. (10) She understood his curiosity when he cried, "I want to watch them grow!"

SECTION 2
PROBLEMS WITH VERBS

AGREEMENT In English we use different forms of the verb, depending upon whether the subject is singular or plural. These are the present tense forms of the verb *to be*:

	Singular	**Plural**
First person:	I am	We are
Second person:	You are	You are
Third person:	He is	They are
	She is	
	It is	

Note that there are three forms, one for the first person singular (*am*), one for the third person singular (*is*), and one for second person singular and all the plurals (*are*). This last is usually called the *plural form*, even though it is used for *you*, whether the *you* means one or a group.

Most present tense verbs have only two forms: one for third person singular, and one for all the others. Look at *to say*, for example:

	Singular	**Plural**
First person:	I say	We say
Second person:	You say	You say
Third person:	He says	They say
	She says	
	It says	

You'll note that the only one that looks different is the third person singular, which has an *s* on the end. This may confuse you; it confuses a number of students. Just keep telling yourself that verbs are the *opposite* of nouns. Nouns are made plural by putting an *s* on the end; verbs are made singular by putting an *s* on the end.

This simple kind of agreement does not usually give you trouble. Very few of you would write, "They says it is going to rain," or, "My father say I can't go." The problems come up in sentences that confuse you about what their subjects really are. Here are some rules to follow:

313

1. Make sure that the verb agrees with the subject, not some modifier of the subject.

   Each <u>of the texts</u> is expensive.
   The selection <u>of fairy tales</u> does not satisfy me.
   The mother hen, <u>as well as her chickens,</u> is for sale.

   In all three examples, the subjects—*each, selection,* and *hen*—are singular, in spite of the underlined modifiers. (Watch out especially for *of* phrases that come after the subject. If they confuse you, put your thumb right over them, so you can concentrate on the real subject.)

2. Subjects connected by *and* are considered plural and take a plural verb (a verb without the *s*), unless the two subjects are considered to be one thing because they are paired so frequently.

   Drinking and driving *do* [plural verb] not *mix.*
   Doors and windows *were* [plural verb] *broken* in the storm.
   but
   Bread and butter *is* [singular verb] easy to digest.

3. Subjects connected by *or* or *nor* take the verb that agrees with the nearest subject. Remember, the *or* is not a plus sign!

   Either the coach or the *players are* mistaken.
   Either the players or the *coach is* mistaken.
   Neither my aunt nor my *uncle is* happy about the divorce.

4. Even if the subject comes after the verb, it still determines the form of the verb.

   Just on top of the hill *were the foot soldiers.*
   (Note that your plural subject is *foot soldiers.*)

5. When a sentence begins with *there,* look for the subject after the verb, and make the verb agree with it.

   There *are* many *people* who dislike the senator.
   There *is* only one *person* who wants to kill him.

6. A subject that is a collective noun—*team, committee, group, class, family*—takes a plural subject when you are considering the members individually and a singular subject when you are considering it as a unit.

   The class *is* in agreement on the senior trip. (singular)
   The family *were living* in four different states at that time. (plural)
   (If this last sounds awkward to you—and it does to me—rephrase it this way: "The family members were living in four different states at that time.")

Try these rules on the next exercises.

2 PROBLEMS WITH VERBS

Exercise 2-1 Rewrite the following sentences, correcting any subject-verb agreement errors.

1. Crazy dreams and delusions of grandeur probably goes together.
2. I have had my share of crazy dreams, but at least one of my nightmares were based on reality.
3. There was a connection between this dream and what had happened that day.
4. When Sydney Harris spoke at my college, introducing him to the students were my job.
5. The introduction was in my dream as well as in real life, but after that, my dream and reality parts company.
6. In my dream, a whole gang of Godfather-type thugs was after Harris, and I had to hide him.
7. There was two hoodlums chasing me down the streets of Chicago, up fire escapes and over roofs.
8. Neither running nor climbing fire escapes are easy for me in real life, but both came easy to me in the dream.
9. Each of the gangsters were fast footed and evil looking, but they were no match for me.
10. Sydney Harris was still safe when I woke up.

Exercise 2-2 Correct all subject-verb agreement errors in the following story. Be able to give a reason for any change you make.

(1) My mother, knowing that children need books, were interested in buying a set of children's encyclopedia for me when I was three years old. (2) The set, together with some self-instructional workbooks, were not too expensive. (3) There were even one book designed to teach children to read. (4) You've seen the kind of book—a word and a picture is linked together, and when the child say what the picture shows, he learns to read the word. (5) Many of the pictures is obvious, but a few presents a challenge to the nonreader. (6) I had a little trouble with some of the pictures that was in the book. (7) The salesman, hoping to increase his commission, were trying to show how quickly the book would teach me to read. (8) He pointed out a picture of a moon; jumping over the moon was a cow. (9) What was the word under the picture? (10) Either *cow* or *moon* were printed under the picture, right? (11) Wrong—the word printed in large letters were *jump*. (12) "What do you see here?" asked the salesman. (13) My answer, after a glance at the letters, was a cow. (14) Now, he should have asked, "What do the cow do?" (15) Instead, he told me to look again. (16) Neither the lettering nor the picture were any help to me, but I wanted to get the right answer, so I tried again. (17) "Bull?" I asked.

WRONG PRINCIPAL PARTS

When you look up a verb in a good dictionary, the forms that you find there are the *principal parts* of the verb, its present-infinitive form (for everything but third person singular), its past-tense form, and its past-participle form (the form to use with *have, has,* or *had*). You won't have any trouble with the principal parts of most verbs, the regular ones. Regular verbs follow the rule of making their past tenses and part participles by adding *d, ed,* or *t* to the present infinitive form. That's why they are regular. They look like this:

Present	**Past**	**Past Participle**
ask	asked	(have) asked
start	started	(have) started
bend	bent	(have) bent

But irregular verbs create all sorts of problems for many of us. They don't follow the rule about forming the past tense and the past participle. In fact, generally their past tense and past participle are different. That's why they are irregular. Many of us are accustomed to hearing nonstandard forms of these irregular verbs all the time, as the irregular verbs are among our most popular verbs. Here are some of the irregular verbs:

Present	**Past**	**Past Participle**
begin	began	(have) begun
break	broke	(have) broken
bring	brought	(have) brought
choose	chose	(have) chosen
come	came	(have) come
do	did	(have) done
draw	drew	(have) drawn
go	went	(have) gone
lay	laid	(have) laid
lie	lay	(have) lain
ride	rode	(have) ridden
ring	rang	(have) rung
run	ran	(have) run
see	saw	(have) seen
set	set	(have) set
sit	sat	(have) sat
speak	spoke	(have) spoken
take	took	(have) taken
write	wrote	(have) written

It is easy to get irregular verbs mixed up, because we often hear people misuse the past tense with helping verbs (*should have came, has ran, might have wrote*) and misuse the past participle by itself (*he done, time run out, they seen*). Try to avoid making these errors in speech; some people react to them the same way most of us do to hearing a fingernail scraped on a blackboard! Whatever you do, make sure you do not make these errors in writing. Check the list to see which verbs you are accustomed to hearing in their nonstandard forms, and then double-check to make sure you have the standard form every time you write these. (It pays to keep the troublesome ones written down on a little card in your wallet. The next time you get stopped by a train, you can spend your time wisely by pulling out your card and reciting, "should have *come*," "should have *come*." This will help you to train your ear to accept the standard forms of the verbs. Once your ear is trained, you can write whatever sounds best to you.)

Even if you have no trouble with any of the other irregular verbs, you may have problems straightening out *lay* and *lie*. Most people do! This *lie* means *recline*, not *tell an untruth*. It is different from *lay*, because you always have to have something to lay—you lay an egg, lay down a burden, or lay a book on a table. You can't use *lay* without an object, unless you're talking about hens, and everybody knows what they lay.

When you're using the verb *lie*, you never have an object; you just lie down, instead of lying any thing down.

Sound simple? It isn't! The real confusion of *lie* and *lay* comes in the past-tense form of *lie*, which is—you guessed it—lay! When you use this, you have to figure out whether you mean the present tense of *lay* or the past tense of *lie*. Both sound and look the same. Perhaps these sentences will help to reduce the confusion. All are correct forms.

Present tense

The judge *lays down the law* all day, and then he *lies* down at night to sleep.

Past tense

The judge *laid down the law* all day yesterday, and then he *lay* down last night to sleep.

The form to use with helping verbs:

The judge *has laid down the law* all day for six years, but he *has lain* down every night for sixty years to sleep.

The "ing" form

The judge *has been laying down the law* for six years, but he *has been lying* down every night for sixty years to sleep.

Of course, you can get rich without knowing any of this if you are a country singer. Many balladeers have made millions in spite of lyrics containing lines like "come lay down beside me" and "lay across my big brass bed." They don't make their millions from me.

If you tell your dog to "lay down," and you get no response, you may have one of the more grammatical dogs. Try the standard English form: "Lie down!"

Exercise 2-3 Choose the standard English form of the irregular verb in each of the following sentences:

1. I have (did, done) some foolish things in my life.

2. One that sometimes keeps me (lying, laying) awake remembering it is picking up a hitchhiker.
3. The story (begun, began) when I was going to the bus depot to pick up my mother in the middle of a terrible blizzard.
4. A friend was driving, and as we (rided, road, rode) past the grocery store, we spotted someone in the swirling snow.
5. We barely (saw, seen) him because visibility was so poor.
6. My friend pulled to a stop, and the man (came, come) to the car.
7. Getting in to (set, sit) down, he said one attention-getting sentence: "I'm an escapee from the state hospital."
8. That (brought, brung) to mind visions of being (taken, took) hostage at gunpoint or (laying, lying) injured in a snow bank while my car sped away.
9. His next sentence (sat, set, sit) our minds at rest: "I want to go turn myself in; it's *cold* out there!"
10. After we had (took, taken) him back to the hospital, I vowed never to pick up a hitchhiker again.

SHIFT IN VOICE OR TENSE

Being consistent in your writing will help your reader to understand your meaning. There are two ways in which your verbs can be inconsistent: shifting voices and shifting tenses.

The voice of a verb shows its relationship to the subject of a sentence. By far the most common form is the active voice, in which the subject does the verb. All of these sentences are in the active voice:

Cats *scratch* furniture.
The bratty child *broke* the lamp.
The school district *has spent* all its money.

But verbs can also be in the passive voice, showing that the subject has the verb done to it. (The subject takes no action; hence, the term *passive*.) These sentences are all in the passive voice:

Furniture *is scratched* by cats.
The lamp *was broken* by the bratty child.
All the school district's money *has been spent*.
All its money *has been spent* by the school district.

Note that changing a sentence from active to passive required changing the subject, too. It would have made no sense to say this: "Cats are scratched by furniture."

When you begin writing a sentence using active verbs and you shift to passive verbs for no apparent reason, you can confuse your reader. This sentence from a student's paper should show you what I mean:

While we drove closer to my home, the suggestion of stopping to get something to eat was decided against, for the rain had suddenly turned into a downpour.

2 PROBLEMS WITH VERBS

Did that *was decided against* sound really strange to you? It did to me. I'd prefer this version:

Driving closer to my home, we decided against stopping to get something to eat, for the rain had turned into a downpour.

You should notice that the passive voice has nothing to do with tense. A verb can be passive in any tense. *Tense* simply refers to the *time* that the verb represents. There are twelve possible tenses in English, although only about half of them are used very often. Here is one verb in all twelve tenses and in both active and passive voices:

	Active	**Passive**
Present:	We kiss.	We are kissed.
Past:	We kissed.	We were kissed.
Future:	We will kiss.	We will be kissed.
Present perfect:	We have kissed.	We have been kissed.
Past perfect:	We had kissed.	We had been kissed.
Future perfect:	We will have kissed.	We will have been kissed.
Present progressive:	We are kissing.	We are being kissed.
Past progressive:	We were kissing.	We were being kissed.
Future progressive:	We will be kissing.	We will be being kissed.
Present perfect progressive:	We have been kissing.	We have been being kissed.
Past perfect progressive:	We had been kissing.	We had been being kissed.
Future perfect progressive:	We will have been kissing.	We will have been being kissed.

Did you notice that in the perfect and progressive tenses, the part of the verb that changes is the helping verb? It is the helping verb that indicates whether you are using present perfect, past perfect, or future perfect, and the same with the progressive tenses.

So when do you use each of these twelve tenses? Well, here are some examples:

Present Tense
This expresses action going on right now, customary action, or timeless action.
We kiss every morning when we first wake up.
We are kissed by the sun's warm rays.

Past Tense
This expresses action before the present time.
We kissed thirty-four times yesterday.
We were kissed by all the aunts at the family party.

Future Tense

This expresses expected action.

We will kiss and end the quarrel, I hope.

We will be kissed by all the uncles before the party ends.

Present Perfect Tense

This expresses action that has occurred in the past but that is not over for all time. It may occur again.

We have kissed under this tree many times.

We have been kissed by everybody at the party now.

Past Perfect Tense

This expresses action that had occurred before some other past event.

We had kissed even before you got your coat off.

We had been kissed fifteen times before the party was an hour old.

Future Perfect Tense

This expresses action that will have happened by a certain time in the future.

We will have kissed 5,000 times before our anniversary.

We will have been kissed to death by the time the party ends.

Present Progressive Tense

This expresses action that is continuing right this very moment. The action sounds more stretched out than it does when you use the present tense.

We are kissing our money goodby when we invest in that stock. (I had to change this kiss to a figurative one, as it is pretty difficult to say anything while you are really kissing!)

We are being kissed by the sun's warm rays.

Past Progressive Tense

This expresses continuing action in the past.

We were kissing when your wife walked in.

We were being kissed every two minutes all night long.

Future Progressive Tense

This expresses action that will be continuing in the future.

We will be kissing like this when you have dentures and I use a cane.

We will be being kissed by the sun for too long if we stay out here until noon.

Present Perfect Progressive Tense

This expresses continuing action that occurred in the past but is not over for all time.

We have been kissing every morning for 110 years.

We have been being kissed by the sun's rays for two hours already.

Past Perfect Progressive Tense

This expresses continuing action that occurred in the past and is over now.

We had been kissing for several minutes when your wife walked in.

2 PROBLEMS WITH VERBS

We had been being kissed for more than an hour before we decided to rebel and kick the next relative who approached either of us.

Future Perfect Progressive

This expresses action that will have been continuing for some time in the future.
We will have been kissing every morning for 110 years next Tuesday.
We will have been being kissed by the sun's rays for two hours by one o'clock.

Thoroughly confused? Don't be! Just remember not to strive for variety by mixing these tenses when there is no logical reason to use more than one tense. You should generally pick one tense and stick with it when you are talking about the same time period. If you use too many tenses, you will only confuse your reader. Consider the following example:

I had often listened to these stories before, but I had never believed them. The story that evening was the most incredible of all. I am asked to believe that four people will jump from the tenth story of a burning building, and all will have lived to talk about it.

The tense problems here could be taken care of by changing the last sentence: I was asked to believe that four people jumped from the tenth story of a burning building, and all lived to talk about it.

Now test your skills with verb tenses by completing this exercise.

Exercise 2-4 Write down all the verbs in each of the following sentences. Identify the tense of each verb by writing down the form (Past perfect, for instance) next to the verb. Finally, if there are any problems with tense or voice shifts, change the faulty verb to a better one, and identify the tense of the new verb.

1. Once upon a time, way back in my family history, there were at least two witches.
2. I say "at least two" because I found out about one only recently.
3. I have heard stories about Martha Emerson, the falsely accused witch, ever since I was a child.
4. However, I only learned of the second witch a year or so ago.
5. Perhaps no one spoke of her because she was an embarrassment—after all, she had been executed.
6. Execution was not Martha Emerson's fate.
7. According to a partial transcript of her trial, which my mother still has, Martha was accused of witchcraft back in the days of the Salem witch trials.
8. Her accuser was a young man of the village; he testified in court that she had come into his room at night and had ridden him with a bit and bridle, making his mouth sore in the morning.
9. Martha said the only thing riding him was his own lust.
10. The judges agreed, apparently, for she was acquitted.

Exercise 2-5   Now correct all the errors in verb form or tense in the following stories. Be able to give a reason for each change you make.

(1) Children often display quite an imagination. (2) When my older son, Greg, was a toddler, he loves to play pretend tricks on us. (3) He would came up to me with an empty hand and say, "Want some candy?" (4) When he done this, I usually pretended to gobble up the candy, but one time Greg's look of horror stops me. (5) "You forgot to unwrap it," he says. (6) I had to pretend to spit out the candy's wrapping. (7) Sometimes he also pretended that he would be sitting the table for breakfast—on the stairs. (8) One time he become quite disgusted with me because I "sat on the toast."

(9) Our family's dog, Toby, spends many hours laying on the floor playing with the boys. (10) Nick, the younger one, held conversations with the dog. (11) Nick's voice is normal when he speaks for himself, but when he spoke for Toby, it gets high and false. (12) When Nick was six years old, one of his comments for Toby was making us all laugh. (13) Speaking for Toby, Nick says, "I knew it was you, Nick, because I could smell your sense of humor!"

SECTION 3
PROBLEMS WITH PUNCTUATION

APOSTROPHES Apostrophes are dying, but they probably will be around at least for the rest of your lifetime. To follow the conventional rules of punctuation, you need to know how to use them. They are used in two different situations.

1. When you join two words into a contraction, you put an apostrophe to show where you have omitted letters.

   don't (omitted *o* in *do not*)
   doesn't (omitted *o* in *does not*)
   it's (omitted *i* in *it is* or *ha* in *it has*)
   I'm (omitted *a* in *I am*)
   I've (omitted *ha* in *I have*)

   This usage seldom causes any trouble, but occasionally some writer will mistakenly put the apostrophe in *I'm* without omitting any letter (*I'am*) or will put the apostrophe where the space is omitted (*does'nt*). If you make these mistakes, there are two ways you can cure yourself of the habit: (1) stop using contractions altogether, and let your writing sound quite formal; or (2) proofread an additional time just to make sure you have the correct forms of contractions.

2. When you want to show that a noun owns the noun that comes right after it in the sentence, you add an apostrophe—or an apostrophe and an *s*—to the first noun. This is the usage that causes 90 percent of the trouble with apostrophes.

   Some of the problems stem from trying to put apostrophes in possessive pronouns. Pronouns, those special words that can take the place of nouns, change their form to show possessive. Possessive pronouns never contain apostrophes, so don't write any of these:

   mi'ne
   your's
   hi's
   her's
   it's

That last one is probably the only one you are tempted to write, but you realize that *it's* means *it is* or *it has* (see the contraction above), so perhaps you write *its'*. Don't write that either; there is no such word. Please make a mental or a written note of this right now: The possessive pronoun meaning *belonging to it* has no apostrophe. Try reading *it's* as *it is* or *it has* every time you see it. If you can't substitute two words for the contraction, you have the wrong form.

If you can eliminate the error with *its*, you can probably reduce your apostrophe problems by about 50 percent. The other half of the problems comes from trying to decide on the apostrophe's position—before or after the *s*. If you are confused, the reason is probably that you were taught several rules about differences in singular forms and plural forms. These may seem inconsistent to you, because they are. Look at a few examples:

Singular	**Plural**
Girl's ball	Girls' ball team
Woman's ball	Women's ball team
Tom Jones' record (sometimes Tom Jones's record)	The Joneses' house

When you try to find some consistency, you can't go by singulars and plurals. After all, you have two singulars ending in apostrophe-*s* and one in *s*-apostrophe. You also have one plural ending in *s*-apostrophe, one ending in apostrophe-*s*, and one ending in *es*-apostrophe. Luckily, there is a consistent rule, but it goes by sound:

Find the basic word, the word that is really doing the owning. Add an apostrophe to it, and then, if you do not already have a zzz sound, add an s.

To find the basic word, change each possessive into a prepositional phrase. Now you have these:

Ball of the *girl* (*Girl' ball* still needs an *s*.)

Ball of the *woman* (*Woman' ball?* No, *woman's ball*.)

Record of Tom *Jones* (*Jones' record* sounds OK, but this one is optional. You won't be wrong if you write *Jones's record*.)

Ball team of the *girls* (*Girls' ball team* is correct.)

Ball team of the *women* (*Women' ball team* still needs that *zzz* sound, so *women's ball team* is correct.)

House of the *Joneses* (Note that the *es* is already there to make it plural, so all you need to add is an apostrophe to make it the *Joneses' house*.)

Now, where would you put apostrophes in these sentences?

Its raining outside, so Bev cant walk over to Johns house to see his new parakeet, Walter. It has a fancy cage with "Walters Estate" written above the door, and it sits on its perch inside and does tricks. John says its fun to see the birds antics, and Bev had planned to take her parakeet, Emily, over there so they

3 PROBLEMS WITH PUNCTUATION 325

could watch both birds performances, but shell have to wait until theres a dry spell. Parakeets shouldnt go out in the rain.

When you have put in all the apostrophes you want, check them against mine:

It's raining outside, so Bev *can't* walk over to *John's* house to see his new parakeet, Walter. It has a fancy cage with *"Walter's* Estate" written above the door, and it sits on its perch inside and does tricks. John says *it's* fun to see the *bird's* antics, and Bev had planned to take her parakeet, Emily, over there so they could watch both *birds'* performances, but *she'll* have to wait until *there's* a dry spell. Parakeets *shouldn't* go out in the rain.

Exercise 3-1 Insert any apostrophes that are needed when you rewrite the following sentences:

1. Have I told you the story of my husbands "arrest"?
2. Its not a long story, but it couldve been.
3. Clydes brother had been visiting us from Arkansas.
4. He was ready to leave—finally—and we went to the station to buy his ticket a couple of hours before the trains departure.
5. The ticket clerks behavior was a little strange, but we tried to ignore it.
6. It wasnt possible to ignore what happened when we returned to meet Arvills train.
7. As soon as wed entered the door, policemen popped up from behind the clerks counter, and other police emerged from the door to the mens room.
8. For some reason, Clydes thoughts turned to his car, parked in a "no parking" zone.
9. Running for the door, he shouted, "Im just moving my car; its right outside."
10. The policemens suspicions were really aroused by this behavior, as they had come to arrest him.
11. One officers hand shot out to grab my husbands arm, and another officer asked for his identification.
12. A third officer took an escaped convicts picture from his pocket and compared the convicts features with Clydes.
13. Fortunately, he could easily see they didnt look alike.
14. "Theres a resemblance," he said, "but theyre not the same person."
15. The convicts freedom ended the next day; he hadnt gotten farther than a neighbors garage.
16. Clydes anger grew when he saw the convicts picture in the paper.
17. "Ive got a lot more hair than hes got!" he protested.

QUOTATION MARKS

Quotation marks are used (1) around titles of short works, such as poems, articles, or chapters, (2) around words talked about as words—unless you can set them in italic type, and (3) around dialogue or exact quotations. You can see all three uses in this sentence:

After he read my poem, "The Male Must Go Through," he asked me, "Are you sure you want to spell 'male' like that?"

The quotation marks around "male" in the question are single, you will note. Since they are already inside quotation marks for the dialogue, they are single to keep them separate from the double quotation marks around the dialogue. Whenever you use a quote within a quote, the interior one goes in single quotes.

Most of the problems you might have in using quotation marks come in combining them with other marks. The example ended in a question mark followed by quotation marks. Why this order? Well, the quotation was the question, so the question mark belonged inside with the rest of the dialogue. If the dialogue had been a statement, but my whole sentence had been a question, the quotation marks would have come first.

Did he say, "You spelled 'male' incorrectly"?

You can follow the same rule with exclamation points but not with other marks of punctuation. The following two rules apply in America:

1. **Periods and commas are insignificant punctuation, and they always go inside the quotation marks, whether they are part of the quoted material or not.**
2. **Colons, semicolons, and dashes always go outside quotation marks.**

The reason I said these rules apply in America is that Great Britain does just the opposite with periods and commas. If you're reading a British book, you'll note that the quotation marks come before the period or comma. A few government offices in the United States have finally started following the example of the British, but this practice will probably be slow to catch on. After all, we have been trying to be different ever since the American Revolution.

Actually, I remember hearing that our practice of putting the periods and commas inside goes all the way back to the Stamp Act, when newspaper printers squeezed everything terribly in order to avoid paying for the extra stamp needed if they had another page. Putting the period or comma inside gave them a tiny bit more space and possibly saved them the price of another stamp. I do not know whether this story is true or not, but it certainly stuck with me and helped me solve a number of punctuation problems. Perhaps it will stick with you, too.

Exercise 3-2 Insert quotation marks (either single or double) wherever they are needed when you rewrite these sentences.

1. Which essay in Taylor's book do you like the best? the teacher asked his class.
2. The students were equally divided between Keys and Me and Body Language Spoken Here.

3 PROBLEMS WITH PUNCTUATION

3. Although they admitted that Spare Me the Details was very well written, they objected to some of its wording.
4. The teacher asked again, Which words don't you like?
5. I was really turned off, one young woman responded, by the word spittle.
6. What didn't you like about the word spittle? the teacher wanted to know.
7. I don't know; it was just another gross detail, and I don't like gross details, said the student.
8. Another student spoke up: Although Spare Me the Details was well written, I would have appreciated being spared some of the nastiest parts of the description!
9. You've all got to be kidding! another student spoke up.
10. Gross details are a fact of life, she said, and words like spittle and belch make the writing realistic and make me like it!

COMMAS, SEMICOLONS, AND COLONS

Oh, no! Here it comes—that one punctuation mark that causes everybody so much trouble, the comma!

You can eliminate some of this trouble if you will remember the difference between using *one* comma and using *two* commas.

1. One comma is used to separate one part of a sentence from another part. If the parts belong together (subject and verb, verb and object, preposition and object), you should *not* put a comma between them. Don't write this sentence:

I just learned that Neil Diamond, has a movie coming out soon.

The comma in the second clause of this sentence separates the subject—*Neil Diamond*—from the verb—*has*.
Use one comma when you want to set off parts, such as when you write these sentences:

An hour after dark but still before midnight, Cinderella's clothes turned to rags. (This comma sets off a long introductory phrase or group of phrases.)

Cinderella, look at your dress! (Here you are setting off the name of the person who is addressed.)

Moreover, you should fire your fairy godmother. (The conjunctive adverb beginning this sentence is set off.)

After Cinderella left, the party was no fun. (There are two reasons for this comma: to set off the dependent clause that begins the sentence, and to keep the reader from thinking *party* is the object of *left* and looking for another subject for the verb *was*.)

2. Two commas are used around words to set off the words from the rest of the sentence. This use does not separate the part of the sentence that comes before the first comma from the part that comes after the second comma. Do write this sentence:

I just learned that Neil Diamond, my favorite musician, has a movie coming out soon.

When you set off the words *my favorite musician* in this way, you are showing that they are not essential to the sentence, that they provide additional material that interrupts the essential parts of the sentence. If the additional words seem to be even more of an interruption, set them off with dashes.

I have just learned that Neil Diamond—I have eleven of his albums—has a movie coming out soon.

These nonessential words that are set off with a pair of commas are called *nonrestrictive modifiers*. They are different from *restrictive modifiers*, which identify some noun or pronoun in the sentence and have to be there for clarity; the essential modifiers restrict the meaning of that noun or pronoun and keep you from confusing it with somebody or something else. Perhaps these examples will help you see when to set a modifier off with commas. All of these sentences are correct.

My husband, Clyde, is proofreading this book. (Since I'm not a bigamist, I've already identified one person by saying "my husband," so the name is just extra information.)

My brother Jay has a new baby. (I have two brothers; if I had only one, I would put commas around *Jay*.)

My oldest son, Greg, drew some pictures for the local edition of this book. (I have two sons but only one oldest son.)

My son Nick, the ten-year-old, will be happy when I finish the book. (Because I have two sons, the name is restrictive, but after I have given his name, anything else I say about him is nonrestrictive. *The ten-year-old* is not necessary to identify him.)

Math teachers who cannot multiply should lose their jobs. (If you set this one off with commas around *who cannot multiply,* you'd be saying that all math teachers should lose their jobs. You'd be treating the clause you set off as if it were nonrestrictive, but really it is important to the sentence.)

A complete grammar text will give you more detailed rules on commas, but these two rules will go a long way.

Semicolons and colons are used in similar situations. When you are writing a sentence with two independent clauses and no conjunction (*and, but, or, nor*), you can sometimes choose either mark of punctuation.

Harley had only one fault; he was impossible to live with.

Harley had only one fault: he was impossible to live with.

Which sentence do you prefer? Either would be okay, but the colon implies a little bit more about the relationship between the clauses. When you see the colon there, you assume that "he was impossible to live with" is an explanation of his one fault. The semicolon does not imply that relationship. In the first sentence, perhaps his one fault was his terrific body odor. That could make him impossible to live with, but it isn't the same thing that the second sentence says.

Semicolons can also be used to separate clauses that would normally be separated by a comma and a conjunction when the clauses themselves have commas in them. Look at this sentence:

I paid for the cake, the ice cream, and the party favors, and Sandra paid for the punch and the prizes.

Do all those commas confuse you? If you like this sentence better, you can write it this way:

I paid for the cake, the ice cream, and the party favors; and Sandra paid for the punch and the prizes.

Note that you "upgrade" the punctuation from a comma to a semicolon in this way *only* when the clauses are both independent. You should not use semicolons with dependent clauses.

Exercise 3-3 Supply all the punctuation needed to make sense of this story when you copy it over.

    I was always an outspoken child and sometimes my bluntness embarrassed other people one victim of my loud mouth was Jimmy Garrett a teenager who lived next door to us when I was not yet in school the scene of his embarrassment was my mothers wedding reception Jimmy was among the guests invited to our house my eavesdropping on my grandfathers conversation with Jimmy caused all the trouble my grandfather who had had too much to drink was trying to explain to Jimmy the meaning of the word inebriated Jimmy asked whats the difference between inebriated and intoxicated Mr Barclay I was four years old I understood their conversation only dimly but I felt that my grandfathers honor was at stake I also remembered some hushed comments Jimmys mother had made about medications her son was taking in one of those unexpected lulls in conversation I bellowed out my grandfathers defense dont you dare call my grandfather constipated youre constipated yourself Jimmy Garrett!

(If it will help you to decide about commas, I will tell you that Mr. Barclay was the only grandfather I had.)

For help on this exercise, see the chart on the next page.

How to Punctuate Clauses

Symbols	Example	Explanation
I = Independent clause (can stand alone as a sentence)		
D = Dependent clause (can't stand alone)		
1. I ; I	You lied to me; I'll never believe you again.	The semicolon joins clauses that could be separate sentences.
2. I , and/but/or I	You lied to me before, but I'll still believe you.	A comma and a conjunction join two clauses that could be separate sentences.
3. I : I	You lied to me: you have a wife and ten kids.	A colon comes after the first would-be sentence and introduces a second would-be sentence that is an explanation or an example of the first.
4. D , I	*Although I was honest with you,* you lied to me.	The first clause could not stand alone; it is joined with a comma to the second clause, a would-be sentence.
5. I D	You lied to me *although I was honest with you.*	Here it is the second clause that can't stand alone; a comma isn't needed unless the sentence is hard to read without one.
6. D , I D	*Although I was honest with you,* you lied to me *when you proposed to me.*	The only clause that could stand alone is the middle one; this is a combination of nos. 4 and 5.
7. I ; D , I	I'll hate you forever; *although I was honest with you,* you lied to me.	Here the middle clause is the only one that could NOT stand alone; this combines nos. 1 and 4.
8. I D ; I	You lied to me *although I was honest with you;* I'll hate you forever.	Again the middle clause is the only one that could NOT stand alone, but here it belongs with the first clause; this combines nos. 1 and 5.
9. I D I	The man *who called himself single* had a wife and ten kids.	Between the subject and the verb of the sentence is a clause that can't stand alone; since that restrictive clause is needed to identify the subject, it is not set off with commas.
10. I , D , I	Petrucio Smith, *who called himself single,* had a wife and ten kids.	Between the subject and the verb of the sentence is a clause that can't stand alone; that clause is *not* needed to identify the subject, so it is set off with commas to indicate that it is nonrestrictive.

SECTION 4

SOME OTHER GRAMMATICAL PROBLEMS

PRONOUNS   Pronouns are very helpful because they enable you to avoid an enormous amount of repetition. Just think what you would sound like if you always had to use a name instead of saying *she, he, they, we,* and *you.* Still, there are a large number of pronouns, and a few of them are confusing.

1. Personal and impersonal pronouns are the commonest and perhaps the most troublesome. They take the place of names or references to items, and they come in three forms:

Subject	**Object**	**Possessive**
I	me	my, mine
you	you	your, yours
she	her	her, hers
he	him	his
it	it	its
we	us	our, ours
they	them	their, theirs
one	one	one's

   (Note that this last, the impersonal or indefinite pronoun, is the only one that has an apostrophe in the possessive form. The others have a special form for the possessive.)

   Obviously, before you can decide which one of these to use, you must know the use in the sentence. If your pronoun will be the object of a verb or a preposition, you will need to use the object form. Many people have difficulty recognizing this when they have a pair of objects. Note the following sentences; they are all correct:

   Bonnie and I went to the store because Mother asked us. (*I* is one of the subjects; *us* is an object of the verb *asked.*)

Mother gave the money to Bonnie and me. (*Me* is one of the objects of the preposition *to*.)

She and I had a fight with Jeff and him. Jeff and he had a fight with her and me. (Can you figure out which are the subjects and which are the objects in the last two sentences?)

2. Relative and interrogative pronouns also have the same three forms, but they are less definite about the nouns they replace.

Subject	**Object**	**Possessive**
who	whom	whose
that	that	of that
which	which (or whom)	of which, whose
whoever	whomever	
whatever		
what		

There are two possible problems with these. First, the object forms *whom* and *whomever* confuse some people.

It may help you to note that many object forms of pronouns have an *m* in them—*me*, *him*, *them*, *whom*, and *whomever*. If you can't decide whether to say *who* or *whom*, just ask yourself, "Would I say *he* or *him*?" If you would say *he*, you need *who*, and if you would say *him*, you need *whom*. Try this suggestion out on these sentences:

_____ did you vote for? (I voted for *him*, so I'm going to say *whom*. Whom did you vote for?)

_____ is your favorite candidate? (*He* is my favorite candidate, so I'll say *who*. Who is your favorite candidate?)

The other problem occurs because some people mix up *whose* with *who's*. The one with the apostrophe means *who is* or *who has*; it's a contraction. Which sentence is correct?

Who's the politician whose daughter was kidnapped?
Whose the politician who's daughter was kidnapped?
(Since "who is daughter was kidnapped" makes no sense, you figured out immediately that the second sentence was wrong, didn't you?)

3. Demonstrative pronouns point out things.

this	that	these	those	such	so
same	the former	the latter	the first		
the second	the third				

These don't cause many problems, but you do sometimes hear someone say, "This here car is giving me trouble," or, "That there dog looks lazy." Putting

4 SOME OTHER GRAMMATICAL PROBLEMS

here or *there* after a demonstrative pronoun is redundant and nonstandard English.

4. Reflexive pronouns end in *self* or *selves*:

myself
yourself
himself
herself
itself
ourselves
themselves (*not* theirselves)
oneself

When the subject is also the one to receive the action of the sentence, you use a reflexive pronoun.

He sent *himself* a love letter.

You also use one for emphasis sometimes.

If you can't go for your father, he will just have to go for *himself.*

Do *not* use a reflexive pronoun when all you need is the object form of the personal pronoun. Don't say this:

The bus almost hit Harry and *myself.* (Some people seem to think this is more polite than *Harry and me;* it isn't, and it is less correct!)

5. Indefinite pronouns include a number of words for somewhat vague ideas or entities:

all	another	any
anybody	anyone	anything
both	each	each one
either	neither	none
nothing	no one	nobody
everyone	everybody	everything
few	many	much
one	oneself	some
somebody	someone	several
such	other	others

About the only problems these cause are agreement problems. Many of these that might appear to be plural are usually considered singular—*everyone, everybody,* and *anyone,* for instance. Remember, if it ends in *one* or *body,* it has to be singular; if it were plural, it would end in *ones* or *bodies.* If you're in doubt about whether an indefinite pronoun is singular or plural, check a dictionary.

Exercise 4-1 Correct any pronoun errors when you rewrite these sentences.

1. Whom hasn't suffered from foot-in-mouth disease at one time or another?
2. I certainly have, and I'm going to have to change the names to avoid a libel suit against myself.
3. When I was an undergraduate, one of mine jobs was editing the community college newspaper.
4. A letter to the editor almost put several members of the staff and me behind bars once.
5. The letter called garbage collectors "scum"; it was clearly not our idea.
6. I thought ourselves might need a lawyer, and I was discussing the problem with the president of the student body, Hugh Smith.
7. Hugh suggested, "I know Andy Schwartzwaller; I could get he to defend you, I think."
8. "I wouldn't *let* him defend me," I replied, remembering sordid stories I had heard about Schwartzwaller.
9. "Everybody know he is the crookedest lawyer in Flint!"
10. Hugh changed the subject, looking as if I had hurt himself.
11. About a week later, the reason for his look was revealed to myself.
12. Hugh was among the class officers whom were mentioned in an article in the daily paper.
13. Who's son do you think he was?
14. His mother was Mrs. Andrew Schwartzwaller!
15. I had inadvertently called his stepfather the crookedest lawyer in Flint.

DANGLING AND MISPLACED MODIFIERS

One of my sons recently brought home a note from school about a book fair. The fair was ending on a Thursday, and the note contained the following comment about that day:

Students may return to purchase extra books, as well as parents, on that day.

I thought I might find myself replaced by a more lenient mother (for only a quarter?), but I wasn't. What the school meant, of course, was this:

Students, as well as parents, may purchase extra books on that day.

This kind of error is called a "misplaced modifier." You can avoid it by checking to see that any modifiers are as close as possible to what they are talking about. How would you correct this misplaced modifier (from a student's paper)?

Like all babies, my parents thought I was cute.

You could produce an awkward but grammatically correct sentence this way:

My parents thought I, like all babies, was cute.

I'd prefer something like this, however:

Like all babies, I was cute—or at least my parents thought so.

Sometimes a modifier is worse than misplaced. No matter how hard you look, you can't find what it should modify anywhere in the sentence. Then you call it a "dangling modifier." Dangling modifiers are very often at the beginning of the sentence. Here are a couple:

Before changing her diaper, the baby was unhappy. (She changed her own diaper? Change this to something like this: Before her father changed her diaper, the baby was unhappy.)

After fasting for two days, the meal seemed delicious. (The meal couldn't fast, so clarify who did. After fasting for two days, George thought the meal was delicious.)

Whenever you begin a sentence with something other than a clause, you need to be especially careful that you have not created a dangling modifier.

Of course, sometimes dangling modifiers are not the first thing in the sentence. Here is one I heard on the radio recently:

On Ladies' Night, when accompanied by a gentleman, any item on the menu is half-price.

After wondering how menu items found escorts, I decided the advertising writer really meant this:

On Ladies' Night, any item on the menu is half-price for women accompanied by gentlemen.

The best way to catch this error in your own writing is to pay attention to *exactly* what you have said. Keep asking yourself, "Is this what I really mean?" After you have caught a few modifier problems, your consciousness will be raised, and you will find you have developed an "ear" for this mistake.

Exercise 4-2 Rewrite these sentences to eliminate any dangling or misplaced modifiers. (Some sentences contain no error; just mark them "OK.")

1. Like most neighborhoods, I grew up in an area that contained some original characters.
2. The Bradford twins were two of these characters, Ginny and Geraldine.
3. There had to be some reason they were three grades behind in school; as soon as I moved into their neighborhood, I began to figure it out.
4. Coming down to greet me, the twins' welcome was very friendly.
5. Wanting to know about the rest of my family, Ginny asked me where my mother was.
6. After seeing my mother at the window, my answer was, "She's looking out at us now."

7. By the time Ginny looked up, my mother had been replaced by our German shepherd.
8. Only slightly puzzled, Ginny's question was this: "Is that your mother?"
9. Mothers were a problem for Geraldine, too, as she insisted her aunt was one.
10. The only problem was that, like many modern women, her aunt's decision was to have no children, and she stuck to that choice.
11. Stubbornly sure of her definition, she was "a mother without children," according to Geraldine.
12. Like Geraldine, Ginny's stubbornness was often evident.
13. Nancy, another neighbor of ours, had to deal with it, too.
14. Returning from a weekend visit, Nancy's explanation was that she had been in Eaton Rapids.
15. "You ate rabbits?" questioned Ginny.
16. Everyone but Ginny laughed at the strange question, who looked puzzled.
17. "It's a *place*," Nancy replied; "it's E-a-t-o-n, not *eating*."
18. After explaining that she didn't eat any rabbits, Ginny still looked puzzled.
19. Keeping her curiosity to herself, for a minute there was silence.
20. Finally, when she could hold in her question no longer, Ginny had to ask it: "How'd they taste?"

FAULTY PARALLELISM

Parallel structure can be very effective when it works well. You'll see what I mean if you read this paragraph from Peter M. Sandman's *The Unabashed Career Guide:*

> If you want to devote your life to teaching young men and women on an advanced level, you have no choice but to become a professor. If you want to add to the sum total of unmarketable human knowledge in some field, you have no choice but to become a professor. If you want to retire from the conflicts of everyday life to think about fundamental questions, you have no choice but to become a professor. Some of the most inspired and inspiring people in this world are professors. Every graduate student has known one such man, and hopes to become another himself. He'll probably fail, of course.

The first three sentences all end with the same independent clause, and the introductory dependent clause in each case begins with *if*. It is not necessary, however, to repeat the exact words to create parallel structure. Whenever the grammatical form is repeated—a series of prepositional phrases, a list of gerunds (verbals ending in *ing* and used as nouns), or a group of short independent clauses, for instance—you have parallel structure. When similar ideas are discussed, the reader expects parallel structure to indicate equivalent value or importance. Differences in grammatical structures may confuse your readers and create awkward rhythms in your sentences. Here are two sentences written by students:

4 SOME OTHER GRAMMATICAL PROBLEMS

I thought he was everything I wanted: sexy, intelligent, smart (GPA = 3.7), and was built like a powerhouse.

There are other reasons that people find it necessary to sell: They cannot afford to maintain their home and a job transfer are good examples.

How would you correct these sentences? Here are some possible ways:

I thought he was everything I wanted: sexy, intelligent, smart (GPA = 3.7), and powerfully built.
I thought he was everything I wanted: sexy as sin, intelligent as a computer, and built like a powerhouse.

There are other reasons that people find it necessary to sell: They cannot afford to maintain their home, or they are transferred to other jobs, for example.
There are other reasons that people find it necessary to sell: Maintenance costs and job transfers are good examples.

You may want to look back at the discussion of parallel structure at the end of Chapter 6 before you attempt this next exercise.

Exercise 4-3 Some of these sentences contain faulty parallelism. Rewrite these to create parallel structure. If there is no problem with parallelism in the sentence, mark it "OK."

1. To write a book, you need some ideas, a supply of paper, and to have a self-correcting electric typewriter.
2. I began this book with the ideas, with the paper, but without having the typewriter.
3. I decided on renting one rather than to buy such an expensive item.
4. My first rental was for a period of two weeks, and I typed every day—every day that I had electricity, that is.
5. The electricity went out once and staying out for fourteen hours.
6. Desperate to complete my typing, I borrowed a manual typewriter from the college, loaded it in my trunk, drove home, and pulling in the driveway only to see the lights come on in the house; I could use the electric typewriter again.
7. After I signed a contract to publish this book, my husband decided I should have my own self-correcting typewriter.
8. It was expensive, but it was the best birthday gift I ever had.
9. With the whole summer for revising and to type the book, I did not feel pressured.
10. Still, I typed nearly every day—every day that the electricity was on, that is.
11. The power went out just once but going out when I really needed it—the night before my deadline.
12. For a few minutes, I delighted in the break I was getting, but soon my delight turned to feeling frustrated: I still had about twenty pages to type.

13. After two hours of sitting in the dark and wait for the power to come on, I gave up and went to bed.

14. If I couldn't type, at least sleeping was possible.

15. Just before two in the morning, the power came on; just before five in the morning, I got up and finished my typing.

Exercise 4-4 This last exercise contains pronoun errors, dangling or misplaced modifiers, and examples of faulty parallelism. Rewrite the story to eliminate all of these problems.

Husbands and wives whom work together sometimes become targets for practical jokers. When we first started teaching, my husband and I worked in a high school where three other married couples also taught. Because of their contrasting personalities and having different approaches to life, one couple attracted most of the teasing. One trick that was played on them turned out to be more a joke on her than on himself. It was a day for conferences, and a group of we teachers decided to have lunch together at a neighborhood restaurant. Arranging it in advance with the waitress, she agreed to present the entire bill to Mr. X. We would then thank him for the lunch, call him a good sport for losing his bet so graciously, and leaving him to pay the bill. Of course, after driving around the block, the bill would be paid on our return. We expected both Mr. and Mrs. X to be flabbergasted, as there had been no bet. He turned the tables on ourselves, however; he played along with the gag. Pretending to be sorry he lost the bet, his reaction really surprised us. Returning from our trip around the block, we found she and him arguing. "How could you make such a bet when you know we can't afford to feed all them people?" she cried. Not wanting to cause a divorce or that she have a stroke, we had to confess the plot. Her anger should have turned against ourselves, but it didn't. She was even angrier at her husband when she realized he had played along with the joke, letting her make a fool of her for nothing.

S E C T I O N 5

SPELLING PROBLEMS

You are probably reading this section for one of two reasons: either it was assigned to you, or you consider yourself a "poor speller." If the first is your reason, you may skim through it quickly, picking up a few pointers on how to improve your generally good spelling. If you are reading this because you think you can't spell, you need to do something right now, before you read any further—change your attitude. Who is a poor speller? If you answered, "Somebody who misspells words," ask yourself this question: "Who misspells words?" The answer is *everybody*.

Everybody who is asked to spell an unfamiliar word, one that is unknown, unheard before, and probably not even seen before, will stumble over it, guess at it, and most likely spell it incorrectly. Spelling a word wrong—or spelling several words wrong—does not make you a poor speller. If you consider yourself a poor speller, it is probably because you pay little attention to your writing and consequently misspell even words that you "know" how to spell, or because you do not know how to spell words that you use every day and that everyone else seems to be able to spell. You may write them three or four different ways, and all of the spellings look equally good to you; in fact, you may write them three or four different ways in the same paper.

Whatever your spelling problem, you can come close to conquering it. I say "come close" because nobody ever learns to spell every word in the English language. There will always be unfamiliar words that you will have to use a dictionary for. What you can do is greatly increase your stock of words that you know how to spell without consulting a dictionary and learn to look up the remaining words quickly. You can turn out papers with no misspelled words, and you don't have to resort to the vocabulary of an elementary school textbook to accomplish this feat. What you must do is resolve to work at it. There is no magic pill that will suddenly fill your brain with all the contents of the dictionary. Learning to spell, like dieting, requires self-discipline and a change of daily habits. The first step is much the same as in dieting: Find out what shape you are really in. Here is a questionnaire to help you "weigh" your spelling abilities.

SURVEYING YOUR SPELLING HABITS

Answer these questions frankly. You need to take an honest look at how big—or small—your problem may be.

1. How many words do you usually misspell in a page of original writing?

2. When you turn in a paper, do you think that all of the words are spelled correctly? Or, do you think that there are probably a few misspelled words, but if you are lucky nobody will notice them? Do you ever write "sp" by a word but turn the paper in that way anyway?
3. When you are copying a paragraph from a book (as when you are quoting), do you sometimes misspell words that were correct in the original?
4. When you get a paper back with "sp" written by several words, do you have to look the words up to see how they are really spelled? Or, do you say immediately, "That was just carelessness; I know how to spell that word"?
5. When you are confused about how to spell a word, what is your first reaction? Look it up in a dictionary? Write out several versions of the word to see which looks best? Ask somebody how to spell it? Smudge your writing so that nobody can tell how you spelled it?
6. Do you reverse letters, writing *frist* for *first*, *buisness* for *business*, and *dose* for *does*?
7. Do you confuse the words you never really learned—but should have—in second grade?

   to/too/two

   there/their/they're

   where/wear

   here/hear

   its/it's

8. Do you misspell words you see every day, such as the name of your street, the place where you work, or the title of your textbooks?
9. Do you have trouble knowing when to double letters? (What is the difference between *mating* and *matting?*)
10. When were you first aware that you were having trouble with spelling?

The answers to these questions should give you some idea of the size of your problem. If you frequently make most of the mistakes mentioned here, turning in papers that you know contain misspelled words, even when you are quoting, you have an attitude problem. Either you think spelling is a hopeless cause, or you think it is beneath you, not really worth bothering about. Let me convince you that both of these ideas are wrong. You can learn how to spell, and you need to do so if you are not to go through life burdened with a serious handicap.

If you frequently misspell words and are never really sure whether your writing is flawed or not, you may never know how many opportunities your handicap has cost you. Few potential employers will take the time to respond to your letter of application with a kind note informing you that they have no use for a *realitor*, a *hygeinest*, or a *proffesional mannager*. Instead, they will toss your letter into the wastebasket. If you have a job and are not receiving expected promotions, you may not be told one of the reasons: Your illegible, confusing memos may be holding you back. (I can just hear some of you saying, "But my secretary will take care of such petty details!" My response is this:

"How do you know he will? If you can't spell, you won't be able to catch his errors, will you? Do you really expect a secretary to have accomplished a feat that is beyond the abilities of the boss?") Even in your love life, you may be handicapped by your insecurity about spelling. You probably know how to spell all the four-letter words, but the longer, more romantic words are generally the ones you need for love letters. If you decide it is better not to write at all, you may receive a "Dear John" letter.

Many people will judge your intelligence, your education, your upbringing, and your social standing by your ability to spell. They may be wrong, but why fight their misconceptions? Learning to spell is much easier than changing the world. In fact, you're taking the first step in that direction right now. There are only five more steps you need to take.

STEPS TOWARD SPELLING ACCURACY

Reading this chapter and answering the questions in the survey about your spelling abilities should help you to accomplish the first part of the six-step process:

1. Be alert to your spelling difficulties.
2. Utilize as many senses as possible when you grapple with a hard word.
3. Learn the useful rules of phonics.
4. Pay attention to word meanings.
5. "Sell" the really hard words to yourself.
6. Try gimmicks to improve your proofreading.

Your awareness of your spelling problems needs to go a little beyond just reading a book, however. This chapter may make you aware of words that are hard for many people to spell, but what you need to know is your own weakness. What words are the real bugaboos for you? List making is practically a necessity if you are going to answer this. Go back over papers you have written and search out those "sp" symbols. Write every word down. Carry your list with you always. Just as dieters refuse to leave the house without their calorie-counters, you should never go out unaccompanied by a spelling list. Your list should be a part of your new way of life as a good speller. Why? What possible use could you have for a spelling list if you're just going to the dentist? Well, suppose you have to wait for a 124-car train to pass before you get to the dentist's office? What better time will you have to practice your "*i*-before-*e*-except-after-*c*s"? Instead of reading about advances in root-canal work while you wait for the previous patient to leave, you can learn to differentiate between *loose* and *lose*. Finally, you may find spelling rules so deadening that you won't need an anesthetic. Just take your mind off the drill by adding *ing* to every word you can think of. You'll be glad you took your spelling list.

Using All Three Senses

I'd love to think of a way you could put your nose or your taste buds to work helping you to become a better speller, but I can't. (If you think of one, please send it to me.) Only three of the five senses are really much good in spelling, but most of us don't use even these. Because we are accustomed to seeing the printed words—and because many of us were taught to read by the "see and say" method—we frequently use only our eyes when we are trying to figure out the spelling of a word. Haven't you done this? You couldn't decide how *embarrass* should be spelled, so you jotted down *embarass*, *embarras*, and *embarrass* in the margin of your paper, hoping that the one that "looked right" would suddenly begin to glow? Perhaps this worked for you. You may have a strong visual sense of how most words should look. If you have, you're probably a pretty good speller. Many people lack this ability; for them, the sense of sound or the sense of touch and movement may be more helpful in improving their spelling.

Spelling entirely by sight may not be easy for you because you have only a hazy idea of what the middles of words ought to look like. Many people have this problem. Speed reading training has taught them to look at the beginning and the end of the word, and their eyes slide right over the middle as if it did not exist. They may be able to read very well this way, but when they have to write, they wish they could just put ——— in the middle of the word, as books used to do for words that were considered unprintable. If you are one of these people, try to involve your ear and your hand when you are learning a difficult word. Here are a few tricks:

1. Spell the word out loud, preferably in rhythm. Say to yourself (or to anyone who will listen), "emb-arr-ass, emb-arr-ass." The chant may stick in your mind, and it will also give you a feel for the number of letters the word contains. Most words that are difficult for me seem to have nine letters, and it helps me to keep this in mind. I just keep doubling almost everything in *comite* until I get to nine letters and have spelled *committee*.

2. Pronounce the word carefully. Ask someone else to listen to you to detect a possible mispronunciation. You may be having trouble with *probably* because you say "probly" or with *explanation* because you say "explaination."

3. If the word is not pronounced as it is spelled, mispronounce it. Don't do this all the time; you just need to do it long enough to learn the correct spelling. For instance, if *mortgage* is a difficult word for you, say that *t. Mort-gage* will sound a little funny, but nobody else needs to hear you.

4. Write or print the word often enough to develop a feel for the movement involved in spelling it correctly. Children with serious spelling difficulties sometimes work with blocks with raised letters or with letters cut from sandpaper. I don't know how useful these would be for adults, but anything that might work is worth a try. (I know of one person who really got the feel for the word *should* when his mother burned it into his hand with a hot needle because he had missed it on a spelling test, but this I do not recommend.)

Psychologists now say that some people are eye-oriented and others are ear-oriented. Discover your own strengths, and use them to help you to become a good speller.

Learning About Phonics

Perhaps you were absent in second grade on the day the rest of the class learned which letters were vowels and which consonants. If you never learned this distinction, the rules of phonics wouldn't make much sense. You can learn it now, as it is a very sensible distinction, and it will be useful to know.

Some letters are formed with the mouth open, and some are formed with it partially shut—the lips together, the tongue against the teeth, or the teeth together. If a sound can be made with the mouth open, the letter that represents it is a *vowel*. A quick trip through the alphabet will show you that there are only five: *a, e, i, o,* and *u*. (You may have a second-grade echo that says "sometimes *y* and *w*." This is true in words like *try* and *now*, but try now to ignore it.) All the rest of the letters are *consonants*. They are less troublesome to spellers because they do not represent as many sounds. Check your spelling list; it probably contains many words with vowels that confuse you.

Vowels can have short or long sounds. Your second-grade echo may remind you that "a long vowel says its name." You can find long vowels in words like *mate, meet, mite, moat,* and *mute*. Note that the long vowel is almost never the only vowel in the word. *Mate, mite* and *mute* all end in silent *e*, and that *e* is necessary to make the *a, i,* and *u* have a long sound. *Meet* and *moat* do not have silent *e* endings, but they have additional vowels right next to the long vowels. When a vowel is the only vowel in a word, it will have a short sound: *mat, met, mitt, Mott, mutt*. The first helpful rule to remember is this: *Words with single vowels have a short vowel sound; words with double vowels or vowels followed by a consonant and a silent* e *have a long vowel sound.*

This rule will be particularly helpful to remember when you are adding endings to words and trying to remember whether or not to double the consonant. Look at the word *write*. The *i* has a long sound because of the silent *e* ending, right? Suppose you want to change it to the noun, *writing*. The *e* is no longer necessary, as the vowel *i* in the ending will keep the first *i* "saying its name." That is why you "drop the *e* before adding *ing*." *The vowel in the* ing *ending has the same effect as the silent* e. The only way you can keep the vowel in the first part of the word short-sounding is to "protect" it with a double consonant before the ending. You see this happening in words like *sitting, hopping* (contrast with *hoping*), *rapping* (very different from *raping*), and *getting*. If you tend to spell *writing* as *writting*, you need to remember that this last word would rhyme with *sitting* and *spitting*. Keep this rule in mind: *When you add an ending to a word, double the final consonant only when the word has a short vowel sound.*

Most rules have exceptions, and of course these do. The exceptions are not too confusing, however. There are some endings that can be added to single consonants *without* making the preceding vowel sound long. You see this happening in such words as *marketable, benefited, traveling,* and *buttoning*. If you followed the rule just given, wouldn't you expect them to contain *tt, ll,* and *nn?* To see why they aren't spelled this way, you need to consider the accent in the original word, that is, where the emphasis is placed when you say the word. Do you say "MAR-ket" or "mar-KET"? "BEN-e-fit" or "ben-e-FIT"? "TRA-vel" or "tra-VEL"? "BUT-ton" or "but-TON"? In each case, you say the first pronunciation, so the last syllable, the one ending in the consonant you are trying to decide whether or not to double, is an unaccented syllable. From this you can figure out another rule: *When you add an ending to a word that already has at least two syllables, the final consonant is not doubled if it is in an unaccented (unemphasized) syllable.*

The other group of exceptions contains words ending in *ce* or *ge*. Consider *manage, change, peace,* and *service.* Now suppose you want to add an ending beginning with *a, o,* or *u, able,* for instance. *After the* g *or* c, *the silent* e *is not dropped,* so we have *manageable, changeable, peaceable,* and *serviceable.*

Check your list of misspelled words to see how many were problems for you because of long and short vowels, doubled consonants, or added endings. If you remember these few rules, you can reduce the errors with these words to almost zero, and your overall spelling will begin to look better already!

There are two other helpful rules of phonics. One also deals with adding endings, this time to words ending in a consonant plus *y*. *When you add any ending other than* ing *to a word ending in a consonant plus* y, *first change the* y *to* i. You can see this if you add the ending in parentheses to the given word:

(es) to bunny   bunnies
(ed) to pry   pried
(ing) to cry   crying
(es) to outcry   outcries
(est) to pretty   prettiest.

The second is the famous rule about *ie* versus *ei*. You have surely heard at least part of it:

I before *e*, except after *c*,
Or when sounded like *a*, as in *neighbor* and *weigh.*

Memorizing this will really help you to straighten out the difference between *believe* and *receive.* The verse is just as useful as "Thirty days hath September." Notice that the *c* must come right before the vowel combination; having a *c* somewhere else in the word doesn't count. That is why *achieve* is not spelled with an *ei* combination; the intervening *h* keeps the *c* from counting. Most words that appear to be exceptions were once pronounced like *a* but have changed in their pronunciation over the years. *Foreign,* for instance, was once pronounced *forayn.* Most of the exceptions are words that do not contain *c* but that are still spelled with *ei: either, seize, protein, weird, height, kaleidoscope, forfeit, seismograph.* The only *ie* word that is likely to cause you trouble because it doesn't follow the rhyme is *financier.* It came into English from French, so it wasn't required to follow the rule. If any of these exceptions are words that particularly bother you, try to memorize them. Perhaps it will help to make up a nonsense sentence composed mainly of words that are exceptions: Weird financiers either seize protein kaleidoscopes at their height or forfeit seismographs.

5 SPELLING PROBLEMS

Being Alert to Meanings

Have you ever looked a word up in the dictionary, spelled it exactly as the dictionary spelled it, and still found it marked "sp" when your paper was returned? If this has happened, you probably were spelling the wrong word. If you use a spelling dictionary instead of a regular dictionary, you may be especially likely to fall into this trap. Finding a word in the dictionary that looks the way you think your word looks is no guarantee that you have found the right word. You have to read the definition, too, to make sure that you really have found the word you want.

Suppose, for instance, you have written, "The bride stumbled as she came down the isle." You may be surprised to find *isle* marked "sp," because you checked it in a dictionary. If you had read the definition, however, you would have found that it meant "an island, especially a small one." Since there are no islands in your church, you can tell you have the wrong word. Knowing what alternate spelling you might look under is not an easy matter, however. You know that the word begins with the long *i* sound, so you might try other vowel combinations, probably *ai* and *ei*. Under *ai* you will find "*aisle:* a part of a church divided laterally from the nave by a row of pillars or columns." That's your word.

As you go over your list of spelling problems, note how many of them are words you confuse with similar sounding words that have different meanings. Here are a few of the most commonly mistaken words. Are any of them difficult for you?

to/too/two
there/their/they're (note that all contain *the*)
then/than
your/you're
its/it's
here/hear
no/know
whether/weather
accept/except
affect/effect
desert/dessert
council/counsel/consul
angle/angel
bare/bear
cite/site/sight
proceed/precede
loose/lose
right/rite/write
role/roll
which/witch

If you are unsure of any of these, check the meaning—not just the spelling—in a good dictionary. Then, make up a sentence containing the confused words, and go over it until you are sure of both spellings. Here are a couple of examples:

I cannot bear to go bare in below-zero temperatures.

The effects of the explosion will affect everyone within fifty miles.

Selling Yourself on the Hard Words

Making up sentences containing words you often confuse for each other is just one form of this next step: Sell the really hard words to yourself. What techniques do advertisers use when they want to get you to remember the name of their product? They make up catchy little jingles, using a combination of music, rhyme, and constant repetition to guarantee that the name will stick in your mind. Why can't you use the same techniques for words that are especially difficult for you?

When you come across a word that is particularly bothersome to you, set it to the music of some commercial you hear frequently. Any seven-letter word could be sung to the tune of "You deserve a break today." If your particular word has only six letters, try the tune of "Things go better with Coke." If you are totally nonmusical, you can at least devise a chant similar to a cheerleader's yell. "Give me an *o-c-c;* give me an *a-s-i;* give me an *o-n.* What have you got? *Occasion!*" (Visual memories can help sell these words to you, too. I learned to spell this particular word by remembering how it looked on a box of all-occasion cards I bought. This memory helped me to avoid doubling the *s*, which would have put an *sh* sound in the word.)

When you use gimmicks, rhymes, or jingles to help you remember, you are depending upon a *mnemonic device*, a catchy little memory-jogger. "Every good boy does fine" and "Mary's violet eyes make John sit up nights proposing" are mnemonic devices you may have used to learn the lines of the musical staff or the planets of the solar system. Perhaps you had trouble spelling *arithmetic* until someone told you "*A* *R*ed *I*ndian *T*hought *H*e *M*ight *E*at *T*urnips *I*n *C*hurch." You can make up your own mnemonic devices to sell yourself on the words that stump you. Here are a few examples:

Maintenance: I want *ten* dollars an hour for doing main*ten*ance work.
Accidentally: Do not accident*ally* shoot your *ally*.
Explanation: *A nation* deserves an expl*anation*.
Eligible: *Eli gives blood* endlessly.
Personnel: People eat raw squid on nine November evenings luxuriously.

Make up your own nonsense devices to help you remember the words that just won't make sense any other way, but don't use these selling gimmicks in place of learning the helpful rules of phonics.

Applying Tricks to Proofreading

If you are the kind of writer who misspells words that you "know" how to spell, you need to concentrate not on gimmicks to help you learn the words but on gimmicks to help you proofread. Any trick that will force you to see the word you have written or typed will help you. Several of these tricks are described in Chapter 10. Here are some suggestions:

1. Slow down. Try to read at half your normal speed or even less. If you must point your finger at every single word to slow yourself down, go ahead and point.

2. Unless your main problem is writing one word when you mean another word, try reading your paper from the last word to the first word. This technique will keep your brain from supplying automatically the word that you expect to fit the sense of the sentence, since the backwards sentence won't make sense at all.

3. Make yourself a bookmark with a window cut in it. The window should be just long enough to fit nine or ten letters into its opening. Move this over your paper, concentrating on just the one or two words revealed in the window of the bookmark.

4. Read your paper out loud. This is not really a gimmick, but it is the best proofreading technique of all, and it should become a habit. Anything that forces you, the writer, to stumble when reading aloud will surely be a barrier to understanding for another reader. Reading aloud helps you to correct problems of grammar, style, and sentence rhythm as well as spelling.

Learning to spell, like dieting, takes time. You won't become an excellent speller overnight. There will always be some words you have to look up in the dictionary; don't be ashamed to use it. (I consulted my dictionary five or six times as I wrote this chapter—most recently to check *overnight* to make sure it was one word.) Try applying the six steps described in this chapter for at least two or three months before you evaluate their effectiveness for you. When this much time has passed, go back to the ten questions at the beginning of this chapter. If you can't honestly see any improvement in your answers, perhaps you have some perceptual problem that is more serious than just being a poor speller. If this is your case, check with the counselors or the reading laboratory at your college to find out where diagnostic tests of learning disabilities are given in your area. Good luck!

A NOTE ON CAPITAL- IZATION

Some writers are mystified about the rules of capitalization. Here is a brief summary:

1. Always capitalize the personal pronoun *I*, the first word in a sentence, the word *God*, and any pronouns that refer to God.

2. Capitalize the first word in a title and all other words except *a*, *an*, *the*, and short prepositions (those less than five letters long).

3. Capitalize all proper names—names of specific people, places, countries, languages, days of the week, months of the year, historical events, and brand names.

4. Capitalize nouns that identify relatives when they replace the relatives' proper names. In other words, if *grandmother* does not come after a possessive pronoun, put a capital *G* on it. When you say, "my grandmother," you are not using the relationship word in place of your grandmother's name (you wouldn't say, "my Lillyn"), so don't capitalize it then.

Here are some sample sentences with the appropriate words capitalized.

Aunt Jane spoke French on Sundays to amuse the pupils at Trinity Lutheran Church.

Was Grandfather born before the Spanish American War?

My aunt called her autobiography *A Woman at the End of Her Rope.*

SECTION 6

USAGE PROBLEMS

The way language is used changes from person to person and from time to time. Look at the word *gay*. Forty years ago, if someone said, "This is a gay restaurant," we would have understood that it had a lively, upbeat atmosphere. Today, in almost everyone's mind, a gay restaurant is one where most of the customers are homosexuals.

How do word meanings change and idioms go from unaccepted to accepted? Why does some slang become a basic part of the language, while other expressions, used by almost as many people, have a rather short life and never get beyond the boundary of slang? The decision is not a democratic one, made by a vote of the speakers. "Hey man, that's, you know, my bag" never became a part of standard English although it was spoken by thousands of Americans in the sixties and early seventies. *Ain't* has been used by millions for a much longer period of time, but it is still not acceptable in a job interview, a sermon, or a business letter. It has made its way into the dictionary, but just look at what two dictionaries have to say about it. The first example is from *Funk & Wagnalls Standard Desk Dictionary* (1976) and the second is from *The American Heritage Dictionary of the English Language* (1973).

> **ain't** (ānt) *Illit. & Dial.* Am not: also used for *are not, is not, has not,* and *have not.*
>
> **ain't, aren't I?** *Ain't* is now nonstandard, although users of standard English sometimes say or write it for amusing effect when they are sure it will not be taken as their normal usage. *Aren't I?* is an ungrammatical locution used to avoid *Ain't I?* when one means *Am I not?*

> **ain't** (ānt). *Nonstandard.* Contraction of *am not.* Also extended in use to mean *are not, is not, has not,* and *have not.*
> Usage: *Ain't,* with few exceptions, is strongly condemned by the Usage Panel when it occurs in writing and speech that is not deliberately colloquial or that does not employ the contraction to provide humor, shock, or other special effect. The first person singular interrogative form *ain't I* (for *am I not* or *amn't I*), considered as a special case, has somewhat more acceptance than *ain't* when employed with pronouns or with nouns. (*Ain't I* has at least the virtue of agreement between *am* and *I*. With other pronouns, or nouns, *ain't* takes the place of *isn't* and *aren't* and sometimes of *hasn't* and *haven't*.) But *ain't I* is unacceptable in writing other than that which is

deliberately colloquial, according to 99 per cent of the Panel, and unacceptable in speech to 84 per cent. The example *It ain't likely* is unacceptable to 99 per cent in both writing and speech. *Aren't I* (as a variant of the interrogative *ain't I*) is acceptable in writing to only 27 per cent of the Panel, but approved in speech by 60 per cent. Louis Kronenberger has this typical reaction: "A genteelism, and much worse than *ain't I.*"

Although there was no national election on *ain't*, this second entry does indicate that somebody voted on it—a Usage Panel, whatever that is. You can find out exactly what that is by reading the introduction to the dictionary, where you will find this note:

> To furnish the guidance which we believe to be an essential responsibility of a good dictionary, we have frequently employed usage-context indicators such as "slang," "nonstandard," or "regional." But going beyond that, we asked a panel of 100 outstanding speakers and writers a wide range of questions about how the language is used today, especially with regard to dubious or controversial locutions. After careful tabulation and analysis of their replies, we have prepared several hundred usage notes to guide readers to effectiveness in speech and writing. As a consequence, this Dictionary can claim to be more precisely descriptive, in terms of current usage levels, than any heretofore published—especially in offering the reader the lexical opinions of a large group of highly sophisticated fellow citizens.

The list of panel members includes three writers represented in this text: Norman Cousins, Sydney Harris, and Gloria Steinem.

Why should a group of editors, professors, writers, and news correspondents have a say in what is good usage when Aunt Tillie wasn't asked? Well, the members of the panel were Uncle Norman, Cousin Sydney, and Aunt Gloria to somebody. They were invited because they read widely and displayed an interest in the language. They were expected to know what was going on in the language currently. You would be wise to take their word about usage whenever you have to speak or write to a "group of highly sophisticated fellow citizens."

When you write for this class and others in college where standard English—perhaps even formal English—is expected of you, there are many words and idioms you should guard against misusing. When you give a speech to the PTA, write a business letter, go for a job interview, or speak at your church, Kiwanis, or high-school reunion, you want to be sure you are using standard English. To help you in this effort, here is an alphabetical list of words, phrases, and idioms that often cause trouble for people. Read through them quickly, pausing at those that cause trouble for you. Perhaps you can get your English instructor to go through the list with you, commenting on the expressions that particularly get under her skin. Those would be good wordings to weed out in a final proofreading of your papers.

a/an

Remember to use *an* only before words beginning with a vowel sound: *an egg, an ostrich, an hour, an honor.* The troublesome words are generally those beginning with *h*, as you have to decide whether the *h* is the first sound you hear.

If the *h* is silent and you hear the vowel that follows it, use *an*. These are correct: *a ham, a hearty meal, a hair, an heir, an honest mistake.*

accept/except

Unless you pronounce words very distinctly, you probably say these words so that they sound alike. Be careful when you write them; use *accept* to mean *receive* and *except* to mean *but* or *excluded*. Everyone *except* George C. Scott *accepted* the Oscar.

advice/advise

The first is a noun; you give it or get it. It rhymes with *ice*. The verb rhymes with *tries* and means *to give advice*. Bankers will *advise* you about your investments, but you don't have to take their *advice*.

affect/effect

Both of these words have both noun and verb meanings, but the meanings you almost always want are these: *Affect* is a verb meaning *influence; effect* is a noun meaning *result*. Inflation *affects* our budgets in several ways, but the *effect* I notice the most is at the grocery store.

all ready/already

When you write this as two words, you mean *prepared* by the second word. The one-word form is an adverb meaning *by this time*. It was *already* too late to go by the time the triplets were *all ready* to leave.

alot

This form is *never* correct. Many students will protest that they have written it that way all their lives. Repetition does not make it acceptable, as there is no divided usage on this word. The term for *a number of people or things* is *lot*. There is no *a* joined to it. *A lot* of people are wrong about this word.

alright

Like *alot*, this is a case of running two words together—*all* and *right*. Although it is somewhat more acceptable than *alot*—two of five recent books on usage I checked called it a "common variant spelling"—it is not the preferred spelling. For many people, it is totally unacceptable, so use *all right*.

altogether/all together

Both of these spellings are correct, but they have different meanings. The one-word form is an adverb meaning *completely*. When you use the separate words, you mean *in a group*. The proposal was *altogether* nonsense, as the committee, meeting *all together* last week, finally agreed.

at

This is frequently used as the last word in a question, but it should not be. It is a preposition, so follow it with an object (*at the corner, at noon*), or leave it out.

Do *not* say, "Where did you park at?" when you could just say, "Where did you park?"

awhile/a while

While is a noun; *awhile* is an adverb. With prepositions, use the two-word form: *for a while, in a while, after a while*. The carpenter rested for *a while*. Then he hammered *awhile* longer.

bad/badly

The *ly* ending turns the adjective into an adverb. Use *bad* to modify nouns or pronouns and *badly* to modify anything else. The workmen did a *bad* job on the plumbing; when they finished, the faucet still dripped *badly*. Most problems occur when the modifier comes after a linking verb like *is*, *seems*, or *feels*. Remember that adjectives come after linking verbs, so use *bad*. "Harry feels *bad*." (In the sentence "Harry feels badly," the verb is not linking. Instead, it refers to Harry's ability to *feel*. If Harry has burned his fingers, nearly destroying his sense of touch, you *should* say, "Harry feels badly." If you are merely discussing Harry's mood, say that he feels *bad*—or be more specific and say that he is depressed, upset, or ill, and avoid the *bad/badly* problem altogether.)

being that

Don't use this for *because*. Say, "Because I like challenges, I took the job," not, "Being that I like challenges I took the job."

beside/besides

When you are talking about *position*, use *beside*. When you mean *in addition to*, use *besides*. I'd like to plant hickory trees *beside* the porch, but *besides* being too expensive, they would require more care than I could give them.

between/among

In the *tween* part of *between*, you can almost see *two* or *twain*, so you can remember to limit it to situations when two people, things, or groups are involved. We divided our lunch equally *between* the two of us. We divided our lunch equally *among* the three of us. (Be sure that *among* is spelled correctly, too. There is no *u* in it!) Sometimes the sense of the sentence makes *among* an awkward choice, even when you are discussing more than two items. If *between* sounds better, use it. *Between* every house on the street was a shared driveway. (I'd prefer recasting this sentence to avoid using either *among* or *between*: Every house on the street shared a driveway with its neighbor.)

can/may

Many texts on usage now say that there is little distinction between these words. In the past, *can* always referred to the ability to do something, but *may* referred to having permission to do it. I know I *can* climb the telephone pole; *may* I try? If you like this distinction, you can certainly continue to use it, but you probably will not be in trouble for not using it in college writing.

6 USAGE PROBLEMS

can't hardly
Since *hardly* has a negative sense to it, this resembles a double negative. Drop the *n't*. He is so drunk he *can hardly* get his car key in the ignition.

can't help but
This has almost the same problem as *can't hardly*. Instead of using the *but*, add *ing* to the word that follows. I *can't help wondering* where Sue is. Jack *can't help thinking* she has left him after all this time.

capital/capitol
The Capitol Building is on Capitol Hill in Washington, D.C.; *capitol* is also used for state government buildings. For all other uses, the word is spelled with an *a*.

center on/center around
Visualize a circle; the center must be *on* a certain point. It does not move around, so you should not say, "center around." The action of this scene *centers on* the father's quarrel with the son.

choose/chose
This is mainly a spelling problem. The form with one *o* is the past tense; it rhymes with *clothes*. The present tense is spelled with double-*o* and rhymes with *views*. I do not *choose* to keep the class that I *chose* last week in registration.

cites/sites/sights
Sight, as in *eyesight*, is seldom a problem. The house was a *sight* after the burglars ransacked it. *Site* is a location. Is this the *site* for the condominiums? When you refer, in a research paper, to a scholar who mentioned another scholar, the word you want is *cite*. Thompson *cited* the work of Seeley and Baker as the basis for his own study.

comply with/comply to
Do not follow *comply* with *to*; the American idiom is *comply with*. I cannot *comply with* the last of your requests.

consensus
A *consensus* is an opinion agreed upon by a group, so a *consensus of opinion*—which you often hear—is a group opinion of opinion. Just say "consensus," if you don't want to be redundant.

continual/continuous
The two meanings here are close, but a *continual* noise is heard over and over again, and a *continuous* noise never stops. An alarm clock that awakens you every five minutes is a *continual* nuisance; one that alarms without a break is a *continuous* nuisance.

council/counsel

A "council" is a governmental group. The verb that sounds just like it but means *to give advice* is spelled *counsel*. Jake's wife *counseled* him not to run for the town *council*.

data

Because *data* came into English from Latin, it forms its plural in a surprising way. Like *phenomena*, it has an *a* ending for the plural. (The singular form is *datum*.) Although you hear people say, "The data is unavailable," and you may even write this in informal English, if you are writing a technical or scientific paper, you should be sure to say, "The *data are* unavailable."

different from/different than

Different from is always acceptable. His second wife looks very *different from* his first. Whether or not *different than* is acceptable depends on the usage text you read. One out of four recently published books says it is preferred if a clause follows. His second wife looks *different than* she did six months ago. Apparently the other three texts would still prefer the longer version necessitated by *different from:* His second wife looks *different from the way* she looked six months ago. My own recommendation is to use *different from* before a noun or pronoun and *different than* before a clause, unless you are writing a very formal paper. Then, you had better forget *different than*.

disinterested

The officials at a football game should be *disinterested;* that is, they should not be favoring either team. They had better not be *uninterested*, or they may miss some of the calls they ought to make. Do not confuse the two meanings.

etc.

Do not use the abbreviation for the Latin words *et cetera* unless you are sure your reader can supply the words you are omitting. Her last job was selling dairy products—milk, butter, eggs, etc. Although that sentence is probably clear, some readers would still prefer dropping it altogether or substituting *and so forth* for it.

everyday/every day

Radio stations used to play a song about an *everyday* housewife almost *every day*. (The one-word form means *ordinary;* the two-word form, *every day,* means *daily*.)

everyone/everybody

The only reason these words cause trouble is that they seem plural although they are treated as singular ideas. It might help to keep in mind that they end in *-one* and *-body*, not *-two* and *-bodies*. When you must replace these with another pronoun, use *his, her,* or *his or her*, not *their*. *Everyone* must carry *his or her* own luggage to the plane. If you don't like this wordy form, change to this one: *All passengers* must carry *their* own luggage to the plane.

factor

This is a perfectly good mathematical term. If you are writing nonmathematical material, try to find a more accurate word. Instead of "Cindy's poor attendance was a major *factor* in her low grade," say, "Cindy's poor attendance was a major *cause* of her low grade."

farther/further

Most speakers prefer *farther* for measurable distances. I live *farther* from the airport than I do from the city limits. For any other use, *further* is the best choice. I refuse to discuss this issue with you any *further*.

fewer/less

After making three cakes, I have *fewer* eggs and *less* milk than I had this morning. What's the difference? The eggs are countable, but the milk is not. You can have *fewer* cartons of milk, but you can't have *fewer* milk. Neither can you have *less* eggs; *less* is always used for items that can't be counted.

flaunt/flout

When you show something off, you are *flaunting* it. If you laugh scornfully at something, you are *flouting* it. In law school he had *flaunted* his legal knowledge, but he *flouted* the courts after graduation by turning to a life of crime.

funny

Do not write this word when you mean *peculiar*. "Horace looked *funny*" could mean either that he looked humorous or that he looked strange. Choose a more descriptive word, phrase, or clause. Horace looked *slightly green*. Horace looked drugged. Horace looked *as if he were hiding a rather unpleasant secret*.

good/well

There is the same distinction between these words that there is between *bad* and *badly*: the first is an adjective (a *good* game, a *good* law, a *good* dog), and the second is an adverb. There seems to be an epidemic in the country right now of people commenting that various sporting teams have "done good" or have "not done so good." Really, it is the commentators who have not done *well*. A team that does not do a *good* job has not done *well*. After verbs of hearing, smelling, and feeling, however, *good* is the appropriate word. "Gee, you smell *good*" refers to the aroma you are giving off. "You smell well" would be an appropriate comment only from a nose doctor.

healthy/healthful

Growing things, like people, animals, and plants, are *healthy*. An activity or a food that is good for you is *healthful*. You should eat *healthful* foods in the right amounts if you want to stay *healthy*.

he or she/his or her

I spent years telling writers that these constructions were wordy and old-fashioned, but I've had to change my advice in the last few years. Women's growing resentment against being included—silently—in the masculine pronouns has made this Victorian-sounding wording modern again. The double pronouns are still wordy, however, so you should avoid them when you can by stating your sentences in the plural: *Students* can validate *their* library cards on Friday. (Try to avoid the awkward singular: Each student can validate *his or her* library card on Friday.)

hopefully

Let's print up some bumper stickers proclaiming "Help stamp out *hopefully*." This has to be the most overused word in the language today. It has replaced *I hope* almost entirely—and inaccurately. It is correctly used to mean *filled with hope:* The Pilgrims embarked *hopefully* on the Mayflower. "Hopefully, I will be able to make my car payment" makes very little sense. Instead, say, "I hope I will be able to make my car payment."

imply/infer

When you hint at something, you *imply* it. If I figure out your hints, I *infer* your meaning from what you said—or didn't say. Gloria *implied* that her husband was unfaithful, but I *inferred* from her behavior that she had several lovers, too.

interesting

Merely stating that something is *interesting* does not increase your readers' interest in your story. Omit the editorial comment and try instead to give details that will arouse curiosity or stimulate thought.

in terms of

Here is another candidate for the bumper stickers; I'd gladly sport a "Down with *in terms of*" banner on my car. Many of the same people who do everything hopefully also must announce their actions *in terms of* decisions, money, or time. In educational circles, "We graded the students in terms of their knowledge" is particularly popular. If you ever have to say this, why not substitute "We graded the students' knowledge"?

in to/into

Into should always indicate movement: The bear waddled *into* his cave. Sometimes *in* is used idiomatically with certain verbs, as in the expression *settle in*. Do not add *to* to this *in*, creating *into;* keep the prepositions in cases like this separate. I haven't yet settled *in to* my new office.

irregardless

This nonstandard word would mean the same thing as *regardless*. It is *not* an acceptable substitute.

is when/is where

When you are defining a term, it is tempting to say the idea "is when" or "is where." Unless you are defining a time (Noon is when the big hand and little hand are both on twelve.) or a place (Home is where you park your car.), eliminate the *when* or *where*. Instead of "Happiness is when someone smiles at you," say, "Happiness is the feeling you get when someone smiles at you."

its/it's

This is a spelling problem, but one more reminder can't hurt: *It's* is a contraction for *it is* or *it has*. The possessive pronoun is *its*. Now that *it's* won three state championships, the school has *its* trophy case filled.

-ize

If you frequently convert nouns into verbs by adding an *ize* ending to them, you will sound too much like an advertising pitchman (pitchperson?). Although the ads are always telling us to *motorize*, *winterize*, and *Midasize*, you should *verbize* your language with great care.

judgment/judgement

The first spelling is the American one; the second is British.

kind of

This expression should be used to mean *a species of*: Here is a *kind of* poisonous snake. Do not use it to mean *rather*, as in "That is *kind of a* nosy question."

lay/lie

The *lie, lied, lied* verb that means *to tell an untruth* is no problem to anyone, but the *lie, lay, lain* verb that means *to recline* or *to stretch out* can be painful. It keeps getting mixed up with *lay, laid, laid*, meaning *to place or put down*. Try to remember these sentences (all are correct): I will *lay my book* aside before I *lie down*. Last night, I *laid my book* aside before I *lay down*. I *have laid my book* aside almost every night before I *have lain down*. Note the difference between placing something—in this case, the book—and stretching out horizontally. The first form requires that you have an object; the second form requires that there be no object. See Section 2 of this Handbook for more help on these confusing verbs. If they still bother you after you have made a sincere effort to straighten them out, avoid them. Say instead, "I will put the book down before I go to bed."

lead/led

A pencil has a *lead*. When you do not mean a chemical element, the word *lead* is pronounced with a long *e* sound and is the present tense of the verb meaning *to conduct*. The guides *lead* tours of the monastery every day. When you put this verb into the past tense, you spell it *led*, but it rhymes with the *lead* in a pencil. The guide who *led* last Friday's tour was the very best. (Do not mistakenly spell this form *lead*.)

lend/loan

The old distinction used to be that you asked the banker to *lend* (verb) you a *loan* (noun). According to two of the four texts on usage I checked, banks may now both *lend* and *loan* money—if you can afford their interest rates. Both forms are becoming accepted as verbs, but there are still a few holdouts who prefer *loan* only as a noun.

like/as

Ever since "like a cigarette should" made one brand of cigarette famous for its questionable grammar, people have argued about the merits of replacing the conjunction *as* with the preposition *like*. In informal writing and in speech, you can get by with introducing a clause with *like:* The physiology text is difficult, *like* I would expect it to be. Still, *as* would sound better and would certainly be the preferred form in formal writing: The physiology text is difficult, *as* I would expect it to be.

lose/loose

If you know how to pronounce these correctly, you probably will not have difficulty spelling them. Both words have a long *oo* sound, as in *toot*. The difference is in the way you pronounce the *s*. *Loose*, meaning *not tight*, has a voiceless *s* sound; place your fingers on your Adam's apple when you say it, and you will feel little movement. Leave your fingers there when you say "lose," meaning *to be defeated* or *to misplace*, and you should feel some vibrations, indicating a voiced *s* sound. To help you remember, *loose* rhymes with *moose*, and *lose* rhymes with *shoes*.

man

Until a few years ago, you could get by with saying "man" and arguing that you meant both sexes. Objections to this use are too frequent to make it acceptable any longer. You can sometimes substitute *people* or *humans* for *man* or *men*. The dinosaurs disappeared before *human beings* walked the earth. (If you said, "before man walked the earth," some feminists might argue that women were here first.)

maybe/may be

The one-word form is an adverb meaning *perhaps*. Do not confuse it with the verb form, *may be*. The party *may be* a disaster, but *maybe* I'll go, anyway. Some texts advise you to avoid this last form altogether, substituting *perhaps*.

me

If you have any notions that *me* is not quite a proper word, discard them. You should always use it to refer to yourself after a preposition or when you are the object or indirect object of a verb. Be especially careful when you are talking about other people in addition to yourself. The following sentences are all correct: The captain gave Roger and *me* orders to return fire. The teacher passed only five other girls and *me*. Between you and *me*, she is a phony.

nice

The vagueness of this word makes it not very desirable. It is not even much of a compliment anymore. Instead of calling someone a "nice person," say that he is *congenial, friendly, good-natured, polite,* or possesses whatever quality makes you consider him "nice."

no one

The British hyphenate this word, but we always write it as two words.

none

At one time, *none* was always considered to be singular, and there are still a few grammarians who insist on its singularity. Now most people say it can be singular or plural, depending on the sense. If *no one* can be substituted for it, use a singular verb: *None of us is* the culprit. If substituting *no persons* for it would make more sense, use a plural verb: Although hundreds of workers pass through this gate each day, *none are* to be seen here at 4:00 A.M.

of

This is a preposition; do not mistake it for a helping verb form (*have*). Although "He *could of been* the driver" may *sound* the same as "He *could have been* the driver," the two do not *look* alike. Only the second one is correct.

off/of

These two prepositions should not be combined. Use *off* by itself or *from,* depending on the meaning. I can't get *off* this horse! (Not "*off of* this horse.") I bought this textbook *from* a former student. (Not "*off of* a former student.")

only

Most of us are careless about the placement of *only* when we speak. I know I catch myself saying, "I only bought $45 worth of groceries," when I mean, "I bought only $45 worth of groceries" (not $55 or $65). *Only*, put between the subject and the verb, implies that I *only bought* the groceries, I didn't adopt them, mortgage them, or do something else more serious than buying them. What I intend to say is *only $45*, of course. The implication is that I could have spent more. In speech, this kind of sloppy placement of *only* is overlooked, but in writing it is considered more of a flaw. Watch where you put *only*. There is a difference between "Her father *only said* they could elope" (he didn't mean it) and "Her father said they could *only elope*" (he wouldn't pay for the wedding).

principal/principle

Since both of these are pronounced the same, these words create only a spelling problem. The one that ends in *-le* always means *rule*, which also ends in *-le*. All other meanings are spelled with the *-al* ending. The *principal* drilled us on the *principles* of safety.

probable/probably

These both mean the same, but *probable* is used to modify nouns (the *probable failure* of the tax proposal) and *probably* to modify verbs, adjectives, or adverbs (the tax proposal will *probably fail*).

proceed/precede

These words are very close, but *proceed* means *to go ahead* or *to continue*, and *precede* means *to come before*. The wedding party proceeds down the aisle, with the bridesmaids *preceding* the matron of honor.

quotes/quotations

Quotes is most acceptable as a verb; for the noun, use *quotations*. Sedgwick *quotes* poetry frequently, but I seldom recognize his garbled *quotations*.

rain/rein/reign

You probably do not get confused about the *rain* that falls from the sky, but you may mix up the king's *reign* with the *rein* you must keep on your emotions.

real

Do not use this for *very* when you write. Although you may say, "The roller coaster was a really thrilling (or real thrilling) ride," in writing you should say, "The roller coaster was a *very* thrilling ride."

reason is because

This is a nonstandard form. Omit *because:* The reason for the failure of the business is Gerald's incomprehensible bookkeeping. (Not "is because of Gerald's incomprehensible bookkeeping.")

rise/raise

When you get up from a chair, you *rise* from it. You must have an object to *raise: Rising* from the chair, he *raised* the phonograph needle from the record.

set/sit

There is the same distinction between these two words: *Set* requires an object, and *sit* has no object. Before I can *sit* on the porch swing, I must *set* down the ladder I'm carrying.

sic

If you are quoting someone who has made a grammatical or spelling error, you are not supposed to correct the mistake. Instead, you point out the error, avoiding the blame for it yourself by putting *sic* (Latin for *thus*) in brackets after the mistake. Your quotation will look like this: "The President has make [sic] himself perfectly clear."

so . . . that

When you use *so* as an adverb, you should follow it with a *that* clause. "The music was so loud" sounds incomplete. Say instead, "The music was so loud that the dancers had to shout their romantic whispers."

supposed to

Do not write, *suppose to*. Even though the *to* may keep you from hearing the *d* at the end of *supposed*, you need the *d* for the past-tense form. Students are *supposed to* remember their past-tense endings.

than/then

Than makes a comparison; *then* clarifies the time. If you were found after being lost on the desert for a week, you might say this: "I'd rather eat *than* sleep." This would mean that you prefer food to rest. If you really wanted both food and rest, but you wanted food *first*, you should say this: "I'd rather eat, *then* sleep."

that/who

When you are talking about people, *that* is a poor substitute for *who*. If you use it, your reader may suspect that you are having trouble deciding between *who* and *whom*. Say, "The woman *who* stole the car was arrested," not, "The woman *that* stole the car was arrested."

there/their/they're

These words sound alike, so they create a spelling problem. Note that each word begins with *the*; there is no form beginning *thi*. When a sentence has the verb before the subject, it may begin with *there*: *There* are four reasons for buying that car. *There* also means the opposite of *here*—a word it also contains. I went *there* just last week. *Their* always means *belonging to them*: The Taylors keep *their* dogs in the house. *They're* is actually two words: *they* and *are*. *They're* coming to visit in April. *They're* going to leave *their* car *there* and rent a smaller one here.

to/too/two

You've solved this spelling problem by now, haven't you? You know that *two* is a number, *to* is a preposition or part of an infinitive (*to go to town*), and *too* is an adverb meaning *also* or *excessively*. It may help you to remember that, in most cases, *too* has the double-*o* emphasized, while *to* can usually be pronounced *ta*. When my *two* brothers went *to* a party, I wanted *to* go, *too*.

try and

Although you may say you are going to *try and study*, this expression is not very logical. It sounds as if the *trying* and the *studying* were two different acts. Your writing should be clearer: I am going to *try to* study.

unique

Some grammatical purists will tell you that *unique* means the *only one of its kind*, so it cannot be modified. Usage appears to be changing on this. You may have noticed that Norman Cousins's essay in this text contains the phrase "its most unique feature" in its first paragraph. Norman Cousins was part of the Usage Panel for the *American Heritage Dictionary*, remember. Still, the best advice is to avoid using *unique* when you really mean merely *unusual*. Save *unique* for the very, very unusual, and you probably won't need to modify it.

utilize

Utilize is just a long way to say *use*. It smacks of jargon and is even a bit precious—especially in the statement, "I utilized the facilities," an overly cute way of saying, "I went to the bathroom."

very/vary

Vary is the verb. Student responses may *vary* from one semester to the next. *Very* is an adverb. The responses are *very* different.

while

This conjunction is overused; it should not replace *and* or *but*. The dogs eat beef, *but* the cats prefer fish. (Not, "The dogs eat beef, *while* the cats prefer fish.")

who/whom

Remember, the subject is *who*, and the object adds an *m*. In some sentences, it is difficult to figure out which form you need because there are several clauses. What would you use here?

The contestant (who, whom) they liked the best was voted "Miss Congeniality."

You may have to rearrange the dependent clause into subject-verb-object (they liked *whom*) to see that *whom* is the answer.

whose/who's

The first of these is a possessive pronoun. The man *whose* house you crashed into is threatening to sue. The second is a contraction meaning *who is* or *who has*. *Who's* got the money for a lawyer?

-wise

Although *clockwise* and *otherwise* are perfectly acceptable words, most newly created words with *wise* endings are frowned upon. *Gradewise*, you won't do well in English class if you insist on adding *wise* to nouns to make adverbs.

would

This is a fine helping verb, but do not use it twice in the same sentence. Specifically, when you have an *if* clause, do not put *would* in it. "We *would* get along better if you *would* just shut up" is wrong. Instead, say, "We *would* get along better if you just shut up."

you

You is a mark of informality in writing. It is not objectionable in most assignments, so long as it is not used to offend your readers. For example, I would never say this: "When you discover that you have venereal disease, you should see a physician at once." Keep this kind of statement impersonal: "Anyone with symptoms of venereal disease should see a physician at once."

your/you're

You know the difference between the possessive pronoun *your* and the contraction *you're*, don't you? *You're* going to get this one right in every one of *your* papers.

INDEX

A

a/an, 350–351
abstraction, ladder of, 64, 67, 75, 78
accept/except, 351
Acronym Game, 17–18
advice/advise, 351
affect/effect, 351
agreement:
    of pronoun and antecedent, 162, 333, 338
    of subject and verb, 59–60, 313–315
ain't, 63, 349–350
Allen-Avery, Julie ("Keys and Me"), 276–278, 326
all ready/already, 351
alot (an error), 351
alright (an error), 351
altogether/all together, 351
among, 352
analogies, 149, 164
analysis:
    assignment, 162–163
    defined, 137
    pitfalls, 138–139
    "practicing" (box), 139
Anderson, Jack ("How to Outsmart the Bureaucrats"), 287–289
Ann Landers Encyclopedia, The, 106–108
apostrophes, 117–118, 323–325
application letter (cover letter), 191–193
argument, 142–152
    by analogy, 149
    assignment, 163–164
    deductive reasoning, 145–158
        "practicing" (box), 147–148
    direct or indirect, 142–143
    fallacies, 146, 151–152
    inductive reasoning, 143–145
        "practicing" (box), 144–145
    refutation, 150–151

argument about the person (fallacy), 152, 164
argument to ignorance (fallacy), 151, 164
as, 358
Asmus, Linda ("Blind Obedience to Authority"), 201–209, 211, 215–217
at, 351–352
Auden, W. H., 21
audience:
    analysis of, 30–35, 39–42
    and paragraphing, 101–103
    and process papers, 135
Austen, Jane, 15
awhile/a while, 352

B

bad/badly, 352
bandwagon fallacy, 151–152, 164
being that (an error), 352
beside/besides, 352
between/among, 352
brackets, 216
bridging sentence, 106
Buchwald, Art ("Body Language Spoken Here"), 282–284, 326

C

can/may, 352
can't hardly (an error), 353
can't help but (an error), 353
capital/capitol, 353
capitalization, 347–348
cause-and-effect essays, 140–142, 163
    assignment, 163
    contributing causes, 140
    necessary causes, 140
    pitfalls of writing, 140–142
    "practicing" (box), 142
    sufficient causes, 140

center on/center around, 353
Chambers, Rick ("Stars and Dollars: The Space Research Controversy"), 152–155
checklists:
  for editing, 169–170
  for proofreading, 170
  for theses, 52
  for writing essay exams, 183–184
choose/chose, 353
circular reasoning, 151, 164
cites/sites/sights, 353
classification:
  assignment, 162–163
  defined, 137
  pitfalls, 138–139
  "practicing" (box), 139
clauses, dependent, 87, 133, 308, 310–311, 327–330, 336, 362
clauses, independent, 87, 133, 307, 310, 328–330, 336
clichés, 70, 72
colons, 133, 328, 330
commas, 133, 327–330
comma splices, 42–43, 91, 310–312
Communications Model, 6–8, 29
comparison/contrast pattern, 124–128, 135–136
comply with/comply to, 353
conclusions, 110
  "practicing" (box), 111
conjunctions, coordinating and subordinating, 87–88, 308, 310
conjunctive adverbs, 87, 311, 327
connotation, 67–68, 74, 79
  "practicing" (box), 68–69
consensus, 353
continual/continuous, 353
contractions, 323, 325, 332
coordination, 87
correlation (mistaken for causation), 141
council/counsel, 354
Cousins, Norman ("A Growing Wealth of Words"), 74–76, 127, 186, 350, 362
cover letters (application letters), 191–193
credibility, 34–35, 141, 150, 218
Crites, Stephen ("New Deal for the Academic Shuffle"), 256–258

D

dangling modifiers, 172, 334–336, 338
dashes, 328
data, 354

deductive reasoning:
  assignment, 164
  defined, 145–146
  "practicing" (box), 147–148
  syllogisms, 145–148
definition, kinds of, 66–68
DeKam, Elizabeth ("One Valuable Value"), 18–20
denotation, 67–68
dialogue, 112–113
  assignment, 120
dictionaries, 67–68, 75, 345, 349–350, 362
different from/different than, 354
disinterested, 354
Dunham, Sherrie ("In Retrospect"), 55–57

E

Eastman, Richard M. ("The Audience as Creative Force"), 38–42
editing:
  checklist, 169–170
  defined, 165
  exercises, 166–168
effect, 351
ellipsis points, 216
endnotes, 208, 218–220
enthymeme, 147
etc., 354
euphemisms, 66
everyday/every day, 354
everyone/everybody, 354–355
exams:
  checklist for writing, 183–184
  preparing for, 178–181
  writing, 181–184
except, 351

F

factor, 355
factual statements:
  assignment, 98–99
  defined, 81–82
  "practicing" (box), 83–84
fallacies, 146, 151–152, 164
farther/further, 355
feedback, 7–8, 173–174
fewer/less, 355
figurative language:
  assignment, 79–80
  kinds of, 69–70, 94
  "practicing" (box), 71–72
flaunt/flout, 355
Flesch, Rudolf, 84

INDEX

Fog Index (readability), 84–85, 87, 99
footnotes. *See* endnotes
Formal English, 62, 77
fragments, 26, 307–310
freewriting, 16–17
Friel, Brian ("Labors of Love"), 129–132, 134
Frost, Robert, 11
funny, 355

G

General English, 62, 77–78
gerunds, 91
Giles, Mark ("Fighters"), 128–129
Ginott, Haim, 56
Goffman, Erving, 20, 25
Gonzales, Lawrence, 92
good/well, 355
Goodman, Ellen ("Men, Women and War"), 95–97, 101, 110, 127, 300–303
Greeley, Roger E., 149
Green, Stan ("A Good Cigar Is a Smoke"), 36–38, 123, 134
Gunning, Robert, 84

H

Harris, Sydney J. ("Defining a Few Terms"), 262–266, 315, 350
healthy/healthful, 355
he or she/his or her, 356
Holler, John ("The Case Against the Drafting of Women"), 300–303
hopefully, 356
Hudson, Richard G., Jr., 143

I

Iacocca, Lee A., 150, 214
ibid., 218
imply/infer, 356
inductive leap, 143–144
inductive reasoning:
   assignment, 164
   defined, 143–144
   "practicing" (box), 144–145
inferences, 82–84, 98–99, 102, 108, 119
   assignment, 98–99
   defined, 82
   "practicing" (box), 83–84
infinitives, 90
Informal English, 63, 77
interesting, 356
in terms of, 356

interviews (employment), 194–198
in to/into, 356
introductions (in essays), 109–111
   "practicing" (box), 111
irony, 142–143
irregardless (an error), 356
Irving, John, 69–70
is when/is where, 357
its/it's, 117, 323–324, 340, 357
-ize, 357

J

Jourard, Sidney, 20, 25
judgment/judgement, 357
judgments, 83, 98–100, 108, 142
   assignment, 98–100
   defined, 83

K

Katz, Dolly, 70
Kelsey, David ("The Swamp"), 93–95, 123–124
kind of, 357
Kison, John ("Safer at Any Speed"), 259–261
Kome, Hal ("Decoding the TV Commercials"), 235–241
Krantz, Judith (from *Princess Daisy*), 101–103

L

labeling (stereotyping), 12–13
Larson, Charles R. ("Competency Tests for Everyone"), 115–117, 119, 186
Lathrop, Richard, 187
lay and *lie*, 317, 357
lead/led, 357
lend/loan, 358
less, 355
Lessing, Doris (from *Shikasta*), 85–86
like/as, 358
lose/loose, 358

M

Macklin, Patricia ("It Is No Secret"), 113–114, 150
Macrorie, Ken, 56
McWhirter, Nickie ("Phooey on the Little Boxes Other People Put Around Us"), 57–59, 101, 119

Maddocks, Melvin ("The Band Plays On"), 271–273
man, 358
March, Francis A., 75
Marlett, Michelle M. ("The Best Teachings"), 292–294
Marsh, Kathy ("Spare Me the Details"), 269–270, 327
may, 352
maybe/may be, 358
me, 358
Mekemson, Tonia ("Brass Rubbings"), 249–252
Mencken, H. L. ("On the Meaning of Life"), 297–299
metaphor, 70–72, 80
mnemonic devices, 346
modifiers, 88, 172, 314, 328, 330, 334–336, 338
  restrictive and nonrestrictive, 328, 330

N

narrowing the topic, 33
nice, 359
Nichols, Dr. Ralph, 3
Nonstandard English, 63, 77–78
no one, 359
norms, perceived, 34

O

Oates, Joyce Carol (from *Bellefleur*), 105
of, 359
off/of, 359
only, 359
Orwell, George ("The Sporting Spirit"), 253–256
outlining, 122–127
  for comparison/contrast essays, 124–127
  for descriptive essays, 123–124
  getting started, 122–123
  for research papers, 215
  rules of, 124
  sentence outlines, 126–127
  and thesis sentence, 124
  topic outlines, 125–127

P

paragraph development:
  chronological order (time order), 104
  climactic order, 105
  contrasting order, 106
  least-serious-to-most-serious, 104–105
  "practicing" (box), 106–108
  shortest example to longest example, 105
  spatial order, 104
paragraphs:
  conclusions, 110–111
  dialogue, 112–113
  introductions, 109–111
  length, 101–103
  summaries, 111–112, 119
parallelism:
  assignment, 100
  faulty, 176–177, 336–338
  in outlines, 127
  "practicing" (box), 91
passive voice, 92
patterns of development:
  cause-and-effect, 140–142
  chronology, 121–122, 134
  comparison/contrast, 124–128, 135–136
  process, 122–123, 134
perception, 29–30
personification, 70–72, 80
Pettus, Theodore ("Q: Why Do You Want to Work Here?"), 194–198
phonics, 343–344
plagiarism, 214, 218
possessives, 323–325, 331
  of nouns, 323–325
  of pronouns, 331
post hoc fallacy, 151, 164
postwriting, 165–171
"practicing" boxes:
  defining yourself, 10–11
  audience analysis, 31–32
  evaluating thesis sentences, 53
  writing thesis sentences, 53
  achieving variety with connotations, 68–69
  recognizing figurative language, 71
  writing figurative language, 72
  identifying factual statements and inferences, 83–84
  writing periodic sentences, 89
  achieving parallel structure, 91
  achieving sentence variety, 92
  methods of paragraph development, 106–108
  writing introductions and conclusions, 111
  developing outlines, 127–128
  analysis and classification, 139
  cause-and-effect analysis, 142
  arguing inductively, 144–145
  arguing deductively, 147–148
  evaluating essay answers, 184–185

premises, 145–148
prewriting:
  and audience analysis, 30
  defined, 9
  techniques, 15–18, 36, 48–49, 50–51, 137, 162
    Acronym Game, 17–18, 48–49
    classification trees, 50–51, 137, 162
    freewriting, 16–17, 48
    journalistic technique, 36, 49
  and voices, 14
Princess Daisy, 101–103
principal/principle, 359
probable/probably, 360
proceed/precede, 360
professional essays:
  "The Many Me's of the Self-Monitor" by Mark Snyder, 20–26, 186
  "The Audience as Creative Force" by Richard M. Eastman, 38–42
  "Phooey on the Little Boxes Other People Put Around Us" by Nickie McWhirter, 57–59, 101, 119
  "A Growing Wealth of Words" by Norman Cousins, 74–76, 127, 186
  "Men, Women and War" by Ellen Goodman, 95–97, 101, 127, 300–303
  "Competency Tests for Everyone" by Charles R. Larson, 115–117, 119, 186
  "Labors of Love" by Brian Friel, 129–132, 134
  "The Age of Indifference" by Philip G. Zimbardo, 155–161, 186
  "Q: Why Do You Want to Work Here?" by Theodore Pettus, 194–198
  "Mommy Goes to Jail" by Judith Viorst, 225–230
  "Memories of a Small Bomb" by Morton Sontheimer, 231–233
  "Decoding TV Commercials" by Hal Kome, 235–241
  "The Arab Stereotype on Television" by Jack G. Shaheen, 241–249
  "The Sporting Spirit" by George Orwell, 253–256
  "New Deal for the Academic Shuffle" by Stephen Crites, 256–258
  "Defining a Few Terms" by Sydney J. Harris, 262–266
  "Memories of the Championship" by Ed Vital, 266–268
  "The Band Plays On" by Melvin Maddocks, 271–273
  "Snapshot of a Dog" by James Thurber, 273–276
  "Some Cheerful Words About Men" by Gloria Steinem, 279–282
  "Body Language Spoken Here" by Art Buchwald, 282–284, 326
  "How to Outsmart the Bureaucrats" by Jack Anderson, 287–289
  "The Place of Sex Among Human Values" by Bertrand Russell, 290–292
  "Music to Get Pregnant By" by Mike Royko, 295–297
  "On the Meaning of Life" by H. L. Mencken, 297–299
pronouns:
  agreement errors, 162, 333, 338
  forms of, 331–334
proofreading:
  checklist for, 170
  defined, 165
  exercises, 166–168
  techniques, 170–171, 347

Q

qualifications brief (résumé), 187–191
quotation marks, 112–113, 325–327
quotes/quotations, 360

R

rain/rein/reign, 360
readability, 84–85, 86, 87, 99, 177
real, 360
reason is because, 360
refutation, 150–151
repetition, 89–90, 93, 100
research paper, 200–221
  assignment, 222
  bibliography, 209, 213–214, 220–221
  endnotes (footnotes), 208, 218–220
  format, 217–221
  introduction, 217
  library research, 212–214
  note-taking, 214
  outlining, 215
  quotations, including, 215–217
  sample paper, 202–209
  topic selection, 210–212
restrictive and nonrestrictive modifiers, 328
résumé. *See* qualifications brief
rewriting, 174–176
rise/raise, 360
Roberts, Paul, 32–33
roles:
  defined, 10
  and prewriting, 14

Royko, Mike ("Music to Get Pregnant By"), 112, 295–297
run-on sentences, 42–43, 310–312
Russell, Bertrand ("The Place of Sex Among Human Values"), 290–292

S

Sandman, Peter M., 336
Schlafly, Phyllis, 96, 151, 282–284
selection, principle of, 122, 293
self-concepts, 11–14
  defined, 11
  development of, 11
  effect on writing, 12
  incompleteness of, 14
self-fulfilling prophecy, 12
semicolons, 133, 310, 311, 328–330
sentence length, 85–87
sentences:
  complex, 88, 89, 100
  compound, 87, 310, 311, 328–330
  compound–complex, 88, 100
  loose, 88–89
  periodic, 88–89
    "practicing" (box), 89
  run-on, 42–43, 310–312
  simple, 87
  varied, 92
    "practicing" (box), 92
set/sit, 360
Shaheen, Jack G. ("The Arab Stereotype on Television"), 241–249
Shaw, George Bernard, 65
Shikasta, 85–86, 89–90
[*sic*.], 214, 360
sights, 353
simile, 70–72, 80
sites, 353
Snyder, Mark ("The Many Me's of the Self-Monitor"), 20–26, 112, 186
Sontheimer, Morton ("Memories of a Small Bomb"), 231–233
so . . . that, 361
spelling, 339–348
  six steps to spelling accuracy, 341
Standard English, 63
Steinem, Gloria ("Some Cheerful Words About Men"), 279–282, 350
Steinmann, Martin, Jr., 31
stereotyping (labeling), 12–13, 34
  of an audience, 34
  dangers of, 12–13
  defined, 12

student essays:
  "One Valuable Value" by Elizabeth DeKam, 18–20
  "A Good Cigar Is a Smoke" by Stan Green, 36–38, 123, 134
  "In Retrospect" by Sherrie Dunham, 55–57
  "The Ticket" by Roberta Thompson, 73–74, 112, 122
  "The Swamp" by David Kelsey, 93–95
  "It Is No Secret" by Patricia Macklin, 113–114, 123–124, 150
  "Fighters" by Mark Giles, 128–129
  "Stars and Dollars: The Space Research Controversy" by Rick Chambers, 152–155
  "Blind Obedience to Authority" by Linda Asmus, 201, 202–209, 211, 215–217
  "Preparing for the Job" by Mary Jo Volosky, 233–234
  "Brass Rubbings" by Tonia Mekemson, 249–252
  "Safer at Any Speed" by John Kison, 259–261
  "Spare Me the Details" by Kathy Marsh, 269–270, 327
  "Keys and Me" by Julie Allen-Avery, 276–278, 326
  "Male Attitudes in the Army" by Laurie Wardell, 284–286
  "The Best Teachings" by Michelle M. Marlett, 292–294
  "The Case Against the Drafting of Women" by John Holler, 300–303
subjects (of clauses):
  agreement with verbs, 59–60, 313–315
  implied, 307
  verbals used as, 309
subordination, 87, 311
summary paragraphs, 111–112, 119
  assignment, 119
  guidelines for, 111–112
supposed to, 361
Swift, Jonathan, 63
syllogisms, 145–148
symbols, 63–66
synonyms, 68, 75

T

tense (of verbs), 98, 318–322
than/then, 361
thank-you letters, 194
that/who, 361

there/their/they're, 361
thesis sentences, 49–54, 59–61, 83, 98–100, 122, 124, 142
    assignment, 59–61
    checklist for, 52
    in chronologies, 122
    defined, 51
    judgments as, 83, 98–100, 142
    placement of, 54
    "practicing" (box), 53
    in outlines, 124
    specifications for, 51–52
Thompson, Roberta ("The Ticket"), 73–74, 112, 122
Thurber, James ("Snapshot of a Dog"), 273–276
to/too/two, 361
topic sentence, 103–108, 118–119
    advantages of, 103
    assignment, 118–119
    defined, 103
    development of, 104–108
transitions, 108
try and (an error), 361

U

undistributed middle term, fallacy of, 146, 164
unique, 362
usage, 349–363
Usage Panel (for dictionaries), 349–350
utilize, 362

V

validity, 145–148
varieties of English, 62–63
verbals, 309, 336
verbs:
    active, 92, 309, 318–322
    agreement with subjects, 59–60, 313–315
    defined, 307
    in essay exam questions, 182–183
    form (wrong principal part), 77, 315–318, 322
    irregular, 316–318
    linking, 93
    passive, 92, 309, 318–322
    plural form, 313
    required in clauses, 307
    tense shifts, 98, 318–322
very/vary, 362
Viorst, Judith ("Mommy Goes to Jail"), 225–230
Vital, Ed ("Memories of the Championship"), 266–268
voice (of a verb), 318–322. *See also* verbs, active and passive
voices and prewriting, 14–15, 17, 18
Volosky, Mary Jo ("Preparing for the Job"), 233–234

W

Wardell, Laurie ("Male Attitudes in the Army"), 284–286
well, 355
while, 362
who, 361
who, whom, 332, 362
whose/who's, 332, 362
-wise, 362
word magic, 66
would, 363
writing:
    advantages of, 4–5
    contrasted with speaking, 5–6
    disadvantages of, 5
    a three-step process, 5–6

Y

Yeats, W. B., 14
you, 363
your/you're, 363

Z

Zimbardo, Philip G. ("The Age of Indifference"), 155–161, 186